Latinos in the New Millennium
An Almanac of Opinion, Behavior, and Policy Preferences

Latinos in the New Millennium is the most current and comprehensive profile of Latinos in the United States to look at their social characteristics, group relations, policy positions, and political orientations. The authors draw on information from the 2006 Latino National Survey (LNS), the largest and most detailed source of data on Hispanics in America. This book provides essential knowledge about Latinos, contextualizing research data by structuring discussion around many dimensions of Latino political life in the United States. The encyclopedic range and depth of the LNS enable the authors to appraise Latinos' group characteristics, attitudes, behaviors, and views on numerous topics. This study displays the complexity of Latinos, from recent immigrants to those whose grandparents were born in the United States.

Luis R. Fraga is Russell F. Stark University Professor and Professor of Political Science at the University of Washington. He also serves as Associate Vice Provost for Faculty Advancement and Director of the Diversity Research Institute.

John A. Garcia is Research Professor and Director of Community Outreach, Inter-University Consortium at the Institute for Social Research, as well as Faculty Associate in the Center for Political Studies at the University of Michigan.

Rodney E. Hero is Professor of Political Science at the University of California, Berkeley.

Michael Jones-Correa is Professor of Government at Cornell University.

Valerie Martinez-Ebers is Professor of Political Science at the University of North Texas.

Gary M. Segura is Professor of American Politics and Chair of Chicano/a Studies at Stanford University.

Latinos in the New Millennium

An Almanac of Opinion, Behavior, and Policy Preferences

LUIS R. FRAGA
University of Washington

JOHN A. GARCIA
University of Michigan

RODNEY E. HERO
University of California, Berkeley

MICHAEL JONES-CORREA
Cornell University

VALERIE MARTINEZ-EBERS
University of North Texas

GARY M. SEGURA
Stanford University

CAMBRIDGE
UNIVERSITY PRESS

CAMBRIDGE UNIVERSITY PRESS
Cambridge, New York, Melbourne, Madrid, Cape Town,
Singapore, São Paulo, Delhi, Tokyo, Mexico City

Cambridge University Press
32 Avenue of the Americas, New York, NY 10013-2473, USA

www.cambridge.org
Information on this title: www.cambridge.org/9781107638730

First published 2012

Printed in the United States of America

A catalog record for this publication is available from the British Library.

Library of Congress Cataloging in Publication data

Latinos in the new millennium : an almanac of opinion, behavior, and
policy preferences / Luis R. Fraga . . . [et al.].
p. cm.
Includes bibliographical references and index.
ISBN 978-1-107-01722-1 (hardback) – ISBN 978-1-107-63873-0 (pbk.)
1. Hispanic Americans – Politics and government – 21st century.
2. Hispanic Americans – Ethnic identity.   3. Hispanic
Americans – Attitudes.   I. Fraga, Luis Ricardo.   II. Title.
E184.S75L3695   2011
305.868′073–dc23   2011027735

ISBN 978-1-107-01722-1 Hardback
ISBN 978-1-107-63873-0 Paperback

Contents

v

Acknowledgments

A book of this scope would not have been possible without the support and contributions of many people and institutions.

We are grateful to all of our funders, including Gil Cardenas at the Institute for Latino Studies at the University of Notre Dame and the Anney E. Casey Foundation; Paul Brest, Hewlett Foundation; Jacqueline Berrien, Ford Foundation; Lande Ajose and Amy Dominguez-Arms, Irvine Foundation; Geri Manion, Carnegie Corporation; Aixa Cintrón, Russell Sage Foundation; Ken Meier, Program in Equity, Representation, and Governance, Texas A&M University; Edward Murguia, Mexican American and Latino Research Center, Texas A&M University; Barbara Sabol, Kellogg Foundation; the Joyce Foundation; the National Science Foundation; and the University of Iowa.

We also want to acknowledge the contributions from the members of our National Advisory Board. The members were: Lawrence Bobo, Harvard University; Bruce Cain, University of California, Berkeley; Robert Huckfeldt, University of California, Davis; Pei-te Lien, University of California, Santa Barbara; Ken Meier, Texas A&M University; Vilma Ortiz, University of California, Los Angeles; Lisandro Pérez, Florida International University; Kenneth Prewitt, Columbia University; Ricardo Ramírez, University of Notre Dame; Denise Segura, University of California, Santa Barbara; Christine Sierra, University of New Mexico; and Carlos Vargas Ramos, Hunter College, City University of New York.

The following served as research assistants at various stages of the project: Francisco Pedraza (now at Texas A&M University), Seth Greenfest, Ann Frost, and Christopher Towler, University of Washington; Morris Levy, University of California, Berkeley; Matthew De Carlo, Cornell

University; Andrew Parker and Jeanette Carmen Bustamante, Stanford University; Ryan Salzman, University of North Texas; and Salvador Peralta (now at the University of West Georgia), Gabriel Sanchez (now at the University of New Mexico), and Marcela García-Castañon (now at the University of Washington), University of Arizona.

We have now been working together for many years on the Latino National Survey. This would not have been possible without the full support of our partners, spouses, and children. In so many ways, it's our families who inspire us to do this work. Thank you and we love you.

1

Latinos in the New Millennium

Knowledge and Misperceptions

Purpose of the Book

Themes and imagery about Latinos in the United States often focus on the rapid and substantial growth of this population and projections about the continuing impact of those demographic changes into the future. Portrayals in policy debates and the media have depicted the central facets of this fast-growing community – where they come from, how they are transforming traditional centers of migration with new destinations, the trials and tribulations of making it in America, and how the greater American society and its institutions respond to Latinos – imperfectly at best. The faces, stories, and life experiences of Latinos tend to be portrayed largely through sketchily drawn caricatures of working-class, immigrant-based communities trying to find an economic foothold to achieve the American dream; yet also holding steadfastly to traditions, cultural beliefs, and practices that sometimes fit uncomfortably with contemporary America.

But how accurate are these sketchy images, individually and collectively? What is the reality of the Latino experience in the United States? How can we better understand the views and perspectives of Hispanics in American society regarding such issues as education, politics, and public policy? What hard evidence can be brought to bear on this large, growing, and complex population that would help us situate the group in the American polity?

This volume sets out a broad-based profile of Latinos in the United States, including their social characteristics, group relations, policy positions, and political orientations. It draws on and provides a guide through the abundant information contained in the Latino National

Survey (LNS), conducted in 2006 – the largest and most detailed source of recent data on Hispanics in the United States. Our central goal is to uncover essential knowledge about Latinos; accordingly, we structure our discussion around various "conventional wisdoms," or what may be stereotypes about the Latino population, and engage each with research data to assess the "wisdom." At the broadest level, the LNS evidence suggests group attitudes and experiences that challenge numerous simplistic characterizations of the Latino population. More important, it also depicts a mosaic, which at the same time coheres around a theme that might be called neoassimilation. That is, although the myths about Latinos tend to suggest separation in one way or another, the actual evidence instead tells a story of immersion and incorporation into the larger American society, albeit with variations on dimensions and in intensity. Only through systematic examination of survey responses, provided in the subsequent chapters, can we begin to appreciate the reality beyond the myths and gain insights into the complex and new assimilation (if that is the correct word) of Latinos.

The Latino National Survey is an especially useful and appropriate vehicle for considering these questions. The LNS offers a number of landmark contributions: First, it is the largest survey of Latinos ever undertaken outside the U.S. census, including 8,634 respondents residing in fifteen states and the District of Columbia. Second, it includes responses from persons with origins in every Latin American country – the full range of an increasingly diverse Hispanic population in the United States – with subgroup samples large enough for separate, reliable analysis for many of these national origin groups. The survey allows for analysis not just of Mexican Americans, Puerto Ricans, and Cubans, once the only Hispanic national origin groups whose views could be studied in any detail, but also of Dominicans, Salvadorans, Guatemalans, Colombians, and Ecuadorians, as well as U.S. residents of other South and Central American origin. Third, the interviews conducted with respondents are incredibly detailed and far ranging. Respondents, speaking in either English or Spanish, participated in telephone survey interviews more than forty minutes in length, answering more than two hundred questions, which spanned topics ranging from attitudes toward the United States and its institutions and political processes to electoral and civic engagement, inter- and intragroup relations, public policy issues and preferences, transnational interactions, and various other aspects of experiences living in the United States.

The encyclopedic range and depth of the Latino National Survey allow us to appraise Latino group characteristics (e.g., nativity, citizenship status, gender), their attitudes and behaviors (e.g., on education, political participation, transnationalism), and their views on a broad range of topics (e.g., partisanship, abortion, political knowledge). This almanac displays the full complexity found in the Latino population. These complexities are reflected in the range of experiences among a population that includes immigrants from Mexico, Cuba, El Salvador, and elsewhere, and their descendants; recent arrivals and those whose grandparents were born in the United States; English, bilingual, and Spanish speakers; and of course, differences in gender, religious affiliation, and generational status in the United States. This diversity is bridged, to some extent, by a set of commonalities, including cultural practices and traditions, shared neighborhoods and social networks, being viewed as a part of single group by non-Hispanics, and engaging in some common sociopolitical objectives. These commonalities mean that Latinos can be analyzed as a single group, whereas the complexities translate into differences in attitudes and behaviors based, among other things, on social class status, primary regions of residence, historically based experiences in the United States, and extent of national origin allegiances. In a sense, we are suggesting that Latinos can share many important experiences and traditions or values but, at the same time, exhibit relevant distinctions. This book describes areas of similarities in circumstances, viewpoints, and behaviors as well as areas of variation; it identifies and explains patterns in the data; and it places these in the broader context of the social science literature.

We hope the fuller assessment of this increasingly important population provided in this study serves a variety of purposes and speaks to several audiences. We hope that it will inform decision makers in and out of politics, policy makers, local community leaders, and interested citizens and that it will help them to better understand the relationships across different aspects of Latino experiences in the United States and to use those insights to stimulate a variety of politically and socially relevant discourses and actions. We hope as well that this array of empirically grounded data illuminates and clarifies the relationship between Latinos and the American political system. In addition, participants in public-policy arenas (whether national, state, or local) can benefit from the analyses found in the substantive chapters that follow in this volume.

Table 1.1. *Population, by Race and Ethnicity: 2000 and 2008*

	2008 Population	2000 Population	Percentage, 2008	Percentage, 2000
Hispanic	46,822,476	35,204,480	15.4	12.5
Native born	28,985,169	21,072,230	9.5	7.5
Foreign born	17,837,307	14,132,250	5.9	5.0
White alone, not Hispanic	198,963,659	194,527,123	65.4	69.1
Black alone, not Hispanic	36,774,337	33,706,554	12.1	12.0
Asian alone, not Hispanic	13,227,070	10,088,521	4.4	3.6
Other, not Hispanic	8,272,186	7,895,228	2.7	2.8
TOTAL	304,059,728	281,421,906	100.0	100.0

Note: Universe is 2000 and 2008 resident population. "Other, not Hispanic" includes persons reporting single races not listed separately and persons reporting more than one race.

Source: Pew Hispanic Center, *Statistical Portrait of Hispanics in the United States, 2008* (http://pewhispanic.org/factsheets/factsheet.php?FactsheetID=58). Pew Hispanic Center tabulations of 2000 Census (5 percent Integrated Public Use Microdata Series [IPUMS]) and 2008 American Community Survey (1 percent IPUMS).

Who Are Latinos in the United States? Rapid Growth, Greater Diversity

To begin, who are Latinos in the United States? In 2008 there were almost 47 million persons of Hispanic origin in the United States, representing 15.4 percent of the total U.S. population (see Table 1.1). Interestingly, the largest contributor to growth in the Latino population is not the increase in the foreign born or immigrants to the United States but an increase in the numbers of the native born, those born in the United States, as we illustrate in Table 1.2. The native born now represent 62 percent of all

Table 1.2. *Change in the Hispanic Population, by Nativity: 2000 and 2008*

	2008 Population	2000 Population	Change, 2000–2008	Percentage Change, 2000–2008	Share of Total Change (%)
Native born	28,985,169	21,072,230	7,912,939	37.6	68.1
Foreign born	17,837,307	14,132,250	3,705,057	26.2	31.9
TOTAL	46,822,476	35,204,480	11,617,996	33.0	100.0

Note: Universe is 2000 and 2008 Hispanic resident population.

Source: Pew Hispanic Center, *Statistical Portrait of Hispanics in the United States, 2008* (http://pewhispanic.org/factsheets/factsheet.php?FactsheetID=58). Pew Hispanic Center tabulations of 2000 census (5 percent Integrated Public Use Microdata Series [IPUMS]) and 2008 American Community Survey (1 percent IPUMS).

Table 1.3. *Population Change, by Race and Ethnicity: 2000 and 2008*

	2008 Population	2000 Population	Change, 2000–2008	Percentage Change, 2000–2008	Share of Total Change (%)
Hispanic	46,822,476	35,204,480	11,617,996	33.0	51.3
Native born	28,985,169	21,072,230	7,912,939	37.6	35.0
Foreign born	17,837,307	14,132,250	3,705,057	26.2	16.4
White alone, not Hispanic	198,963,659	194,527,123	4,436,536	2.3	19.6
Black alone, not Hispanic	36,774,337	33,706,554	3,067,783	9.1	13.6
Asian alone, not Hispanic	13,227,070	10,088,521	3,138,549	31.1	13.9
Other, not Hispanic	8,272,186	7,895,228	376,958	4.8	1.7
TOTAL	304,059,728	281,421,906	22,637,822	8.0	100.0

Note: Universe is 2000 and 2008 resident population. "Other, not Hispanic" includes persons reporting single races not listed separately and persons reporting more than one race.
Source: Pew Hispanic Center, *Statistical Portrait of Hispanics in the United States, 2008* (http://pewhispanic.org/factsheets/factsheet.php?FactsheetID=58). Pew Hispanic Center tabulations of 2000 census (5 percent Integrated Public Use Microdata Series IPUMS) and 2008 American Community Survey (1 percent IPUMS).

Latinos, and they make up an overwhelming majority of all Hispanics younger than the age of 18.

Table 1.3 provides more detailed information about the relative size of the native- and foreign-born populations among Latinos in the United States. Overall, from 2000 to 2008 there was a 33 percent increase in the Latino population. We can see that the increase in native-born Latinos (7.9 million) was almost double the increase in the number of foreign-born Latinos (3.7 million) in this nine year period. The Hispanic population in the United States not only shifted more toward the native born over this period but also became significantly more diverse, internally.

Table 1.4 presents figures for Latinos in the United States by country of origin. Historically, the Mexican-origin population has made up a majority of all Latinos, and this continues to be the case today. In 2008, Mexican-origin Hispanics made up 65.6 percent of all Latinos in the United States. Puerto Ricans have, historically, made up the second-largest Hispanic-origin group, and that is also true today. Since the 1960s, Cuban Americans have been the third-largest Latino subgroup. However, by the conclusion of the 2010 census or soon thereafter, the Salvadoran- and Dominican-origin populations in the United States will both surpass

Table 1.4. *Nativity by Detailed Hispanic Origin, 2008*

	Total	Native Born	Foreign Born	Percentage Foreign Born
Mexican	30,746,270	19,374,561	11,371,709	37.0
Puerto Rican	4,150,862	4,105,196	45,666	1.1
All Other				
Spanish/Hispanic/Latino	1,777,278	1,535,661	241,617	13.6
Cuban	1,631,001	651,511	979,490	60.1
Salvadoran	1,560,416	550,557	1,009,859	64.7
Dominican	1,334,228	570,180	764,048	57.3
Guatemalan	985,601	301,803	683,798	69.4
Colombian	881,609	295,298	586,311	66.5
Spaniard	629,758	541,359	88,399	14.0
Honduran	607,970	190,986	416,984	68.6
Ecuadorian	590,602	198,497	392,105	66.4
Peruvian	519,349	159,540	359,809	69.3
Nicaraguan	351,704	129,094	222,610	63.3
Venezuelan	210,337	55,195	155,142	73.8
Argentinean	204,707	68,804	135,903	66.4
Panamanian	153,245	77,314	75,931	49.5
Chilean	127,747	47,888	79,859	62.5
Costa Rican	121,655	48,849	72,806	59.8
Bolivian	93,745	33,383	60,362	64.4
Uruguayan	60,730	16,067	44,663	73.5
Other Central American	43,352	16,989	26,363	60.8
Other South American	21,945	9,211	12,734	58.0
Paraguayan	18,365	7,226	11,139	60.7
Total	46,822,476	28,985,169	17,837,307	38.1

Note: Universe is 2008 Hispanic resident population. Hispanic populations are listed in descending order of total population size.

Source: Pew Hispanic Center, *Statistical Portrait of Hispanics in the United States, 2008* (http://pewhispanic.org/factsheets/factsheet.php?FactsheetID=58). Pew Hispanic Center tabulations of 2000 census (5 percent Integrated Public Use Microdata Series IPUMS) and 2008 American Community Survey (1 percent IPUMS).

that of Cubans in the United States. The populations of Salvadoran and Dominican Americans are both younger, more recent immigrant groups, thus leading to more rapid population increases.

Will the rapid increase in the Latino population continue into the future? Table 1.5 presents the distribution of Latinos and non-Hispanic whites by age, displayed as an age pyramid, as well as a comparison of the age structure of foreign-born and native-born Latinos. In the case of the former, Table 1.5 indicates that the population concentration for Latinos

Table 1.5. *Age and Gender Distributions for Race, Ethnicity, and Nativity Groups: 2008*

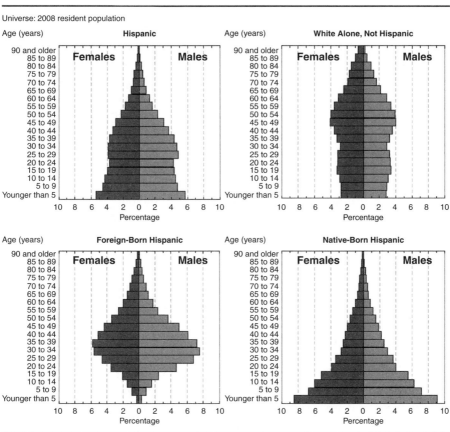

Source: Pew Hispanic Center, *Statistical Portrait of Hispanics in the United States, 2008* (http://pewhispanic.org/factsheets/factsheet.php?FactsheetID=58).

is among the younger age groupings (i.e., those younger than 30 years old), whereas the population bulge for non-Hispanic whites is greatest in the age 45–60 categories.

The youthfulness of Latinos is illustrated most vividly with the native-born Latinos. The age pyramid among the native born is a classic inverted triangle, in which the largest age groupings are at the younger portion of the pyramid. In contrast, the age pyramid for foreign-born Latinos has its greatest population concentration in the age 20–44 categories and is more heavily male than female. The upshot of Table 1.5 is that, on average, Latinos are substantially younger than the overall population, and Latinos born in the United States are younger than those immigrating from abroad; as a result, Hispanics will disproportionately contribute to future population growth in the United States for the foreseeable future.

The next tables reflect two other pertinent aspects of Latinos in the twenty-first century: their language use and their distribution across regions. Table 1.6, on language spoken at home, indicates the extent of English spoken in the household and the level of English-language proficiency among Latinos. The table distinguishes between Latinos younger and older than 18 years old. More than 80 percent of all younger Latinos (who are predominantly native born) speak only English or speak English very well. Among Latino adults, not surprisingly, 86 percent of the native born speak only English or speak English very well. However, if we look at just the immigrant population, we see the uneven pace of language acquisition. Among younger foreign-born Latinos (younger than age 18), 60 percent speak English very well, and 40 percent speak the language less than very well (although it is likely that many are in the earlier stages of English acquisition). By contrast, among foreign-born adults, almost 73 percent of them speak English less than very well.

On the one hand, these data suggest that English-language acquisition is nearly universal in the first generation in the United States, a result consistent with a generation of literature on assimilation (see Alba and Nee 2003; Bean and Stevens 2005). Children of immigrants are English dominant or fluent. On the other hand, given that two-thirds of Latinos older than age 18 are foreign born, Spanish-language use will still be widespread for many years. And although some of the foreign born are long-term residents with ample opportunity to accumulate English skills, others are recent arrivals for whom the process of English-language acquisition is nascent.

Finally, even as Latinos in the United States have, over the first decade of this century, become younger and more diverse, they have also become more dispersed across the United States. There still remain "traditional" areas of residence, such as California, Texas, Florida, and New York, but even within these states, there is a great deal of dispersion away from historical areas of concentration – the immigrant gateways to new areas – to suburbs and secondary cities. Overall, there are simply many more places where Latinos now reside. And although almost one-half of all Latinos still live in either California or Texas, as Table 1.7 indicates, states like Nevada, Georgia, North Carolina, and Arkansas have become more recent destinations for Latinos.

Table 1.6. *Language Spoken at Home and English-Speaking Ability, by Age, Race, and Ethnicity: 2008*

| | Younger Than 18 | | | | 18 and Older | | | |
| | Only English Spoken at Home | Language Other Than Only English at Home | | | Only English Spoken at Home | Language Other Than Only English at Home | | |
		English Spoken Very Well	English Spoken Less Than Very Well	Total		English Spoken Very Well	English Spoken Less Than Very Well	Total
Hispanic	3,658,165	5,293,445	1,835,129	10,786,739	6,197,053	10,929,705	13,693,453	30,820,211
Native born	3,603,805	4,577,981	1,318,381	9,500,167	5,572,470	6,990,123	1,822,660	14,385,253
Foreign born	54,360	715,464	516,748	1,286,572	624,583	3,939,582	11,870,793	16,434,958
White alone, not Hispanic	28,633,770	1,388,432	363,785	30,385,987	148,367,008	6,255,723	2,938,099	157,560,830
Black alone, not Hispanic	7,096,108	321,554	96,728	7,514,390	24,638,587	1,211,577	675,445	26,525,609
Asian alone, not Hispanic	740,363	992,095	330,958	2,063,416	2,103,620	4,072,320	4,154,000	10,329,940
Other, not Hispanic	1,996,628	218,012	46,508	2,261,148	3,943,595	692,753	296,160	4,932,508
TOTAL	42,125,034	8,213,538	2,673,108	53,011,680	185,249,863	23,162,078	21,757,157	230,169,098
Percentage distribution								
Hispanic	33.9	49.1	17.0	100.0	20.1	35.5	44.4	100.0
Native born	37.9	48.2	13.9	100.0	38.7	48.6	12.7	100.0
Foreign born	4.2	55.6	40.2	100.0	3.8	24.0	72.2	100.0
White alone, not Hispanic	94.2	4.6	1.2	100.0	94.2	4.0	1.9	100.0
Black alone, not Hispanic	94.4	4.3	1.3	100.0	92.9	4.6	2.5	100.0
Asian alone, not Hispanic	35.9	48.1	16.0	100.0	20.4	39.4	40.2	100.0
Other, not Hispanic	88.3	9.6	2.1	100.0	80.0	14.0	6.0	100.0
All	79.5	15.5	5.0	100.0	80.5	10.1	9.5	100.0

Note: Universe is 2008 resident population age five and older.

Source: Pew Hispanic Center, *Statistical Portrait of Hispanics in the United States, 2008* (http://pewhispanic.org/factsheets/factsheet.php?FactsheetID= 58).

Table 1.7. *Change in the Hispanic Population, by State: 2000 and 2008*

	2008 Population	2000 Population	Change, 2000–2008	Change, 2000–2008 (%)
California	13,434,896	10,928,470	2,506,426	22.9
Texas	8,815,582	6,653,338	2,162,244	32.5
Florida	3,846,267	2,673,654	1,172,613	43.9
New York	3,232,360	2,854,991	377,369	13.2
Arizona	1,964,625	1,292,152	672,473	52.0
Illinois	1,961,843	1,527,145	434,698	28.5
New Jersey	1,424,069	1,117,604	306,465	27.4
Colorado	993,198	735,769	257,429	35.0
New Mexico	895,150	759,343	135,807	17.9
Georgia	780,408	434,375	346,033	79.7
North Carolina	678,023	377,084	300,939	79.8
Nevada	672,393	393,397	278,996	70.9
Washington	642,959	444,718	198,241	44.6
Pennsylvania	588,950	399,736	189,214	47.3
Massachusetts	556,573	428,530	128,043	29.9
Virginia	528,002	333,482	194,520	58.3
Connecticut	424,191	330,952	93,239	28.2
Oregon	417,152	273,209	143,943	52.7
Michigan	408,695	319,463	89,232	27.9
Maryland	372,650	230,992	141,658	61.3
Utah	323,938	214,750	109,188	50.8
Indiana	322,148	201,203	120,945	60.1
Ohio	296,059	218,350	77,709	35.6
Wisconsin	286,382	191,097	95,285	49.9
Oklahoma	278,676	186,340	92,336	49.6
Kansas	268,964	173,746	95,218	54.8
Tennessee	234,868	142,732	92,136	64.6
Minnesota	217,551	116,692	100,859	86.4
Missouri	182,059	118,235	63,824	54.0
South Carolina	177,999	94,652	83,347	88.1
Idaho	159,257	100,271	58,986	58.8
Arkansas	155,309	85,303	70,006	82.1
Louisiana	152,781	92,836	59,945	64.6
Nebraska	147,968	80,204	67,764	84.5
Alabama	128,586	111,634	16,952	15.2
Iowa	124,030	72,152	51,878	71.9
Rhode Island	120,662	89,870	30,792	34.3
Hawaii	108,663	87,853	20,810	23.7
Kentucky	100,366	56,922	43,444	76.3
Delaware	62,506	37,301	25,205	67.6

Note: Universe is 2000 and 2008 Hispanic resident population.
Source: Pew Hispanic Center, *Statistical Portrait of Hispanics in the United States, 2008* (http://pewhispanic.org/factsheets/factsheet.php?FactsheetID=58).

The states with the fastest-growing Latino populations in the United States have all been in the South or Midwest. Finally, the dispersion of Latinos across regions has also altered the mix of Latino subgroups in many states. For example, the influx of Puerto Ricans and Central Americans into Florida has made Cuban Americans a minority of Hispanics in a state in which they have, over the past three decades, dominated Latino politics. Although persons of Mexican origin are still the dominant group in Southern California, there has been a substantial influx of Central Americans, especially Salvadorans and Guatemalans.

Substantial growth in the Latino population will not change in the near future, as evidenced by our brief demographic profile. So do these demographic changes translate into sociopolitical relationships and consequences for American politics and policy? These broader consequences of demographic change are the focus of this work. The continuation of this introductory chapter will highlight some existing notions about the Latino community and how identifying and understanding the complexities of this large community can enable us to frame or reframe contemporary issues before the body politic. In addition, the identification of these questions serves as the backdrop for the subsequent chapters that explore matters of community, intergroup relations, attitudes and political behaviors, political participation, and transnational activities.

Common Knowledge or Misperceptions?

Despite the easy availability of basic demographic data, like that presented here, there is a host of commonly held, though often mistaken, impressions, notions, and "facts" about Latinos in the United States that are deeply engrained in the broader discourse and difficult to dispel. Although this book does not consider all of these, it does provide a profile of a large, diverse community in all its complexity, in a way that undermines the kind of easy dualities that caricature who Latinos are and what they are about. The LNS allows us to explore and confront various dimensions of this assumed common knowledge, or the "facts" that many people believe about Latinos in the United States.

Latinos Are Predominantly an Immigrant Community
One piece of this "common knowledge" is that Latinos are all immigrants, and not only immigrants, but primarily illegal immigrants. Thus characterized, Hispanic Americans' civic incorporation, capacity for political

participation, views of policy, and so on, are all seen as shaped and constrained by their immigrant status. The LNS corroborates that a majority of the adults in the population are foreign born. The large majority of foreign-born Latinos, however, are legal residents, not undocumented migrants. At the same time, there is a substantial population of Latinos whose families have resided in the United States for several generations. Had the LNS surveyed all Latinos (persons younger than the age of 18 as well as adults), then native-born Latinos would have made up the majority of those interviewed. Well more than 80 percent of all Latino children (more than 86 percent in the 2000 census) are born citizens of the United States.

During the 1980s and 1990s, Latino population growth was driven by immigration, but by the early part of the twenty-first century, this growth was being fueled by the native-born children of immigrants, and Latinos were rapidly becoming primarily a U.S.-born population. This trend will only continue. A significant proportion of the Hispanic population is not only U.S. born, but their parents and sometimes grandparents were born in the United States as well. Recognizing the Latino immigrant experience is certainly important, yet only or overly emphasizing this aspect obscures the full range of experiences and perspectives of Latinos in America.

Latinos Are Isolated from Mainstream Society

The view of Latinos as a predominately immigrant community is sometimes accompanied by the perception that Latinos are culturally impenetrable, unwilling, or (worse) unable to assimilate to American norms and values. This, of course, presupposes that Latinos hold norms and values at odds with American traditions. As a consequence, many observers have been concerned that Latinos do not blend well into America's sociocultural fabric and, in fact, are a strain tugging at this delicate cloth (Buchanan 2002; Huntington 2005). The evidentiary basis of these claims has always been weak (Segura 2005), and these arguments are more expressions of long-established xenophobia in American cultural life rather than anything particular to these immigrants (Fraga and Segura 2006). What evidence there is indicates that, on the contrary, Latinos' orientations and attitudes are very consistent with American core values and traditions, and they have been for some time (de la Garza et al. 1996). Even looking only at the Latino foreign born, as a whole the group evidences consistent values and beliefs that are entirely compatible with the American dream and ethos. The LNS allows us to differentiate respondents' views by time spent in the United States and by generation, and we can track the evolution of assimilation on several dimensions (e.g., English-language use, rates of exogamy, educational attainment) across time. Thus examined, the evidence suggests nuance and variation that are often overlooked in popular discourse on the topic.

Latinos "Stick to Their Own Kind"

Latinos are sometimes portrayed as clannish, preferring to interact only with fellow country persons. Latinos are often residentially concentrated in neighborhoods and often have coworkers who are of their same ethnic background. Are Latinos' social networks defined by neighborhoods, or by workplace settings, or by their ancestral ties, and do any of these links matter? The LNS questions on inter- and intragroup relations and interactions include items inquiring about the composition of respondents' friendship and work networks. For many first-generation Latinos, much of their social network is composed of their fellow coethnics, but these friends and coworkers increasingly come from all parts of Latin America and include native-born Latinos and non-Latinos as well. The longer individuals reside in the United States, the more likely their social networks are to include non-Latinos, and increasingly non-Latino family members or significant others. The extent of interactions with non-Latinos indicates no inherent aversion or attraction to any specific group. Our discussion here gives a more complex portrayal of relationships between Latinos and other racial-ethnic groups.

Latinos' Country-of-Origin Ties Supersede Their U.S. Ties

Although Latinos may be "assimilating," they also seem to retain ties to their countries of origin through a system of regularized contacts and allegiance. These ties include recurring trips to their hometowns, the sending of remittances, the formation of hometown association in the United States, support for their country of origin in a variety of venues, and a strong desire to return to their "mother country." These ties are seen by some commentators as going against the grain of integration into American civil society. However, although first-generation Latinos maintain some ties to their countries of origin, these often reflect family bonds. Over time, especially with family reunification in the United States, these connections are weakened. As we discuss in this almanac, there is a dramatic drop-off of transnational ties in the second generation and beyond. The "dream of return" – the desire many immigrants have to return back home eventually to retire or to convert their accumulated wealth into a prosperous business venture – is more myth than reality. Rootedness in

American society, U.S.-born children and/or spouses, lifestyle preferences, mobility and economic opportunity, and attachment to the United States seriously minimize the proclivity to move back to one's home country.

Latinos Are Following European Ethnics in Fully Assimilating and Losing All but a Symbolic Ethnic Identity

Given the evidence for assimilation among Latinos, does this pattern mean that Latinos will follow the path of European national origin groups and become primarily "symbolic" ethnics? This possibility suggests that Latino ethnicity might increasingly take the form of some degree of group pride and recognition, but it will not be central to people's daily lives. Again, the evidence presented in this work strongly suggests that for many respondents their sense of themselves includes an attachment to their ancestry, cultural traditions, ethnically dense social networks, and group identification as both members of their national origin group and as Latinos or Hispanics. Many Latinos feel that sociopolitical incorporation in the United States does not entail shedding their cultural traditions and practices to meld into American society. Instead, for Latinos, "being American" is part of a broader canvas of self-identifications, so that their sense of being American is at once both authentic and inclusive. This almanac explores Latinos' relationships with American identity and cultural affinities in depth.

National Origin Identities Are Disappearing and Melding into a Pan-Ethnic Hispanic Identity

American commentators often refer to persons who speak Spanish or who come from Latin American nations or are ancestrally connected to these countries as "Hispanic" or "Latino." Indeed, this book likewise follows the practice of describing individuals with a family origin in Latin America as "Latino" or "Hispanic." The blending of persons from many cultural traditions, dialects, histories, and different ties to the United States can reflect a community in formation that extends beyond country-of-origin identities (e.g., Peruvian, Cuban, Mexican). Or it may reflect an artificial characterization of a "community" whose supposed existence lies more in the mass media treatment of these social categories of Latinos or Hispanics than in any reality. In the public domain, the aggregation of such a diverse set of people may simply be a convenient shorthand map of persons who share some commonalities while minimizing substantive and discernible differences. Do persons with family ties to Latin America really see themselves as having something in common with others sharing a similar heritage?

The artificiality versus reality of the socially constructed notion of Latino and/or Hispanic has been continually debated. The LNS results indicate that respondents feel a sense of Latino identity even across differences in national origin, nativity, generational status, and language use. Seeing themselves in these terms creates a sense of identification and affinity but can also serve as a basis for collective expressions. Interestingly, seeing oneself as Latino and/or Hispanic does not come at the expense or the discarding of national pride or identification (for either one's country of origin or the United States). This almanac's analysis of Latino identity goes beyond simple univariate, or single-variable, labels, to uncover respondents' multiple identities.

Latinos Are Adopting La raza cósmica *and See Themselves as Racially Distinct in the United States*

Ongoing conversations about the changing racial and ethnic makeup of the United States have introduced the possibility that the predominant racial classification scheme of black and white does not fully reflect the country's increasing racial diversity. Latinos can be characterized as a multiracial group made up of persons from a number of national origins. At the same time, however, it is possible that the central role of race in American life and a sense of otherness among Latinos may be a basis for Hispanics to view themselves in racial terms. If Latinos were to adopt a separate racial identity, not simply an ethnic identity, this would challenge the prevailing black-white racial paradigm. Vasconcelos's (1997) concept of Latinos as a *raza cósmica* – a race that is itself an amalgam of other races – is one way to describe Latinos as a racialized minority. One indication that this might be occurring is the high proportion of Latinos who place themselves in the "some other race" category in many recent government surveys. Do Latinos think of themselves ethnically, racially, or both? If Latinos see themselves as a distinct race in America, how might this affect their relationships with other groups in American society?

Of course, a critical complication of this question is the widely varied racial histories of the Latin American societies from which Latino immigrants come. Although some societies like Mexico are predominantly mestizo – meaning European and Native American mixtures – others are African and European, or even all three. Moreover, there is significant variation within nations, with some Latinos being entirely of African,

European, or Native American ancestry even in nations whose population includes many more individuals of mixed or uncertain ancestry. Race
in the Americas is, at the very least, a difficult concept.

The LNS includes a set of questions that tap various ways in which
race is identified and measured, asking respondents to place themselves
in the census's conventional racial categories, to identify the lightness or
darkness of their skin color, and to indicate whether they agree (or not)
with the characterization of Latinos as a distinct race. On the basis of
responses to these questions, this book explores the relationship between
Latinos and race in the United States, as well as the possible implications
of these choices for their relationship with other racial-ethnic groups.

Discrimination Binds Latinos Together

As mentioned earlier, underlying our examination of Latinos here in this
almanac is an assumption that the persons whom we designate as Latinos
or Hispanics actually share an affinity and identification with one another.
But how might this identity come about? One explanation might be the
way that other members of American society treat Latinos. Differential
treatment or discriminatory behavior based on a set of stereotypes (e.g.,
phenotype, language, accent, cultural practices) can shape and reinforce
a sense of group identity. What is the extent of discriminatory behavior
experienced by Latinos? In what settings does it occur, and who are the
perpetrators? Whether or not our LNS respondents directly experience
acts of discrimination, how do they perceive the general treatment of
Latinos?

Our examination of the LNS data indicates that a noticeable percentage of Latinos feel that they have been treated unfairly in a variety of
public settings. Their perception of why they have been discriminated
against ranges from their accent to their phenotype, foreign-born status,
gender, and so on. A sizable number of those who indicated that they
have experienced unfair treatment answer that "being Latino" is itself
the basis for this discrimination. But this unfair treatment is complex: for
example, the LNS provides evidence that a significant fraction of this negative treatment toward Latinos is from other Latinos. This intra-Latino
discriminatory behavior could have implications for positive intragroup
relations among Latino subgroups and cooperative endeavors. For the
most part, however, the data presented in this almanac clearly indicate
that Latinos feel that they are different, as a group, from others, and
have a sense of affinity with other Latinos. Being discriminated against

or feeling that Latinos are treated unfairly also plays a role in developing a sense of group identity.

Latinos Do Not Support Their Children's Educational Aspirations and Are Not Involved with Their Schools

Latinos are assimilating to some degree into American society, but dimensions of assimilation associated with upward mobility (i.e., educational attainment) has more of a downward trajectory than an upward mobility. If this is the case, social structures such as the educational system are limiting opportunities rather facilitating Latinos' gains in education and conversion to better labor market returns. This downward mobility would reflect a failure of the educational system to integrate these newcomers. One blue-ribbon report after another assessing the U.S. educational system, especially the K–12 levels, clearly indicates relatively poor educational performances and experiences for many Latino children. Patterns of high dropout, lower graduation, high grade repetition, and limited English proficiency levels have not improved in decades. This is partly because of the continued immigration of Latinos, who arrive with lower educational levels, as well as a greater concentration of poverty among Latino households. These are major culprits that deter educational advancement for Latinos. In addition, a lesser commitment to educational achievement and lower educational trajectories are also cited as obstacles to educational gains. For their part, Latino parents are characterized as less interested in their children's education, and they are said not to encourage their children to excel in school. If only Latino parents would be more supportive and involved themselves with educators and in their schools, the criticism goes, it might be possible for their children to experience greater educational progress.

The LNS provides an overview of the educational aspirations of Latino parents for their children and the amount of contact and participation that Latino parents have with teachers, administrators, and school boards. The evidence here shows that, if the educational system is failing Latino children, it is not because their parents are disengaged from their education. The data indicate, instead, a great deal of involvement and support from Latino parents for their children in the educational arena. The data also suggest a gap, however, between parental aspirations and expectations: Latino parents with high educational aspirations for their children may have lower expectations. In general, this would suggest that despite parents' desires for their children's educational success, they introduce reality factors (i.e., poorer quality education, less resource to commit to education, systemic bias/discrimination, etc.) that can undermine their children's realizing these educational aspirations. So, do Latino parents' lower expectations of their child's opportunity structure diminish their commitment to being engaged in the educational arena? Does immigrant status among parents (which can include limited knowledge and understanding of the American educational system as well as limited English abilities) affect their involvement? Given the espoused commitment to family and their future, how do the persistent negative educational outcomes point to blaming the Latino community? And what are Latino parents' assessments about the problem areas for their children in the educational system? These queries are explored in Chapter 13.

Hispanic Machismo Creates a Gender Divide

One of the prevailing notions about Latinos is a stereotype about patriarchy and male dominance, with men primarily directing the lives of family members, especially those of women. The concept of machismo symbolizes the male-centric notion of power and authority. Latinos' views about gender roles and the appropriate areas of independent decision making and the status of women represent possible obstacles for collective endeavors among Latinas and Latino men, and they may depart from more general American egalitarian ideas. The LNS explored gender issues with a battery of questions on issues of equal pay for men and women, whether women should have the primary responsibility for child rearing, access to birth control, and whether both sexes can serve equally well as political leaders. This allows us to explore whether the existence of macho orientations is so pervasive that it colors all situations or whether it is applied selectively. The LNS finds that views on gender are not very consistent with popular perceptions, but they do vary by such factors as nativity, generation, and socioeconomic status.

Latinos Do Not Naturalize

Are Latino immigrants who retain regularized contact with their countries of origin and hold strong affinities less likely to naturalize? The LNS data make it possible to trace immigrant status and the propensity to naturalize. Historically, rates of naturalization among Latinos, especially those of Mexican origin, have been noticeably lower than for other immigrant groups. More recently, there has been an increase in naturalization, but indicators suggest that anti-immigrant sentiment and restricted rights for permanent-resident aliens have spurred these increases rather than any change in the personal attributes of the foreign born (Pantoja, Ramirez, and Segura 2001). Chapter 2, which explores naturalization and citizenship, indicates that Latinos' decisions of whether to naturalize is dependent less on Latinos' affiliation with the United States or their desire to be part of civil society and more on practical considerations. These include knowledge about the procedures and requirements to pursue naturalization, the rising costs of filing for naturalization, and access to English classes.

Latinos Do Not Participate

Latinos are regularly depicted as politically passive or apolitical. The general political science literature finds a positive correlation between an individual's levels of trust, efficacy, and alienation, and his or her ties to and involvement in the political process. In addition, these orientations are related to both civic and political engagement. Presumably then, Hispanics' feelings of low trust, high alienation, and low political interest could account for their lower rates of participation. But this is not what the LNS data indicate. We look extensively at the patterns of Latinos' political orientations, taking into account the crosscutting dimensions of nativity and generational status, and we look at their views on the proper role of government. The large majority of Latinos are neither alienated nor mistrustful. Many keep informed about politics and follow U.S. politics. Regarding the role of government, the LNS indicates that the foreign born in particular clearly exhibit a self-help or self-reliant orientation; many respondents also indicate that they prefer some distance between individuals and government. And, like many Americans, Latinos have reservations about the responsiveness of government. However, the LNS data also indicate that many Latinos expect government to provide economic assistance, social welfare programs, health-care coverage, and educational equity initiatives. The data indicate that Latino political behavior derives from a complex constellation of attitudes.

Latinos Are Predominantly Conservative

An emerging characterization of Latinos as political actors in American politics is that they are a rather traditional and conservative group, reflected in the importance they attach to religion, family, and the values of self-reliance. The salience of morality and religion for Latinos means that issues such as abortion, capital punishment, and same-sex unions might be pivotal in determining Latinos' issue agenda and partisan support. As a result, it is not uncommon for Latinos to be considered potential

recruits into the conservative wing of American politics. The discussion in
this volume sorts out their ideological distribution along a conservative-
liberal continuum and untangles its underlying elements. In doing so, the
evidence challenges the idea of ideology as a one-dimensional concept in
which the basis for one being a conservative, liberal, or moderate is determined by a common set of moral values. Given that Latinos are viewed
as socially conservative and as holding traditional values, does this mean
that Latinos are uniformly anti-abortion, opposed to same-sex unions,
and advocates for prayer in school or other elements of morally defined
policy agenda? Is an agenda centered on "moral" issues the core of Latinos' policy interests and their primary set of concerns? This seems not
to be the case; instead, our exploration of the data finds more complex
patterns and traits associated with Latinos' political ideology.

Latinos' Affiliation with the Democratic Party Is Waning
The prevailing perspective on partisan affiliation is that Latinos' long
historical attachment with the Democratic Party predisposes them to be
Democrats. This view was reinforced in 2008, when almost 70 percent
of Latino voters supported Barack Obama for president. However, in
2004 the Democratic candidate, John Kerry, received about 60 percent
of Hispanic votes, whereas the Republican candidate, George W. Bush,
received slightly more than 40 percent of the Latino vote (the largest percentage for any Republican presidential candidate). So, is the percentage
of Latinos' voters supporting the Republican ticket in presidential election years consistent? Will the Democratic Party still be able to count
on Hispanic voters for their membership and support? Does variation in
Democratic Party support among Latinos voters represent soft levels of
partisan loyalty and backing?

This book explores partisan affiliations and the strength of party loyalty across dimensions of nativity, generation, and socioeconomic status,
focusing on a number of key questions. Given that a substantial percentage of adult Latinos are immigrants, how they do relate to the major
American political parties? If they develop a sense of dissatisfaction with
or distance from the Democratic Party, does this result in more tenu-
ous support, or does it suggest a potential shift to the Republican Party?
The political ramifications of partisanship and of how Latinos are fitting
themselves into the party system, as illustrated in the LNS, provides a
fuller picture of the nature of partisanship in American politics. Finally,
what are the linkages between Latinos' policy preferences and partisan
support? For example, what is the link between immigration reform,

which emphasizes a normalized status of undocumented migrants in the United States and has been a major policy priority among Latinos, and partisan attachment? How does the policy deadlock on this issue, with few initiatives from either major party beyond a focus on border-security measures, affect Latinos' partisan identification and support? Our data provide tentative clues to the answers to these complex questions.

Latinos' Electoral Choices Are Heavily Influenced by a Coethnic Candidate on the Ballot

The perceptions discussed earlier of Latinos as clannish and as maintaining distinctive cultural practices might lead one to believe that voting choices would be significantly influenced if a Latino or Latina were running for office. The assumption is that voters generally vote for candidate(s) of their same racial-ethnic background. Although some may see this as selecting political representatives simply on the basis of their descriptive attributes – because an officeholder shares a group's characteristics – others might interpret it as supporting an individual whose experiences and interests are similar to those of voters. But how does this play in practice? If candidates speak Spanish and are Latino, will this sway Latino voters to cast their ballot for those candidates? The findings in this almanac do not support this simplistic depiction. Where does issue salience come into the calculus of Latino vote choice? Would a Latino vote for a non-Latino if his or her issue positions were more congruent with the voter's issue concerns and preferences? How does the sense of group affiliation and affinity come into play when Latinos vote? What are the attributes of Latinos associated with a greater or lesser probability of supporting a Latino or Latina candidate, even if he or she ran as a Republican? Are there conditions under which the race-ethnicity of the candidate would be much less relevant for voter choice? These questions are explored in the almanac.

Latinos' Policy Concerns Are Limited Only to Immigration

If many Latino adults are immigrants, does this mean that immigration policy is their primary, driving policy concern? Are Hispanics' views on immigration similar across national origin lines, across generation, across socioeconomic status, and with language use? The insights from the LNS allow us to explore the saliency of immigration relative to other policy areas and concerns among Latinos. We probe for Latinos' policy salience by posing two questions: one about the major issues confronting the nation and, in contradistinction, another about the most important issues confronting Latinos. Are the same sets of issues cited in response to both questions? In short, how different are Latinos' policy concerns and priorities from those of other Americans? The LNS results presented here indicate that immigration is an important issue for Latinos, with a high degree of consensus on preferred policy solutions. At the same time, the ranking of Latino policy interests reflects their struggles to make it in American society in terms of "bread-and-butter issues": the quality of their children's schools and educational opportunities, safety from crime, access to health care, and employment prospects. Together with immigration, these represent a fuller picture of Latinos' policy agenda.

The Latino Almanac's Organization and Content

At the beginning of this introductory chapter, we discussed the growing presence and significance of Latinos in American society and the body politic. Pausing for a brief demographic glimpse of this growing community, we highlighted past and future contributors to an expanding population base. With increasing attention from the media and in politics, and with the increased availability of survey data describing their views and political stances, Latinos have become less invisible. However, at the same time, Latinos find it hard to have their voices heard and their issues addressed by major political institutions, mainstream media outlets, and formal decision-making establishments. Moreover, the "common knowledge" about Latinos is often incorrect.

Our intention with this almanac is to provide an accessible and well-documented profile of the Latino community, with particular attention to LNS questions that shed light on Latinos' attitudes about various assimilation-related issues. We emphasize issues that have engendered interest and, indeed, concern in the general population on the basis of often incorrect assumptions and stereotypes. We hope that in doing so, community-based organizations, members of the mass media, elected and appointed officials, Latino interest groups, and interested citizens will have a source of baseline knowledge with which to analyze Latinos' integration into and engagement with civil society in the United States.

The Data: LNS Survey Description and Methodology

To explore immigrant assimilation over time, political attitudes and behaviors, social networks, and the like, we use the Latino National Survey. The 2006 Latino National Survey (LNS) has 8,634 completed interviews of self-identified Latino and/or Hispanic residents of the United States. Interviewing began on November 17, 2005, and continued through August 4, 2006.[1] The survey instrument contained approximately 165 distinct items, ranging from demographic descriptions to political attitudes and policy preferences, as well as a variety of social indicators and experiences. The mean interview length was 40.6 minutes.

The survey was conducted using computer-assisted telephone interviewing software by Interviewing Service of America, headquartered in Van Nuys, California. All interviewers were bilingual – English and Spanish. Respondents were greeted in both languages and immediately offered the opportunity to interview in either. Interviewers were provided with a consent script to allow them to opt out of the survey, should they choose to do so.

Respondents were selected from a random sample of Latino households in the areas covered. The sample was drawn by Geoscape International, a research and sampling firm in Miami that has particular expertise in identifying Hispanic households. The sample was drawn from a household database of approximately 11 million households in the United States that are identified as Latino or Hispanic.

The Latino National Survey covers fifteen states and the District of Columbia metropolitan area (including counties and municipalities in Virginia and Maryland). The universe of analysis contains more than 90 percent of the U.S. Hispanic population. States were selected, first, on the basis of the overall size of the Latino and/or Hispanic population. In addition, four states – Arkansas, Georgia, Iowa, and North Carolina – were added in an attempt to capture the evolving nature of emerging populations in states without lengthy histories of large Latino populations. Both Georgia and North Carolina, however, rank twelfth and fourteenth, respectively, in terms of Latino population size and would have been included on that basis alone.

The sample is stratified by geographic designation, which means that each state sample is a valid, stand-alone representation of that state's Latino population. State sample sizes vary, but all national figures reported are appropriately weighted such that the numbers are accurately

---

[1] A hiatus in the interviewing occurred from December 15 to January 10 to account for the large number of potential respondents in the sample who were likely to be unavailable during that period. Completed interviews in that time-frame represent only callbacks of interviews begun on an earlier date.

representative of the universe covered by the study. The national margin of error is approximately ±1.05 percent. The smallest sample size for any unit was four hundred, which yields a margin of error of less than ±5 percent for each state.

Sampling in a number of states was internally stratified. In each case but California, internal strata were represented proportionately in the final sample and imposed solely to ensure that lower-density regions were in the final sample. In California, additional strata were imposed in a proportional fashion, owing in part to the larger sample size, to allow for greater between-region comparisons. Even though the sample frame was a subset of the fifty states, the states selected and Latino respondents chosen represent more than 90 percent of all Latinos residing in the United States. Through the use of weighting and estimation techniques it is possible to calculate national-level results with the computed national-level weights so that they remain representative of the national Latino population.

The Substantive Areas of the Latino Almanac

The range and extent of the LNS allows us to cover a wide range of socially and politically relevant topics. This is organized by key subject areas. We begin with in-depth demographic profiles of Latinos in the United States; by national origin; and in the case of Mexico, by state of origin. If respondents were born in Mexico, the LNS asked what state they came from. By identifying immigrants' home states, it is possible to discern geographic patterns in the waves of migration, and the characteristics and profiles of these migrants can be compared across their Mexican states of origin. In addition, comparisons can be made on generational status in the United States using indicators of assimilation, socioeconomic status, and a host of political behaviors and attitudes. The extent of the demographic characteristics will enable readers to see variations and similarities among Latinos in the LNS survey.

Although we did not design *Latinos in the New Millennium* to be only a political reference book, the insight and value-added nature of this project is the collective background and experience of the contributors as longtime and well-established observers and analysts of Latino politics. We begin the political side of this almanac with an examination of core political values that are central to the American political system. Matters such as trust in government, sense of civic engagement, expectations about the role of government in civil society, beliefs about fairness, and access for all persons in society are covered. How well do Latinos feel that they understand American political institutions and processes? The logical extension of core values is putting such values into practice.

A significant portion of this book covers the scope of political participation of Latinos in the United States. This includes their levels of knowledge about the political system, their civic engagement, their electoral involvement (e.g., registration status, voting, campaigns, contributions), their frequency of contact with public officials, their assessment of and membership in political parties, the factors determining their vote choice, their actual vote choices, their views on the importance of supporting coethnic candidates, and their political ideology. In addition, in a separate chapter we explore how being Latino affects one's identification of salient policy issues and policy preferences for a wide range of social, cultural, and economic issue areas. How do Latinos evaluate officeholders?

We pay close attention to the policy area of education. Historically, education has been at the core of Latinos' concerns, and improving the educational experiences of their children has been a key priority for Latino parents. We investigate the range of experiences that Latino parents have for their children, their educational aspirations and expectations for their children, and the contact they have with key actors in the educational system (e.g., teachers, school administrators, principals, school board members). We also explore the extent and satisfaction of their children's participation in bilingual programs. Finally, we asked parents to assess their children's education and schools. In doing so, we can construct a fuller picture of the intersection of Latinos and the educational system.

We describe a Latino population as if this population constituted a distinct group and/or identifiable community in America. Yet we do not stop with that assumption; we explore the possible bases for a viable ethnic community by looking at their experiences of discrimination, perceived individual and group sense of commonality of circumstances and common issues areas, cultural similarities, the concept of linked fate, and competitive or cooperative relations among other Latino subgroup members and with other racial and ethnic groups. Our analysis explores both intragroup relations among members of the different Latino national origin subgroups, as well as Latinos' views about African Americans, non-Hispanic whites, and Asian Americans (asked in certain states with significant Asian American populations). This analysis can gauge social distance between the named groups and possible areas of common interests.

This almanac also addresses the issue of Latino transnationalism – ties to their countries of origin – and Hispanics' views about gender roles and women's roles in public life. With the foreign born making up a majority of all adults, transnationalism – the sustained interactions and exchanges transcending national boundaries and maintained by a system of social networks and institutional structures – plays an important role in Latino daily life. The transnational transactions explored in the LNS occur between individuals and communities in the form of capital flows, trade, citizenship affiliations and activities, political incorporation, intergovernmental organizations, social movements, familial ties, social identities, and influence on policy. More specifically, the LNS describes the extent of contacts, visits, remittances, civic and political engagement in the countries of origin, and attention to country-of-origin politics. We explore these questions: To the extent that transnationalism occurs, is it limited primarily to the immigrant generation? Do institutions in countries of origin facilitate and encourage regularized transnational ties? Are there political ramifications for the civic and political engagement for Latinos who are transnationally engaged?

Finally, we provide some insights about media use and sources for Latinos. Given the choices of print and television, how does one's media source affect political knowledge and interest? Does the language of the media source produce any differences among Latinos? How accessible are computers and the Internet for Latino households? Though somewhat limited, the battery of media-related items does provide information not only about use of and sources of political information but also about the levels of political interest among Latinos. As with the other sections, comparisons are made by differentiating LNS respondents by nativity, generational status, citizenship, gender, and other pertinent characteristics.

Our analysis is presented through a combination of bivariate tables and narratives that highlight important relationships. In the case of the former, nativity and generational status are commonly considered major factors in the assimilation process that should help inform potential differences or widespread consensus. Where there are variations, other key crosscutting variables, such as educational attainment, gender, socioeconomic status, income, and so on, are introduced into our discussion. We provide some coverage of the extant knowledge in each topic area and summarize the key findings.

In our concluding chapter, we revisit the themes of complexities and similarities and their political significance for the Latino population. We also summarize the major findings of each chapter and provide some general conclusions about the current and future status of Latinos in American society and its politics. By summarizing the resultant analyses and interpretations, we hope to assist in the formation of basic understandings and insights that can be gleaned from the LNS. One possible outcome for readers are policy discussions informed by the LNS results and analyses. These political discussions could center on more effective approaches for political mobilization, increasing political interest, and understanding what affects Latinos' vote choice. This idea of linking research with policy and political applications is a major consideration in the preparation of this work. Unfortunately, much of the attention on Latinos has been couched in a variety of positive, negative, promising, alarming, speculative, and emotional ways. Our interest lies in facilitating interest in this significant group in American society and the American political system by pursuing discourse, scrutiny, planning, and evaluation of the future of Latinos in the American context.

Bibliography

Alba, Richard and Victor Nee. 2003. *Remaking the American Mainstream: Assimilation and Contemporary Immigration*. Cambridge, MA: Harvard University Press.

Bean, Frank and Gilian Stevens. 2005. *America's Newcomers and the Dynamics of Diversity* (American Sociological Association Rose Monographs). New York: Russell Sage Foundation Press.

Buchanan, Patrick J. 2006. *State of Emergency: The Third World Invasion and Conquest of America*. New York: St. Martin's Press.

De la Garza, Rodolfo, A. Falcón, and F. Chris García. 1996. "Will the Real Americans Please Stand Up: A Comparison of Anglo and Mexican American Support for Core American Values." *American Journal of Political Science* 40, no. 2: 335–51.

Fraga, Luis Ricardo. 2009. "Building through Exclusion: Anti-Immigrant Politics in the United States." In *Bringing Outsiders In: Transatlantic Perspectives on Immigrant Political Incorporation*, ed. Jennifer L. Hochschild and John Mollenkopf, 176–92. Ithaca, NY: Cornell University Press.

Fraga, Luis Ricardo, John A. Garcia, Rodney E. Hero, Michael Jones-Correa, Valerie Martinez-Ebers, and Gary M. Segura. 2010. *Latino Lives in America: Making It Home*. Philadelphia: Temple University Press.

Fraga, Luis R., and Gary Segura. 2006. "Culture Clash? Contesting Notions of American Identity and the Effects of Latin American Immigration." *PS: Political Science and Politics* 4, no. 2 (June): 279.

Huntington, Samuel. 2005. *Who Are We? The Challenges to America's National Identity*. New York: Simon and Schuster.

Ngai, Mae. 2004. *Impossible Subjects: Illegal Aliens and the Making of Modern America*. Princeton, NJ: Princeton University Press.

O'Brien, Soledad. 2009. *Latino in America*. CNN documentary. http://www.cnn
.com/SPECIALS/2009/latino.in.america/.

Pantoja, Adrian D., Ricardo Ramirez, and Gary M. Segura. 2001. "Citizens by
Choice, Voters by Necessity: Patterns in Political Mobilization by Naturalized
Latinos." *Political Research Quarterly* 54, no. 4: 729–50.

Segura, Gary. 2005. Review of Who Are We?: The Challenges to America's
National Identity Perspectives on Politics Vol. 3, No. 3, pp. 640–42.

Smith, Rogers. 1997. *Civic Ideals: Conflicting Visions of Citizenship in U.S.
History*. New Haven, CT: Yale University Press.

Suro, Roberto, and Jeffrey S. Passel. 2003. *The Rise of the Second Generation:
Changing Patterns in Hispanic Population Growth*. Washington, D.C.: Pew
Hispanic Center.

Vasconcelos, Jose and Didier T. Jaen (Translator). 1997. The Cosmic Race / La
raza cosmica (Race in the Americas). Baltimore: The Johns Hopkins University
Press.

2

A Demographic Profile of Latinos in the United States

Introduction: The Changing Demographics of the Latino Community

Over the past twenty years there have been significant changes in the demographics of the Latino population in the United States. These have occurred in five areas. First, and most important, the Latino population is now much larger than previously, and it represents a larger share of the national population. The Latino population grew 58 percent between 1990 and 2000 and increased 43 percent between 2000 and 2010. The 2000 census revealed that Latinos were 12.5 percent of the U.S. population, surpassing African Americans as the largest minority group (who accounted for only 12 percent). The most recent data from the 2010 census indicate that the Latino population has grown to 16.3 percent of the U.S. population, and that trend is expected to continue for decades to come. Indeed, the Pew Research Center projects that Latinos will make up about 30 percent of the U.S. population by 2050 (Passel and Cohn 2008).

Second, we are continuing to see both immigration and native births driving Latino population growth. Immigration has increased in part as a result of expanding employment opportunities, as well as new immigration policies. The Immigration Reform and Control Act of 1986 (IRCA), for instance, regularized the immigration status of a significant number of people, many of whom were then able to sponsor additional family members to enter the country. The Illegal Immigration Reform and Immigrant Responsibility Act (IIRIRA) of 1996 had the unintended effect of encouraging undocumented migrants to remain in the country rather than risk apprehension by traveling between a home country and the United States (U.S. Commission on Immigration Reform 1997). The largest source of Latino population growth is not immigration, however, but native births. For example, from 2000 to 2006, the Latino population grew by 10.2 million, 58.6 percent of which was due to native births (Nasser 2008).

A third important change is that the national origin of the Latino population is becoming increasingly diverse, even as the population with roots in Mexico continues to be predominant. In 1990, people of Mexican decent represented 60.3 percent of Latinos in the United States; Puerto Ricans, 12.2 percent; and Cubans, 4.7 percent. By 2010, persons of Mexican origin comprised a significantly larger majority of Latinos: approximately 65.4 percent. Substantial immigration from Central America and the Latin Caribbean, however, reduced the percentage of Latinos of Puerto Rican origin to 9.1 percent and of Cuban origin to 3.5 percent, whereas Salvadorans grew to account for 3.6 percent. Salvadorans, together with Dominicans, Guatemalans, Columbians, Ecuadorians, and those from unspecified countries now constitute 22 percent of the total U.S. Latino population (Saenz 2010).

Fourth, a growing share of Latino immigrants is choosing to naturalize. Past research shows that Latino immigrants, especially Mexicans, have lower rates of naturalization than other immigrant groups (DeSipio 1996). Changes in Mexican nationality law, however, as well as the natural progression to citizenship eligibility of those newly documented by IRCA, resulted in a boom in Latino naturalization in the early and mid-1990s. In California, this boom was accelerated further by the politicization of ethnicity that resulted from immigrant-targeted ballot initiatives and immigrant-unfriendly provisions of the 1996 Personal Responsibility and Work Opportunity Reconciliation Act (i.e., the federal welfare reform act).

More recently, the number of Latinos applying for citizenship surged nationwide. Officials attribute this increase to several factors, including citizenship campaigns across the country, the announcement of a significant increase in application fees beginning July 2007, the charged political climate of the immigration debate, and the 2008 presidential elections (Chishti and Bergeron 2008). One result is that, although Mexicans still have a comparatively lower tendency to become U.S. citizens, the number of naturalized citizens from Mexico rose by 144 percent from 1995 to 2005 – the highest rate of increase of any major sending country (Passel and Cohn 2008).

Finally, there have been dramatic changes in the geography of Latinos in the United States. Latinos no longer live primarily in the Southwest, Florida, New York City, and Chicago; the 2010 census shows that Latinos now have a clear national presence. In 1990, Latinos were the largest minority group in only sixteen of the fifty states, and their share of the population exceeded 5 percent in only fifteen states. By 2010, Latinos outnumbered all other minorities in twenty-seven states, and their population exceeded 5 percent in thirty-two states (U.S. Census Bureau 2010). The importance of this geographic dispersion should not be underestimated. There is every reason to expect that the experiences of Latinos vary widely across political and institutional contexts. For instance, one would expect Latinos living in emerging communities to have significantly different social experiences from those living in long-established Latino enclaves.

Adapting to American Society? Indicators of Latino Assimilation

One of the primary challenges for Latinos, irrespective of their citizenship or generational status, is to survive and thrive in American society. Like most Americans, Latinos would like to have sufficient economic security, physical safety, and personal freedom to allow themselves and their families to live happy and prosperous lives. In spite of these typically American desires, critics of Latino immigration, especially of immigration from Mexico, warn that Latinos must assimilate into mainstream society, or they will not share in this American dream (Huntington 2004). To what extent is this criticism valid? Is it actually based on a misperception of Latinos, who are in fact already successfully integrating into American society? As we outline the demographic profile of Latinos today, we highlight several population characteristics that are commonly used as indicators of assimilation, such as English proficiency, education, outgroup marriage, homeownership, and military service. This should allow us to assess the portrayal of Latinos used by those who are critical, or perhaps just fearful, of the growing presence of Latinos in the United States.

Demographic Characteristics of Latino National Survey Respondents

With many of the previously described demographic changes in mind, the sampling design of the Latino National Survey was intended to provide a comprehensive and up-to-date representation of the Latino population on the U.S. mainland. In part, our objectives were to compile a data set or a source of information that (1) would allow users and/or readers to test conclusions of earlier survey research and (2) allow them to explore new topics of study that reflect the changing Latino population. For example, we purposely oversampled Latinos living in states, cities, and towns that are considered new destination communities. However, in other circumstances, the over- or underrepresentation of certain types of individuals may be the unintended consequence of respondent bias. For example, if the level of English proficiency reported by the U.S. Census Bureau is accurate, Spanish speakers were somewhat more likely than English speakers to complete our survey (data not shown). We also experienced some difficulty in successfully interviewing respondents who self-reported at the lowest income and/or education categories (see Table 1.14 and Table 1.10).

With these qualifications in mind, this chapter presents a comprehensive national profile of Latinos based on the demographics of the respondents to the Latino National Survey (LNS). Whenever possible, we comment on how our LNS respondents compare with demographic information provided by the U.S. Census Bureau and other sources, such as the Pew Hispanic Research Center.

Generation and Citizenship Status

As previously noted, the growth in the U.S. Latino population is a function of both immigration and native births. According to population estimates of the U.S. Census Bureau, approximately 40 percent of Latinos are foreign born. Among those foreign born who are eligible to naturalize, an estimated 46 percent are U.S. citizens. Mexicans have the lowest naturalization rates (35 percent), and Cubans have the highest, at 67 percent (Passel 2007). In 2000, 28 percent of Latinos were second generation – that is, children of immigrants – and 32 percent were third generation or more. However, because Latino native births now exceed the immigration rate, the distribution of generations is projected to shift. By 2010, the percentage of first-generation Latinos was projected to decrease to 38 percent, whereas the percentage of second-generation Latinos will increase to 32 percent (Suro and Passel 2003).

Table 2.1 shows the numbers and percentages of immigrant (first generation) and U.S.-born (2+ generation) LNS respondents by their national origins. As Table 2.1 shows, the foreign born are overrepresented in the LNS when compared with census estimates: about

Table 2.1. *Country of Origin, by Generation and Citizenship*

Response		First Generation			2+ Generation	
		Noncitizen	Citizen	Total	Citizen	Total
Mexico	Freq.	2,969	1,016	3,985	2,049	6,034
	Row%	49.20	16.84	66.04	33.96	100.00
	Col%	76.74	49.73	67.41	75.39	69.92
Puerto Rico	Freq.	0	383	383	291	674
	Row%	0.0	56.82	56.82	43.18	100.00
	Col%	0.00	18.75	6.48	10.71	7.81
Cuba	Freq.	77	169	246	72	318
	Row%	24.21	53.14	77.35	22.65	100.00
	Col%	1.99	8.27	4.16	2.65	3.68
Dominican	Freq.	136	110	246	65	311
Republic	Row%	43.73	35.37	79.10	20.90	100.00
	Col%	3.52	5.38	4.16	2.39	3.60
El Salvador	Freq.	249	112	361	63	424
	Row%	58.73	26.41	85.14	14.86	100.00
	Col%	6.44	5.48	6.11	2.32	4.91
Guatemala	Freq.	126	36	162	12	174
	Row%	72.41	20.69	73.10	6.90	100.00
	Col%	3.26	1.76	2.74	0.44	2.02
Colombia	Freq.	53	54	107	15	122
	Row%	43.44	44.26	87.70	12.30	100.00
	Col%	1.37	2.64	1.81	0.55	1.41
Other Central	Freq.	101	60	161	16	177
America	Row%	57.06	33.90	90.96	9.04	100.00
	Col%	2.61	2.94	2.72	0.59	2.05
Other South	Freq.	154	97	251	26	277
America	Row%	55.60	35.02	90.62	9.38	100.00
	Col%	3.98	4.75	4.25	0.96	3.21
Spain	Freq.	4	6	10	49	59
	Row%	6.78	10.17	16.95	83.05	100.00
	Col%	0.10	0.29	0.17	1.80	0.68
"Don't know,"	Freq.	0	0	0	60	60
refused, and	Row%	0.0	0.0	0.0	100.00	100.00
U.S.A.	Col%	0.00	0.00	0.00	2.20	0.69
response						
TOTAL	Freq.	3,869	2,043	5,912	2,718	8,630
	Row%	44.83	23.67	68.50	31.50	100.00
	Col%	100.00	100.00	100.00	100.00	100.00

Note: First/2+ generation: chi-square (7 d.f.) 91.039 (P = 0.000). Citizen/noncitizen (first generation only): chi-square (7 d.f.) 44.940 (P = 0.003). Dichotomous measures taken from responses to questions asking where individuals were born (first generation) and where their families are from (second generation). Island-born Puerto Ricans coded as first generation. Question wording: "Where were you born?" and "Which country does most of your family come from?"

68 percent of the LNS respondents are first generation. To a certain extent, this overrepresentation was intentional, as we set out to oversample individuals from newly emerging Latino destinations. It is possible, however, that the LNS may come somewhat closer to capturing the true proportion of Latinos who are foreign born because of undercounting problems with the census, especially among those who are undocumented and/or highly transient (Ericksen 2001). If the census numbers are accurate, then the proportion of those with origins in Mexico are unintentionally overrepresented in the LNS sample. Otherwise, the proportions for each of the other countries reflect the LNS principal investigators' intent and should allow us to provide a comprehensive and accurate assessment of Latinos living in the United States today.

English Proficiency
English proficiency is widely considered the single most important element of cultural adaptation for immigrants who seek to be successful outside of their ethnic enclaves (Alba and Nee 2003). Yet the size of the Latino immigrant population relative to the size of its U.S.-born population, coupled with the steady stream of Spanish-speaking people into the country, could lead one to expect a limited level of English proficiency among Latinos.

Our survey found that English-speaking skills are indeed limited among first-generation respondents, with 43 percent speaking "just a little" English and 16 percent "not at all." Yet the data in Figure 2.1 show that about 27 percent of noncitizens speak English "pretty well" or "very well." Not surprisingly, given the language requirements for naturalization, citizens are significantly more English proficient than noncitizens. In fact, about two-thirds of the naturalized citizens speak English "pretty well" or "very well." Only about 6 percent of U.S.-born Latinos (2+ generation) reported any limitations to their spoken-English abilities.

Race

The discovery following the 2000 census that the size of the Hispanic or Latino population had surpassed the size of the African American population understandably generated considerable attention and plenty of headlines. However, the census contained another interesting piece of news regarding the racial identification of Latinos. Forty-two percent rejected the specified racial categories, such as "white," "black," "Asian," and so on, opting instead to identify themselves as "[s]ome other race," most often writing in *Hispanic* or a similar term. In contrast, only

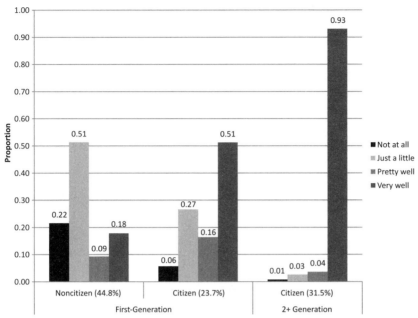

Figure 2.1. English Proficiency, by Generation and Citizenship
Question wording: "How good is your spoken English? Would you say you could carry on a conversation in English (both understanding and speaking) very well, pretty well, just a little, or not at all?" Individuals who answered the survey in English were coded as speaking English "very well."

0.02 percent of the non-Hispanic population reported "[s]ome other race." Approximately 6 percent of all Latinos reported two or more races, compared with just less than 2 percent of all non-Hispanics. In the 2000 census, nearly half (48 percent) of Latinos reported white only, whereas 2 percent reported Black or African American alone. This represents small but significant declines for both groups from the 1990 census, −4 percent and −1 percent, respectively (Grieco and Cassidy 2001). However, some analysts believe that changes in the 2000 census that reversed the order of the ethnicity and race questions from the 1990 census, asking the Hispanic origin question before the race question, likely influenced Latinos' response to the race identification question (Logan 2003). Also, for the first time, census respondents in 2000 were allowed the option of selecting one or more race categories to indicate their racial identities.

The LNS data shows that the tendency to view Latinos as a separate and distinctive race appears to have become even stronger by 2006, as

Table 2.2. *Respondent's Race, by Generation and Citizenship*

Response		First Generation			2+ Generation	
		Noncitizen	Citizen	Total	Citizen	Total
White	Freq.	868	486	1354	528	1882
	Row%	64.11	35.89	71.94	28.06	100.00
	Col%	22.14	24.36	22.89	19.43	21.80
Black, African	Freq.	28	14	42	22	64
American or	Row%	66.67	33.33	65.63	34.38	100.00
Negro	Col%	0.71	0.70	0.71	0.81	0.74
American Indian or	Freq.	82	27	109	39	148
Alaskan Native	Row%	75.23	24.77	73.65	26.35	100.00
	Col%	2.09	1.35	1.84	1.43	1.71
Asian Indian	Freq.	4	3	7	3	10
	Row%	57.14	42.86	70.00	30.00	100.00
	Col%	0.10	0.15	0.12	0.11	0.12
Native Hawaiian or	Freq.	4	10	14	8	22
Pacific Islander	Row%	28.57	71.43	63.64	36.36	100.00
	Col%	0.10	0.50	0.24	0.29	0.25
Some other race	Freq.	2564	1314	3878	1999	5877
	Row%	43.63	22.36	65.99	34.01	100.00
	Col%	65.39	65.86	65.55	73.55	68.07
Refused	Freq.	371	141	512	119	631
	Row%	72.46	27.54	81.14	18.86	100.00
	Col%	9.46	7.07	8.65	4.38	7.31
TOTAL	Freq.	3921	1995	5916	2718	8634
	Row%	66.28	33.72	68.52	31.48	100.00
	Col%	100.00	100.00	100.00	100.00	100.00

Note: First/2+ generation: (141 d.f.) 2.020 (P = 0.000). Citizen/noncitizen (first generation only): (81 d.f.) 1.740 (P = 0.001). Island-born Puerto Ricans coded as first generation. Question wording: "What is your race?"

shown in Table 2.2. The LNS question was constructed using answer options similar to the racial question in the 2000 census. The LNS respondents were asked: "What is your race? Are you White, Black, American Indian, Asian, Native Hawaiian/Pacific Islander, some other race or more than one?" More than two-thirds of the LNS respondents report their race as "other," with about 65 percent of first-generation respondents (nearly evenly divided among noncitizen and citizen respondents) identifying as "other," and more than 73 percent of second generation and beyond identifying as such. The second largest response

Table 2.3. *Gender, by Generation and Citizenship*

| Response | | First Generation | | | 2+ Generation | |
		Noncitizen	Citizen	Total	Citizen	Total
Male	Freq.	1934	902	2836	1251	4087
	Row%	68.19	31.81	69.39	30.61	100.00
	Col%	49.34	45.21	47.95	46.01	47.34
Female	Freq.	1986	1093	3079	1468	4547
	Row%	64.50	35.50	67.71	32.29	100.00
	Col%	50.66	54.79	52.05	53.99	52.66
TOTAL	Freq.	3920	1995	5915	2719	8634
	Row%	66.27	33.73	68.51	31.49	100.00
	Col%	100.00	100.00	100.00	100.00	100.00

Note: First/2+ generation: (75 d.f.) 255.341 (P = 0.000). Citizen/noncitizen (first generation only): (75 d.f.) 1013.033 (P = 0.000). Island-born Puerto Ricans coded as first generation. Question wording: no question, gender was determined by the interviewer.

category is "white," with more than 22 percent of first-generation respondents identifying as white and just less than 20 percent of second generation and beyond identifying as such. The remaining respondents are divided, in small groups, among the remaining categories, with the fewest identifying as Asian or Pacific Islander. Obviously, the proportion of respondents who identified as white is much lower than in the 2000 census, but the percentage who indicated more than two races was also lower (less than 3 percent; data not shown).When LNS respondents were asked a follow-up question ("Do you feel that Latinos/Hispanics make up a distinctive racial group in America?"), 51 percent reiterated that they view Latinos and/or Hispanics as a distinctive race.

Gender

It is worth noting that LNS respondents are nearly evenly divided between men and women, regardless of citizenship status and generation. The data in Table 2.3 show that among first-generation noncitizens, nearly half are male (49.34 percent) and half are female (50.66 percent). Among first-generation citizens, again nearly half are male (45.21 percent) and slightly more than half are female (54.79 percent). Similarly the second-generation and beyond respondents are nearly evenly divided, with about 46 percent of respondents being male and about 53 percent being female.

Table 2.4. *Marital Status, by Generation and Citizenship*

Response		First Generation			2+ Generation	
		Noncitizen	Citizen	Total	Citizen	Total
Single	Freq.	1451	575	2026	1401	3427
	Row%	71.62	28.38	59.12	40.88	100.00
	Col%	37.02	28.82	34.26	51.53	39.70
Not married but	Freq.	332	68	400	115	515
living together	Row%	83.00	17.00	77.67	22.33	100.00
	Col%	8.47	3.41	6.76	4.23	5.97
Married but not	Freq.	176	71	247	50	297
living together	Row%	71.26	28.74	83.16	16.84	100.00
	Col%	4.49	3.56	4.18	1.84	3.44
Married	Freq.	1773	1026	2799	960	3759
	Row%	63.34	36.66	74.46	25.54	100.00
	Col%	45.24	51.43	47.33	35.31	43.54
Divorced	Freq.	127	153	280	132	412
	Row%	45.36	54.64	67.96	32.04	100.00
	Col%	3.24	7.67	4.73	4.85	4.77
Widowed	Freq.	60	102	162	61	223
	Row%	26.91	45.74	72.65	27.35	100.00
	Col%	1.53	5.11	2.74	2.24	2.58
TOTAL	Freq.	3919	1995	5914	2719	8633
	Row%	66.27	33.73	68.50	31.50	100.00
	Col%	100.00	100.00	100.00	100.00	100.00

Note: First/2+ generation: (1 d.f.) 2.796 (P = 0.201). Citizen/noncitizen (first generation only): (1 d.f.) 13.181 (P = 0.011). Island-born Puerto Ricans coded as first generation. Question wording: "What is your current marital status?"

Marital Status

In addition to asking the gender of each respondent, we also elicited information on marital status. Table 2.4 reports that immigrants (first generation), both citizen and noncitizen, are substantially more likely to be married – even if they are not living together – than the U.S.-born citizens. This confirms the findings of other recent studies that many Latino immigrants arrive already married (Lee and Edmonston 2005). Fifty-one percent of first-generation respondents are married, compared to just 39 percent of second-generation and beyond respondents. This is the only major difference between the foreign born and the U.S. born with respect to marital status, as the proportions of divorced and widowed are roughly the same.

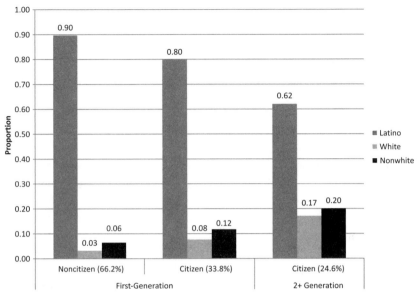

Figure 2.2. Race of Spouse, by Generation and Citizenship
Question wording: "What is your spouse's race and ethnicity?"

Race of Spouse

Following the practice of many subordinate (minority) groups in the United States, Latinos are significantly more likely to marry Latinos than non-Latinos (see Figure 2.2). Overall, 80 percent of the married LNS respondents reported being married to Latino spouses. Latino assimilation or incorporation into American society is evident in the out-group marriage trend with citizenship and later generations. Among noncitizens, about 90 percent have Latino spouses, compared to 80 percent of naturalized citizens with Latino spouses. Later generations are even less likely to be married to Latino spouses, only 62 percent. Interestingly, if they are not married to Latinos, later generations are most likely to have nonwhite spouses (20 percent), just as immigrants have spouses whose racial identity is nonwhite.

Religious Affiliation and Practices

It is widely known that the predominant religious identity or affiliation for Latinos is Catholicism. Census data from 2000 and more recent studies of the religious life of Latinos in the United States suggest that about three-fourths of Latino immigrants self-identify as Catholics. Yet the level of Catholicism declines with each generation. The level of religiosity, such as attendance at religious services, also declines with each generation. However, a significant percentage of Latinos identify as "born-again or spirit-filled" and participate in religious worship that has been characterized as part of a worldwide charismatic or renewalist movement (Espinosa, Elizondo and Miranda 2005; Pew Forum on Religion and Public Life 2008). These previously reported trends are evident in the LNS survey results.

Table 2.5 shows the religious affiliation of LNS respondents. Approximately three-fourths (73.50 percent) of first-generation respondents indicate they are Catholic. However, there are slightly more Catholics among noncitizens (75.39 percent) than naturalized citizens (69.79 percent). The percentage of Catholics among U.S.-born citizens (second generation and beyond) is lower still, about 66 percent. If the data are further broken down by generation (data not shown), there is a modest but steady decline in the numbers of Catholics with each generation: from 73 percent in the first generation, to 70 percent in the second generation, 65 percent in the third generation, and only 58 percent in the fourth generation. About 20 percent of the respondents report affiliations with other Christian denominations, but the percentage of respondents in each Protestant denomination is small. Overall, Latinos seem more likely than non-Latinos to identify with a particular religious denomination; a recent national survey by the Pew Forum on Religion and Public Life (2008) shows that 16 percent of the general population self-identifies as "unaffiliated," which includes atheists, agnostics, and simply nonreligious people, whereas only about 7 percent of the LNS respondents report no religious affiliation.

The strength of the charismatic movement among the LNS respondents can be seen in the data in Figure 2.3. When asked whether they consider themselves "born-again Christian, spirit-filled Christian or involved in the charismatic movement," more than one-third of the respondents, irrespective of generation, said yes. However, those born in the United States were definitely more likely than immigrants to respond in the negative; 54 percent of the second generation and beyond said no, compared to 42 percent of the immigrants. It is also worth noting that a higher percentage of immigrants refused to answer the question or said that they "didn't know." It may be that some of the recent immigrants simply did not understand the terminology used in the question.

Table 2.5. *Religion, by Generation and Citizenship*

Response		First Generation			2+ Generation	
		Noncitizen	Citizen	Total	Citizen	Total
Jehovah's Witness	Freq.	108	59	167	57	224
	Row%	64.67	35.33	74.55	25.45	100.00
	Col%	2.75	2.96	2.82	2.10	2.59
Catholic	Freq.	2956	1393	4349	1782	6131
	Row%	67.97	32.03	70.93	29.07	100.00
	Col%	75.39	69.79	73.50	65.56	71.00
Assemblies of God	Freq.	67	33	100	53	153
	Row%	67.00	33.00	65.36	34.64	100.00
	Col%	1.71	1.65	1.69	1.95	1.77
Southern Baptist	Freq.	43	39	82	83	165
	Row%	52.44	47.56	49.70	50.30	100.00
	Col%	1.10	1.95	1.39	3.05	1.91
Pentecostal	Freq.	148	95	243	108	351
	Row%	60.91	39.09	69.23	30.77	100.00
	Col%	3.77	4.76	4.11	3.97	4.06
Other Protestant	Freq.	216	97	313	97	410
	Row%	52.68	23.66	76.34	23.66	100.00
	Col%	5.51	4.86	5.29	3.57	4.75
Mormon	Freq.	21	14	35	25	60
	Row%	60.00	40.00	58.33	41.67	100.00
	Col%	0.54	0.70	0.59	0.92	0.69
Jewish	Freq.	4	5	9	6	15
	Row%	44.44	55.56	60.00	40.00	100.00
	Col%	0.10	0.25	0.15	0.22	0.17
Don't identify with any denomination	Freq.	218	128	346	237	583
	Row%	63.01	36.99	59.35	40.65	100.00
	Col%	5.56	6.41	5.85	8.72	6.75
Other	Freq.	140	133	273	270	543
	Row%	51.28	48.72	50.28	49.72	100.00
	Col%	3.57	6.66	4.61	9.93	6.29
TOTAL	Freq.	3921	1996	5917	2718	8635
	Row%	66.27	33.73	68.52	31.48	100.00
	Col%	100.00	100.00	100.00	100.00	100.00

Note: First/2+ generation: (2 d.f.) 11.730 (P = 0.000). Citizen/noncitizen (first generation only): (2 d.f.) 1.050 (P = 0.349). Island-born Puerto Ricans coded as first generation. Question wording: "Stop me when I get to the correct one. With what religious tradition do you most closely identify?"

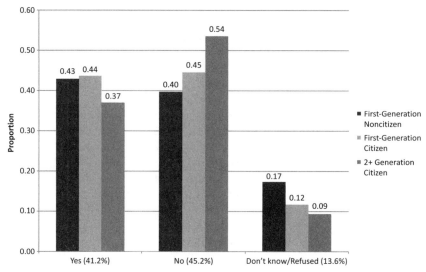

Figure 2.3. Considered Born Again, by Generation and Citizenship
Question wording: "Do you consider yourself a born-again Christian, spirit-filled Christian, or involved in the charismatic movement?"

If church attendance is an indicator of the level of religiosity, Latinos are fairly devote; more than 50 percent say that they attend church once a week or even more frequently (see Table 2.6). However, the first generation is more religious than later generations on the basis of this measure. Second generation and beyond Latinos are considerably more likely than first-generation Latinos to say they never attend church or attend only on major religious holidays, at approximately 35 percent for second generation and beyond, compared to 24 percent for the first generation.

Education
Latinos continue to have lower educational attainment than most subgroups in the U.S. population (Pew Hispanic Center 2008). Although more than 75 percent of non-Hispanic whites have a high school degree or GED (Snyder, Dillow and Hoffman 2009), only about 64 percent of the LNS respondents say they have achieved this minimal level (see Table 2.7). First-generation noncitizens are most likely to have less than a high school education: approximately 4 percent say they have no education, 28 percent have eighth grade or less, and 21 percent have some high

Table 2.6. *Attendance at Religious Services, by Generation and Citizenship*

		First Generation			2+ Generation	
Response		Noncitizen	Citizen	Total	Citizen	Total
More than once a	Freq.	559	382	941	392	1333
week	Row%	59.40	40.60	70.59	29.41	100.00
	Col%	14.26	19.13	15.90	14.42	15.44
Once a week	Freq.	1519	754	2273	930	3203
	Row%	66.83	33.17	70.96	29.04	100.00
	Col%	38.75	37.76	38.41	34.20	37.09
Once a month	Freq.	821	335	1156	421	1577
	Row%	71.02	28.98	73.30	26.70	100.00
	Col%	20.94	16.78	19.54	15.48	18.26
Only on major	Freq.	474	238	712	526	1238
religious holidays	Row%	66.57	33.43	57.51	42.49	100.00
	Col%	12.09	11.92	12.03	19.35	14.34
Never	Freq.	484	255	739	419	1158
	Row%	65.49	34.51	63.82	36.18	100.00
	Col%	12.35	12.77	12.49	15.41	13.41
Don't know	Freq.	45	21	66	21	87
	Row%	51.72	24.14	75.86	24.14	100.00
	Col%	1.15	1.05	1.12	0.77	1.01
Refused	Freq.	18	12	30	10	40
	Row%	60.00	40.00	75.00	25.00	100.00
	Col%	0.46	0.60	0.51	0.37	0.46
TOTAL	Freq.	3920	1997	5917	2719	8636
	Row%	66.25	33.75	68.52	31.48	100.00
	Col%	100.00	100.00	100.00	100.00	100.00

Note: First/2+ generation: (1 d.f.) 67.960 (P = 0.000). Citizen/noncitizen (first generation only): (1 d.f.) 7.570 (P = 0.006). Island-born Puerto Ricans coded as first generation. Question wording: "How often do you attend religious services?"

school. Second generation and beyond are most likely to have attended college: approximately 33 percent say they have some college, 13 percent report having four-year college degrees, and 7 percent say they have graduate and professional degrees. The education levels of foreign-born Latino citizens are generally higher than noncitizens but not as high as later generations. Not too surprisingly, a large majority of the first-generation respondents have completed their education somewhere other than the United States or Puerto Rico (66 percent). As Figure 2.4 shows, this is

Table 2.7. *Education, by Generation and Citizenship*

Response		First Generation			2+ Generation	
		Noncitizen	Citizen	Total	Citizen	Total
None	Freq.	140	34	174	18	192
	Row%	80.46	19.54	90.63	9.38	100.00
	Col%	3.57	1.70	2.94	0.66	2.22
Eighth grade or	Freq.	1080	327	1407	82	1489
below	Row%	76.76	23.24	94.49	5.51	100.00
	Col%	27.55	16.38	23.78	3.02	17.25
Some high school	Freq.	815	278	1093	375	1468
	Row%	74.57	25.43	74.46	25.54	100.00
	Col%	20.79	13.93	18.48	13.81	17.01
GED	Freq.	127	73	200	65	265
	Row%	63.50	36.50	75.47	24.53	100.00
	Col%	3.24	3.66	3.38	2.39	3.07
High school	Freq.	1032	474	1506	763	2269
graduate	Row%	68.53	31.47	66.37	33.63	100.00
	Col%	26.33	23.75	25.46	28.09	26.29
Some college	Freq.	463	466	929	891	1820
	Row%	25.44	25.60	51.04	48.96	100.00
	Col%	11.81	23.35	15.70	32.81	21.08
4-year college	Freq.	152	211	363	338	701
degree	Row%	41.87	58.13	51.78	48.22	100.00
	Col%	3.88	10.57	6.14	12.44	8.12
Graduate or	Freq.	111	133	244	184	428
professional	Row%	45.49	54.51	57.01	42.99	100.00
degree	Col%	2.83	6.66	4.12	6.77	4.96
TOTAL	Freq.	3920	1996	5916	2716	8632
	Row%	66.26	33.74	68.54	31.46	100.00
	Col%	100.00	100.00	100.00	100.00	100.00

Note: First/2+ generation: (11 d.f.) 6.450 (P = 0.000). Citizen/noncitizen (first generation only): (11 d.f.) 8.580 (P = 0.000). Island-born Puerto Ricans coded as first generation. Question wording: "What is your highest level of formal education completed?"

particularly true among noncitizens, among whom more than three-quarters report having completed their education elsewhere.

Further evidence of the absence of education among Latinos is presented in Table 2.8, which reports the educational attainment of LNS respondents' parents. The table reveals that most parents did not finish high school. This is particularly true among noncitizens, of whom

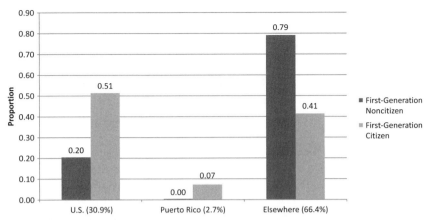

Figure 2.4. Where Education Was Completed, Foreign-Born Respondents Only
Question wording: "Where did you complete your highest level of education?"

Table 2.8. *Parents' Education, by Generation and Citizenship*

Response		First Generation			2+ Generation	
		Noncitizen	Citizen	Total	Citizen	Total
Neither of them	Freq.	2365	996	3361	952	4313
finished high school	Row%	70.37	29.63	77.93	22.07	100.00
	Col%	60.32	49.92	56.81	35.01	49.95
At least one of them	Freq.	835	467	1302	828	2130
finished high school	Row%	64.13	35.87	61.13	38.87	100.00
	Col%	21.30	23.41	22.01	30.45	24.67
At least one of them	Freq.	134	124	258	336	594
went to college	Row%	51.94	48.06	43.43	56.57	100.00
	Col%	3.42	6.22	4.36	12.36	6.88
At least one of them	Freq.	132	175	307	312	619
got a college degree	Row%	43.00	57.00	49.60	50.40	100.00
	Col%	3.37	8.77	5.19	11.47	7.17
At least one or both	Freq.	108	116	224	178	402
of them received an	Row%	48.21	51.79	55.72	44.28	100.00
advanced degree	Col%	2.75	5.81	3.79	6.55	4.66
Don't know	Freq.	347	117	464	113	577
	Row%	60.14	20.28	80.42	19.58	100.00
	Col%	8.85	5.86	7.84	4.16	6.68
TOTAL	Freq.	3921	1995	5916	2719	8635
	Row%	66.28	33.72	68.51	31.49	100.00
	Col%	100.00	100.00	100.00	100.00	100.00

Note: First/2+ generation: (1 d.f.) 1.306 (P = 0.334). Citizen/noncitizen (first generation only): (1 d.f.) 0.023 (P = 0.908). Island-born Puerto Ricans coded as first generation. Question wording: "Which of the following best describes your parents' educational attainment?"

60 percent report that neither parent finished high school, and an additional 21 percent say that only one parent finished high school. The situation improves with naturalized citizens and U.S.-born Latinos, but nonetheless, large majorities still report that one or both parents never finished high school.

Economic Status: Objective and Subjective Measures

The vast majority of Hispanic immigrants come to the United States seeking better economic opportunities (data not shown). However, as noted earlier, Latinos desire a better life for themselves and their families, and most believe in the American dream, which they define in terms of steady, good-paying jobs; homeownership; and financial security (Fraga et al. 2010). How are Latinos faring? Tables 2.9–2.10 and Figures 2.5–2.6 are intended to answer this question.

In the 2000 census, Latinos had the highest participation rate in the labor force among all racial ethnic groups (Therrien and Ramirez 2001). Table 2.9 reports the employment status of the LNS respondents. A comfortable majority are employed full-time (55 percent), as well as a small percentage who also work more than one job (2.5 percent). Noncitizens are somewhat more likely than citizens to work full-time (59 percent compared to 54 percent and 50 percent, respectively), whereas U.S.-born citizens are somewhat more likely than immigrants to be working only part-time or to be full-time students. Interestingly, more than 10 percent of noncitizens do not work outside the home, compared to less than 5 percent of the second generation and beyond.

What level of wages do Latinos receive for their work? This is a sensitive question that many people prefer not to answer. In an effort to increase the level of response, LNS respondents were provided with several ranges of income and asked to select the one that best described the total income earned by all members of their household in 2004. Even with this less specific questioning, about 23 percent still refused to provide this information. Among those who did respond, it appears that income increases with naturalization and later generations, as indicated in Table 2.10. More noncitizens are in the two lowest income brackets: 22 percent have household incomes less than $15,000, and 24 percent have income between $15,000 and $24,999. More second generation and beyond respondents had annual household incomes greater than $65,000. More first-generation citizens had incomes greater than those of noncitizens but less than those of the second generation and beyond.

Table 2.9. *Employment Status, by Generation and Citizenship*

Response		First Generation			2+ Generation	
		Noncitizen	Citizen	Total	Citizen	Total
Employed full-time	Freq.	2299	1076	3375	1373	4748
	Row%	68.12	31.88	71.08	28.92	100.00
	Col%	58.65	53.88	57.04	50.50	54.98
Working more than one job	Freq.	100	47	147	72	219
	Row%	68.03	31.97	67.12	32.88	100.00
	Col%	2.55	2.35	2.48	2.65	2.54
Employed part-time	Freq.	260	151	411	364	775
	Row%	63.26	36.74	53.03	46.97	100.00
	Col%	6.63	7.56	6.95	13.39	8.97
Engaged in occasional labor or day labor	Freq.	158	46	204	40	244
	Row%	77.45	22.55	83.61	16.39	100.00
	Col%	4.03	2.30	3.45	1.47	2.83
Currently unemployed	Freq.	403	127	530	183	713
	Row%	76.04	23.96	74.33	25.67	100.00
	Col%	10.28	6.36	8.96	6.73	8.26
A full-time student	Freq.	122	96	218	306	524
	Row%	23.28	18.32	41.60	58.40	100.00
	Col%	3.11	4.81	3.68	11.25	6.07
Retired or permanently disabled	Freq.	91	309	400	252	652
	Row%	22.75	77.25	61.35	38.65	100.00
	Col%	2.32	15.47	6.76	9.27	7.55
Not working outside the home	Freq.	487	145	632	129	761
	Row%	77.06	22.94	83.05	16.95	100.00
	Col%	12.42	7.26	10.68	4.74	8.81
TOTAL	Freq.	3920	1997	5917	2719	8636
	Row%	66.25	33.75	68.52	31.48	100.00
	Col%	100.00	100.00	100.00	100.00	100.00

Note: First/2+ generation: (4 d.f.) 113.670 (P = 0.000). Citizen/noncitizen (first generation only): (4 d.f.) 44.460 (P = 0.000). Island-born Puerto Ricans coded as first generation. Question wording: "What is your employment status?"

Although many Latinos have low household incomes, only about 13 percent at the time of the survey received any kind of government assistance (see Figure 2.5). About 22 percent of second generation and beyond have received public assistance in the past, compared to only 15 percent of the first generation. Noncitizens are the least likely to have received government assistance.

Table 2.10. *Household Income, by Generation and Citizenship*

Response		First Generation			2+ Generation	
		Noncitizen	Citizen	Total	Citizen	Total
Less than $15,000	Freq.	860	234	1094	223	1317
	Row%	78.61	21.39	83.07	16.93	100.00
	Col%	21.94	11.73	18.50	8.21	15.26
$15,000–24,999	Freq.	936	307	1243	347	1590
	Row%	75.30	24.70	78.18	21.82	100.00
	Col%	23.88	15.39	21.01	12.78	18.42
$25,000–34,999	Freq.	511	296	807	328	1135
	Row%	63.32	36.68	71.10	28.90	100.00
	Col%	13.04	14.84	13.64	12.08	13.15
$35,000–44,999	Freq.	265	229	494	299	793
	Row%	53.64	46.36	62.30	37.70	100.00
	Col%	6.76	11.48	8.35	11.01	9.19
$45,000–54,999	Freq.	132	150	282	252	534
	Row%	46.81	53.19	52.81	47.19	100.00
	Col%	3.37	7.52	4.77	9.28	6.19
$55,000–64,999	Freq.	79	123	202	205	407
	Row%	19.41	30.22	49.63	50.37	100.00
	Col%	2.02	6.17	3.42	7.55	4.72
More than $65,000	Freq.	117	256	373	519	892
	Row%	31.37	68.63	41.82	58.18	100.00
	Col%	2.98	12.83	6.31	19.11	10.33
Refused	Freq.	1020	400	1420	543	1963
	Row%	71.83	28.17	72.34	27.66	100.00
	Col%	26.02	20.05	24.01	19.99	22.74
TOTAL	Freq.	3920	1995	5915	2716	8631
	Row%	66.27	33.73	68.53	31.47	100.00
	Col%	100.00	100.00	100.00	100.00	100.00

Note: First/2+ generation: (d.f.) (P = 0.000). Citizen/noncitizen (first generation only): (d.f.) 0.000 (P =). Island-born Puerto Ricans coded as first generation. Question wording: "Which of the following best describes the total income earned by all members of your household during 2004?"

Because of the reluctance of people in general to provide their annual income and perhaps the reluctance of Latinos to accept government assistance, a better indicator of how Latinos are faring financially may be the prevalence of homeownership (see Figure 2.6). Although two-thirds of the noncitizens are renters (67 percent), citizens, irrespective of their generation status, are most likely to own their homes (59 percent).

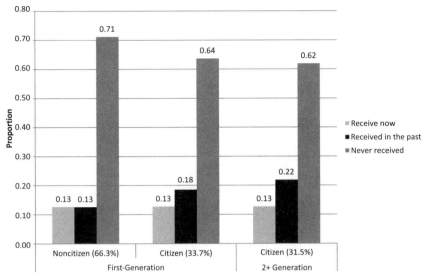

Figure 2.5. Received Government Assistance
Question wording: "Do you receive now or have you ever received any kind of government assistance?"

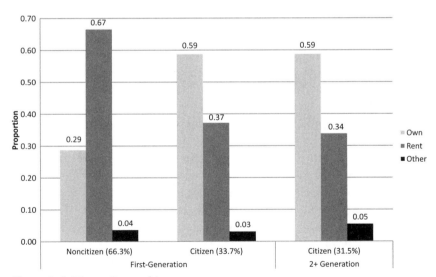

Figure 2.6. Home Ownership
Question wording: "Do you own or rent your residence in the United States?"

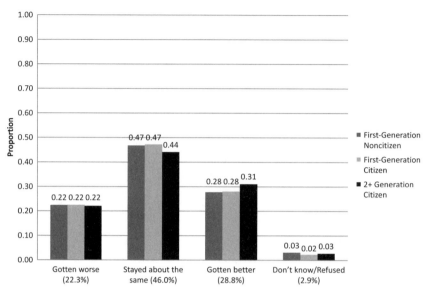

Figure 2.7. Financial Situation, by Generation and Citizenship
Question wording: "What about your personal financial situation? Over the past year, has it gotten better, stayed about the same, or gotten worse?"

Overall, the objective indicators of employment, income, and home ownership show that economic status improves for Latinos with citizenship and generation. How does this objective assessment compare with the subjective opinions of Latinos regarding their financial situations? To answer this question, LNS respondents were asked whether their personal financial situation had gotten worse, stayed about the same, or gotten better over the past year. Figure 2.7 displays their answers. It is important to remember that this question was asked in 2006, before the downturn in the economy. Interestingly, there are only small differences between respondents in different categories of generation and citizenship. About 22 percent across the categories perceive that their financial status has gotten worse. Most believe that their personal financial situation had stayed about the same over the previous year. Approximately 47 percent of the first generation say their financial status had stayed about this same, whereas about 44 percent of the second generation and beyond express this sentiment. Twenty-eight percent of the first generation felt that their financial status had improved, compared with 31 percent of the second generation and beyond.

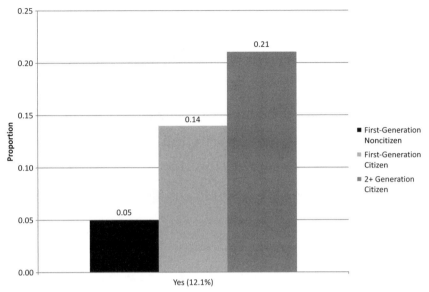

Figure 2.8. Union Membership, by Generation and Citizenship
Question wording: "Are you or anyone in your household a member of a union?"

Union Membership

Compared to other major racial ethnic groups in the United States, Latinos are the least likely to be union members. According to a recent report of the U.S. Bureau of Labor Statistics (2010), black workers were most likely to be union members (14 percent), then non-Hispanic whites (12 percent), Asians (11 percent), and finally Latinos (10 percent). These statistics are closely reflected in total percentage of LNS respondents who are union members (12 percent; see Figure 2.8). However, union membership increases with citizenship and generation, and union members usually have higher pay than nonunion members in the same occupations. Only about 5 percent of noncitizens are union members, compared with about 14 percent of first-generation citizens. Membership climbs to 21 percent among the second generation and beyond.

Military Service

The past twenty years have witnessed dramatic increases in the percentage of Latinos among active-duty enlisted personnel. According to Department of Defense military enrollment records, Latinos accounted for fewer than 5 percent of enlisted personnel in 1977, but their numbers had

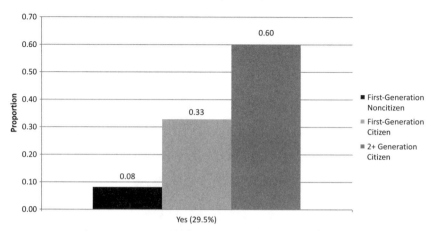

Figure 2.9. Military Service (Self or Family), by Generation and Citizenship
Question wording: "Have you or any close member of your family ever served in the U.S. military?"

increased to about 13 percent by 2006 (Segal and Segal 2007). Almost 30 percent of the LNS respondents have served themselves or have close family members with military service (see Figure 2.9). The prevalence of military service increases significantly with citizenship and generational status. Among the first generation, only about 8 percent of noncitizens have military service in their background, but almost 33 percent of naturalized citizens do. The percentage with personal or family service in the military almost doubles (60 percent) among the second generation and beyond.

Conclusion

The ways that Latinos are becoming a part of the American fabric are similar to the behaviors followed by previous waves of immigrants (Sassler 2006). Judging from the information presented here, there are clear signs that Latinos are integrating into American society – through English-language acquisition, out-group marriage, religion practices, and military service. There is also evidence that Latinos are advancing economically, as citizens and later generations are increasingly more likely than noncitizens to be college educated and homeowners with higher incomes. However, the road to full participation in American society is not as easy or as direct as some might characterize it (Park 1950; Huntington 2004): even as Latinos make progress in each of the indicators of assimilation that we examined, they also continue to struggle with low levels of educational achievement. Meanwhile, education continues to be the primary means through which Americans of all backgrounds and incomes gain the skills that are likely to lead to significant upward social, economic, and political mobility in the United States (Hochschild 1995; Hochschild and Scovronick 2004).

Bibliography

Alba, Richard and Victor Nee. 2003. *Remaking the American Mainstream: Assimilation and Contemporary Immigration.* Boston: Harvard University Press.

Chishti, Muzaffar and Claire Bergeron. 2008. "Hispanic Vote Goes for Obama But May Not Lead to Quick Action on Immigration Reform." *Migration Information Source*, Migration Policy Institute, February 17. Accessed at http://www.migrationinformation.org/USFocus/display.cfm?ID=701.

DeSipio, Louis. 1996. *Counting on the Latino Vote: Latinos as a New Electorate.* Charlottesville, VA: University of Virginia Press.

Ericksen, Eugene. 2001. "An Evaluation of the 2000 Census: Final Report to Congress." U.S. Census Monitoring Board, Suitland, MD, September 1, pp. 15–42. http://govinfo.library.unt.edu/cmb/cmbp/reports/final_report/fin_sec3_evaluation.pdf.

Espinosa, Gastón, Virgilio Elizondo, and Jesse Miranda, eds. 2005. *Latino Religions and Civic Activism in the United States.* New York: Oxford University Press.

Fraga, Luis R., John A. Garcia, Rodney E. Hero, Michael Jones-Correa, Valerie Martinez-Ebers, and Gary M. Segura. 2010. *Latino Lives in America: Making It Home.* Philadelphia: Temple University Press.

Grieco Elizabeth M., and Rachel C. Cassidy. 2001. "Overview of Race and Hispanic Origin." *Census 2000 Brief.* 1:1. http://www.census.gov/prod/2001pubs/cenbr01–1.pdf.

Hochschild, Jennifer L. 1995. *Facing Up to the American Dream: Race, Class, and the Soul of the Nation.* Princeton, NJ: Princeton University Press.

Hochschild, Jennifer L., and Nathan Scovronick. 2004. *The American Dream and the Public Schools.* New York: Oxford University Press.

Huntington, Samuel P. 2004. *Who Are We? The Challenges to America's National Identity.* New York: Simon and Schuster.

Lee, Sharon M., and Barry Edmonston. 2005. "New Marriages, New Families: U.S. Racial and Hispanic Intermarriage." *Population Bulletin* 60(2) 3–36.

Logan, John R. 2003. "How Race Counts for Hispanic Americans." Lewis Mumford Center for Comparative Urban and Regional Research, University of Albany, Albany, NY. http://mumford.albany.edu/census/BlackLatinoReport/BlackLatino01.htm.

Nasser, Haya El. 2008. "Births Fueling Hispanic Growth." *USA Today.* http://www.usatoday.com/news/nation/2008-06-29-hispanics_n.htm. June 30, 2008.

Park, Robert E. 1950. *Race and Culture.* Glencoe, IL: Free Press.

Passel, Jeffery S. 2007. "Growing Share of Immigrants Choosing Naturalization." Pew Research Center, Washington, D.C. http://pewhispanic.org/files/reports/74.pdf.

Passel, Jeffery S., and D'Vera Cohn. 2008. "U.S. Population Projections: 2005–2050: Social and Demographic Trends Report." Pew Research Center, Washington, D.C. http://pewhispanic.org/files/reports/85.pdf.

Passel, Jeffrey S., and D'Vera Cohn. 2010. "How Many Hispanics? Comparing New Census Counts with the Latest Census Estimates." Pew Hispanic Center, Washington, D.C. http://pewhispanic.org/files/reports/139.pdf.

Pew Forum on Religion and Public Life. 2008. "The U.S. Religious Landscape Survey." Pew Research Center, Washington, D.C. http://religions.pewforum.org/reports.

Pew Hispanic Center. 2003. "Hispanics in the Military Fact Sheet." Pew Hispanic Center, Washington, D.C. http://www.pewhispanic.org/files/factsheets/6.pdf.

Pew Hispanic Center. 2008. "Statistical Portrait of Hispanics in the United States, 2006." Pew Hispanic Center, Washington, D.C. http://pewhispanic.org/factsheets/factsheet.php?FactsheetID=35.

Saenz, Rogelio. 2010. "Latinos in America 2010." *Population Bulletin Update,* December 2010. http://www.prb.org/pdf10/latinos-update2010.pdf.

Sassler, Sharon L. 2006. "School Participation among Immigrant Youths: The Case of Segmented Assimilation in the Early 20th Century." *Sociology of Education* 29: 1–24.

Segal, Mady W., and David R. Segal. 2007. "Latinos Claim Larger Share of US Military Personnel." Population Reference Bureau, Washington D.C., October. http://www.prb.org/Articles/2007/HispanicsUSMilitary.aspx.

Snyder, T.D., Dillow, S.A., and Hoffman, C.M. 2009. *Digest of Education Statistics 2008* (NCES 2009-020). National Center for Education Statistics, Institute of Education Sciences, U.S. Department of Education.Washington, DC.

Suro, Roberto, and Jeffery Passel. 2003. "The Rise of the Second Generation: Changing Patterns in Hispanic Population Growth." Pew Hispanic Center, Washington, D.C. http://www.hablamosjuntos.org/resources/pdf/PHC_Projections_final_(October_2003).pdf.

Therrien, Melissa, and Roberto R. Ramirez. 2001. "The Hispanic Population in the United States: Population Characteristics." *Current Population Reports* P20–535. Washington, D.C.: U.S. Census Bureau.

U.S. Bureau of Labor Statistics. 2007. "Union Members in 2006." http://www.bls.gov/news.release/pdf/union2.pdf.

U.S. Bureau of Labor Statistics. 2010. "News Release: Union Members 2009." Document USDL-10-0069. http://www.bls.gov/news.release/pdf/union2.pdf.

U.S. Census Bureau. 2006. "Table 1. Income and Earnings Summary Measures by Selected Characteristics: 2004 and 2005." *Income, Poverty, and Health Insurance Coverage in the United States: 2005.* http://www.census.gov/prod/2006pubs/p60231.pdf.

U.S. Census Bureau. 2007. "Table 1a. Percent of High School and College Graduates of the Population 15 Years and Over, by Age, Sex, Race, and Hispanic Origin: 2006." *Educational Attainment in the United States: 2006.* http://www.census.gov/population/www/socdemo/education/cps2006.html.

U.S. Census Bureau. 2007. "Hispanic Population in the United States 2006: March CPS." http://www.census.gov/population/www/socdemo/hispanic/ho06.html.

U.S. Census Bureau. 2010. "2010 Census Data: Redistricting Data." http://2010.census.gov/2010census/data/.

US Commission on Immigration Reform. 1997. Binational Study on Migration: Executive Summary. Washington, D.C.: US Commission on Immigration Reform. September.

U.S. Department of Labor. 2007. "Union Members in 2006." Department of Labor Statistics, Washington, D.C. http://bollettinoadapt.unimore.it/allegati/07_3_71_SINDACATO.pdf.

3

Core Values

Beliefs and the "American Creed"

Few issues regarding Latinos, particularly Latino immigrants, have been as normatively controversial as perceptions and assessments of the extent to which they hold and embrace core American beliefs and values. But identifying, and measuring, "core" values and beliefs in American politics has never been a simple task in the first place. Both the media and the political realm offer frequent assertions about the existence of an "American Creed," but there is some debate about what the specific elements of such a creed might be and the importance of each of the values that might constitute that creed, both in its own right and relative to others (see Fraga and Segura 2006). Ideas such as democracy, liberty, equality (of opportunity), and individual achievement (self-reliance) are all considered part of the American creed (Citrin et al. 1990). However, scholars suggest that values, such as equality and the potential need for a firm equality of condition, are pivotal. Moreover, numerous scholars have claimed there is no single tradition but multiple political traditions in American politics (Smith 1993), the existence of which belie the assertion of a singular American creed.

Of these multiple traditions it is the liberal tradition that is generally considered the most prominent. This is, the tradition that stresses freedom, liberty, individualism, and equality of opportunity as the defining elements of American political thought. Individualism is often associated with (strong) beliefs in self-reliance, hard work, and taking responsibility for one's own economic and social situation. There is also a corollary assumption that equality of opportunity is inherently important and an essential structural feature linked to individual beliefs about self-reliance and hard work. Also influential is the civic republican tradition that promotes civic engagement, community, and fraternity as essential traits of American society. We discuss civic engagement in Chapter 7, but readers will find aspects of community integrated into topics throughout the book. A third tradition, ascriptive hierarchy, focuses on traits such as race-ethnicity, gender, and class,which have served as ostensible justifications for exclusion and/or an unequal status by those who would argue that some individuals and groups are less (or more) deserving or worthy of a legitimate place in the American polity (Smith 1993; see Elazar 1966). We chose to focus our survey questions on issues associated with individualism, self-reliance, and equality of opportunity that are most closely associated with the liberal tradition because of that tradition's ostensible primacy among American political values, and because Latinos' beliefs in such values has often been an implicit and sometimes explicit basis on which Latinos are "evaluated" by the larger society.

Though limited in volume and scope, previous research has found Latinos' beliefs and values indicative of the liberal strand of American thought to be quite compatible with those of the broader society. One study (de la Garza et al. 1996, 335), for example, found that "at all levels of acculturation, Mexican Americans are no less likely and often more likely to endorse values of individualism" than the American public in general. There may be several reasons for this, but one reason suggested by de la Garza and colleagues is that the implicit assumption of the American creed that self-reliance, individualism, and the like are uniquely American is dubious. That is, various groups, and perhaps especially groups that include populations who have immigrated to the United States in search of improved economic well-being, such as Latinos, probably embrace such values as much as American citizens generally.

Analyses

A number of questions in the LNS were asked that provide insights into the extent to which Latinos subscribe to some of the key ideas of liberalism. The questions cover a range of topics, from the role of hard work, to whether there should be equal rights for all (regardless of a persons' beliefs) that are indicative of liberal views. We assess responses to the questions relative to generation and citizenship, national origin, income and education, and gender.

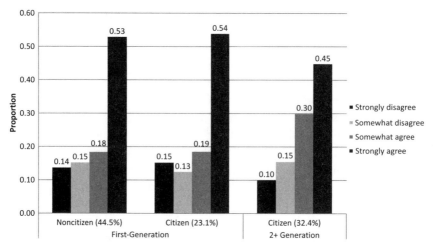

Figure 3.1. Individual Is Responsible for Lack of Success, by Generation and Citizenship
Question wording: "Most people who don't get ahead should not blame the system; they have only themselves to blame."

Perceptions of Blame and Failure to Get Ahead

One way of assessing views on self-reliance and individualism is to consider whether individuals think their economic situation results entirely or primarily from their own behavior or whether they attribute their situation to other, external, factors, such as "the system." On the whole, whether citizen or noncitizen, first generation or second generation and beyond, large majorities of Latinos – more than 70 percent – agree somewhat or strongly that they have "only themselves to blame" if they "don't get ahead." Among the first generation (noncitizens and citizens) more than half strongly agree; this strength of conviction diminishes among the second generation and beyond, where 45 percent hold the strong view, as shown in Figure 3.1. However, about 30 percent of the second generation and beyond still somewhat agree as to where individual responsibility for economic success lies, which is about half higher than for the first generation. There is, then, a decline from the first and the second generation and beyond in strongly attributing self-blame, but there is a greater tendency to agree somewhat. Indeed, the second generation and beyond actually is more likely than the first generation to agree with this expression of personal responsibility. Overall, these responses suggest a substantial self-reliance and/or individualist orientation, with, however, some modest shifts by generation.

For all the national origin groups, the leading response is strong agreement that people have "only themselves to blame" for not getting ahead; when combined with those who somewhat agree, there is 70 percent or more agreement across the groups (with the exception of Salvadorans, at 67 percent), and Cubans generally express the strongest belief in self-reliance, at about 80 percent, which can be seen in Table 3.1. Yet along with this overall high degree of individualism there is substantial "system blame" among respondents, in that upward of 20 percent of each group somewhat or strongly disagree that people have "only themselves to blame."

Across every income level, the leading response, for roughly half of respondents, is that they strongly agree that people "have only themselves to blame" for not getting ahead; further, in every income group, "somewhat agree" is the second most common response. Together, between 70 percent and 75 percent of each income group strongly or somewhat agrees. The only notable difference is that those in the two highest levels show more agreement than do those at the several income levels below them (see Figure 3.2).

As seen with some frequency in our various analyses, responses to questions often look fairly similar when examined from the standpoint of income or education. Interestingly, this is the case regarding those who feel strongly that individuals "have only themselves to blame . . . for not getting ahead." Here, those at the highest income and education levels are a bit less likely to agree than are those at the lower income and education levels (see Figure 3.3 and compare to Figure 3.2). And women are only slightly less likely to agree that they "have only themselves to blame . . . for not getting ahead" (Figure 3.4). Overall, the extent of a sense of personal responsibility seems very strong (though not universal) and varies some by generation, national origin, and socioeconomic status. The level of individualism apparent among the respondents suggests substantial affinity for this important dimension of liberal ideas.

Whether Poor People Can Get Ahead with Hard Work

Along with individual responsibility, a belief in the value and promise of hard work is generally considered part of a liberal outlook in American politics. The high proportion of Latinos who strongly and/or somewhat agree that "poor people can get ahead in the United States if they work hard" indicates that they believe strongly in something akin to the American dream and, by association, an American creed based in liberal values.

Table 3.1. *Perception of Blame for Failure to Get Ahead, by National Origin*
Category: Political Views, Role/View of Government

Response		Cuba	Dominican Republic	El Salvador	Mexico	Puerto Rico	Other Central America	Other South America	Other	Missing	Total
Strongly disagree	Freq.	38	41	58	713	68	35	50	8	12	1024
	Row%	3.76	4.05	5.70	69.62	6.66	3.39	4.90	0.75	1.19	100.00
	Col%	12.72	14.58	15.79	12.76	10.68	10.74	14.37	9.85	16.60	12.79
Somewhat disagree	Freq.	23	42	65	831	86	52	50	17	8	1172
	Row%	1.97	3.56	5.51	70.89	7.36	4.41	4.23	1.42	0.65	100.00
	Col%	7.65	14.70	17.49	14.88	13.51	15.98	14.22	21.50	10.44	14.65
Somewhat agree	Freq.	52	34	71	1259	164	73	70	28	18	1770
	Row%	2.93	1.95	4.03	71.13	9.26	4.12	3.96	1.60	1.03	100.00
	Col%	17.14	12.13	19.29	22.54	25.69	22.55	20.08	36.42	24.79	22.12
Strongly agree	Freq.	189	166	175	2782	320	164	179	25	35	4036
	Row%	4.68	4.12	4.34	68.93	7.93	4.06	4.44	0.62	0.87	100.00
	Col%	62.50	58.59	47.43	49.82	50.12	50.73	51.33	32.23	48.17	50.44
TOTAL	Freq.	302	284	369	5585	638	323	349	78	73	8002
	Row%	3.78	3.55	4.62	69.79	7.98	4.04	4.36	0.97	0.92	100.00
	Col%	100.00	100.00	100.00	100.00	100.00	100.00	100.00	100.00	100.00	100.00

Note: National origin: (24 d.f.) 73.9072 (P = 0.0010). Question wording: "Would you strongly agree, somewhat agree, [or] strongly disagree with the following statement, or do you have no opinion? 'Most people who don't get ahead should not blame the system; they have only themselves to blame.'"

60

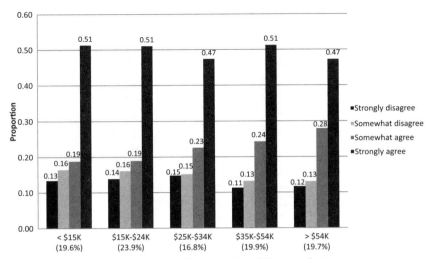

Figure 3.2. Individual Is Responsible for Lack of Success, by Income
Question wording: "Most people who don't get ahead should not blame the system; they have only themselves to blame."

The extent of strong agreement is highest among first-generation noncitizens (79 percent) and is only slightly less so (76 percent) among first-generation citizens, as shown in Figure 3.5. The proportion of second generation and beyond Latinos who strongly agree about the utility of

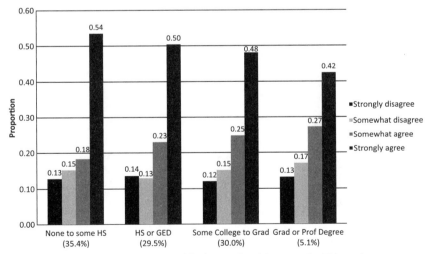

Figure 3.3. Individual Is Responsible for Lack of Success, by Education
Question wording: "Most people who don't get ahead should not blame the system; they have only themselves to blame."

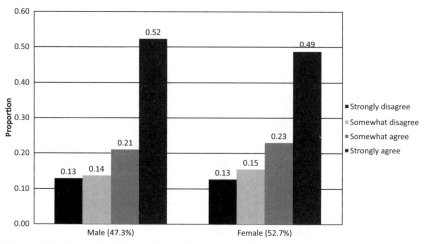

Figure 3.4. Individual Is Responsible for Lack of Success, by Gender
Question wording: "Most people who don't get ahead should not blame the system; they have only themselves to blame."

hard work is somewhat less than among the first generation (by about 12 percent). But almost a quarter of the second generation and beyond agree somewhat. Although the decline in strong agreement is noteworthy (and reminiscent of the pattern of responses found apportioning blame for

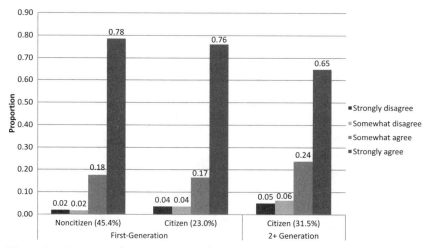

Figure 3.5. Poor People Can Get Ahead through Hard Work, by Generation and Citizenship
Question wording: "Poor people can get ahead in the United States if they work hard."

"not getting ahead"), that 90 percent of the second generation and beyond is in either strong or somewhat agreement about the rewards of hard work, is an important finding. Unlike our previous question, fewer second generation and beyond have this view than those in the first generation. The reasons for this decline are not entirely clear, but one possibility is that some disillusionment may set in if economic prosperity does not increase at the pace the respondent might have hoped for or expected.

There is a strong sense across national origin groups that "poor people can get ahead in the United States if they work hard." For all but the Puerto Rican respondents, greater than 90 percent somewhat or strongly agree with the statement, and in every instance, "strongly agree" is by far the leading response (Table 3.2). Even among Puerto Ricans, almost two-thirds strongly agree, with an additional 22 percent of the respondents somewhat agreeing – meaning that 86 percent are in agreement. Clearly, a belief in the benefits of hard work run wide and deep across the national origin groups.

Across income levels there are high levels of strong agreement that "poor people can get ahead in the United States if they work hard"; specifically, more than two-thirds and up to about three-fourths of each income level group strongly agree. Interestingly, as Figure 3.6 demonstrates, the greatest extent of strong agreement comes from those at the three lowest levels of income (75 percent among those with incomes less than $15,000, $15,000–$24,000, and $25,000–$34,000). Furthermore, for each income group, 90 percent or more somewhat or strongly agree. There are, likewise, high levels of strong agreement across education levels (Figure 3.7). Specifically, well more than two-thirds and up to about three-fourths of each education level grouping strongly agree about the likely benefits of hard work. Note that the broadest level of strong agreement comes from those at the lowest levels of education (78 percent among those with high school education or less). And in each education grouping, 90 percent or more somewhat or strongly agree. Thus, although there is some variability by socioeconomic status, the similarities across strata are striking. Men and women about equally express agreement that hard work will lead to economic advantages, as is reflected in Figure 3.8.

Does Access to More Opportunities Affect Life Advancement?

Who gets what chances in life vary dramatically, and how people view their own opportunities and those that are available to others can likewise vary considerably. Because we are interested in Latinos' view of the idea

Table 3.2. *Ability of Poor People to Get Ahead with Hard Work, by National Origin*

Category: Political Views, Role/View of Government

Response		Cuba	Dominican Republic	El Salvador	Mexico	Puerto Rico	Other Central America	Other South America	Other	Missing	Total
Strongly disagree	Freq.	14	18	7	178	42	12	6	2	6	285
	Row%	5.11	6.26	2.30	62.54	14.88	4.18	1.96	0.77	0.20	100.00
	Col%	4.57	5.97	1.63	3.03	6.70	3.50	1.52	2.83	7.21	3.39
Somewhat disagree	Freq.	10	7	16	195	42	9	20	3	4	307
	Row%	3.27	2.28	5.19	63.57	13.55	3.03	6.66	1.10	1.34	100.00
	Col%	3.16	2.35	3.96	3.32	6.58	2.74	5.58	4.36	5.21	3.65
Somewhat agree	Freq.	41	46	56	1139	140	61	100	28	15	1624
	Row%	2.52	2.83	3.43	70.13	8.60	3.76	6.15	1.69	0.90	100.00
	Col%	12.85	15.39	13.83	19.35	22.08	17.97	27.26	35.52	18.60	19.34
Strongly agree	Freq.	253	228	324	4372	409	258	241	44	54	6183
	Row%	4.09	3.68	5.24	70.72	6.61	4.17	3.89	0.72	0.88	100.00
	Col%	79.42	76.28	80.58	74.30	64.64	75.79	65.64	57.28	68.97	73.62
TOTAL	Freq.	318	298	402	5885	632	340	367	77	79	8398
	Row%	3.79	3.55	4.79	70.07	7.53	4.05	4.36	0.92	0.94	100.00
	Col%	100.00	100.00	100.00	100.00	100.00	100.00	100.00	100.00	100.00	100.00

Note: National origin: (24 d.f.) 123.1202 (P = 0.0000). Question wording: "For the following question, please indicate how much you agree with the statement: 'Poor people can get ahead in the United States if they work hard.'"

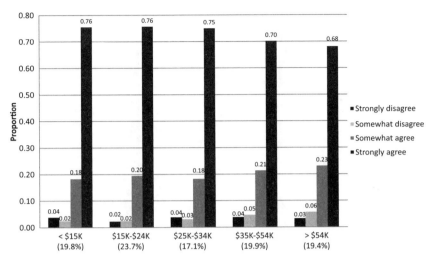

Figure 3.6. Poor People Can Get Ahead through Hard Work, by Income
Question wording: "Poor people can get ahead in the United States if they work hard."

of equal opportunity, we asked respondents whether it was "a problem if some people have more of a chance in life than others." The responses varied dramatically, particularly across citizenship status and generations. Overall, a clear majority (about 57 percent) agreed strongly or somewhat that difference in life chances is not really a big problem. However, among

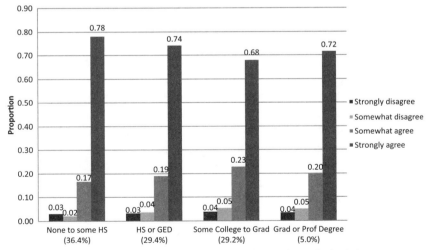

Figure 3.7. Poor People Can Get Ahead through Hard Work, by Education
Question wording: "Poor people can get ahead in the United States if they work hard."

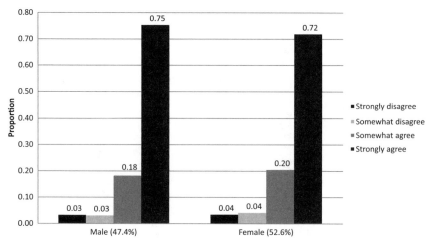

Figure 3.8. Poor People Can Get Ahead through Hard Work, by Gender
Question wording: "Poor people can get ahead in the United States if they work hard."

the second generation and beyond, a majority (53 percent) disagree somewhat or strongly with the idea; that is, they do not find it appropriate that some might have "more of a chance in life than others." This latter view might be interpreted in various ways, but one possibility is that differences in life chances are considered inconsistent with the value of and belief in equal opportunity in economic and social realms. Understood this way, then, the views of a majority of the second generation and beyond could be viewed as affirming the principle of equal opportunity. There is a rather large difference between the second generation and beyond and the first generation on this issue, as seen in Figure 3.9. Roughly 13 percent to 17 percent fewer noncitizen and/or first-generation respondents either strongly or somewhat disagree with the statement. Whether this can be considered acceptance of inequality and/or a weak belief in or embrace of equality of opportunity is not obvious. However, the general patterns and views differ across citizenship and generation.

The views of respondents regarding the importance of equal opportunity show strong similarities across national origin groups. We found that there is considerable agreement – indeed, strong agreement is the most common response for every national origin group – ranging from 30 percent agreement among Puerto Ricans to 45 percent among Dominicans. Yet the second leading answer to this question, when assessed by nationality, is most often strongly disagree. The 30 percent of strong agreement

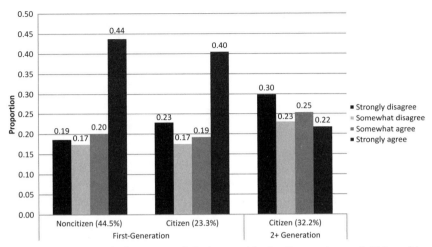

Figure 3.9. Unequal Chance in Life Is Acceptable, by Generation and Citizenship **Question wording:** "It is not really that big of a problem if some people have more of a chance in life than others."

among Puerto Ricans, shown in Table 3.3, is almost matched by the 28 percent who strongly disagree. In general there seems to be considerable overall agreement that difference is life chances is not really a big problem, as well as division and/or ambivalence within some of national groups, especially Puerto Ricans, on this question.

Our understanding of how Latinos feel about equal opportunity gains considerable nuance when the income of the respondents is taken into consideration. This is laid out in Figure 3.10. Clear majorities of all income groups – except those at the highest level ($54,000 and more) – somewhat or strongly agree. Those with the lowest levels of income appear the most accepting of unequal life chances. They are the most likely to strongly agree that "some people hav[ing] more of a chance in life than others" is not a problem. Strong agreement on this issue is about half as common among the highest income levels than among the lowest; the monotonic pattern of decreasingly strong agreement from the lowest to highest income levels is likewise striking.

The impact of education levels on perceptions of equal opportunity is somewhat similar to that of income but in certain ways is more pronounced. Slight majorities of those with at least some college education strongly or somewhat disagree with the notion that unequal access to opportunities in society is acceptable. Considerably fewer, about 30 percent to 40 percent, of those who have never been to college, and 35 percent

Table 3.3. *Perception of Role of Chance in Life Advancement, by National Origin*
Category: Political Views, Role/View of Government

Response		Cuba	Dominican Republic	El Salvador	Mexico	Puerto Rico	Other Central America	Other South America	Other	Missing	Total
Strongly disagree	Freq.	67	68	78	1296	178	62	86	16	14	1863
	Row%	3.59	3.62	4.17	69.52	9.54	3.33	4.63	0.85	0.74	100.00
	Col%	21.87	23.19	20.51	23.14	28.08	19.39	24.70	22.83	19.75	23.24
Somewhat disagree	Freq.	53	50	68	1103	120	58	51	25	16	1544
	Row%	3.46	3.24	4.39	71.46	7.77	3.78	3.27	1.63	1.01	100.00
	Col%	17.47	17.15	17.88	19.70	18.93	18.26	14.45	35.97	22.50	19.25
Somewhat agree	Freq.	58	44	78	1225	146	70	77	18	19	1735
	Row%	3.33	2.55	4.51	70.62	8.40	4.04	4.46	1.03	1.07	100.00
	Col%	18.86	15.18	20.63	21.88	23.01	21.93	22.17	25.58	26.66	21.64
Strongly agree	Freq.	128	130	155	1976	190	129	135	11	22	2875
	Row%	4.45	4.50	5.40	68.72	6.61	4.49	4.70	0.38	0.75	100.00
	Col%	41.80	44.47	40.98	35.28	29.99	40.41	38.68	15.62	31.09	35.86
TOTAL	Freq.	306	291	379	5599	633	320	349	70	69	8017
	Row%	3.82	3.63	4.73	69.84	7.90	3.99	4.36	0.87	0.87	100.00
	Col%	100.00	100.00	100.00	100.00	100.00	100.00	100.00	100.00	100.00	100.00

Note: National origin: (24 d.f.) 65.7410 (P = 0.0061). Question wording: "Would you strongly agree, somewhat agree, strongly disagree with the following statement, or do you have no opinion? 'It is not really that big of a problem if some people have more of a chance in life than others.'"

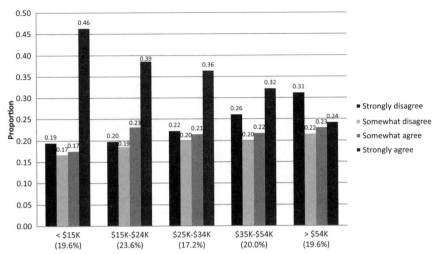

Figure 3.10. Unequal Chance in Life Is Acceptable, by Income
Question wording: "It is not really that big of a problem if some people have more of a chance in life than others."

with up to a high school education (or less) strongly or somewhat disagree on this point (see Figure 3.11). In short, the more educated are more likely than the less educated to view inequality of opportunity as problematic. As with most other questions, we found that there is

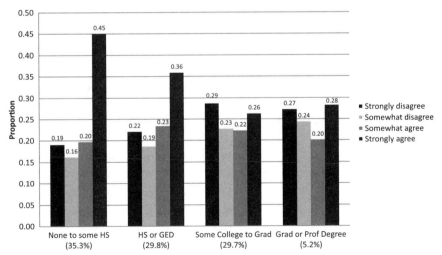

Figure 3.11. Unequal Chance in Life Is Acceptable, by Education
Question wording: "It is not really that big of a problem if some people have more of a chance in life than others."

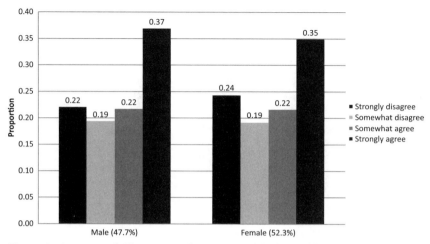

Figure 3.12. Unequal Chance in Life Is Acceptable, by Gender
Question wording: "It is not really that big of a problem if some people have more of a chance in life than others."

essentially no difference by gender on this question (the details of which can be found in Figure 3.12).

Support for Equal Rights Regardless of Political Belief

Another, important element of the American political values system that is found in a number of forms, including the American creed, concerns views about civil liberties, such as freedom of belief, association, speech, religion, and the like. We included in the LNS a question that would help assess respondents' attitude about civil liberties. Respondents were asked about their level of (dis)agreement with this statement: "No matter what a person's political beliefs are, they are entitled to the same legal rights and protection as anyone else." As seen in Figure 3.13, across citizenship status and across the first generation and the second generation and beyond, most were supportive though somewhat reserved in their feeling about equal rights; three-quarters agreed somewhat and (varying a bit by citizenship and generation) between 3 percent and 7 percent agreed strongly. There was relatively little variation across generation and/or citizenship status. More than 80 percent of all respondents agree somewhat or strongly, which suggests solid commitment for this value, associated with tolerance in a liberal democracy.

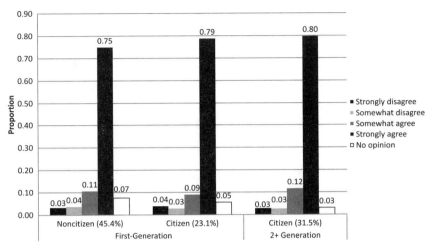

Figure 3.13. Equality of Right, without Regard to Political Views, by Generation and Citizenship

Question wording: "Would you strongly agree, somewhat agree, somewhat disagree, [or] strongly disagree with the following statement, or do you have no opinion: 'No matter what a person's political beliefs are, they are entitled to the same legal rights and protections as anyone else.'"

Regarding national origin groups, the generally high levels of support are clearest among Cubans and Puerto Ricans, who have 88 percent and 85 percent, respectively, of (some degree) of agreement; Mexicans are bit behind at 82 percent and show slightly less strong support and more "no opinion" responses, as shown in Table 3.4. Salvadorans also demonstrate a more tepid response than do the other larger national origin groups. The other groups also rather strongly support the idea; however, there is a greater likelihood for them to report "no opinion."

Support for this proposition increases with income level, particularly in the "somewhat agree" responses (Figure 3.14). There is a marked growth – from 73 percent to 84 percent – in levels of those who somewhat agree moving from the lowest (less than $15,000) to the highest ($54,000 and more) income levels; there is a similar, if more modest, pattern for the "strongly agree" responses (although the percentage of "strongly agree" responses is low, on the whole). The impact of education on tolerance for different beliefs is quite similar to that of income, which can be seen in Figure 3.15; this is another instance where the two socioeconomic status variables follow each other closely, although it is not always the case (as we have seen). As is the case for many, though hardly all, of the previous

Table 3.4. *Support for Equal Rights, by National Origin*

Category: Political Views, Specific Issues Views

Response		Cuba	Dominican Republic	El Salvador	Mexico	Puerto Rico	Other Central America	Other South America	Other	Missing	Total
Strongly disagree	Freq.	14	6	15	208	17	2	17	1	6	285
	Row%	4.87	1.93	5.21	72.81	5.82	0.76	6.10	0.48	2.03	100.00
	Col%	4.25	1.78	3.60	3.44	2.52	0.63	4.65	1.73	6.90	3.30
Somewhat disagree	Freq.	5	12	16	191	15	18	12	1	4	275
	Row%	1.92	4.22	5.73	69.63	5.51	6.61	4.43	0.41	1.53	100.00
	Col%	1.61	3.74	3.82	3.16	2.30	5.27	3.26	1.44	4.99	3.18
No opinion	Freq.	18	23	39	666	68	38	40	14	6	911
	Row%	1.98	2.48	4.25	73.10	7.45	4.21	4.38	1.54	0.61	100.00
	Col%	5.50	7.27	9.39	11.02	10.30	11.13	10.67	17.83	6.64	10.55
Somewhat agree	Freq.	273	253	311	4620	537	271	290	61	62	6677
	Row%	4.08	3.79	4.65	69.19	8.04	4.05	4.34	0.92	0.93	100.00
	Col%	83.29	81.70	75.34	76.43	81.52	78.62	77.45	77.88	73.82	77.33
Strongly agree	Freq.	18	17	32	360	22	15	15	1	6	486
	Row%	3.60	3.51	6.66	74.04	4.56	3.09	3.05	0.18	1.32	100.00
	Col%	5.35	5.51	7.85	5.96	3.36	4.36	3.97	1.13	7.64	5.63
TOTAL	**Freq.**	327	310	413	6045	659	344	374	79	84	8634
	Row%	3.79	3.59	4.78	70.01	7.63	3.99	4.33	0.91	0.97	100.00
	Col%	100.00	100.00	100.00	100.00	100.00	100.00	100.00	100.00	100.00	100.00

Note: National origin: (32 d.f.) 69.5299 (P = 0.0240). Question wording: "Would you strongly agree, somewhat agree, somewhat disagree, strongly disagree with the following statement or do you have no opinion: 'No matter what a person's political beliefs are, they are entitled to the same legal rights and protections as anyone else.'"

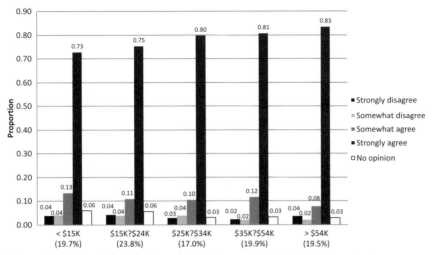

Figure 3.14. Equality of Right, without Regard to Political Views, by Income
Question wording: "Would you strongly agree, somewhat agree, somewhat disagree, [or] strongly disagree with the following statement, or do you have no opinion: 'No matter what a person's political beliefs are, they are entitled to the same legal rights and protections as anyone else.'"

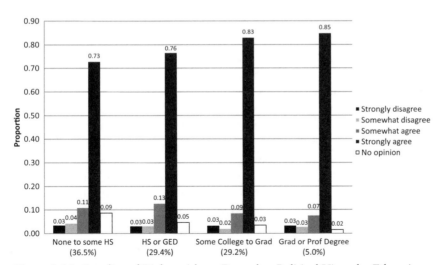

Figure 3.15. Equality of Right, without Regard to Political Views by Education
Question wording: "Would you strongly agree, somewhat agree, somewhat disagree, [or] strongly disagree with the following statement, or do you have no opinion: 'No matter what a person's political beliefs are, they are entitled to the same legal rights and protections as anyone else.'"

questions covered in this chapter, there is essentially no difference by gender on acceptance of the right of individuals to have equal rights to different views; support for this general indicator of views on civil liberties varies not at all between Latinas and Latinos (data not shown).

Conclusion

Do Latinos hold beliefs consistent with core American values? This chapter assessed Latinos' responses to several LNS questions concerning values associated with the most prominent of the American political traditions, liberalism – specifically, individualism and self-reliance, the value and importance of hard work, views regarding (un)equal life chances, and beliefs regarding assurances of equality in civil liberties. Latinos' views as expressed in the LNS appear quite compatible and consistent with core American values. Those views vary somewhat according to generation, citizenship, national origin, and socioeconomic status, but not always in the way one might expect; across the question responses, gender had little or no impact.

Latinos generally demonstrate a high level of agreement that individual responsibility, rather than "the system," is to be blamed for failure to succeed in life. They likewise indicate a strong belief that the poor can get ahead with hard work in the United States. Thus, on the two questions in the LNS that most directly tap central aspects of the American creed, Latinos strongly adhere to the relevant values. Although there is some modest variation across subgroups by generation and so on, the overall orientation on these questions is strong.

Assessing Latinos' responses to the question of whether it is "really not much of a problem if some people have more of a chance in life than others" is more complicated. Equality of opportunity is a supposedly important premise in the American belief system because it concerns the openness and fairness of the social and economic structure in which members of the society live and seek to prosper; as such, it is in important ways external to individual initiative and linked to attitudes that are part of self-reliance and hard work. Conditions that deviate from equality of opportunity, such as some people having more of a chance in life than others, could be viewed as undermining a core value. A (slight) majority of the second generation and beyond disagree strongly or somewhat that differential life chances are not a big problem, which might be understood as objecting to inequality of opportunity and, in turn, as endorsing the important American opportunity ethos. Yet that this is a bare majority, and that majorities of the first generation seem not to find a problem, indicates further complexity. Latinos' responses to this issue generally seem the most varied of the several values questions. Thus, Latinos' ideas about the social structure of equality in the United States are apparently more difficult to describe and explain in general, shown by variation in responses across the subgroups. However, Latinos' views do not seem to indicate challenges to American values, as some critics say.

Finally, Latinos offer substantial, though not unqualified, support for the view that equal rights should not be curtailed because of differences in one's views, a dimension of civil liberties. A large portion of respondents somewhat agree, but relatively few strongly agree, that there should be equal rights to believe and speak out without penalty. Latinos' solid level of support on this issue is probably not all that different from that of the general population.

In summary, Latinos' values seem strongly consistent with several values integral to the liberal strand of American creed. This is especially so concerning individual responsibility and hard work. Their values regarding (in)equality of opportunity and civil liberties are not quite as simple, but there is no obvious reason to suggest that they stray much (if at all) from the American core values.

Bibliography

Citrin, Jack, Beth Reingold, and Donald P. Green. 1990. "American Identity and the Politics of Ethnic Change," *Journal of Politics* (52) 4: 1124–54.

de la Garza, Rodolfo O., Angelo Falcon, and F. Chris Garcia. 1996. "Will The Real Americans Please Stand Up: Anglo and Mexican-American Support of Core American Political Values" *American Journal of Political Science* (40) 2 (May): 335–51.

Elazar, Daniel J. 1966. *American Federalism: A View from the States.* New York: Crowell.

Fraga, Luis. R., and Gary M. Segura. 2006. "Culture Clash? Contesting Notions of American Identity and the Effects of Latin American Immigration" *Perspectives on Politics*, 4(2): 279–87.

Smith, Rogers M. 1993. "Beyond Tocqueville, Myrdal, and Hartz: The Multiple Traditions in America," *American Political Science Review* 87 (3) (September): 549–66.

4

Latino Identities

Commonalities and Competition

This chapter explores the attachment Latinos feel to group identities, ranging from their attachment to their compatriots from their same country of origin to their affinity with pan-ethnic identification such as Latino or Hispanic, and their identification as American. The identity labels individuals choose have consequences for the belief and attitudes individuals hold and the way that individuals act. These consequences are political because they shape both the manner that individuals think of themselves collectively and the way that they calculate the costs and benefits of collective action.

Collective action is at the root of politics. Without the coordinated effort of groups of people, the redistribution of public goods, which is at the root of all politics, cannot occur. There are, however, very different conceptions of collective action, with two principle approaches in the social science literature: in the first, collective action is considered the result of the amalgamation of individual interests, and in the second, it is the consequence of mobilized group identities.

The first approach, often associated with rational-choice accounts of politics (Downs 1957; Olson 1971), envisions collective action taking place only if the benefits of this action to the individuals involved outweigh the costs. Collective action will be achieved only if individuals see their self-interest bound up with the goals set out for the group. Collective action is more likely to occur if individuals receive selective incentives or side payments to act collectively, and less likely if the goals are public goods, which, once achieved, are freely available to all. Collective action in which the end goal is a public good inevitably encounters free-rider problems. Within this framework, the choice to free ride is a rational one, with individuals leaving the costs of collective action to others, while remaining in the position to join in reaping the benefits of that action. Collective action, seen this way, is characterized by the barriers to group mobilization rather than its possibilities, and it is considered more exceptional than commonplace. At its most basic, in this view, if individuals think that they will receive little or no material benefit from acting in concert with others, then they will not do so. However, more nuanced rational-choice theories of collective action take into account the expressive benefits of acting as part of a group. These include feelings of efficacy, empowerment, satisfaction, and self-worth that are psychological rather than material and are generated simply as a result of taking part in the group, regardless of the success of the group's efforts or the achievement of its goals (Moe 1980; Chong 1991).

Casting the rewards of group mobilization in terms of psychological benefits rather than as concrete, material gains for individuals shifts the calculus of costs and benefits, and opens up the possibility that collective mobilization may have a more social rather than simply individualistic basis. This brings us to the second approach to collective action: collective action as the consequence of mobilized group identities. In this perspective, the key to individuals acting in concert is their common identification as members of a group. Individuals do not act in politics solely as individuals, but because they believe they are a part of group. This basis of group membership can range from an identification with a geographic area, like a particular town or city, with a state or country, with a type of place (e.g., rural versus urban), with an organization (e.g., church, an interest group, a political party, a government), or with a group of people (identified, either by themselves or others, by a set of common markers, such as gender, ethnic origin, race, and religion).

In this view, however, mobilization does not come about simply because individuals are objectively members of a group, whether it is a religious denomination, a racial category, or a national origin group. For group identities to serve to mobilize people politically, two preconditions must be met: individuals must recognize themselves as members of the group, and individuals must be conscious of the political value of acting as a group (Miller et al. 1981; Shingles 1981; Garcia 1982; Conover 1984, 1988; Dawson 1994; Omi and Winant 1995; Cole, Tucker, and Ostrove 1998). These are by no means obvious outcomes, and their presence or absence presumably explains why a great many groups are not politically engaged as groups per se, and why many individuals who might objectively be considered members of politicized groups might not be politically engaged themselves.

There is a substantial literature on the importance of group identification among racial and ethnic minorities in general, and Latinos more specifically (e.g., Keefe and Padilla 1987). In general, this literature focuses on Latino ethnic identification (e.g., Garcia 1982; Jones-Correa and Leal 1996; Lee and Bean 2004), and to some extent on the link between identification and outcomes, such as partisanship, ideology, issues positions, and intergroup relations (e.g., Kaufmann 2003; Lopez and Pantoja 2004; Nicholson, Pantoja, and Segura 2005; Sawyer 2005). This literature fits squarely in the second approach to collective action in politics, asking, "Do people in fact identify as members of a group, and do these group membership have political ramifications, affecting individuals' attitudes, beliefs, and actions?" This is not to claim that individuals do not choose policy positions and so on for instrumental reasons as well, but rather to underline that identity choices fundamentally shape political attitudes and behaviors for Latinos in the United States.

In what follows we seek to define the identities that Latinos in the United States adopt as they settle, adapt, and integrate into American society: how Latinos identify as members of their national origin group, as a pan-ethnic group with other Hispanics or Latinos, and as Americans. We also explore other dimensions of Latino identity as well: Do Latinos see themselves as members of a distinct racial group? How do parents identify the children of mixed Latino and/or non-Latino marriage? Also, do Latinos in the United States feel that they should blend in with mainstream culture or remain culturally distinct? Do they feel that Latinos should retain Spanish or learn English? The tables in this chapter illustrate how Latino respondents' identity choices are constructed through their social networks: through the friendships they have and relationships with their coworkers. Latinos can feel competitive as well as close to other coethnics as well: the tables in this chapter illustrate perceptions of competition across various issues, such as employment, education, and politics. The chapter concludes by looking more closely at how Latinos perceive other Americans' views of what it means to be American: does being American require being born in the United States, speaking English, being white, or being Christian? The findings in each of the tables are presented by citizenship status and generation in the United States.

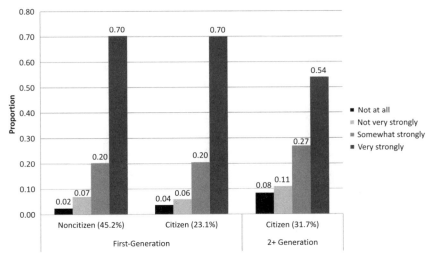

Figure 4.1. Strength of Identification with Country of Origin, by Generation and Citizenship
Question wording: "In general, how strongly or not do you think of yourself as [national origin descriptor]?

Latino Identities in America

Approximately two-thirds of all adults of Latin American origin in the United States were born outside of the United States. We would expect, then, that many Latinos identify strongly with their country of origin. Figure 4.1 illustrates this clearly. About 90 percent of all foreign-born respondents identify very strongly or somewhat strongly with their country of origin. That connection does not significantly diminish with naturalization: first-generation citizens identify as strongly with their country of origin as their nonnaturalized counterparts: 90 percent of naturalized citizens identify very strongly or somewhat strongly with their country-of-origin label, the same as the 90 percent of foreign-born noncitizens. However, there is a substantial decrease in the percentage of those who identify with their country of origin between first generation and second generation and beyond Latinos. The proportion of respondents who identify very strongly is 70 percent for the first generation, but only 54 percent for those respondents born in the United States. These decreases are paralleled by increases in the "somewhat strongly" and "not very strongly" responses, which suggests a steady decline in country-of-origin identity across generations in the United States.

As is the case with country-of-origin identity, a sense of identification as Latino and/or Hispanic is shared – at least to some extent – by

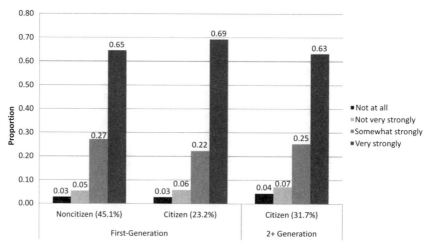

Figure 4.2. Strength of Identification as Hispanic/Latino, by Generation and Citizenship
Question wording: "In general, how strongly or not do you think of yourself as Hispanic or Latino?"

virtually all U.S. Latinos. Overall, only about 3 percent identify "not at all" as Latino, whereas only an additional 6 percent identify "not very strongly." About 65 percent of Latinos identify very strongly as either Hispanic or Latino. Moreover, there are relatively minor (though statistically significant) differences between generations, and between naturalized and nonnaturalized first-generation immigrants, as documented in Figure 4.2. First-generation citizens are most likely to identify strongly as Latino and/or Hispanic, with 69 percent asserting that they identify very strongly, and another 22 percent saying that they identify somewhat strongly. Native-born Latinos are least likely to identify as Latino or Hispanic, with 63 percent identifying very strongly, and 25 percent identifying somewhat strongly. One possibility is that, for the foreign born, *Latino* has a meaning closer to "Latin American origin"; this might help explain its adoption even by recent immigrant arrivals to the United States (Oboler 1995). Another is that media and governmental use of these pan-ethnic labels "Hispanic" and "Latino" has helped foster a sense of common identity, or at least the language of common identity, even among new immigrants. Whichever the case, it is clear that over the past fifteen years the number of Latinos identifying by these pan-ethnic labels has increased substantially: large majorities of every generation and national-origin group feel comfortable adopting these terms to describe themselves,

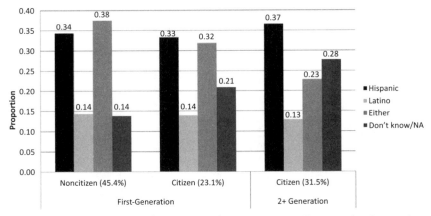

Figure 4.3. Preferred Term for Persons of Latin American Descent, by Generation and Citizenship

Question wording: "The most frequently used terms to describe persons of Latin American descent living in the United States are 'Hispanic' and 'Latino.' Of the two, which do you prefer, or do you not care about this terminology?"

with the exception of Cuban Americans. Even among Cubans, a plurality prefer these pan-ethnic labels.

The data show that large majorities of respondents to the Latino National Survey were very strongly attached to pan-ethnic identities, either Latino or Hispanic. Figure 4.3 shows that across generations, and for both citizens and noncitizens, the term *Hispanic* is preferred by more than a two-to-one margin over the term *Latino* (35 percent versus 14 percent). Native-born respondents are slightly more likely to choose *Hispanic*, with 37 percent preferring this term. However, slightly more than half of respondents say that either term is acceptable, or they refuse to provide an answer (i.e., "don't know/don't care"), which indicates that most either see these identity labels as interchangeable or see the choice between them as of little consequence. There are only trivial differences between the native born and the foreign born, and between citizens and noncitizens in terms of preferring Latino or Hispanic, but first-generation respondents are more likely to state that either term is acceptable, whereas respondents born in the United States tend more toward the "don't know/don't care" viewpoint. The end results are similar: both new arrivals and those born in the United States see the two terms as interchangeable.

Persons of Latin American ancestry in the United States may think of themselves as part of a larger Latino or Hispanic ethnic group, but do

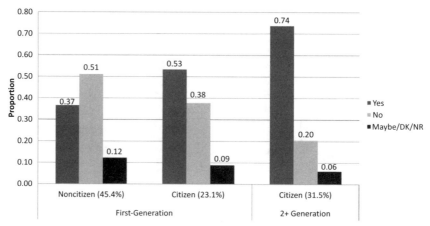

Figure 4.4. Latinos Are a Distinct Racial Group in the United States, by Generation and Citizenship

Question wording: "In the U.S., we use a number of categories to describe ourselves racially. Do you feel that (Latinos/Hispanics) make up a distinctive racial group in America?"

they think of themselves racially? The Latino National Survey results provide some evidence for the racialization of Latinos (De Genova 2003). More than half of all respondents (52 percent) in the LNS indicated that they believed that Latinos/Hispanics were a distinct racial group, the equivalent of the African American, Asian, or white racial categories used by the census. Interestingly, there are rather large intergroup differences in opinions regarding whether Latinos represent a distinct racial group. Among first-generation immigrants, naturalized citizens are more likely than noncitizens to view Latinos as a racial group by 16 percentage points: 53 percent to 37 percent, respectively. Even more striking, Hispanics are considered a distinct racial group by three-quarters (74 percent) of all respondents born in the United States, compared with 42 percent of those born outside the United States: a more than 30-percentage-point difference. These differences suggest that assimilation – as indicated by time in the United States – may lead to racialization, leading Latinos to see themselves not only as an ethnic group but also as a racial group. In summary, the results presented in Figure 4.4, building on the findings presented in previous tables, indicate that not only are respondents comfortable identifying pan-ethnically as either Latino or Hispanic, but also for a majority of respondents this group identity becomes part of a racial rather than simply an ethnic set of identifiers.

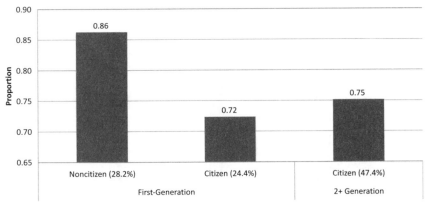

Figure 4.5. Children of Non-Latino Partner and/or Spouse Are Latino, by Generation and Citizenship
Question wording: Ask if R's spouse/partner is non-Latino and has children: "Do you consider your children Latina/o?"

One question is whether Latino identity, whether interpreted as an ethnic label or a racial label, might diminish over time or through intermarriage, or whether it will persist. The existing literature assumes that intermarriage is a culminating step on the pathway to assimilation into American culture; presumably specific ethnic identities fade away with intermarriage (Gordon 1964; Lieberson 1981; Alba and Nee 2003). Latino National Survey data indicate that pan-ethnic Latino or Hispanic identities are in fact fairly resilient, even with intermarriage. For instance, as Figure 4.5 indicates, Latinos who marry non-Latinos remain very likely to identify their children as Latino as well, with 78 percent indicating that they think of their children as Latino or Hispanic.

Somewhat surprisingly, there is no significant difference across generations in how they view the identity of the children they have with non-Latino spouses and/or partners. Identification of children of interethnic marriages as Latino is higher among noncitizens (86 percent) than among first-generation citizens (72 percent) or those born in the United States (75 percent), although out-marriage is a much smaller percentage of total marriages in the first generation than among Latinos born in the United States. The U.S.-born Latinos are more likely to outmarry than the foreign born, although out-marriage rates in general have declined as the number of Latinos in the United States has increased, and Latinos are more likely to interact largely with other Latinos (Qian and Lichter 2007). In any case, the data presented in Figure 4.5 point to the persistence of Latino identity even with intermarriage – at least through parental eyes. How

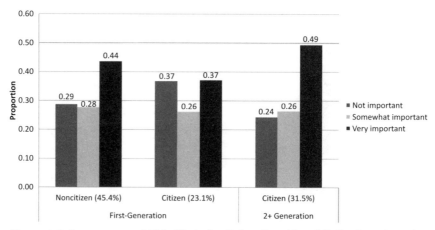

Figure 4.6. Importance of U.S. Birth for Being Considered Fully American, by Generation and Citizenship
Question wording: "When you think of what it means to be fully American in the eyes of most Americans, do you think it is very important, somewhat important, or not important to have been born in the United States?"

these children will identify once they reach adulthood is an open question (see Rumbaut and Portes 2001).

Along with wanting to know how our respondents think about their identities as Latinos, we were curious as to how they think about their attachments to an American identity and how they conceived of that identity. Figures 4.6–4.9 address what they believe American society demands of them before they can be truly accepted – if ever – as American. Figure 4.6 shows what respondents think the importance is, to other Americans, of the idea that one must be born in the United States to be "fully American." Fully 71 percent of respondents believe that being born in the United States is either very or somewhat important to be accepted as American.

The proportion of respondents who believe that being born in the United States is not important to being American is highest, perhaps unsurprisingly, among naturalized Latino citizens – 37 percent of this group believe that birthplace does not determine one's American identity, compared with 29 percent of first-generation noncitizens and 24 percent of those born in the United States. This may be indicative of either personal experience or motivated reasoning, or both – those who are not born in the United States are significantly less likely to feel that most Americans believe in the importance of being born in the United States as an important part of being American.

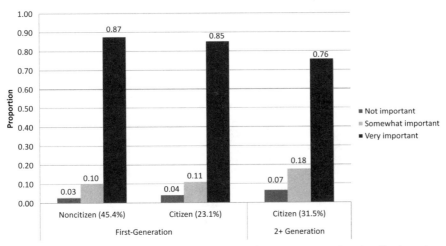

Figure 4.7. Importance of English Proficiency for Being Considered Fully American, by Generation and Citizenship
Question wording: "When you think of what it means to be fully American in the eyes of most Americans, do you think it is very important, somewhat important, or not important to speak English well?"

Figure 4.7 indicates there is relative consensus across citizens and noncitizens, and across generations, on the importance of speaking English for being considered fully American. Of respondents, 83 percent consider English proficiency very important, and only 4 percent overall disregard its importance. This matches the findings presented in Figure 4.12, in which Latinos themselves placed almost-unanimous emphasis on the importance of learning English. However, the degree of importance placed on English as a qualification for being fully American differs between generations. Respondents born in the United States are less likely than first-generation immigrants to view English as very important (76 percent of Latinos born in the United States say English is "very important" to being American, whereas the figure for the first generation as a whole is 87 percent – an 11-percentage-point difference). Thus, although all Latinos seem to agree on the centrality of English to commonly held notions of what it means to be American (note that across generations fewer than 5 percent think English is not important at all to most people's views of being fully American), those born in the United States seem to believe that it is slightly less central to understandings of American identity.

Although most respondents are skeptical of the role that race plays in the definition of being fully American in the United States, the data in

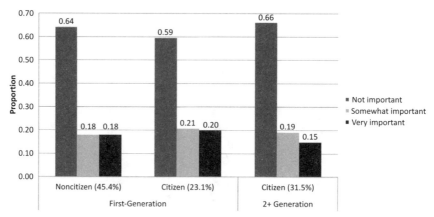

Figure 4.8. Importance of Being White for Being Considered Fully American, by Generation and Citizenship
Question wording: "When you think of what it means to be fully American in the eyes of most Americans, do you think it is very important, somewhat important, or not important to be white?"

Figure 4.8 indicate that a strikingly large percentage of Latinos – 36 percent overall – do believe that most Americans think it is either somewhat important or very important to be white to be considered fully American. These perceptions about race as a defining factor in American identity may be linked to Latinos' beliefs about the Hispanic and/or Latino as a racial group, however unlike the findings presented in Figure 4.4, the findings here do not seem to increase across generations. The perception of the importance given to race as a factor in being American seems slightly more prevalent among naturalized than nonnaturalized first-generation respondents (see Figure 4.8), although it is slightly less prevalent among second generation and beyond respondents than among those born outside of the United States.

Although Latinos remain for the most part skeptical about race as a centrally defining factor in American identity, most Latinos (about 60 percent in all) think that it is at least somewhat important to be Christian to be seen as fully American in the eyes of most Americans. As shown in Figure 4.9, this perception is less prevalent among naturalized (compared with nonnaturalized) first-generation immigrants, as well as among second generation and beyond compared with first-generation respondents. Among Latinos born in the United States, fully 46 percent believe that being Christian is not central in most Americans' understanding of what it means to be fully American. This suggests that assimilation (as indicted

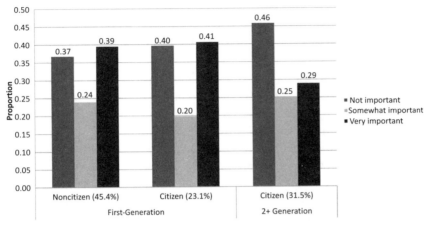

Figure 4.9. Importance of Being Christian for Being Considered Fully American, by Generation and Citizenship
Question wording: "When you think of what it means to be fully American in the eyes of most Americans, do you think it is very important, somewhat important, or not important to be White?"

by naturalization and being born in the United States) does decrease the perceived importance of being Christian for fully American status, although among all groups, the majority of respondents believe that it is at least somewhat important.

Given this understanding of some characteristics of Americans, how "American" do Hispanics see themselves, and how does this differ as they remain in the United States? Figure 4.10 shows that 68 percent of all Latinos consider themselves either very strongly or somewhat strongly

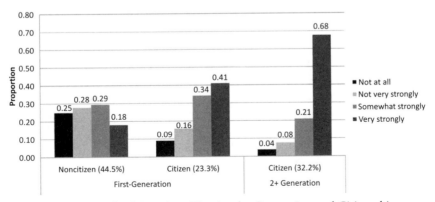

Figure 4.10. Strength of American Identity, by Generation and Citizenship
Question wording: "In general, how strongly or not do you think of yourself as American?"

American. Predictably, there are large intergroup differences in the strength of attachments to American identity, most prominently those between first and second generation and beyond Latinos, that is, Latinos who are born abroad and those born in the United States. Sixty-eight percent of Latinos born in the United States consider themselves strongly American (another 21 percent consider themselves somewhat American), but this percentage diminishes to 41 percent for naturalized citizens, and to only 18 percent for foreign-born noncitizens.

Only about 14 percent of all respondents do not consider themselves American to any degree ("not at all"). Twenty-five percent of first-generation noncitizens and 9 percent of naturalized citizens consider themselves "not at all" American, but only 4 percent of Latinos born in the United States do so. As the assimilation literature would predict (Alba and Nee 2003), on the whole, the vast majority of Latinos identify as American at least to some degree, but the strength of this identification increases parallel to integration into American society (i.e., with time spent in the United States, naturalization as a U.S. citizen, and being born in the United States). This seems a straightforward intuition. The most surprising finding in Figure 4.10, perhaps, is that a large proportion – 47 percent – of foreign-born Latinos identify as either somewhat or very strongly American, even without being citizens.

Respondents were also asked to choose between three forms of self-identification: identification with their country of origin, a pan-ethnic identification as Latino or Hispanic, and their identification as American. Keep in mind that in real life, people are rarely, if ever, forced to choose among their identities; people can have and use identities defined by gender, occupation, race, and/or religion simultaneously. What Figure 4.11 presents is a forced choice: respondents' preferred identity option among the three choices.

The distribution of responses indicates that 80 percent of all respondents identify as either Latino and/or Hispanic or with their country of origin, with a relatively equal split between them. However, although only 4 percent of noncitizens choose American as their primary identity, this jumps to 15 percent among those who are naturalized and to 37 percent among those born in the United States, the modal, or most common, response given. Nevertheless, even among these second generation and beyond respondents, for those born in the United States, both Latino and/or Hispanic (36 percent) and country-of-origin (24 percent) identity are still quite high, which suggests the durability of these identity ties even among individuals born in the United States.

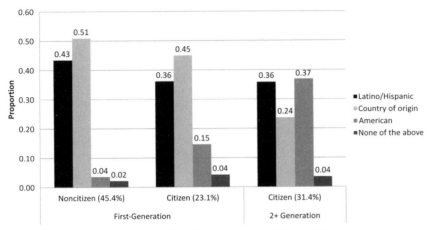

Figure 4.11. Preferred Identity, by Generation and Citizenship
Question wording: "Of the three previous terms, 'Latino or Hispanic,' '[national origin descriptor],' or 'American,' which best describes you?"

It could be that the persistence of pan-ethnic and country-of-origin identities (even though identification as American increases over time and generation in the United States) has implications for other social and cultural indicators of integration, such as learning English. There has certainly been a great deal made of the contention that Latinos supposedly do not want to learn English. Is this contention true?

The LNS results show precisely the opposite: 91 percent of all respondents feel that learning English is very important, and about 98 percent of respondents consider learning English either somewhat or very important. Furthermore, there are only slight differences in these opinions by citizenship status and generation (Figure 4.12). If anything, the importance given to learning English declines slightly with time in the United States and over generation: 95 percent of foreign-born noncitizens believe that it is very important to learn English, 92 percent of all naturalized citizens believe this is true, and 87 percent of all Latinos born in the United States believe learning English is very important. This opinion is so widely and strongly held as to be, in public opinion terms, practically unanimous: Latinos emphatically believe in the importance of learning English.

Interestingly, however, just as Latinos in the United States feel that learning English is very important, they also believe that it is important to retain Spanish. Eighty-five percent of Latinos in the LNS sample believe that it is very important to retain the ability to speak Spanish. This percentage, like the percentages presented in Figure 4.12 for learning English,

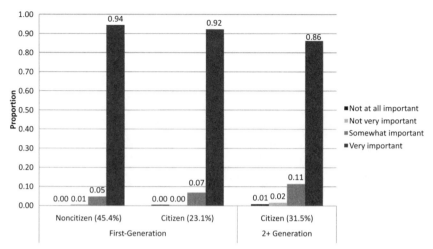

Figure 4.12. Importance of Everyone in the United States Learning English, by Generation and Citizenship
Question wording: "How important do you think it is that everyone in the United States learn English?"

does not differ between naturalized and nonnaturalized first-generation immigrants: 88 percent of foreign-born noncitizens and 89 percent of foreign-born citizens believe it is very important to maintain the ability to speak Spanish, as documented in Figure 4.13. However, there are some generational differences: among second-generation and beyond

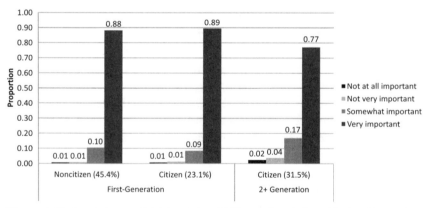

Figure 4.13. Importance of Maintaining Ability to Speak Spanish, by Generation and Citizenship
Question wording: "How important do you think it is for you or your family to maintain the ability to speak Spanish?"

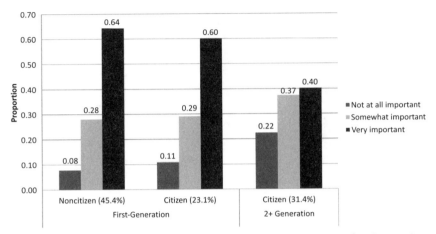

Figure 4.14. Importance of Changing to Blend into U.S. Society, by Generation and Citizenship
Question wording: "How important is it for (Latinos/Hispanics) to change so that they blend into the larger American society?"

respondents, speaking Spanish is rated "very important" by 77 percent of respondents, compared with 89 percent among the first generation. Latinos born in the United States seem to downgrade the importance of speaking Spanish a bit, from "very important" to "somewhat important."

Note that the responses given in the LNS to questions about learning English and retaining Spanish are aspirational. This is to say that even though 95 percent of noncitizen Latinos believe it is important to learn English, because they were born in Latin America, a much smaller percentage actually speak English fluently. Similarly, although very high percentages of the second generation and beyond speak English as their native tongue, Latinos born in the United States are more likely to support the view that Latinos should retain the ability to speak Spanish, even if they no longer use it as their primary language. As Figure 2.1 indicates, by the second generation there is already a linguistic transition under way from Spanish dominance to English. Those born in the United States to foreign-born parents may understand and speak Spanish, but their dominant language is English. By the third generation (U.S.-born Latinos born to U.S.-born parents), English-language dominance is complete, and Spanish-language ability is relatively rare.

Like Figures 4.12 and 4.13, which present Hispanics' views on learning English and retaining Spanish, Figures 4.14 and 4.15 suggest that Latinos hold seemingly divergent views about assimilation into American society.

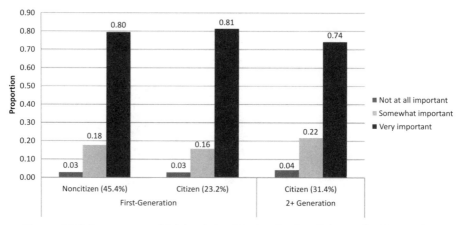

Figure 4.15. Importance of Maintaining Distinct Latino Cultures, by Generation and Citizenship
Question wording: "How important is it for (Latinos/Hispanics) to maintain their distinct cultures?"

On the one hand, the data in Figure 4.14 suggest that a strong majority of Latinos see "blending in" to American society as either very (56 percent) or somewhat (31 percent) important.

However, the belief in the importance of "blending in" to U.S. society declines with generations in the United States. Sixty-three percent of first-generation respondents think that "blending in" is very important, compared with only 40 percent of those born in the United States. The inverse of this finding is that only 9 percent of the first generation believes that blending into U.S. society is not important, but this view is held by 22 percent of Latinos born in the United States. Among first-generation citizens and noncitizens the differences are less stark. In fact, a slightly larger proportion of first-generation citizens (vis-à-vis noncitizens) believe that blending is somewhat important.

One interpretation of these findings is that those born outside the United States feel strong pressures to acculturate to U.S. society, and so place a greater emphasis on fitting in. Latinos born in the United States, however, have in fact already "blended in" linguistically and culturally, and so, paradoxically, place less of an emphasis on the need to further do so. An ancillary interpretation might be that Latinos who are born and grow up in the United States adopt an appreciation of the very American value of diversity, and so see less need to adopt a belief in "blending in," even as, as posited earlier, they do so in practice.

Although the belief in whether or not it is important for Latinos to blend into U.S. society diminishes over generations in the United States (see Figure 4.14), there is relatively little disagreement among Latinos regarding the importance of maintaining a distinctly Latino culture. Between 74 and 81 percent of all respondents, regardless of time spent or generation in the United States, agree that it is very important, whereas only between 2 percent and 4 percent feel that it is not at all important. There are no significant differences between naturalized and non-naturalized first-generation respondents, whereas the differences across generations are only minor. Clearly, there is consensus in the Latino community that maintaining the culture is of at least some importance, and this consensus transcends citizenship and generational boundaries.

The pattern of responses for "maintaining a distinct Latino culture" is similar to the pattern exhibited in Figure 4.13, which graphed responses to the question asking Latinos to rank the importance of maintaining an ability to speak Spanish. In that instance as well, overwhelming majorities of Hispanics across generations declared that Latinos should keep their ability to speak Spanish. In that case we argued that this belief was aspirational and that respondents held on to the belief in the importance of speaking Spanish even as it is clear that the ability to speak Spanish declines with time spent in the United States and across generations. The responses to the question asking whether Latinos should maintain a distinct culture may be equally aspirational, although the evidence here is less clearcut.

What is evident is that identities and the values attached to identities, such as maintaining and/or learning a language or culture, overlap in complex and seemingly contradictory ways. Latino respondents wish to identify both pan-ethnically with other Latinos and as American; they value learning English but also want to retain the ability to speak Spanish; they want to blend in to American society but also want to maintain a distinct cultural identity. For Hispanics these are not either-or options; rather, what might appear to be contradictory tendencies from an outsider's perspective is the attempt, by Latinos themselves, to form an amalgam of identities that make sense of their diverse attachments as Americans and their histories and ancestries in Latin America.

Interestingly, the persistence of Latino ethnic identity over time and generation is not paralleled by Latinos' social isolation in ethnic social networks. A bare majority of the friendship networks of first-generation noncitizen respondents are mostly Latino and/or Hispanic, but the percentage with all or mostly Latino friends declines with time in the United

Table 4.1. *Race-Ethnicity of Friendship Network, by Generation and Citizenship* **Category:** Identity/Assimilation, Latino Identity/Assimilation

Response		First Generation			2+ Generation	
		Noncitizen	Citizen	Total	Citizen	Total
Mix of all of the above	Freq.	841	674	1515	907	2422
(do not read)	Row%	55.51	44.49	62.55	37.45	100.00
	Col%	21.83	34.37	26.06	33.73	28.48
Mostly (Latino/Hispanic)	Freq.	1918	600	2518	628	3146
	Row%	76.17	23.83	80.04	19.96	100.00
	Col%	49.78	30.60	43.31	23.35	37.00
Mostly white	Freq.	124	106	230	225	455
	Row%	53.91	46.09	50.55	49.45	100.00
	Col%	3.22	5.41	3.96	8.37	5.35
Mixed (Latino/Hispanic)	Freq.	817	442	1259	661	1920
and white	Row%	64.89	35.11	65.57	34.43	100.00
	Col%	21.20	22.54	21.65	24.58	22.58
Mostly black	Freq.	11	8	19	42	61
	Row%	57.89	42.11	31.15	68.85	100.00
	Col%	0.29	0.41	0.33	1.56	0.72
Mixed (Latino/Hispanic)	Freq.	119	113	232	186	418
and black	Row%	28.47	27.03	55.50	44.50	100.00
	Col%	3.09	5.76	3.99	6.92	4.92
Other	Freq.	23	18	41	40	81
	Row%	56.10	43.90	50.62	49.38	100.00
	Col%	0.60	0.92	0.71	1.49	0.95
TOTAL	Freq.	3853	1961	5814	2689	8503
	Row%	66.27	33.73	68.38	31.62	100.00
	Col%	100.00	100.00	100.00	100.00	100.00

Note: First/2+ generation: one way (6 d.f.) 80.370 (P = 0.000). Citizen/noncitizen (first generation only): one way (6 d.f.) 37.310 (P = 0.000). Categories "Mostly Asian" and "Mixed Asian/Latino" are eliminated from this table and included only for residents of California, Texas, New York, and Illinois. Island-born Puerto Ricans are coded as first generation. Question wording: "How would you describe your friends? Are they [read response items]."

States and by generation. Only 31 percent of foreign-born Latino citizens have mostly Latino friends. Among Latinos born in the United States only one in four −23 percent – have mostly Latino friends, as Table 4.1 shows.

Among noncitizens the next more common response category after "mostly Latino" friends is a "mix of all": 21 percent indicate that they have friends from all ethnic groups, with a preponderance of no single group. This percentage increases to 34 percent among the native born, where those answering a "mix of all" outnumber those saying they have "mostly Latino" friends. That said, relatively few Latinos seem to have "mostly blacks" as friends; fewer than 6 percent indicate their friends are either "mostly black" or "mixed Latino/Hispanic and black." Equally few (5 percent) list their friends as being "mostly white,"although respondents are much more likely to indicate a mix of whites and Latinos as their friends: 22 percent of the foreign born and 25 percent of the native born give this response. Although the findings suggest that Latinos' assimilation over time in the United States promotes greater diversification of friendship networks, and a move away from insular, Latino-only social circles, this social diversification is more likely to include whites than blacks. However, this may be a function of the demographics of the areas in which Latinos live rather than an indication of black-Latino relations, a topic that deserves further study (Barreto and Sanchez 2009; Jones-Correa 2009).

As with friendship networks, the LNS data indicate a shift between foreign-born Latinos and those born in the United States, as well as between naturalized and nonnaturalized first-generation immigrants from "mostly Latino/Hispanic" workplaces to more racially and/or ethnically mixed work places (see Table 4.2). Forty-four percent of nonnaturalized first-generation Latinos say their workplaces are mostly Latino – this is their modal response, the largest response category. The modal response for naturalized foreign-born Latinos shifts to "mix of all" (30 percent), as it is for Latinos born in the United States as well (26 percent).

However, to a greater degree than friendship networks, the changes in the ethnic and racial composition of coworkers over time in the United States reflect a shift to more interaction with "mostly white" coworkers, with (also unlike friendship networks) a slight decrease in "mixed Latino/Hispanic and white" circles. A substantial percentage, even among noncitizen Latinos, work in either mostly white or mixed Latino/white workplaces (30 percent); this proportion increases to 41 percent for the native born. Few Latinos work in workplaces that have either mostly black or mixed Latino-black workforces. These make up 3.6 percent of workplaces among the first generation, and only 6.7 percent among Latinos born in the United States. This suggests contact with black Americans increases over time (doubling between the first and second generation), but that for second-generation Latinos, most of their interactions in the workplace are with whites or with a mix of racial groups. Thus, although

Table 4.2. *Race-Ethnicity of Coworkers, by Generation and Citizenship* **Category**: Identity/Assimilation, Latino Identity/Assimilation

Response		First Generation			2+ Generation	
		Noncitizen	Citizen	Total	Citizen	Total
Mix of all of the above	Freq.	699	520	1219	613	1832
(do not read)	Row%	57.34	42.66	66.54	33.46	100.00
	Col%	20.48	30.41	23.79	26.14	24.53
Mostly (Latino/Hispanic)	Freq.	1487	434	1921	513	2434
	Row%	77.41	22.59	78.92	21.08	100.00
	Col%	43.57	25.38	37.50	21.88	32.59
Mostly white	Freq.	288	262	550	516	1066
	Row%	52.36	47.64	51.59	48.41	100.00
	Col%	8.44	15.32	10.74	22.00	14.27
Mixed (Latino/Hispanic)	Freq.	755	345	1100	467	1567
and white	Row%	68.64	31.36	70.20	29.80	100.00
	Col%	22.12	20.18	21.47	19.91	20.98
Mostly black	Freq.	32	23	55	54	109
	Row%	58.18	41.82	50.46	49.54	100.00
	Col%	0.94	1.35	1.07	2.30	1.46
Mixed (Latino/Hispanic)	Freq.	88	76	164	102	266
and black	Row%	33.08	28.57	61.65	38.35	100.00
	Col%	2.58	4.44	3.20	4.35	3.56
Other	Freq.	64	50	114	80	194
	Row%	56.14	43.86	58.76	41.24	100.00
	Col%	1.88	2.92	2.23	3.41	2.60
Total	Freq.	3413	1710	5123	2345	7468
	Row%	66.62	33.38	68.60	31.40	100.00
	Col%	100.00	100.00	100.00	100.00	100.00

Note: First/2+ generation: one way (6 d.f.) 62.590 (P = 0.000). Citizen/noncitizen (first generation only): one way (6 d.f.) 37.270 (P = 0.000). Categories "Mostly Asian" and "Mixed Asian/Latino" are eliminated from this table and included only for residents of California, Texas, New York, and Illinois. Island-born Puerto Ricans are coded as first generation. Question wording: "How would you describe your co-workers? Stop me when I get to your answer. Are they [read response items.]"

assimilation (i.e., naturalization and being born in the United States) promotes greater diversity of both friends and coworkers, in the workplace these ties largely take place between Latinos and whites.

One might read these findings as largely reflecting the racial and ethnic composition of a society that is, as of 2010, still two-thirds white racially, but they suggest perhaps that even among Latinos born in the United

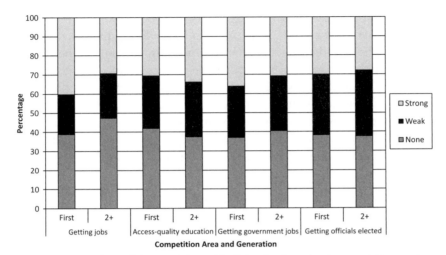

Figure 4.16. Feeling of Competition with Other Latinos, by Area and Generation
Question wording: "Some have suggested that [respondent's country of origin group] are in competition with other Latinos. After each of the next items, would you tell me if you believe there is strong competition, weak competition, or no competition at all with other Latinos
. . . in getting jobs?
. . . having access to education and quality schools?
. . . getting jobs with the city or state government? having (respondent's country of origin group's] representatives in elected office?"

States, black-Latino interactions are still relatively less common. Note, too, that even in the second generation, 22 percent of Latinos are still working in workplaces with mostly other Latinos. This likely reflects the occupational segregation and spatial concentration of Latinos both regionally and locally, perhaps more than it suggests any preference for social ties with one racial group over another – but this too is an area for further exploration (Rodrigues and Segura 2004).

Figure 4.16 sums up the results of four distinct questions measuring feelings of competition among Latinos. These questions ask respondents to gauge how much competition they believe exists among Latinos in the area of employment, in access to a quality education, in getting a government job, and in getting officials elected. The chart graphs responses into three categories: strong competition, weak competition, or no competition. Feelings of competition are fairly consistent across these four issues, with between 30 percent and 40 percent of Hispanics indicating that they felt competition with other Latinos in each area. Feelings of competition are also fairly consistent across generations, with responses of first-generation Latinos matching relatively closely the responses of Hispanics born in the United States (data not shown). Only in the area of employment (both in the private and in the public sectors) do foreign-born Latinos feel that there is significantly greater competition with other Latinos. What this figure indicates on the whole is that, despite strong attachments to identities they hold in common with individuals from their same country of origin, and with other Latinos, one-third of Latinos nonetheless still feel that competition exists with others who share these identities.

Conclusion

The data presented in this chapter reflect the complexity of Latino identities. On the one hand, Latinos hold on to their identification with their countries of origin and with the larger identities for those with ancestry from Latin America – Hispanic and Latino. Respondents to the LNS feel that Hispanics should retain Spanish and maintain a distinct culture. On the other hand, even as Hispanics wish to recognize their distinctiveness – through their identity choices, culture, and language – they also almost unanimously recognize the importance of acquiring English, with large majorities indicating that Latinos need to "blend in" with the larger culture. Feelings of common sentiment with other Latinos do not stop a substantial minority of Hispanics from feeling competitive with one another across a number of different arenas, ranging from work to the political arena. Nor does it seem to prevent Latinos over time from taking jobs in increasingly ethnically and racially diverse workplaces and having increasingly diverse groups of friends.

The way Latinos make their identity choices will inevitably play out in the political sphere. Decisions about labels, language, friends, and social networks all shape Latinos' insertion in to American political life and their adoption of an American identity. Clearly, Latinos see "becoming American" in complicated ways – both blending in and staying true to themselves simultaneously. This complexity is reflected as well in how Hispanics interpret the importance other Americans place on factors like being born in the United States, speaking English, being white, and being Christian. If they are skeptical of the importance of race for the definition of "being fully American," substantial minorities and sometimes majorities are feeling their way toward trying to understand how birthright, citizenship, language, and religion fit in with notions of American identity. In this they are very much like all other Americans.

Bibliography

Alba, Richard D., and Victor Nee. 2003. *Remaking the American Mainstream: Assimilation and Contemporary Immigration.* Cambridge, MA: Harvard University Press.

Barreto, Matt, and Gabriel Sanchez. 2009. *"Black-Brown Relations in the New South." Paper presented at the conference "Undocumented Hispanic Migration: On the Margins of a Dream,"* Connecticut College, New London, CT, October 16–18.

Chong, Dennis. 1991. *Collective Action and the Civil Rights Movement.* Chicago: University of Chicago Press.

Cole, Elizabeth, Alyssa Tucker, and Joan M. Ostrove. 1998. "Political Participation and Feminist Consciousness among Women Activists of the 1960s." *Political Psychology* 19: 349–71.

Conover, Pamela. 1984. "The Influence of Group Identifications on Political Perception and Evaluation." *Journal of Politics* 46(3): 760–85.

Conover, Pamela. 1988. "The Role of Social Groups in Political Thinking." *British Journal of Political Science* 18(1): 51–76.

Dawson, Michael C. 1994. *Behind the Mule: Race and Class in African American Politics.* Princeton, NJ: Princeton University Press.

Downs, Anthony. 1957. *An Economic Theory of Democracy.* New York: Harper and Row.

Garcia, John A. 1982. "Ethnicity and Chicanos: Measurement of Ethnic Identification, Identity, and Consciousness." *Hispanic Journal of Behavioral Sciences* 4(3): 295–314.

Gordon, Milton M. 1964. *Assimilation in American Life.* New York: Oxford University Press.

Jones-Correa, Michael. 2009. "Commonalities, Competition and Linked Fate: Race Relations in New and Traditional Immigrant Receiving Areas." Paper presented at the conference "Still Two Nations? The Resilience of the Color Line," Duke University, Durham, NC, March 19–21.

Jones-Correa, Michael, and David Leal. 1996. "Becoming 'Hispanic': Secondary Panethnic Identification among Latin American-Origin Populations in the United States." *Hispanic Journal of Behavioral Sciences* 18(2): 214–54.

Kaufmann, Karen M. 2003. "Cracks in the Rainbow: Group Commonality as a Basis for Latino and African-American Political Coalitions." *Political Research Quarterly* 56(2): 199–210.

Keefe, Susan E., and Armando M. Padilla. 1987. *Chicano Ethnicity.* Albuquerque: University of New Mexico Press.

Lee, Jennifer, and Frank D. Bean. 2004. "America's Changing Color Lines: Race/Ethnicity, Immigration, and Multiracial Identification." *Annual Review of Sociology* 30: 221–42.

Lieberson, Stanley. 1981. *A Piece of the Pie: Blacks and White Immigrants since 1880.* Berkeley: University of California Press.

Lopez, Linda, and Adrian D. Pantoja. 2004. "Beyond Black and White: General Support for Race-Conscious Policies among African Americans, Latinos, Asian Americans and Whites." *Political Research Quarterly* 57(4): 633–42.

Miller, Arthur, Patricia Gurin, Gerald Gurin, and Oksana Malanchuk. 1981. "Group Consciousness and Political Participation."*American Journal of Political Science* 25(3): 494–511.

Moe, Terry M. 1980. *The Organization of Interests: Incentives and the Internal Dynamics of Political Interest Groups.* Chicago: University of Chicago Press.

Nicholson, Stephen, Adrian Pantoja, and Gary Segura. 2005. "Race Matters: Latino Racial Identities and Political Beliefs." Paper presented at the annual meeting of the American Political Science Association, Washington, D.C., August 31–September 4.

Oboler, Suzanne. 1995. *Ethnic Labels, Latino Lives, Identity and the Politics of (Re)Presentation in the United States.* Minneapolis: University of Minnesota Press.

Olson, Mancur. 1971. *Logic of Collective Action: Public Goods and the Theory of Groups.* Cambridge, MA: Harvard University Press.

Omi, Michael, and Howard Winant. 1995. *Racial Formation in the United States.* New York: Routledge.

Qian, Zhenchao, and Dan Lichter. 2007. "Social Boundaries and Marital Assimilation: Interpreting Trends in Racial and Ethnic Intermarriage." *American Sociological Review* 72(February): 68–94.

Rodrigues, Helena Alves, and Gary M. Segura. 2004. "A Place at the Lunch Counter: Latinos, African-Americans, and the Dynamics of American Race Politics." Presented at the conference "Latino Politics: The State of the Discipline," Texas A&M University, College Station, TX, April 30–May 1.

Rumbaut, Ruben, and Alejandro Portes. 2001. *Ethnicities: Children of Immigrants in America.* Berkeley: University of California Press.

Sawyer, Mark. 2005. "Racial Politics in Multiethnic American: Black and Latina/o Identities and Coalitions." In *Neither Enemies nor Friends: Latinos, Black, Afro-Latinos*, ed. Anani Dzidzienyo and Suzanne Oboler. New York: Palgrave Macmillan, 265–80.

Shingles, Richard. 1981. "Black Consciousness and Political Participation: The Missing Link." *American Political Science Review* 75(1): 76–91.

5

Latino Transnationalism

Continuities and Breaks with Countries of Origin

Transnationalism refers to the persistent ties that immigrants and their descendants have with their countries of origin. These ties can be social, such as maintaining contact with their friends and family; economic, for example, continuing to own land and businesses; or political, for instance, having an interest in, and taking part in, their country of origin's politics. Researchers characterize these transnational ties as made up of multiple attachments that stretch across national borders to make up a unified social world that is simultaneously located in two different places (Basch, Glick Schiller, and Szanton-Blanc 1994; Smith and Guarnizo 1998; Levitt and Glick Schiller 2004). Two leading immigration scholars describe how this occurs:

Over time and with extensive movement back and forth, communities of origin and destination increasingly comprise transnational circuits – social and geographic spaces that arise through the circulation of people, money, goods and information.... Over time, migrant communities become culturally "transnationalized," incorporating ideologies, practices, expectations, and political claims from both societies to create a "culture of migration" that is distinct from the culture of both the sending and receiving nation. (Massey and Durand 1992, 8)

In this view, nation-states are seen as increasingly less relevant as an organizing principle of social interaction (Basch et al. 1994; Glick Schiller 1999; Portes 1999), facilitated by the ease of international travel and communication in an era of e-mail and Internet cafes, video-conferencing parlors in which immigrants can see and talk to the family they have left behind, instant money transfers, and cheap airfare.

Scholars generally use a few key indicators as measures of transnational ties: (1) the existence of organizational networks, such as immigrant hometown associations (Orozco 2000; Alarcón 2002; De la Garza and Hazan 2003); (2) immigrant attitudes and behaviors, such as engagement in remittance practices (i.e., immigrants sending money back to relatives in their countries of origin; Conway and Cohen 1998; Flores-Macias 2009); (3) travel back to immigrants' countries of origin; and (4) the desire to one day live there again (Guarnizo 2000; Waldinger 2008. However, despite general agreement that the phenomenon of transnationalism exists, a number of disagreements and debates persist (Jones-Correa 2003; Waldinger and Fitzgerald 2004).

This chapter presents evidence from the Latino National Survey on the forms of Latinos' ties to their countries of origin while addressing three open questions about transnationalism:

First, does transnationalism decline with time in the United States? Levitt (2003), among others, argues for the persistence of transnationalism, whereas DeSipio (2000) points to indications that transnational behaviors like remittances fade the longer one spends in the United States. Do transnational ties, such as remittances, decline as DeSipio suggests? And do different kinds of transnational ties decline equally?

Second, does transnationalism persist in some form across generations? Levitt and Waters's (2003) volume brings together a group of scholars who put forward preliminary arguments about the persistence of transnationalism among the children of immigrants. Although most contributors posit that transnationalism will continue in some form for the children of immigrants, it is not clear what that form will be. Jones-Correa (2003) asks, supposing that transnationalism persists beyond first-generation immigrants, what forms does transnationalism take, and what percentage of the second generation is likely to engage in these forms?

Third, are there differences across national origin groups? The literature on transnationalism suggests that ties to country of origin play out differently for different national origin groups (Guarnizo, Portes, and Haller 2003). Political transnationalism, such as making donations or voting in country-of-origin elections, is thought to be weaker among Colombians, for instance, than among Dominican immigrants in the United States (Guarnizo et al. 2003; DeSipio and Pantoja 2004). Immigrants from countries closer geographically to the United States, which often have close historical ties to the United States, are also thought to be more likely to take part in the transnational circuit of travel, remittances, and return. Are there differences in transnational ties for different

Latino groups, and do these differences play out the way the literature suggests?

This chapter examines Latino transnational behaviors in the United States, among the first generation – those who migrate to the United States – and then among subsequent generations. The chapter is divided into two sections, the first presenting findings for first-generation immigrants, those born abroad and immigrating to the United States, and the second presenting results for the second generation, those born in the United States to immigrant parents. In this chapter the evidence is presented largely as figures rather than as tables. For the first-generation figures, transnational ties are presented by time in the United States and by country of origin. For the second generation, transnational ties are presented by country of origin alone.

Some explanation of the graphs that follow is in order. In the first section, which focuses on the first generation alone, each figure indicates levels of contact on the y-axis (vertical) and years in the United States on the x-axis (horizontal). There are six panels in each figure, one for each of six national origin groups or regions. As noted in the figures' keys, the first is for Mexican immigrants to the United States; the second, for Puerto Ricans; the third, for Cubans; the fourth, for Dominicans; the fifth, for immigrants from South America; and the sixth, for immigrants from Central America.

The LNS has 8,634 respondents in all; 5,704 are of Mexican origin, 822 are of Puerto Rican origin, 430 are of Cuban origin, 335 are of Dominican origin, 425 are of South American origin, and 740 are of Central American origin. Among those born abroad who came to the United States as immigrants, those figures are 3,885 Mexicans, 434 Puerto Ricans, 344 Cubans, 290 Dominicans, 392 South Americans, and 687 Central Americans. That is to say that 71 percent of respondents in the LNS from these six countries and/or regions are born outside the continental United States, and 66 percent are foreign born (68 percent of Mexican-origin respondents are foreign born, as are 82 percent of Cuban-origin respondents, 86 percent of Dominican respondents, 92 percent of South American respondents and 93 percent of Central American respondents).

The inclusion of Puerto Rican respondents in these analyses requires a discussion of its own. Although Puerto Ricans, whether born on the mainland United States or on the island of Puerto Rico, are U.S. citizens at birth (and have been since 1917), historically there has been a sizable migration of Puerto Ricans from the island to the mainland, and in some cases, from the mainland back to the island. This migration pattern, and the fact that Spanish is the principal language on the island of Puerto Rico and not on the mainland United States, with attendant differences in culture and politics, led us to conceptualize the social dynamics of Puerto Rican migration as having more than a passing resemblance to migration from elsewhere in Latin America and to conceptualize continuing ties between Puerto Ricans on the mainland and Puerto Ricans on the island as transnational ties. This may attract some controversy, but this approach has some backing in the literature (Rodriguez 1993, Duany 2002, DeSipio and Pantoja 2004). Where the sample sizes are large enough (for Mexican, Puerto Rican, Cuban and Dominican respondents), results are presented by country of origin. For South and Central Americans, however, results are clustered by region. Although Central and South Americans might be analyzed separately for the foreign born, the size of the second generation in the United States for these national origin groups is too small to allow for separate country-by-country analysis. Indeed, the data by generation should be accompanied by a caveat: except for Mexican-origin immigrants and their children, as well as Puerto Ricans, the number of those born in the mainland United States is too small to be more than indicative of the trends in transnational ties (the n for adults eighteen and older born in the United States for each of these six groups is as follows: Mexican-origin, 1,189; Puerto Rican, 388; Cuban, 76; Dominican, 45; South American, 33; Central American, 53). Although research on the second generation has begun (Portes and Rumbaut 2001; Rumbaut and Portes 2001, Levitt and Waters 2003, Kasinitz et al. 2009), more in-depth analysis of the second generation may require more time for this second generation to mature and come of age in the United States.

A basic measure of transnationalism is the degree to which immigrants maintain contact with their friends and family. It is difficult to imagine any kind of transnational social network existing in the absence of these kinds of contacts with family and friends. The LNS asks about frequency of contact, without asking specifically about the kind of contact (e.g., it does not distinguish between e-mail, mail, phone, and other kinds of contact). The data in Figure 5.1 are coded with answers to the question of frequency of contact with friends and family from 0 to 3, with 0 being "never" having contact, 1 indicating contact once every several months, 2 indicating contact once a month or more, and 3 being contact once a week or more.

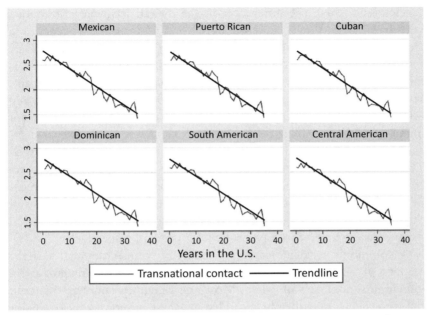

Figure 5.1. Contact with Friends and Relatives in Immigrant's Country of Origin over Time in the United States, by Country of Origin, among First-Generation Immigrants
Question wording: "How often do you have contact with friends and family in [R's country of origin]?" ($N = 6,184$).

Two results are striking. The first is that there is no significant difference in the change in rates of contact across time for across any of the six groups. Indeed, the graphs for all six categories (corresponding to Mexican, Puerto Rican, Cuban, Dominican, South American, and Central American respondents) look remarkably similar. The second is that for all six groups, rates of contact fall significantly over time. At year 1 the rate of contact with family and friends among first-generation Latino immigrants is, on average 2.75, or almost once a week or more: contact early on for all immigrants is both frequent and common. By year 20, contact with friends and family has fallen to an average of once a month or more, and by year 35 the average response is 1.5, or contact somewhere between once every several months and once a month. The decline in contact does not indicate that contact with family and friends stops altogether in the first generation, but there is a pattern of steady decline over time in the United States among first-generation immigrants.

That said, there are differences in the overall frequency of contact with friends and family across national origin groups. First-generation Dominicans are the most likely to have weekly contact: 72 percent. Only 13 percent of Cubans – perhaps understandably given their status as long-term exiles – give a similar response. The percentages for Mexicans, South Americans, and Central Americans are 64 percent, 61 percent, and 60 percent, respectively. Puerto Ricans born on the island, though not immigrants, have similar rates of contact, at 53 percent. The percentages for no contact at all are the inverse of those for frequent contact. Thirty-four percent of Cuban respondents, for instance, say they have no contact at all with friends and family in Cuba, whereas only 5 percent of Dominicans say the same thing about contact with their country of origin. Similar percentages for Mexicans, South Americans, and Central Americans are 9 percent, 5 percent, and 7 percent, respectively.

A commonly used indicator of immigrant transnational ties is the amount of remittances – funds sent back to family or hometowns in immigrants' countries of origin. Most first-generation immigrants remit funds to their family members. Added up, these remittances are a major source of foreign-exchange earnings for many countries in Latin America and, indeed, around the world: more than $35 billion were sent to Latin America by immigrants in the United States in 2007 (Flores-Macias 2009). However, remittance behavior is not stable over time. The average frequency of remittances for first-generation immigrants peaks before year 10 in the United States and then declines precipitously over the following twenty years, as indicated in Figure 5.2.

The responses to the question "How often do you send money?" are coded here from 0 to 5, with 0 being "never," 1 indicating less than once a year, 2 indicating once a year, 3 indicating once every few months, 4 being once a month, and 5 indicating more than once a month. At year 10 the average remittance frequency for first-generation Latino immigrants is every few months; by year 35 in the United States, the average frequency is between once a year and never.

The distribution for remittances, it should be noted, falls into two clusters. In general, the most common, or modal, response given by respondents is that they do not remit at all. Thirty-six percent of Mexican, 73 percent of Puerto Rican, 57 percent of Cuban, 37 percent of Dominican, 45 percent of South American, and 21 percent of Central American respondents say they do not remit at all. However, across groups at least half of respondents say they remit funds at least once a year or more. The top remitters are the Central Americans: their modal response is once a

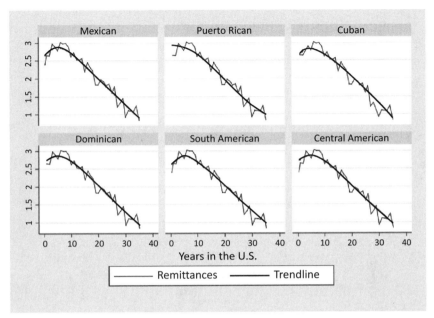

Figure 5.2. Frequency of Remittances to Immigrant's Country of Origin, over Time in the United States, by Country of Origin, among First-Generation Immigrants
Question wording: "How often do you send money?" ($N = 6,096$).

month or more (41 percent); 57 percent say they send remittances once a month or more. Overall, the results indicate that Puerto Ricans and Cuban Americans are the least likely to remit, and that Central Americans and, to a lesser extent, Dominicans are the most likely.

Figure 5.3 indicates that the amount remitted stays fairly constant for the first generation, across years spent in the United States, with the average amount falling somewhere around $400 at year 1 in the United States and ending slightly higher by year 35. The amount remitted by Cuban Americans, however, does increase fairly dramatically from around $300 to around $600 over time in the United States. For the other five national origin groups and/or regions, average remittances stay fairly constant across the first generation.

Puerto Rican respondents born on the island exhibit many of the same classic indicators of transnational behavior as their foreign-born counterparts. Although Puerto Ricans are U.S. citizens, in some ways, as reflected by the figures in this chapter, they act like immigrants, maintaining

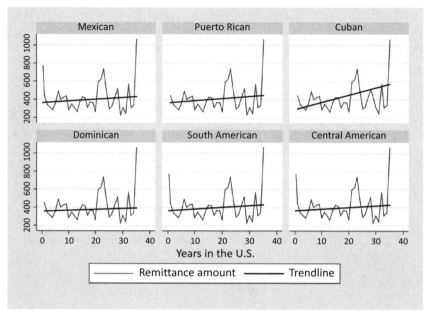

Figure 5.3. Average Remittance Amount to Immigrant's Country of Origin, over Time in the United States, by Country of Origin, among First-Generation Immigrants
Question wording: "What is the average amount you send each time?" ($N = 3,714$).

contact with friends and family, for instance, and sending remittances to family back in Puerto Rico from the mainland.

Just as contact with friends and family declines over time, so does immigrants' desire to return to live in their country of origin. Figure 5.4 shows that at year 1, more than 60 percent of all first-generation immigrants say they plan to return at some point to live in their country of origin (the flip side to this figure is that even at year 1, 30 percent or more say they plan to stay in the United States permanently). The percentage indicating they plan to return to live in their country of origin declines over time, so that by year 35 in the United States only about 15 percent say they have any intention of returning. These trend lines vary only marginally across national origin group and/or region; with the pattern for Puerto Ricans again very similar to that for their foreign-born counterparts.

Among foreign-born respondents, the least likely to indicate that they would like to return are, not surprisingly, Cuban refugees, who arrived

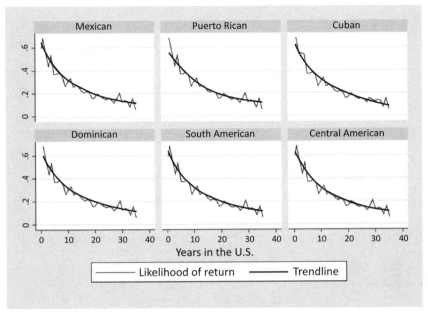

Figure 5.4. Plans to Return to Country of Origin, over Time in the United States, by Country of Origin, among First-Generation Immigrants
Question wording: "Do you have plans to go back to [R's country of origin] to live permanently?" (*N* = 6,096).

to the United States fleeing the Castro regime in Cuba beginning in 1960: only 7 percent of Cuban respondents say they have plans to return. Seventeen percent of Puerto Rican respondents say they have plans to return the island. For the remaining countries and regions, about one in four respondents indicate that they have plans to go back. The figures are 29 percent for Mexican respondents, 26 percent for Dominican respondents, 24 percent for South American respondents, and 28 percent for Central American respondents.

There may be several concurrent explanations for the findings of diminished expectation of return with time in the United States: the first is self-selection. By year 35 in the United States presumably at least some immigrants who planned to return at year 1 have done so. The decline in intention to return among Latino immigrants who have lived longer in the United States may reflect the fact that as time goes on, the immigrants most likely to return have already returned, and the those that are left have made the decision to remain. The second explanation is people's changing intentions and assimilation: many immigrants arrive to their receiving

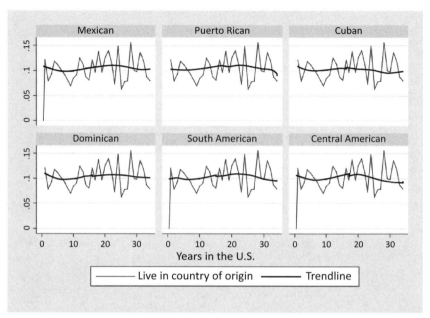

Figure 5.5. Return to Immigrant's Country of Origin to Live for a Time, over Time in the United States, by Country of Origin, among First-Generation Immigrants
Question wording: "Have you ever returned to live (rather than just visit) there for a portion of time?" ($N = 6,184$).

country thinking they will return, but quickly life intervenes. They may marry, have children, buy a home, get a job, and make a career. In short, they settle in. The fact that by year 35 people indicate they are staying may reflect that they have given up on the myth of return – the idea that at some point they may go back, even though it is increasingly unlikely, the longer they stay in the United States (Guarnizo 1997, Jones-Correa 1998; Barreto and Muñoz 2003). The final explanation for the decrease in plans to return may simply be that with more time in the United States immigrants have less to return to: their family may have already joined them in the United States, or have passed away, or simply become more distant. In any case, it is clear that immigrants spending more time in the United States are less likely to express the desire to return.

If most immigrants quickly decide to remain in the United States, and most, over time, give up any notion of going back to their countries of origin to live, how many of those who are currently residing in the United States have actually returned to spend some length of time in their countries of origin for more than a visit? Figure 5.5 indicates that

11 percent of Latino immigrants, a not insubstantial portion, have return-ed at some point to spend some time living in their country of origin.

As with other indicators of transnationalism, this variable varies some-what across national origin group and region. Not surprisingly, fewer than 2 percent of first-generation Cuban respondents say they have returned to live for any extended period in Cuba. Although they are not immigrants per se, 19 percent of Puerto Rican respondents born on the island but living on the mainland say they have moved for a time to Puerto Rico. Eleven percent of Mexican first-generation respondents, 13 percent of Dominicans, 11 percent of South Americans, and 9 percent of Central Americans indicate that they, likewise, had moved back to live for a while in their country of origin before returning to live in the United States. These figures confirm what Figure 5.5 indicates as well: aside from the Cuban and Puerto Rican outliers, about one in ten first-generation immigrants move back to their country of origin to live for some time before returning once again to live in the United States.

Transnationalism depends on the attachments immigrants retain to their countries of origin. We might expect immigrants with children remaining in their countries of origin to retain these attachments more than immigrants who have their children with them in the United States (Hondagneu-Sotelo and Avila 1997). Eleven percent of LNS respondents say they have children whom they support financially outside the United States. Figure 5.6 indicates that very soon after Latino immigrants' arrival to the United States, the percentage with dependents younger than age eighteen begins to drop off, either because their dependents grow older or because their children join them in the United States. At year 1 in the United States an average of 20 percent of Latino immigrants have chil-dren in their countries of origin whom they support financially. By year 20 in the United States, this percentage is down to 10 percent, and by year 35 the percentage is closer to 0 percent.

As with other indicators of transnational ties, there is some variation by national origin. Cubans, not surprisingly, and Puerto Ricans perhaps more so, are the two respondent groups least likely to be providing finan-cial aid to underage minors outside the mainland United States. Central American respondents are the most likely to have children outside the United States: 18 percent. Also, 11.6 percent of Mexican respondents, 10.3 percent of Dominican respondents, and 8.9 percent of South Amer-ican respondents indicate that they support children outside the United States as well. The fact that respondents have children outside the United States is linked to remittance frequency. Note, for example, that among the national origin groups represented in the LNS, Central Americans

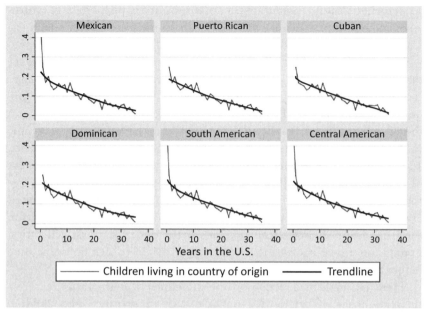

Figure 5.6. Support of Children in Country of Origin, over Time in the United States, by Country of Origin, among First-Generation Immigrants
Question wording: "Do you have children under 18 that you assist financially living in another country?" ($N = 6,096$).

have both the highest percentage of children abroad and the highest frequency of remittances. This is not coincidental.

Along with dependents, having a home, property, or a business in their country of origin is also a likely indicator of immigrants' transnational ties. One-third – 32 percent – of all Latino first-generation immigrants indicate that they owned a home, property, or business in their country of origin. Figure 5.7 shows that at year 1 in the United States the average percentage across national origin groups and regions is near 45 percent. This percentage declines over time in the United States. By year 20, perhaps 30 percent of first-generation Latinos own property, a home, or a business in their countries of origin, and by year 35 the figure is less than 20 percent.

Among first-generation immigrant respondents to the LNS, Central and South Americans are the most likely to have some kind of property in their country of origin (40 percent in each group). Thirty-three percent of Mexicans, 23 percent of Puerto Ricans, 11 percent of Cubans, and

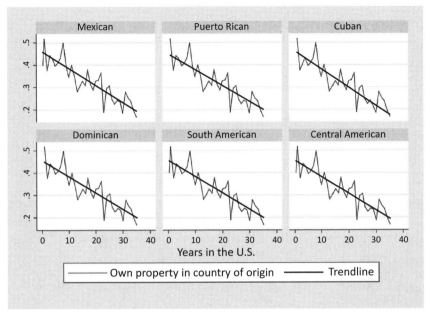

Figure 5.7. Ownership of Home, Business or Property in Immigrant's Country of Origin, over Time in the United States, by Country of Origin, among First-Generation Immigrants
Question wording: "Are you the owner of land, a house or a business in [R's country of origin]?" (*N* = 6,184).

32 percent of Dominican first-generation immigrants to the United States own property back in their countries of origin.

Once again, the data indicate a gradual decline of possible transnational indicators with time in the United States, with the pattern holding across all six national origin groups, for Puerto Ricans and Cubans as much as for Dominicans and Central Americans. It is worth noting, however, that even in year 35 one in five immigrants still owns some kind of property in their country of origin, and that immigrants with property interests, almost by definition, have greater ties to their countries of origin than those who do not.

Although the pattern for most first-generation immigrant transnational behaviors either declines or holds steady over years spent in the United States, this is not true for immigrant travel to their country of origin. In Figure 5.8 responses to this question are coded from 0 to 5, with 0 indicating having never traveled to country of origin, 1 being traveled more than five years ago, 2 indicating travel once in the previous five

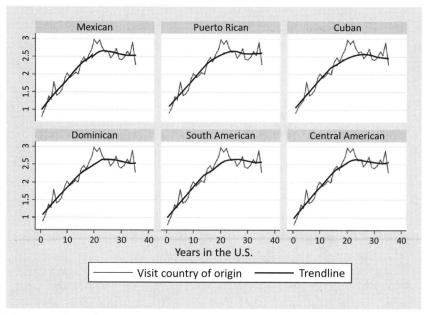

Figure 5.8. Travel to Visit Immigrant's Country of Origin, over Time in the United States, by Country of Origin, among First-Generation Immigrants
Question wording: "How often do you visit (R's country of origin)?" ($N = 5,946$).

years, 3 indicating travel once in the previous three years, 4 indicating travel once a year, and 5 being travel more than once a year. At year 1 in the United States, the average response for Latino immigrants is about 1: most have never traveled back to their country of origin. Travel increases over time in the United States: by year 10 the mean response is 2, traveled once in the previous five years. Frequency of travel peaks for immigrants from all national groups and regions at year 20. At that point the average response is 2.5: immigrants indicate they have traveled to their country of origin between three and five years ago. After year 20 frequency of travel begins to level off.

Interestingly, this general pattern holds for both Puerto Rican migrants to the mainland and Cuban refugees. There are a couple of possible explanations for the pattern observed here. The first is that for some immigrants, particularly those coming as undocumented migrants or even those traveling as legal permanent residents, there are legal complications restricting travel. With time in the United States those legal restrictions may ease, allowing for greater opportunities to travel to countries of origin. Over time Cuban refugees increasingly find ways to travel back to Cuba. Second, immigrants' resources increase over time in the United States; basic needs are taken care of, and immigrants have more disposable income to spend on travel. In this, Puerto Rican migrants act much like immigrants from Latin America.

About 11 percent of all Latino first-generation immigrants indicate they travel more than once a year to their countries of origin; another 21 percent say they travel yearly. But 33 percent say they have never traveled to their country of origin, and 13 percent say they traveled there more than five years ago. Travel as an indicator of transnationalism is bifurcated, then, with a third of respondents indicating no travel at all, and a third indicating frequent (once a year or more) travel.

We see this in the individual country and region of origin data as well. Dominican respondents travel the most frequently to their country of origin, with 49 percent of first-generation immigrants saying they travel once a year or more. Puerto Ricans are the next most frequent travelers, with 37 percent indicating travel once a year or more to the island. Thirty-five percent of Mexican respondents said they traveled at least once a year to their country of origin; the figures for Cubans, South Americans, and Central Americans were considerably lower: 5 percent for Cuban respondents, 24 percent for South Americans, and 24 percent for Central Americans. Note, however, that, with the exception of Puerto Ricans and Dominicans (16 percent and 14 percent, respectively), the modal response for first-generation immigrants is never to have traveled to their countries of origin: 32 percent of Mexican respondents, 68 percent of Cuban respondents, 27 percent of South American respondents, and 41 percent of Central American first-generation respondents indicated they had never traveled back to their countries of origin.

In Figure 5.9 we see that fewer than 6 percent of all first-generation respondents indicate any kind of participation in clubs or associations connected with their countries of origin. Participation in any kind of organized activity – political or otherwise – is low across all national origin groups, with the trajectory of participation over time not varying substantially across national origin groups. Nonetheless, there are differences in participation by country of origin: 10 percent of Dominican first-generation respondents participate in voluntary associations connected to their country of origin, as do 9 percent of South Americans, 6 percent of Central Americans, 5 percent of Puerto Ricans and Cubans, and 4 percent of Mexicans.

In all cases, participation in country-of-origin-related voluntary associations declines slightly over time. But what is notable is how slight the

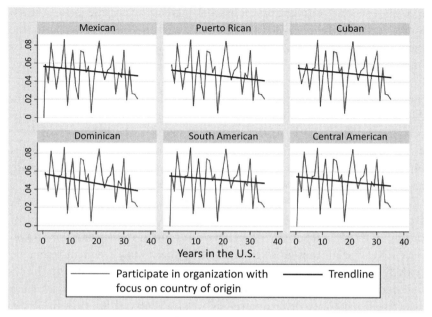

Figure 5.9. Participation in a Voluntary Organization or Hometown Association Linked to Country of Origin, over Time in the United States, by Country of Origin, among First-Generation Immigrants
Question wording: "Do you participate in the activities of a club, association or federation connected to the town or province your family came from in [country of origin]?" ($N = 6,096$).

decline actually is compared to other measures of transnational affiliation: for first-generation immigrants as a whole, at year 1 participation is slightly less than 6 percent, and at year 30 it is somewhere between 4 and 5 percent. It is also not entirely clear what this relatively stable pattern of participation means: Does it indicate that immigrants are still attached to their countries of origin, even across time? Is it a reflection that these organizations shift their attention to concerns in the United States as immigrants stay in the United States over longer periods of time? This debate continues to play out in the literature (Orozco 2000; De la Garza and Hazan 2003; Waldinger and Soehl 2009). Figure 5.10 describes participation rates for citizens and noncitizens, and for the first generation and successive generations, in greater detail.

Figure 5.10, like Figure 5.9 presented earlier, indicates that only 5.4 percent of first-generation respondents participate in clubs or other associations connected with their countries of origin. However, strikingly, there

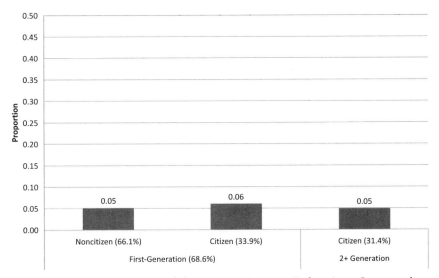

Figure 5.10. Participation in Clubs, Associations, or Federations Connected to Country of Origin, by Generation and Citizenship
Question wording: "Do you participate in the activities of a club, association or federation connected to the town or province your family came from in [country of origin]?"

are no significant differences between citizens and noncitizens or between generations, even though one might anticipate that first-generation Latinos are more likely to engage in civic participation connected with their countries of origin. Participation in voluntary associations linked to immigrants' country of origin hardly declines in the first generation or into the second (we return to this in our discussion of second-generation transnationalism). This finding suggests that this kind of voluntary participation may be more dependent on intergenerational transmission than on immigrants' naturalization status or birthplace. In other words, parents who participate pass on this tendency to their children (as well as, perhaps, their positions and social connections within these organizations), and this transmission endures through naturalization and generations.

Political transnationalism – immigrants' interest and involvement in their country of origin – is much more limited than other forms of transnational ties. Few immigrants engage in it (Guarnizo et al. 2003; Waldinger and Lim 2009; Waldinger, Porzecanski, and Soehl 2009). The broadest indicator of political transnationalism is simply paying attention to political news from one's country of origin. Figure 5.11 illustrates a slight but steady decline in attention to country-of-origin politics across years spent

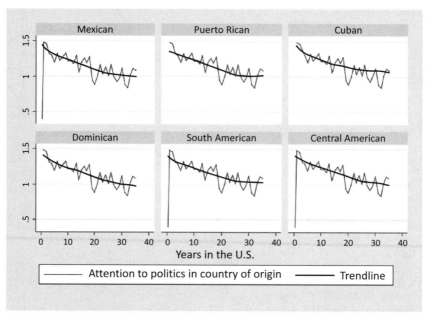

Figure 5.11. Attention to Politics in Country of Origin, over Time in the United States, by Country of Origin, among First-Generation Immigrants
Question wording: "How much attention would you say you pay to politics in [country of origin]? Would you say you pay a lot of attention, some attention, a little attention, or none at all?" ($N = 6,096$).

in the United States. This is true for all six countries and regions charted herein. The response categories are coded from 0 to 3, with 0 indicating no attention to country of origin politics, 1 indicating "a little," 2 indicating "some," and 3 signifying "a lot." Among first-generation Latino immigrants the average level of interest in country-of-origin politics declines from between "a little" and "some" interest at year 1 in the United States to only "a little" for immigrants living in the United States for thirty-five years.

There are differences across national origin groups: 32 percent of first-generation Cuban respondents say they pay a lot of attention to country-of-origin politics, but only 12 percent of Mexican immigrants do. The figure for Dominicans, South Americans, and Central Americans is 26 percent, 27 percent, and 18 percent, respectively. Eighteen percent of Puerto Rican respondents born on the island say they follow political news on the island closely. There are also dissimilarities at the other end of the scale: 41 percent of Puerto Ricans born on the island say they

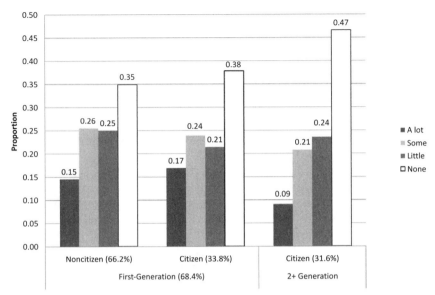

Figure 5.12. Attention Paid to Politics in Country of Origin, by Generation and Citizenship
Question wording: "How much attention would you say you pay to politics in [country of origin]? Would you say you pay a lot of attention, some attention, a little attention, or none at all?"

follow political news of the island not at all; as do 41 percent of Central American respondents and 40 percent of Cuban respondents. Similar figures are 37 percent of Mexicans, 31 percent for Dominicans, and 28 percent for South Americans. Educational levels across national origin groups probably play some role in explaining differences across national origin groups, with Cuban and South Americans having higher levels of education, on average, than Mexican and Central American residents in the United States. The higher the educational level, the more likely an individual is to follow politics.

Figure 5.12 indicates that first-generation citizens actually pay slightly more attention to country-of-origin politics than do noncitizens, although these findings likely reflect selection bias: those who naturalize are more likely to follow politics in general, as well as to have the education and other resources and characteristics associated with political engagement. Note, however, that first-generation citizens are slightly more likely to report having no interest in country-of-origin politics than noncitizens. As might be predicted, attention to politics in Latinos' countries of origin

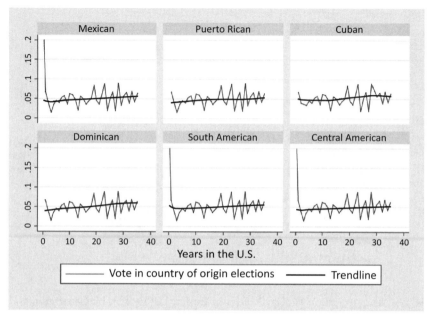

Figure 5.13. Vote in Country-of-Origin Elections after Arrival to the United States, over Time in the United States, by Country of Origin, among First-Generation Immigrants
Question wording: "Have you ever voted in [R's country of origin] elections since you've been in the U.S.?" ($N = 6,184$).

declines between the first and subsequent generations (we return to this finding in a later section).

Despite the fact that several of the main Latin American sending nations allow their nationals in the United States to participate in their countries' electoral politics directly from the United States (e.g., Colombia) and some allow their nationals to vote on returning to their country of origin (e.g., the Dominican Republic; Jones-Correa 2001; McCann, Cornelius, and Leal 2009), few foreign-born Latinos avail themselves of this option. An average 4.5 percent of first-generation Latinos report that they had voted in their country of origin's elections after arriving to the United States.

The trend lines shown in Figure 5.13 for foreign-born Latinos' electoral participation in Dominican or Mexican politics across time in the United States are not perceptibly different from that of Central Americans, although Central Americans cannot participate in their country of origin's elections without returning to register and vote there. In all cases, the trend lines point to a slight increase in participation over time. But there are differences in levels of participation by national origin group: 11 percent of first-generation Dominican respondents say they have participated in their country of origin's elections; the figure for Mexican respondents is 3.3 percent, for Central Americans it is 3.4 percent, and for South Americans it is 17.1 percent. It is no accident that Dominicans and South Americans – the two groups most likely to allow voting in country-of-origin elections from the United States – also have the highest participation rates in country-of-origin elections: essentially, easier access to the ballot means higher turnout.

The percentage of Puerto Rican respondents who say that they have returned to the island to vote is 4.6 percent, not dissimilar from the percentages for first-generation immigrants, and the trend line for participation for Puerto Ricans born on the island who have returned to vote in elections on the island after migrating to the United States is also similar to those of first-generation immigrants. This underlines the fact that migrants from Puerto Rico to the mainland also behave transnationally even though they are U.S. citizens. Finally, it is striking that the average of those participating in electoral politics hardly shifts at all with years spent in the United States: 5 percent say they have participated in their country of origin's politics at year 1 and at year 35 in the United States. This suggests that electoral participation in country-of-origin politics does not occur only soon after arrival to the United States. Rather, either immigrants enter and exit transnational participation, with a small percentage constantly cycling through to participate, or alternatively, there is a small minority of immigrants (5 percent or fewer) who remain engaged in country-of-origin politics, no matter how long they live in the United States.

The data deserve a caveat: it is odd that any foreign-born Cubans say they have returned to participate in Cuban elections, given that there have not been free and competitive elections in Cuba for decades. If anything, this should be a reminder to take these findings with a grain of salt: when the number of respondents is very small (3 respondents of 322 first-generation Cuban respondents responded yes to this question, for a 0.92 participation rate), the chances of oddities in the data (e.g., misunderstanding of the questions, poor recollection) to emerge is all the higher.

Although only a small minority – 5 percent – of Latino first-generation respondents in the LNS participated in the electoral politics of their country of origin, an even smaller minority – fewer than 2 percent – indicated

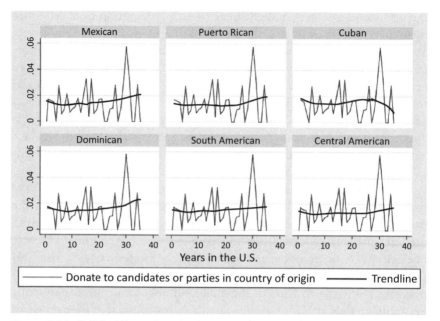

Figure 5.14. Political Donations in Country of Origin after Arrival to the United States, over Time in the United States, by Country of Origin, among First-Generation Immigrants
Question wording: "Since coming to the U.S., have you contributed money to a candidate or party in your country of origin?" ($N = 6,096$).

they have contributed money to a candidate or political party in their country of origin. The highest percentage of reported donations were from Dominican respondents, with 5 percent of respondents indicating they had made donations to a candidate or party from the Dominican Republic. This is in keeping with what the literature suggests about transnational Dominican political involvement (Graham 1996, 1997; Guarnizo et al. 2003). One percent of first-generation Mexican respondents, 2.6 percent of Puerto Ricans, fewer than 1 percent of Cuban respondents, 3 percent of South Americans, and 2 percent of Central American respondents had made similar donations.

The trend lines in Figure 5.14 are similar to the pattern for the figures on electoral participation in country-of-origin politics: the figures are similar for all six countries and regions (though trending down, unsurprisingly, for Cuban donations). Once again, donations of Puerto Ricans residing in the mainland to Puerto Rican candidates and parties is about as high as that for any of the other regions. Once again, the relative steadiness of the trend lines can be interpreted one of two ways: as indicating that a small percentage of immigrants is constantly cycling through to make donations or as indicating that a very small minority has the inclination and means to donate their resources to country-of-origin politicians, and this minority of the foreign born persists in their engagement across time in the United States.

Transnationalism across Generations

The general pattern in the first generation is of significantly declining ties over time among immigrants with their countries of origin, although for a minority of respondents these ties persist. How will the second generation's ties and loyalties play out? Do the children of immigrants keep up the transnational ties of their parents, or do they abandon them in favor of new ties in the United States? Does second-generation transnationalism exist? How extensive is it?

Research on the second generation suggests that there is some persistence of transnational ties into the second generation. Rumbaut (2003) and Kasinitz and colleagues (2003) both draw on survey samples to show that at least some of the second generation engages in regular transnational behavior. They also find important variations in this behavior. For instance, Kasinitz and colleagues (2003), in their study of eighteen-to thirty-two-year-old children of immigrants in New York City, find that transnational behaviors vary significantly by country of origin, with a third of Dominicans and South Americans having strong transnational ties (meaning that they have traveled frequently to, send remittances to, and/or speak the language of their country of origin), compared with fewer than 10 percent of Russian Jews and Chinese immigrants. In addition, those children of immigrants who rely on ethnic media or belong to ethnic organizations are more likely to exhibit transnational behaviors. Rumbaut (2003), drawing on a San Diego–based survey of immigrant children in their twenties (largely of Mexican, Filipino, Vietnamese, and Chinese origin), finds similar patterns of variance. He, too, finds that transnational behaviors vary across country of origin. Children of Mexican immigrants are much more likely to travel to their parents' home country (particularly with Mexico just across the border from San Diego) and to continue to speak their parents' native language, whereas children of Filipino origin are more likely to send remittances.

Yet having confirmed the existence of transnational behaviors among the second generation, both of the larger survey studies find that even occasional transnational practices are limited to less than half of their samples, and those with regular, repeated transnational behaviors account, on the whole, for a small percentage of their second-generation respondents (about 10 percent in both surveys). An overwhelming majority of the children of immigrants are deeply rooted in the United States. Rumbaut's (2003) San Diego survey finds, for example, that by their twenties, 88 percent of respondents consider the United States their home, 84 percent are U.S. citizens (even among young adults of Mexican origin this figure is still 81 percent), 66 percent say they prefer using English (an additional 32 percent say they are equally comfortable in English and their parents' native language). Seventy-two percent have never sent remittances, and 75 percent have visited their parents' country fewer than two times in their lives.

In the New York study, Kasinitz and colleagues (2003) report similar findings with regard to language (56 percent prefer English), travel (73 percent have traveled to their parent's home country three or fewer times), and remittances (71 percent have never remitted money). In New York City, 78 percent of the children of immigrants are U.S. citizens (including 58 percent of those not born in the United States). Seventy percent are registered to vote in the United States, and 53 percent voted in 1996. Respondents were more interested in New York City politics than in the politics of their countries of origin. For at least some of the groups examined, transnational practices seem to decrease with age (for South Americans and West Indians), and for Dominicans, the more likely immigrants are to have U.S. citizenship, the less likely they are to exhibit transnational behavior. How accurate and generalizable are these findings? These data are useful, but the disagreements in the literature about the persistence of transnationalism, particularly across generations, remain unresolved (Levitt and Waters 2003; Jones-Correa 2003). We turn to the evidence from the Latino National Survey, with its larger and more diverse pool of respondents, to move the debate forward.

As in Figure 5.1, Figure 5.15 indicates that contact with friends and family declines over years spent in the United States for first-generation immigrants from Latin America. Recall that the data are coded with answers to the question of frequency of contact with friends and family from 0 to 3, with 0 being "never" having contact, 1 indicating contact once every several months, 2 indicating contact once a month a more, and 3 being contact once a week or more. For first-generation respondents the average frequency of contact with friends and family in their countries of origin is about once a month. However, frequency of contact with

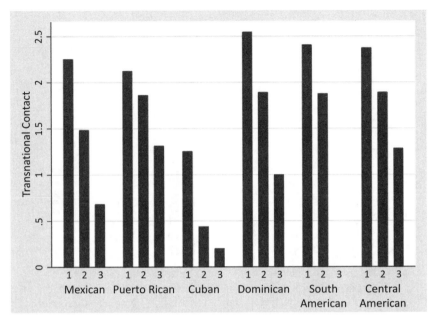

Figure 5.15. Contact with Friends and Family in Country of Origin, by Country of Origin, across Generation of Immigrants
Question wording: "How often do you have contact with friends and family in [R's country of origin]?" ($N = 8,488$).

friends and family in countries of origin drops significantly below that for second- and third-generation respondents across all national origin groups.

For Mexican-origin respondents, for example, the frequency of contact in the first generation is somewhat more than once a month. For second-generation respondents who are born in the United States as the children of immigrants, frequency of contact with friends and family drops off to an average of somewhere between once a month and once every several months. By the third generation, Mexican respondents report frequency of contact with friends and family in Mexico to somewhere between once every several months and never.

The highest levels of contact in the first generation are among Dominican, South American, and Central American immigrants; the lowest is among Cuban refugees. Among second-generation respondents, the highest levels of contact are among Puerto Ricans, Dominicans, South Americans, and Central Americans – for each of these groups, frequency of contact approaches once a month. Not surprisingly, given the nature of

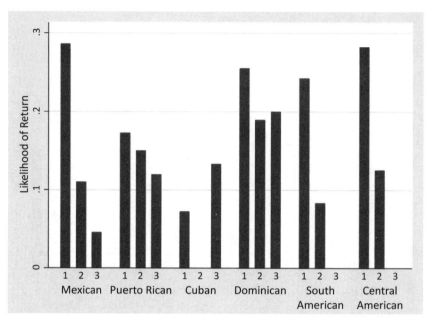

Figure 5.16. Plans to Return to Country of Origin, by Country of Origin, across Generation of Immigrants
Question wording: "Do you have plans to go back to [R's country of origin] to live permanently?" ($N = 8,634$).

the migration from Cuba to the United States, Cuban respondents have the least contact with family and friends among the six national origin groups, across generations.

Figure 5.4 presented the results for the question posed to Latino first-generation immigrants about their plans to return to their countries of origin. Figure 5.16 presents similar findings across immigrant generations. While among first-generation respondents 26 percent indicate that they have plans to return to their countries of origin, these percentages drop across generations; for second-generation respondents only 12 percent give this response, and among third-generation respondents (those whose grandparents were immigrants but who were born to parents born in the United States), 6 percent indicated they had plans to go to live in their country of origin.

These figures for all Latinos are mirrored almost exactly in Figure 5.16 in the results for Mexican-origin respondents. For every other national origin group, across generations there is a similar decline in respondents' stated plans to return. (Note again that, given the small sample sizes for

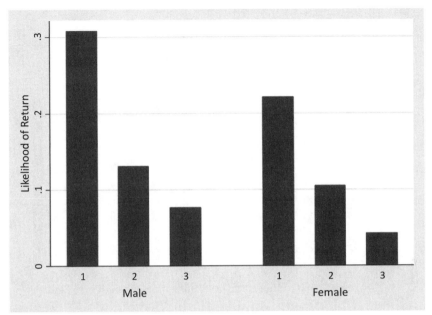

Figure 5.17. Plans to Return to Country of Origin, by Gender, across Generation of Immigrants
Question wording: "Do you have plans to go back to [R's country of origin] to live permanently?" ($N = 8,634$).

particular national origin groups, the key to interpreting the graph is to focus on trends rather than particular results. Thus, although there is a slight uptick in the graph for third-generation Dominican respondents, it is important to keep in mind that the response size here is only three individuals).

Figure 5.17 shows a slightly different look at the same data, looking at the question of return through the lens of gender rather than country of origin. Some scholars have argued that gender is critical to understanding the dynamics of immigration (Hondagneu-Sotelo 1994; Mahler and Pessar 2001; Pessar and Mahler 2001; Goldring 2001), and in particular the decision to stay and settle permanently in immigrants' new country of residence, in this case, the United States (Jones-Correa 1998b; Pessar 1986). Figure 5.17 confirms that across generations women are more likely than men to indicate a preference for settling in the United States rather than going back to live in their countries of origin.

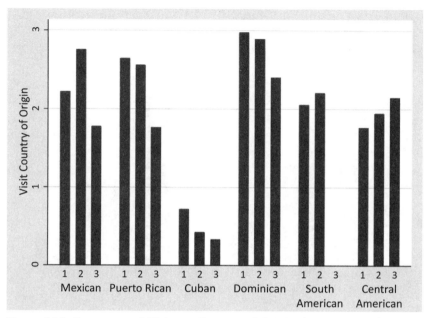

Figure 5.18. Frequency of Visits to Country of Origin, by Country of Origin, across Generation of Immigrants
Question wording: "How often do you visit [R's country origin]?"; recoded as average by generation.

All in all, trends for the second and successive generations continue those of the first: plans to return decline within and across generations, with women less likely to express plans to return than men. That said, one in four first-generation immigrants still have some intention to return, and among the children of immigrants born in the United States, one in ten still have plans to live in their parents' country of birth. How realistic these plans are, or how likely they are to be acted on, is difficult to know, but any uncertainty about future commitments is likely to have an effect on other social and political behaviors (Jones-Correa 1998).

Immigrants' visits to their country of origin increase substantially over time for first-generation immigrants in the United States (Figure 5.8). For the most part, the likelihood of visiting continues to increase, or holds steady, among the children of immigrants (Figure 5.18). Recall that the responses to this question are coded from 0 to 5, with 0 being having never traveled to country of origin, 1 being traveled more than five years ago, 2 indicating traveled once in the previous five years, 3 indicating traveled once in the previous three years, 4 being travel once a year, and 5 indicating travel more than once a year.

For Mexican-origin respondents travel to Mexico increases from an average of "travel in the previous five years" to an average closer to "travel in the previous three years." Travel reported by Puerto Rican and Dominican second-generation respondents also approximates these levels. Travel by second-generation South American and Central American second-generation respondents appears less frequent (approximately "travel in the previous five years") but is still higher in the second generation than in the first. The exception is Cuban Americans, for whom travel to Cuba is understandably low in the first generation and is lower still as reported by respondents from successive generations. Again, keep in mind that all these data for the second and third generation are based on small sample sizes and so should be interpreted as trends rather than as definite figures.

In our discussion of the findings in Figure 5.6, we noted that having children who remain in the country of origin is likely to be a strong predictor, along with property ownership (Figure 5.7), of transnational ties. Unfortunately, the LNS does not have data on property ownership in countries of origin beyond the first generation. However, the question about providing financial support to children younger than eighteen years old was asked of all respondents with children. Figure 5.19 indicates that 16 percent of first-generation respondents indicated they had children they supported financially abroad. But among second-generation respondents there were none – except for a very small percentage of second-generation Puerto Rican respondents (i.e., Puerto Ricans born on the mainland United States rather than on the island) who indicated that they supported children on the island. In other words, by the second generation, immigrants' nuclear families are universally located entirely in the United States.

One indicator of the likelihood of the persistence of transnational ties in the first and successive generations is whether Latino immigrants and their descendents marry other Latinos. Previous research has found that children of immigrants have high rates of out-marriage: in the 1980s at least a quarter of Asian and Latino immigrants married outside their broad racial-ethnic categories (as defined by the census) in the first generation; half did so by the second generation (Farley 1998). Qian and Lichter (2007) find that evidence for continued considerable out-marriage in the 1990s and early 2000s, but they note that the exogamy may be lower as a result of higher immigrant populations. Keep in mind that any figures for

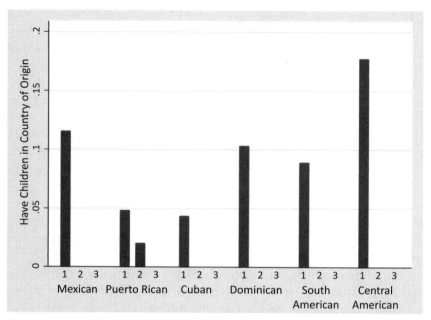

Figure 5.19. Children Younger Than 18 Living in Country of Origin, by Country of Origin, across Generation of Immigrants
Question wording: "Do you have children under 18 that you assist financially living in another country?" (*N* = 4,289).

out-marriage would certainly be higher if they took into account those marrying out of their national origin (rather than racial-ethnic) group. In New York City, for instance, there are increasing numbers of pairings among Latinos of different national origins (e.g., Puerto Rican and Mexican, Colombian and Dominican).

Figure 5.20 graphs the percentage of respondents with a Latino and/or Hispanic spouse or partner. Among first-generation immigrants, 59 percent are married or partnered to another Latino or Latina. This implies that 40 percent of foreign-born Latino immigrants – a sizable percentage – are married or have partners who are not Latino or Latina. Among second-generation respondents, only 35 percent of the children of immigrants are married or partnered to a Latino or Latina. And among third-generation respondents that percentage declines to less than 10 percent. Marriage patterns among Latinos indicate considerable social and marital assimilation, with the majority of respondents born in the United States having non-Latino partners. Because long-term relationships like marriage imply social ties and responsibilities, it is unlikely that Latinos who

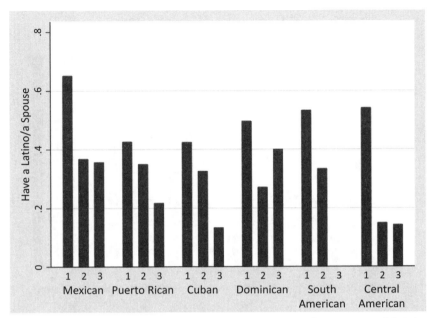

Figure 5.20. Respondent Has a Latino Spouse or Partner, by Country of Origin, across Generation of Immigrants
Question wording: "What is your spouse/partner's race and ethnicity?"; recoded so that 1 = Latino spouse, and 0 = non-Latino spouse ($N = 8,634$).

out-marry to other racial-ethnic groups will have the same strength and frequency of transnational ties as those who marry or partner with other Latinos. However, because transnational ties are often so localized – with immigrants having connections to specific to towns and provinces (Levitt 2001) – it may be the case that even having a Latino partner with origins from another Latin American country results in attenuated transnational ties.

Figure 5.20 shows that first-generation Mexican immigrants (group 1 in the figure) are the most likely to marry other Latinos: 65 percent do so. This is in keeping with the sociological literature, which describes how the larger the pool of available marriage partners from one's own ethnic group, the likelier it is that members of that group find a partner from within that group rather than out-marry. The lowest rates of partnering and/or marriage with other Latinos in the first generation are for Central and South Americans (46 percent and 47 percent, respectively).

Among second-generation respondents, the highest rate of marriage and/or partnering with other Latinos is once again highest among

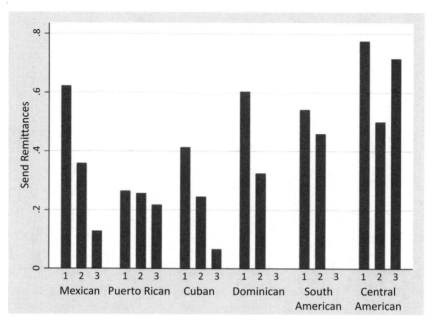

Figure 5.21. Remittances to Country of Origin, by Country of Origin, across Generation of Immigrants

Question wording: "How often do you send money?"; recoded to 1 = remit once a year or more, and 0 =less than yearly or never (*N* = 6,096).

Mexican-origin residents, but this time only 37 percent are endogamous: 63 percent marry or partner with non-Latinos. The group with the lowest percentage marrying and/or partnering with other Latinos in the second generation are Dominican Americans, at 27 percent.

Figure 5.21 indicates that frequency of sending remittances declines not only within the first generation, as indicated by Figure 5.2, but also across generations. The question "How often do you send money?" is coded here with 1 equaling sending money once a year or more and 0 being less than once a year or never. This trend shows clearly for each national origin and/or regional group (except for Central Americans, who appear to show a jump in their frequency of remittances in the third generation). But this result is likely a statistical anomaly: there are only seven third-generation Central American respondents in the survey, so the results are not statistically significant. Fifty-nine percent of first-generation immigrants send funds to friends and family once a year or more, but only 33 percent do in the second generation and only 13 percent among third-generation immigrants.

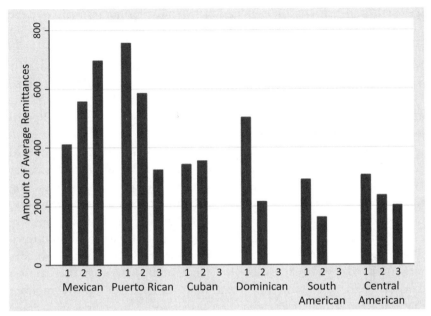

Figure 5.22. Average Amount of Money Sent to Country of Origin, by Country of Origin, across Generation of Immigrants
Question Wording: "What is the average amount you send each time?" (*N* = 3,714).

Mexican immigrants, given their larger group size and longer history in the United States (the LNS includes 3,885 first-generation Mexicans, 600 second-generation respondents of Mexican origin, and 632 third-generation respondents), show a clear pattern: in the first generation more than 60 percent of Mexican-origin respondents remit at least once a year or more; in the second generation fewer than 40 percent remit that often, and by the third generation only one in ten remit once a year or more.

As noted in Figure 5.2 first-generation Central American, Dominican, and Mexican-origin immigrants are the most frequent remitters, but interestingly, among second-generation respondents, Central and South Americans are the most likely to continue remitting once a year or more, whereas the frequency of Dominican and Mexican remittances drop off more drastically after the first generation.

Figure 5.3, which graphed changes in amounts remitted among first-generation respondents, indicated that there was a slight upward trend in the amounts remitted, even as there was a downward trend in the frequency of remittances to immigrants' countries of origin. In Figure 5.22

we see these trends continue, at least for Mexican-origin residents – in the first generation the average amount remitted is approximately $400, but among second-generation respondents, the amount remitted is closer to $600, and in the third generation the amount remitted is approximately $700. The sample size is large enough for Mexican respondents, so these figures are likely reliable. However, for other national origin groups the amount remitted decreases rather than increases over generation. Remittances for Puerto Ricans (the group with the second-largest group of second-generation immigrants) falls substantially in the second and third generations. Every other national origin group (albeit with much smaller sample sizes for second and later generations, which makes interpreting trends a bit dicier) shows declines in remittance amounts over generations. It could be that Mexican-origin residents in the United States are an exception, with continuing family ties well into the second and third generations, ties that encourage the continuation of remittances, whereas those ties fade for other national origin groups. However, the data on contact, children supported abroad, and out-marriage do not indicate that Mexican-origin respondents are exceptional. Increases in average amounts of remittances may simply reflect increases in disposable income among Mexican Americans.

As noted in the discussion for Figures 5.10–5.12, political transnationalism – immigrants' interest and involvement in their country of origin – is limited when compared to other forms of transnational ties, and few immigrants engage in it. In the first generation, interest in politics in immigrants' countries of origin falls over time in the United States. With response categories coded from 0 to 3, with 0 indicating no attention to country of origin politics, 1 indicating "a little," 2 indicating "some," and 3 signifying "a lot," among first-generation immigrants, interest in country of origin politics falls just above the levels indicating "a little" interest in politics. This varies somewhat by country of origin. The strongest interest in country-of-origin politics is found among Cuban and South American first-generation respondents (reflecting, in part, higher levels of education among the two groups). Among second-generation respondents – the children of immigrants – attention to politics falls slightly among Mexican Americans and more dramatically among Dominican and South American respondents, to levels indicating "a little" interest in country-of-origin politics. For Puerto Ricans, Cuban Americans, and Central Americans, interest in country-of-origin politics actually increases slightly, if not significantly. For third-generation respondents, interest in politics in immigrants' countries of origin falls across all national origin and regional groups.

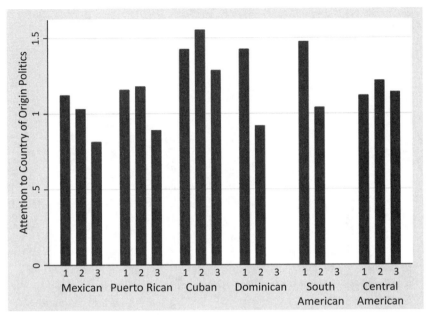

Figure 5.23. Attention to Politics in Country of Origin, by Country of Origin, across Generation of Immigrants
Question wording: "How much attention would you say you pay to politics in [country of origin]? Would you say you pay a lot of attention, some attention, a little attention, or none at all?" ($N = 6,096$).

Participation in voluntary associations, like hometown associations and regional federations, linked to immigrants' countries of origin is low in the first generation – 5 percent of immigrants belong to these kinds of voluntary organizations overall. As we saw in Figure 5.9, the exceptions are among Dominicans and South Americans, both of whom have significantly higher rates of participation in these kinds of voluntary organizations. Interestingly, Figure 5.24 shows that second-generation Latino immigrants' participation in these kinds of organizations actually increases slightly: 6 percent of second-generation immigrants say they participate in these voluntary organizations.

Participation rates are still fairly low, even for groups with the highest levels of participation: 12 percent of second-generation Cuban American respondents, for instance, indicate that they participate in these type of associations, as do 13 percent of South Americans. These data should not be overinterpreted, as the trends for the second generation are based on very small samples of respondents. For example, the Cuban data are based on a total sample of forty-nine Cuban American second-generation

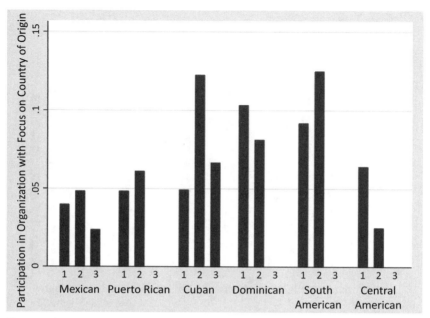

Figure 5.24. Participate in Organization Directed at Country of Origin, by Country of Origin, across Generation of Immigrants
Question wording: "Do you participate in the activities of a club, association, or federation connected to the town or province your family came from in [R's country of origin]?" ($N = 8,634$).

respondents, of whom six indicated that they participate in these kinds of voluntary organizations. The equivalent figures for South Americans are twenty-four overall, with three indicating participation. Figure 5.24 illustrates trends rather than exact figures. Nonetheless, the overall results indicate that participation in country-of-origin-oriented voluntary organizations increases slightly or at least holds steady among second-generation immigrants.

Conclusion

This chapter presents a complex view of transnationalism, presenting evidence from the Latino National Survey that suggests that Latinos maintain affective ties to their countries of origin, but that these – on the whole – diminish with time in the United States in the first generation and across generations in the United States. Despite the ties Latinos have to their countries of origin, the findings indicated in the tables and figures in this chapter show declines in the frequency of immigrants' contacts with friends and family over time in the United States; in the frequency of their monetary remittances to the friends and family in the country of origin; in their support of children living in the country of origin; in their ownership of homes, land, or businesses in the country of origin; and in their plans to return to their country of origin. Very soon after arriving to live in the United States, Latino immigrants overwhelmingly indicate that their plans are to remain in this country. Latino out-marriage to non-Latinos increases with time in the United States and across generations. Overall, these results point to a process of immigrant settlement in the United States.

These findings from the LNS corroborate other sources, suggesting that immigrants and their children in the United States are here to stay and are increasingly incorporated in the social and political life of this country. Other indicators of immigrant settlement in the United States indicate, for instance, the following:

- Immigrants are no more likely to return to their countries of origin today than they were a century ago, and their children, not surprisingly, are even less likely to do so (U.S. Immigration and Naturalization Services 1992, table 2).
- Immigrants have had higher rates of citizenship acquisition since the mid-1990s than previously, and relatively few immigrants (and even fewer of their children) actively acquire dual nationality or take advantage of provisions for voting abroad (Jones-Correa 2001).
- Immigrants are increasingly homeowners, settling as stable residents in neighborhoods across the United States (Joint Center for Housing Studies 2008.
- Immigrants and their children learn English; indeed, their children become English dominant (Portes and Rumbaut 2001; Rumbaut and Portes 2001).

Taken overall, these data provide evidence for the linear assimilation of immigrants – immigrants are further incorporated into society over time and with each successive generation.

There are two caveats to this conclusion: the first is that transnational ties can be uneven across national origin groups: Cuban Americans, for obvious reasons related to their status as refugees rather than economic immigrants, are often outliers, with significantly fewer sending remittances, traveling, or planning to return to their country of origin. Although most immigrants indicate their intentions to remain in the United States, higher percentages of first- and second-generation immigrants from the Dominican Republic indicate a desire to return to live permanently in their country of origin than do Latinos hailing from other countries. And Puerto Rican attitudes and behaviors, particularly on issues related to their ties to the island of Puerto Rico, are sometimes indistinguishable from those of immigrants from elsewhere in Latin America, despite the facts that Puerto Rico is a commonwealth of the United States and all Puerto Ricans are U.S. citizens.

The second caveat is that transnational ties do not entirely fade away among first-generation Latino immigrants or even among the native born. Although ties to countries of origin decline, at times dramatically, in some instances these ties can be persistent. For instance, remittances and contact with family in Latino immigrants' countries of origin both decline over time and generation, but a significant minority is still engaged in both, even in the second generation. Travel to immigrants' countries of origin increases steadily with years spent in the United States, but this might be explained by the regularization of immigrants' legal status and increasing resources allowing for travel. Other measures better reflect the persistence of transnational ties; while the percentage of individuals engaged in these practices is low, the levels of participation are remarkably persistent. For example, participation in voluntary associations linked to the country of origin is low overall; this level of participation is constant across years in the United States and among the second generation. Likewise, although only a small percentage of respondents indicated that they participated in a voluntary association linked to their country of origin, had voted in their country of origin elections (both around 5 percent), or had donated to politicians or political parties in their country of origin (about 2 percent), these percentages stay steady across years spent in the United States. Transnational ties can maintain a small but loyal following, even as they decline overall over time.

Bibliography

Alarcón, Rafael. 2002. "The Development of Hometown Associations in the United States and the Use of Social Remittances in Mexico." Washington, D.C.: Inter-American Dialogue.

Barreto, M., and J. Muñoz. 2003. "Re-Examining the 'Politics of In-Between': Political Participation among Mexican Immigrants in the United States." *Hispanic Journal of Behavioral Sciences* 25(4): 427–47.

Basch, Linda, Nina Glick Schiller, and Cristina Szanton-Blanc. 1994. *Nations Unbound: Transnational Projects, Postcolonial Predicaments, and De-territorialized Nation-States*. Basel, Switzerland: Gordon and Breach Publishers.

Conway, Dennis, and Jeffrey Cohen. 1998. "Consequences of Migration and Remittances for Mexican Transnational Communities." *Economic Geography* 71(1): 26–44.

De la Garza, Rodolfo, and Myriam Hazan. 2003. *Looking Backward, Moving Forward: Mexican Organizations in the U.S. as Agents of Incorporation and Dissociation.* Claremont, CA: Tomás Rivera Policy Institute.

DeSipio, Louis. 2000. "Sending Money Home...for Now: Remittances and Immigrant Adaptation in the United States." Working paper, Inter-American Dialogue and Tomás Rivera Policy Institute (January). Claremont, CA.

DeSipio, Louis, and Adrian Pantoja. 2004. "Puerto Rican Exceptionalism? A Comparative Analysis of Puerto Rican, Mexican, Salvadoran and Dominican Transnational Civic and Political Ties." Paper presented at the conference "Latino Politics: The State of Discipline," Texas A&M University, College Station, TX, April 30–May 1.

Duany, Jorge. 2002, *The Puerto Rican Nation on the Move: Identities on the Island and in the United States.* Chapel Hill: University of North Carolina Press.

Farley, Reynolds. 1998. "Presentation to the Race Advisory Board, President's Initiative on Race." http://clinton3.nara.gov/Initiatives/OneAmerica/farley.html.

Flores-Macias, Gustavo. 2009. "Making Migrant-Government Partnerships Work: Insights from the Logic of Collective Action." Working paper, Cornell University.

Glick Schiller, Nina. 1999. "Transmigrants and Nation-States: Something Old and Something New in the U.S. Immigrant Experience." In *The Handbook of International Migration: The American Experience*, ed. Charles Hirschman, Philip Kasinitz, and Josh DeWind, 94–119. New York: Russell Sage Foundation.

Goldring, Luin. 2001. "The Gender and Geography of Citizenship in Mexico-U.S. Transnational Spaces." *Identities: Global Studies in Culture and Power* 7: 501–37.

Graham, Pamela 1996. "Re-Imagining the Nation and Defining the District: The Simultaneous Political Incorporation of Dominican Transnational Migrants." Ph.D. dissertation, University of North Carolina.

Graham, Pamela. 1997. "Nationality and Political Participation in the Transnational Context of Dominican Migration." In *Caribbean Circuits: Transnational Approaches to Migration*, ed. P. Pessar, 91–126. Staten Island, NY: Center for Migration Studies.

Guarnizo, Luis E. 1997. "The Emergence of a Transnational Social Formation and the Mirage of Return Migration among Dominican Transmigrants." *Identities* 4(2): 281–322.

Guarnizo, Luis E. 2000. "Notes on Transnationalism." Paper presented at the workshop "Transnational Migration: Comparative Theory and Research Perspectives." Wadham College, University of Oxford, U.K., July 2000.

Guarnizo, Luis E. 2001. "On the Political Participation of Transnational Migrants: Old Practices and New Trends." In *E Pluribus Unum? Contemporary and Historical Perspectives on Immigrant Political Incorporation,* ed. Gary Gerstle and John Mollenkopf, 213–63. New York: Russell Sage Foundation.

Guarnizo, Luis E., Alejandro Portes, and William Haller. 2003. "Assimilation and Transnationalism: Determinants of Transnational Political Action among Contemporary Migrants." *American Journal of Sociology* 6(May): 1211–48.

Hondagneu-Sotelo, Pierrette. 1994. *Gendered Transitions: Mexican Experiences of Immigration.* Berkeley: University of California Press.

Hondagneu-Sotelo, Pierrette, and Ernestine Avila. 1997. "I'm Here, but I'm There: The Meanings of Latina Transnational Motherhood." *Gender and Society* 11(October): 548–71.

Joint Center for Housing Studies. 2008. *The State of the Nation's Housing.* Cambridge, MA: Harvard University. http://www.jchs.harvard.edu/publications/markets/son2008/son2008.pdf.

Jones-Correa, Michael. 1998a. *Between Two Nations: The Political Predicament of Latinos in Queens.* Ithaca, NY: Cornell University Press.

Jones-Correa, Michael. 1998b. "Different Paths: Gender, Immigration and Political Participation." *International Migration Review* 32(2): 326–49.

Jones-Correa, Michael. 2001. "Under Two Flags: Dual Nationality in Latin America and Its Consequences for Naturalization in the United States." *International Migration Review* 35(4): 997–1029.

Jones-Correa, Michael. 2003. "The Study of Transnationalism among the Children of Immigrants: Where We Are and Where We Should Be Headed." In *The Changing Face of Home: The Transnational Lives of the Second Generation*, ed. Peggy Levitt and Mary Waters, 221–41. New York: Russell Sage Foundation.

Kasinitz, Philip, Mary C. Waters, John H. Mollenkopf, and Merih Anil. 2003. "Transnationalism and the Children of Immigrants in Contemporary New York." In *The Changing Face of Home: The Transnational Lives of the Second Generation*, ed. Peggy Levitt and Mary Waters, 96–122. New York: Russell Sage Foundation.

Kasinitz, Philip, Mary C. Waters, John H. Mollenkopf, and Jennifer Holdway. 2009. *Inheriting the City: The Children of Immigrants Come of Age.* New York: Russell Sage Foundation.

Levitt, Peggy. 2001. *The Transnational Villagers.* Berkeley: University of California Press.

Levitt, Peggy. 2003. "The Ties That Change: Relations to the Ancestral Home over the Life Cycle." In *The Changing Face of Home: The Transnational Lives of the Second Generation*, ed. Peggy Levitt and Mary Waters, 123–44. New York: Russell Sage Foundation.

Levitt, Peggy, and Nina Glick Schiller 2004. "Transnational Perspectives on Migration: Conceptualizing Simultaneity." *International Migration Review* 38: 595–629.

Levitt, Peggy, and Mary Waters, eds. 2003. *The Changing Face of Home: The Transnational Lives of the Second Generation.* New York: Russell Sage Foundation.

Mahler, Sarah J., and Patricia Pessar. 2001. "Gendered Geographies of Power: Analyzing Gender across Transnational Spaces." *Identities: Global Studies in Culture and Power* 7: 441–59.

Massey, Douglas, and Jorge Durand. 1992. "Continuities in Transnational Migration: An Analysis of Thirteen National Communities." Paper presented at the conference "New Perspectives on Mexico-U.S. Immigration," Mexican Studies Program, University of Chicago, October 23–24.

McCann, James, Wayne A. Cornelius, and David Leal. 2009. "Absentee Voting and Transnational Civic Engagement among Mexican Expatriates." In *Consolidating Mexico's Democracy*, ed. Jorge Dominguez and Chappell Lawson. 89-108. Baltimore: Johns Hopkins University Press.

Orozco, Manuel. 2000. "Latino Hometown Associations as Agents of Development in Latin America." Working paper, Inter-American Dialogue and Tomás Rivera Policy Institute. Washington, D.C.

Pantoja, Adrian. 2005. "Transnational Ties and Immigrant Political Incorporation: The Case of Dominicans in Washington Heights, New York." *International Migration* 43(4): 123–46.

Pessar, Patricia R. 1986. "The Role of Gender in Dominican Settlement in the United States." In *Women and Change in Latin America*, ed. J. Nash and H. Safa, 273–94. South Hadley, MA: Bergin and Garvey.

Pessar, Patricia, and Sarah Mahler. 2001. "Gender and Transnational Migration." Working paper 01-06e, Center for Migration and Development, Princeton University, Princeton, NJ.

Portes, Alejandro. 1999. "Immigration Theory for a New Century: Some Problems and Opportunities." Pp. 21–33 in *The Handbook of International Migration: The American Experience*, edited by C. Hirschman, P. Kasinitz, and J. DeWind. New York: Russell Sage Foundation.

Portes, Alejandro, and Ruben Rumbaut. 2001. *Legacies: The Story of the Second Generation*. Berkeley: University of California Press.

Qian, Zhenchao, and Daniel T. Lichter. 2007. "Social Boundaries and Marital Assimilation: Interpreting Trends in Racial and Ethnic Intermarriage." *American Sociological Review* 72(February): 68–94.

Rodriguez, Clara E. 1993 "Puerto Rican Circular Migration: Revisited." *Latino Studies Journal* 4(2): 93–113.

Rumbaut, Ruben. 2003. "Severed or Sustained Attachments? Language, Identity, and Imagined Communities in the Post-Immigrant Generation." In *The Changing Face of Home: The Transnational Lives of the Second Generation*, ed. Peggy Levitt and Mary Waters, 43–95. New York: Russell Sage Foundation.

Rumbaut, Ruben, and Alejandro Portes. 2001. *Ethnicities: Children of Immigrants in America*. Berkeley: University of California Press.

Smith, Michael Peter, and Luis Guarnizo. 1998. *Transnationalism from Below*. New Brunswick, NJ: Transaction Publishers.

U.S. Immigration and Naturalization Service. 1992. *Statistical Yearbook of the Immigration and Naturalization Service*. Washington, D.C.: U.S. Government Printing Office.

Waldinger, Roger D. 2008. "Between 'Here' and 'There': Immigrant Cross-Border Activities and Loyalties." *International Migration Review* 42(1): 3–29.

Waldinger, Roger D., and David Fitzgerald. 2004. "Transnationalism in Question." *American Journal of Sociology* 109(5): 1177–95.

Waldinger, Roger D., and Nelson Lim. 2009. "Homeland Calling? Political and Social Connectivity across Borders." http://works.bepress.com/roger_waldinger/36.

Waldinger, Roger, Rafael Porzecanski, and Thomas Soehl. 2009. "Caged: Expatriate Voting and Its Limits." http://works.bepress.com/roger_waldinger/34.

Waldinger, Roger D., and Thomas Soehl. 2009. "Making the Connection: Latino Immigrants and Their Cross-Border Ties." http://works.bepress.com/roger_waldinger/37.

6

Intergroup Relations

A Diverse Latino Community

It is clear that Latinos exhibit a diverse "profile," along the lines of nativity, language use, degree of assimilation, and sense of own group identity (or identities), not to mention the usual sociodemographic characteristics (e.g., class, educational attainment, income levels). At the same time, Latinos are clustered together as both members of national origin groups and as members of a pan-ethnic confederation. This section of the book looks at this complex group to explore the extent of commonalities and contrasts among this growing and diverse set of Latino respondents in the Latino National Survey. In addition, we explore Latinos' perceptions and experiences of living in the United States, as well as the nature and extent of intergroup connections with other groups (e.g., whites, African Americans and Asian Americans). In doing so, we can examine how much nativity and citizenship status affects Latinos views, attitudes, and experiences.

We begin the focus with the LNS respondents' views about their life chances and opportunities in America, their experiences with discriminatory treatment in a variety of settings, and their perceptions about intergroup relations. The "outside" groups identified are whites (or Anglos), African Americans, and Asian Americans. As Latinos represent a pan-ethnic grouping (i.e., transcending national origin identities), we also examine intragroup relations and attitudes about the various Latinos subgroups. These types of queries can provide us with a benchmark view of how Latinos are fitting in our sociopolitical system and can allow us to compare views among key subgroup distinctions under the "Latino" umbrella.

A significant portion of the LNS sample is foreign born, and this is an important variation in the overall Latino community. Concerns about political incorporation and integration, the extent of intergroup contact and familiarity, and experiences in the broader American society of the foreign born can serve to frame their attitudes and assessments of life in the United States. In addition to nativity, such characteristics as primary language use, length of time in the United States, age at immigration, and citizenship status can differentiate attitudes, informational levels, and political behaviors among the foreign born (Garcia 2009). Even though a significant portion of the LNS sample is foreign born, there are variations among the native born in the number of generations that their families have lived in the United States. Accordingly, the presentation of LNS survey responses is organized by nativity and citizen status to provide distinctions about the perceptions and incidence of discriminatory treatment and intergroup relations regarding Latinos.

The results of past studies have suggested that, on the whole, Latinos' perceive some but not especially high levels of discrimination by non-Latinos (see Hero 1992). A 1976 study found that 49 percent of Mexican Americans in Denver, Colorado, versus 76 percent of blacks, thought they were treated unfairly compared to Anglos regarding housing, and then regarding jobs (51 percent; 80 percent for African Americans) and schools (35 percent; 74 percent for African Americans). These results indicate that Mexican Americans had lower socioeconomic status than blacks (and Anglos) in Denver at the time (Lovrich and Marenin 1976). The bases for Mexican Americans' perception of discrimination is subject to a number of interpretations, including that discrimination is subtler to Mexican Americans; they were not yet an "awakened" minority (Lovrich and Marenin 1976), and the questions asked did not or could not tap less visible or institutional types of discrimination.

A 1989 survey suggested that "racial prejudice and discrimination" was a substantial but not overwhelming concern of the "Spanish surnamed" in Colorado Latin American Research and Service Agency (LARASA 1989). When asked if they were very concerned (scored as 3), concerned (scored as 2), or not concerned (scored as 1) about discrimination and prejudice, the average response was 2.46 (i.e., concerned to very concerned); 55 percent said "very," 36.3 percent said "concerned," and 8 percent said "not concerned." These and later data indicated that Latinos have perceived higher levels of discrimination toward them.

The Latino National Political Survey (LNPS; De la Garza et al. 1992) presented a complex picture of Latino citizens' perceptions of discrimination. On the one hand, less than a majority of Latino citizens – Mexican Americans, Puerto Ricans, and Cubans – said they had personally experienced discrimination, ranging from a high of 39 percent (among Mexican Americans) to a low of about 17 percent (Cubans). Furthermore, the overwhelming majority of Latinos – more than 90 percent – who had contacted government officials felt that they had been treated "as well as others" (i.e., non-Latinos).

When the LNPS respondents were asked about their perception of discrimination directed toward specific Latino subgroups (i.e. Mexican Americans, Puerto Ricans, and Cubans), there was noticeable variation. A range of 66.7 percent (Cubans) to about 80 percent (among Mexicans) of Latino citizens perceived some or a lot of discrimination against Mexican Americans. Majorities of each of the three Latino subgroups perceived discrimination against Puerto Ricans, and about three-fourths of Puerto Ricans did so. Interestingly, Cubans perceived discrimination against Cubans to a lesser degree than did Mexican Americans and/or Puerto Ricans – 47 percent of Cuban citizens perceived discrimination against their group, compared with 70 percent and 58 percent of Mexican Americans and Puerto Ricans, respectively, who perceived discrimination toward Cubans. A noteworthy observation is that the difference between Latinos' actual experience with discrimination and their perceptions of discrimination against members of their group is such that they perceive higher levels of discrimination than what they have experienced individually.

In addition, actual and perceptions of perceived discrimination can be experienced at various times over a person's life. Thus, perceptions of differential treatment and actual discriminatory experiences, based on race and/or ethnicity or gender, can affect attitudes and behaviors whether or not the person has experienced discrimination directly. The question of one's disadvantaged position can connect an individual to his or her own group or to other groups that share a similar "disadvantaged" status. This can motivate Latinos to consider pursuing collaborative efforts to take on a common "oppressor." Or conversely, another response would be to close ranks and see other groups as contributing to that disadvantaged status and/or as competitors for scarce resources (i.e., an inside versus outside group distinction).

The LNPS data on noncitizens' perceptions of discrimination is an important distinction to make among Latinos. Although Latino noncitizens (Mexican and Cuban) were less likely to say that they had personally experienced discrimination than their citizen counterparts (26 percent and

10 percent of Mexican-American and Cuban citizens versus 39 percent and 11 percent of Mexican and Cuban noncitizens, respectively), noncitizens overwhelmingly (more than 90 percent) said that they had received equal treatment from the public officials they had contacted. A substantial two-thirds of Mexican and almost half of Cuban noncitizens perceived some or a lot of discrimination against Mexican Americans, but this is somewhat less than was the case for citizens. About a third of Mexican and of Cuban noncitizens perceived some or a lot of discrimination against Puerto Ricans, a much smaller proportion than held among citizens. Majorities of both Mexican (55 percent) and Cuban (69 percent) noncitizens said that there was only a little or no discrimination toward Cubans. Indeed, more than half of Cuban noncitizens replied "none" to the question on discrimination against Cubans. Overall, Cubans, both citizens and noncitizens, were the least likely to say that they had experienced discrimination and the least likely to perceive discrimination against the several Latino groups, themselves included.

In the Pew Hispanic Center and Kaiser Family Foundation National Survey of Latinos, "Latinos overwhelmingly say that discrimination against Latinos is a problem both in general as well as in specific settings such as schools and the workplace" (74). An overwhelming majority (83 percent) of Hispanics also report that discrimination by Hispanics against other Hispanics is a problem, and almost half (47 percent) feel that this is a major problem. Latinos are most likely to attribute this type of discrimination to disparities in income and education, although a substantial number also feel that Latinos discriminate against other Latinos because they or their parents or ancestors are from a different country of origin.

In addition, another Pew survey (March 2004) in five states found that about "three in ten Latinos from California (30 percent), Texas (34 percent), Florida (27 percent), New York (28 percent) and New Jersey (34 percent) report themselves, a family member, or a close friend have experienced discrimination from non-Latinos during the last five years because of racial or ethnic background. Similar percentages also report receiving poorer service than other people at restaurants or stores (41 percent of all Latinos), being called names or insulted (30 percent) or not being hired or promoted for a job (14 percent) because of their race or ethnic background." The "vast majority of Latinos feel that discrimination" against them is "a problem in schools (75 percent) and the workplace (78 percent), and in preventing Latinos in general from succeeding in America (82 percent)." Latinos attribute discrimination from non-Latinos primarily to language and/or physical appearance (Pew Hispanic Center 2004).

This same five-state Pew survey found that large numbers of respondents believed that Latinos discriminating against other Latinos is a problem. "The majority of Latinos in New York (54 percent) and New Jersey (55 percent) reports that Latinos discriminating against other Latinos is a major problem, which is similar to what is reported by Latinos in California (50 percent) and Texas (47 percent), and only slightly higher than what is reported by Latinos in Florida (42 percent)" (Pew Hispanic Center 2004, 4). As intergroup relations are another focus of this section, a general review of this research literature follows.

Intergroup Relations and Coalition Formation

Browning, Rogers-Marshall, and Tabb's (1990) analysis used the idea of political incorporation so that successful minority mobilization in urban communities included (1) a critical minority mass, (2) a minimum amount of support from the electorate, and (3) sophisticated organizational development and political experience (Browning et al. 1984). At the same time, other research (Giles and Evans 1986) indicates that significant obstacles exist for the formation and maintenance of any interethnic and/or racial coalition. In short, the extant research literature on coalition formation can provide some insights into intergroup relations.

Coalitions are action-oriented ventures among similarly situated groups. Thus, political activation and collective efforts depend on common experiences, values and priorities, levels of political incorporation of each minority group, and the groups' collective standing in U.S. political system. Individuals who are inclined to act politically will require some organizational structure and leadership to seek and realize common goals. The leadership cadre helps to frame the issues and develop effective strategies for group actions. It is these linkages and common threads that identify some necessary conditions for coalition formation, and specifically for cooperative connections between Latinos and non-Latinos rather than conflictual or competitive encounters.

Early works on the possibility of coalitions between Latinos and the African American community have centered on their common bases of distinct social and/or political circumstances and interests. Carmichael and Hamilton (1967) identified some necessary requisites for coalition formation, including (1) the recognition of each party's respective self-interests, (2) that each party's respective self-interests benefit from alliances, (3) that each party has an independent base of support, and (4) a focus of the coalitional effort that deals with specific and identifiable goals. In essence, the Rainbow Coalition strategy of Jesse Jackson in the 1988 presidential campaign was to build a coalition based on reciprocity, leverage, and common interests (Henry and Muñoz 1991). More recently, the successful presidential campaign of Barack Obama extended its outreach and organization to be more inclusive of different minority communities and nonminorities. Given these conditions, the experiences and situations associated with minority groups serve as the basis to understand coalition formation.

Work by Uhlaner (1991) examined the basis for coalitions between Latinos and African Americans that relied less on common issue interests and more on levels of perceived discrimination. The discriminatory experiences of minority group members, although varying in degrees, can serve as a foundation for intergroup coalitions. Yet Uhlaner (1991) suggests that, although sympathy may be generated across minority groups, the response can be greater competitiveness or antagonism. That is, recognition of differential treatment across groups could lead specific minority groups to feel more disadvantaged than others and to become inclined to protect their own group more. Hence, the level of one's perceived discrimination is related to the strength of an individual's racial or ethnic identity and the impact of prejudice on one's special interests or specific issues or problems (Uhlaner 1991).

Thus, the key for coalitions, from this perspective, lies with assessments of one's own disadvantaged status and his/her interconnectedness to other minority groups. Each group can be confronting similar problems and a common target. Although the emphasis of this perspective is at the individual level, the dynamics of coalition formation relies heavily on organizations and leaders to channel perceived common interests and discrimination toward specific activities. Studies of minority elites have demonstrated that early socialization experiences, including experiences with discrimination and prejudice, have influenced individuals toward activism and advocacy for their groups (De la Garza and Vaughn 1984; Marable 1985). Besides one's actual experience with discrimination, levels of perceived prejudice and discrimination directed toward one's group could affect one's attitudes, orientations, and behaviors.

Common Status Goals and a Common Target

In addition to the elements of discrimination and minority group status, the other key element regarding coalitions center is common status goals rather than welfare goals (Carmichael and Hamilton 1967; Sonenshein 1990). For example, political ideology (e.g., liberalism, orientations toward social change) serves as the underlying base for coalitions; self-interests are secondary. In this manner, the coalition is based on a moral, sentimental, and friendly basis with direct appeals to one's conscience. Thus, the basis for coalition formation lies with the recognition among minority groups that they share a common opponent and objectives. Political coalitions are viable if both minority groups see themselves as combating the "white power structure" (McClain and Karnig 1990, pp. 542–43). At least some minimum level of trust between the minority groups is essential for any degree of success.

Work by Oliver and Johnson (1984), for example, indicates a low level of trust between Latinos and African Americans in Los Angeles. The element of inter-group trust is a key ingredient for successful coalitions. Finally, the need for coalitions may be lessened if minority groups operate in independent arenas of decision making. A wide range of factors affects the formation of coalitions. These range from the relative size of each minority group, similarity of perceived interests, levels of organizational development and leadership, effects of perceived and actual discrimination, and social distance (Dangelis 1977). In addition, if the social distance, in terms of social status and class, between the two groups is close, then coalitions are more feasible (Giles and Evans 1986; Sniderman Tetlock and Carmines 1993; Dreyer et al. 1988).

The presence of sizable Latino and African American communities has become more evident in major urban areas. The work by McClain and Karnig (1990) identifies almost fifty cities with populations of more than twenty-five thousand in which Latinos and African Americans each constitute more than 10 percent of the total population. Recent works on Los Angeles (Waldinger and Bozomehr 1996; Yu and Chang 1995) have introduced the growth of Asians and Latinos in the metropolitan area with corresponding political and economic developments. In addition, the unsuccessful mayoral attempt by Michael Wu and the first attempt by Antonio Villaraigosa did evidence efforts to form a multiethnic and multiracial coalition, although it was unsuccessful. At the same time, the mayoral elections of Tom Bradley (Los Angeles, 1973–1993), David Dinkins (New York, 1990–1993), Federico Peña (Denver, 1983–1991), Wellington Webb (Denver, 1991–2003), and Harold Washington (Chicago, 1983–1987) represent cases in which interminority coalitions have proved successful. In the case of Antonio Villaraigosa, his coalitional electoral strategy proved successful on his second attempt.

Recent gains in political representation by minority group members have altered the political alignments and networks in Los Angeles local politics. More recently, significant gains among Latinos in the California

Assembly and leadership positions have come about, in part, as a result of working coalitions. Thus, Los Angeles can serve as a prototype urban laboratory community in which greater opportunities and cumulative experiences exists for interracial and interethnic coalitions. At the same time, political competition among Latinos, Asians, and African Americans is still evident in Los Angeles.

Urban research on minority representation of either African Americans or Latinos in local government (Eisinger 1982; Fraga, Meier, and England 1986; Robinson and Dye 1978; McManus and Cassel 1982) has concentrated on each group being independent, yet cooperating with other minority communities with some regularity. Works by Falcón (1988) and McClain and Karnig (1990) have focused on these group's struggles to achieve greater political power and economic mobility. More specific work on coalitions between these two groups has focused on electoral coalitions, such as Jackson's Rainbow Coalition or specific local community efforts and issues.

This discussion of coalitions has centered on common group interests, experiences, and conditions. In addition, coalitions have been maintained on ideological bases regarding social equality (Henry and Muñoz 1991) and self-interests, which serve as political motivation and linkage for intergroup activities. Members of different groups weigh the degree of overlapping self-interests and calculate a cost-benefit ratio for the individual group benefits that could be garnered through cooperative endeavors. By their very nature, these interracial coalitions tend to be short-lived and sustained by specific and identifiable goals (Henry and Muñoz 1991).

In this context of perceptions, actual experiences, differential treatment, and possible positive intergroup relations, the LNS provides survey data through which we can explore the contemporary world of Latinos in the United States. Readers will learn not only if respondents experience discriminatory treatment or not but also, if so, the setting in which it took place. Moreover, the LNS asked about their perception of whites (or Anglos), African Americans, and Asian Americans.

Latinos' Experiences in the United States: Treatment in a Variety of Settings

Our initial assessment of Latinos and their experiences and perceptions of others in American society confirms a set of community attachments and affinities that include fellow national origin members as well as other Latinos. This affinity can be the result of experiences and cultural and

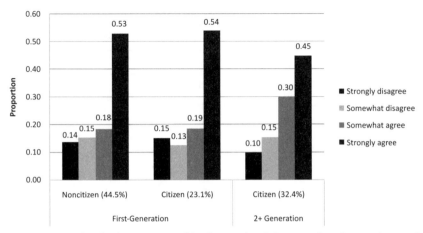

Figure 6.1. Individual Is Responsible for Lack of Success, by Generation and Citizenship
Question Wording: "Latinos can get ahead in the United States if they work hard? 4 = Strongly Agree, 3 = Somewhat Agree, 2 = Somewhat Disagree, 1 = Strongly Disagree, 5 = DK/NS."

linguistic commonalities that transcend national origin group membership. In a positive light, they can be viewed as bridges, but not all commonalities are pleasant. Contact and experiences with non-Latinos, especially negative or discriminatory actions, can serve to accent group distinctiveness and motivate some Latinos to close ranks. Readers will find in the tables that follow answers to a series of questions that gauge Latinos' outlook about their life chances and their experiences of discrimination.

This examination begins with an assessment of Latinos' perceptions about the opportunity structure in the United States. We start by asking whether respondents believe that applying themselves diligently will result in personal advancement, which is broken down in Figure 6.1 by generation (first generation, foreign born) and citizenship status. Latinos, overall, believe that hard work will advance their opportunities and achievements in this country. There is a slight decrease in this belief among the second generation and beyond, especially among those who strongly agree. But if one combines the "somewhat agree" and "strongly agree" responses for the second generation and beyond, their totals are slightly larger than among their first-generation counterparts. Overall, the pattern is consistent across generations.

The response was similar when respondents were asked whether poor people can get ahead in the United States if they work hard. This was

Table 6.1. *Poor People Get Ahead, by Generation and Citizenship*
Category: Community, Crime/Discrimination

Response		First Generation			2+ Generation	
		Noncitizen	Citizen	Total	Citizen	Total
Strongly disagree	Freq.	56	48	104	76	180
	Row%	53.85	46.15	57.78	42.22	100.00
	Col%	1.43	2.41	1.76	2.80	2.09
Somewhat disagree	Freq.	53	50	103	106	209
	Row%	51.46	48.54	49.28	50.72	100.00
	Col%	1.35	2.51	1.74	3.90	2.42
Somewhat agree	Freq.	636	323	959	618	1577
	Row%	66.32	33.68	60.81	39.19	100.00
	Col%	16.22	16.19	16.21	22.74	18.27
Strongly agree	Freq.	3077	1512	4589	1853	6442
	Row%	67.05	32.95	71.24	28.76	100.00
	Col%	78.49	75.79	77.58	68.18	74.62
Don't know	Freq.	98	62	160	65	225
	Row%	61.25	38.75	71.11	28.89	100.00
	Col%	2.50	3.11	2.70	2.39	2.61
TOTAL	Freq.	3920	1995	5915	2718	8633
	Row%	66.27	33.73	68.52	31.48	100.00
	Col%	100.00	100.00	100.00	100.00	100.00

Note: First/2+ generation: (2 d.f.) 195.100 (P = 0.000). Citizen/noncitizen (first generation only): (2 d.f.) 254.370 (P = 0.000). Island-born Puerto Ricans are coded as first generation. Question wording: "For the following questions, please indicate how much you agree with each statement: 'Poor people can get ahead in the U.S. if they work hard.'"

consistent across generations and citizenship status. For those who did not strongly agree with this statement, many somewhat agreed, as shown in Table 6.1. There is virtually no difference between first-generation citizens and noncitizens. Interestingly, first-generation Latinos (irrespective of citizenship status) are more likely to strongly agree with this statement than their second generation and beyond counterparts. There is a similar pattern in Figure 6.1, where the drop-off of "strongly agree" responses among the second generation and beyond is less than in the first-generation group, but overall, both groups agree that poor people can get ahead if they work hard. A possible explanation for this pattern is Latinos' frame of reference for assessing opportunity structures. That is, first-generation Latinos evaluate the fruits of their labor in terms of what would have resulted if they had stayed in their home country, whereas native-born Latinos evaluate their status in comparison with

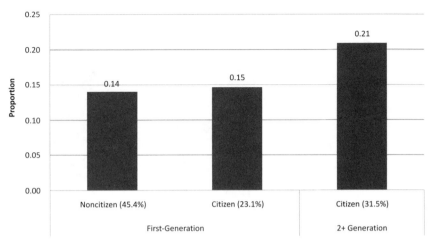

Figure 6.2. Unfairly Fired or Denied a Promotion, by Generation and Citizenship
Question Wording: "In the following questions we are interested in your beliefs about the way other people have treated you in the U.S. Have you ever . . . Been unfairly fired or denied a job or promotion? 1 = Yes, 2 = No, 3 = DK/NA."

other native-born Americans (Schmidt et al. 2009; Ramakrishnan and Bloemraad 2008). Overall, the idea of America as the land of opportunity is held by most people, regardless of economic status (Fraga and Segura 2006).

Discriminatory Experiences among Latinos

Given the strong belief in the ability of all Americans to succeed, how do the individual experiences of Latinos coincide with that notion? What is the role of discrimination or lack thereof? To find out, we asked a number of questions in the Latino National Survey on whether Latinos had experienced discriminatory treatment in a variety of settings, beginning with the workplace.

Only one in seven respondents felt that he or she had been unfairly fired or denied promotion. However, there are some differences by generations (Figure 6.2). One-fifth of second generation and beyond respondents answered affirmatively; among first-generation Latinos, there were no differences according to citizenship status. Note, though, that the wording of this item does not allow us to distinguish whether the basis for the work status was the result of being fired or passed over for promotion.

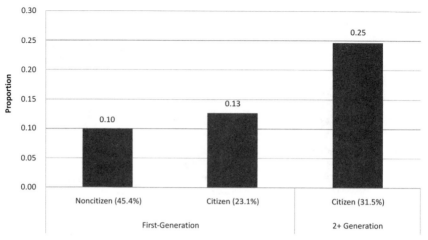

Figure 6.3. Unfairly Treated by the Police, by Generation and Citizenship
Question Wording: "In the following questions we are interested in your beliefs about the way other people have treated you in the U.S. Have you ever...Been unfairly treated by the police? 1 = Yes, 2 = No, 3 = DK/NA."

Another site of discriminatory treatment is interactions with law enforcement. The respondents were asked whether they had "ever been unfairly treated by the police." The vast majority of respondents have not been treated unfairly by the police, as Figure 6.3 makes clear. This is particularly true for the first generation, where about 87 percent have not been treated unfairly by police, whereas about 74 percent of the second generation and beyond responded similarly. It should be noted that the wording of this item referred to any law enforcement agency, such that distinctions between local police, Immigration and Customs Enforcement (ICE), Border Patrol, and so on are not possible. Among the first generation, there was a slightly higher positive response among citizens (12.68 percent versus 9.95 percent). It is difficult to know whether these levels are representative of the general population or other minority group members. An initial examination of responses across generations indicates that this area of contact with law enforcement officials can differentiate the LNS respondents as to their perceptions of opportunity structures and possible obstacles. At the same time, our identification of generational effects would direct further analysis to include other characteristics, such as education level, income, country of origin, and gender. At the same time, we would have to incorporate information about their countries of

Table 6.2. *Housing Discrimination, by Generation and Citizenship*
Category: Community, Crime/Discrimination

| Response | | First Generation | | | 2+ Generation | |
		Noncitizen	Citizen	Total	Citizen	Total
Yes	Freq.	183	112	295	213	508
	Row%	62.03	37.97	58.07	41.93	100.00
	Col%	4.67	5.61	4.99	7.83	5.88
No	Freq.	3679	1846	5525	2458	7983
	Row%	66.59	33.41	69.21	30.79	100.00
	Col%	93.83	92.48	93.38	90.40	92.44
Don't know or	Freq.	59	38	97	48	145
not applicable	Row%	60.82	39.18	66.90	33.10	100.00
	Col%	1.50	1.90	1.64	1.77	1.68
TOTAL	Freq.	3921	1996	5917	2719	8636
	Row%	66.27	33.73	68.52	31.48	100.00
	Col%	100.00	100.00	100.00	100.00	100.00

Note: First/2+ generation: (15 d.f.) 79.165 (P = 0.000). Citizen/noncitizen (first generation only): (d.f.) 0.000 (P =). Island-born Puerto Ricans are coded as first generation. Question wording: "Have you ever been unfairly prevented from moving into a neighborhood because the landlord or a realtor refused to sell or rent you a house or apartment?"

origin, income levels, educational attainment, and gender to examine the persistence of generational differences.

Yet another common site of discrimination is renting or buying housing. We asked respondents, "Have you ever been unfairly prevented from moving into a neighborhood because the landlord or a realtor refused to sell or rent you a house or apartment?" Very few responded yes (Table 6.2). This was true across generations, with about 93 percent of first-generation respondents saying they had not encountered this type of trouble and about 90 percent of the second generation and beyond giving the same response. Statistically, there was a significant relationship between generations of Latinos, as the second generation and beyond perceived more discrimination in housing.

More prevalent for our respondents was the perception of discrimination at public restaurants or stores. Although the majority of respondents say that they have never been treated unfairly or badly at restaurants or stores, this was particularly true among the first generation (86.6 percent). Although still constituting a majority, only about 66 percent of the second generation and beyond have never been treated unfairly or badly at restaurants or stores. This difference, shown in Figure 6.4, is

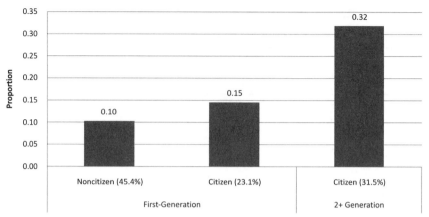

Figure 6.4. Treated Unfairly or Badly in Restaurants or Stores, by Generation and Citizenship
Question Wording: "In the following questions we are interested in your beliefs about the way other people have treated you in the U.S. Have you ever... Been treated unfairly or badly at restaurants or stores? 1 = Yes, 2 = No, 3 = DK/NA."

statistically significant between first and subsequent generations. Thus, we see some noteworthy differences between the immigrant generation and native-born Latinos.

We tried to gain some additional insight into why this might be, and so asked people what they thought "was the main reason for [their] experience(s)." Most respondents who said they had been treated unfairly believe it was because they are Latino (30.3 percent of first generation and 29.6 percent of the second generation and beyond). A rather large percentage of the second generation and beyond believe that they were treated unfairly because of their skin color (20.5 percent), whereas only about 8 percent of the first generation think so, as reflected in Table 6.3. Among the first generation, a fairly large percentage believed they were treated unfairly because of their language or accent (17.3 percent) or because of their status as an immigrant (12.8 percent). As with all surveys, one does not always succeed in presenting all the possible answers or respondents are reluctant to be pinned down to a specific answer. This was the case with this question, where a large percentage of both the first and second generation and beyond chose the generic "for some other reason" as their answer (11.7 percent of the first generation and 21.4 percent of the second generation and beyond). Without detailed explanations, it is difficult to interpret the reticence of the second generation and beyond. The importance of immigrant versus native-born status is

Table 6.3. *Reason for Unfair Treatment, by Generation and Citizenship*
Category: Community, Crime/Discrimination

Response		First Generation			2+ Generation	
		Noncitizen	Citizen	Total	Citizen	Total
Being Latino	Freq.	319	187	506	390	896
	Row%	63.04	36.96	56.47	43.53	100.00
	Col%	30.01	30.81	30.30	29.55	29.97
Being an	Freq.	172	42	214	12	226
immigrant	Row%	80.37	19.63	94.69	5.31	100.00
	Col%	16.18	6.92	12.81	0.91	7.56
Your national	Freq.	64	52	116	110	226
origin	Row%	55.17	44.83	51.33	48.67	100.00
	Col%	6.02	8.57	6.95	8.33	7.56
Your language	Freq.	198	91	289	64	353
or accent	Row%	68.51	31.49	81.87	18.13	100.00
	Col%	18.63	14.99	17.31	4.85	11.81
Your skin color	Freq.	84	62	146	271	417
	Row%	57.53	42.47	35.01	64.99	100.00
	Col%	7.90	10.21	8.74	20.53	13.95
Your gender	Freq.	12	14	26	40	66
	Row%	18.18	21.21	39.39	60.61	100.00
	Col%	1.13	2.31	1.56	3.03	2.21
Your age	Freq.	19	26	45	86	131
	Row%	42.22	57.78	34.35	65.65	100.00
	Col%	1.79	4.28	2.69	6.52	4.38
Other	Freq.	113	83	196	282	478
	Row%	57.65	42.35	41.00	59.00	100.00
	Col%	10.63	13.67	11.74	21.36	15.99
Don't know or	Freq.	82	50	132	65	197
not applicable	Row%	62.12	37.88	67.01	32.99	100.00
	Col%	7.71	8.24	7.90	4.92	6.59
TOTAL	Freq.	1063	607	1670	1320	2990
	Row%	63.65	36.35	55.85	44.15	100.00
	Col%	100.00	100.00	100.00	100.00	100.00

Note: First/2+ generation: (2 d.f.) 33.190 (P = 0.000). Citizen/noncitizen (first generation only): (2 d.f.) 13.770 (P = 0.000). Island-born Puerto Ricans are coded as first generation. Question wording: "There are lots of possible reasons why people might be treated unfairly, what do you think was the main reason for your experience(s)?"

highlighted by the frequency of reasons related to language and accent and being an immigrant. Again, the tendency among the second generation and beyond to indicate their Latino background as a primary reason for discriminatory treatment seems driven by a sense of feeling like an American minority.

Table 6.4. *Race of Person Giving Unfair Treatment, by Generation and Citizenship*

Category: Community, Crime/Discrimination

Response		First Generation			2+ Generation	
		Noncitizen	Citizen	Total	Citizen	Total
White	Freq.	583	399	982	952	1934
	Row%	59.37	40.63	50.78	49.22	100.00
	Col%	54.84	65.63	58.77	72.07	64.64
Black	Freq.	125	65	190	72	262
	Row%	65.79	34.21	72.52	27.48	100.00
	Col%	11.76	10.69	11.37	5.45	8.76
Asian	Freq.	57	8	65	57	122
	Row%	87.69	12.31	53.28	46.72	100.00
	Col%	5.36	1.32	3.89	4.31	4.08
Latino	Freq.	194	71	265	104	369
	Row%	73.21	26.79	71.82	28.18	100.00
	Col%	18.25	11.68	15.86	7.87	12.33
Don't know or not applicable	Freq.	104	65	169	136	305
	Row%	61.54	38.46	55.41	44.59	100.00
	Col%	9.78	10.69	10.11	10.30	10.19
TOTAL	Freq.	1063	608	1671	1321	2992
	Row%	63.61	36.39	55.85	44.15	100.00
	Col%	100.00	100.00	100.00	100.00	100.00

Note: First/2+ generation: (3 d.f.) 14.950 (P = 0.000). Citizen/noncitizen (first generation only): (3 d.f.) 2.210 (P = 0.085). Island-born Puerto Ricans are coded as first generation. Question wording: "In the most recent incident you experienced what was the race or ethnicity of the person(s) treating you unfairly?"

Who is engaging in the discriminatory behavior described by some respondents? We followed up by asking about the race of the person who perpetrated the act of discrimination. Most respondents who have been treated unfairly indicated that the perpetrator was white (50.8 percent of first generation versus 49.2 percent of the second generation and beyond), with "another Latino" the second most common choice (see Table 6.4). That said, first-generation Latinos reported (by a 2:1 margin) in greater numbers that another Latino had treated them unfairly. At the same time, first-generation noncitizens are more likely to have faced discriminatory behavior in which either whites or other Latinos were the perpetrators. There is a body of literature about the transformation of an immigrant group into one of perceived minority group status as they reside in the host country (Wilson 1973). For the most part, this transformation is affected by nature of their reception in the host country and changing

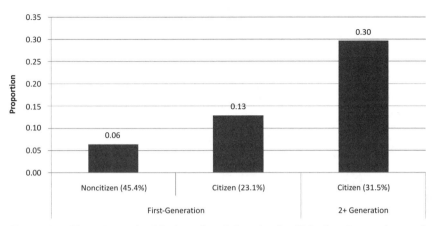

Figure 6.5. Have Been the Victim of a Crime in the U.S., by Generation and Citizenship
Question Wording: "Have you ever been the victim of a crime in this country? 1 = Yes, 2 = No, 3 = DK/RF."

social group comparisons between their immigrant cohorts who remained in their home country and social groups in the host country, which are largely defined in racial-ethnic and/or class groupings.

Following on this, we wondered whether respondents had ever been the victim of a crime. Overall, slightly less than one in seven Latinos responded that they had been. Although about 90 percent of first-generation respondents had not been a crime victim and about 8 percent had, among the second generation and beyond, almost 30 percent had (almost 70 percent had not), as shown in Figure 6.5. Interestingly, among the first-generation Latinos, twice as many naturalized citizens as noncitizens had been victims of crime. The generational differences are noteworthy, as there are developing patterns of how nativity status affects the experiences of Latinos in the LNS, as shown in Table 6.11 (see page 171).

With fewer than one-third of respondents reporting to have been crime victims, those who had been were asked, "Was the person who committed the crime Hispanic, white, black, or don't you know?" Among those who have been the victim of a crime in the United States (see Table 6.5), many reported that the perpetrator of the crime was Hispanic. Among the first generation, about 26 percent report that the perpetrator was Hispanic, with first-generation noncitizens being more likely to respond in this manner (32.53 percent first-generation noncitizen and 21.01 percent first-generation citizen). Among the second generation and beyond, about 22 percent reported that the perpetrator was Hispanic. The next

Table 6.5. *Race of Perpetrator, by Generation and Citizenship*
Category: Community, Crime/Discrimination

Response		First Generation			2+ Generation	
		Noncitizen	Citizen	Total	Citizen	Total
Black	Freq.	65	58	123	134	257
	Row%	52.85	47.15	47.86	52.14	100.00
	Col%	26.10	22.57	24.31	16.67	19.62
White	Freq.	48	47	95	146	241
	Row%	50.53	49.47	39.42	60.58	100.00
	Col%	19.28	18.29	18.77	18.16	18.40
Hispanic	Freq.	81	54	135	183	318
	Row%	60.00	40.00	42.45	57.55	100.00
	Col%	32.53	21.01	26.68	22.76	24.27
Other	Freq.	12	10	22	37	59
	Row%	54.55	45.45	37.29	62.71	100.00
	Col%	4.82	3.89	4.35	4.60	4.50
Don't know	Freq.	43	88	131	304	435
	Row%	32.82	67.18	30.11	69.89	100.00
	Col%	17.27	34.24	25.89	37.81	33.21
TOTAL	Freq.	249	257	506	804	1310
	Row%	49.21	50.79	38.63	61.37	100.00
	Col%	100.00	100.00	100.00	100.00	100.00

Note: First/2+ generation: (1 d.f.) 294.423 (P = 0.000). Citizen/noncitizen (first generation only): (1 d.f.) 212.246 (P = 0.000). Island-born Puerto Ricans are coded as first generation. Question wording: "Was the person who committed the crime Hispanic, white, black, or don't you know?"

most likely race of the perpetrator varies by generation. Among the first generation, about 24 percent said the perpetrator was black, whereas only about 16 percent of the second generation and beyond reported that the perpetrator was black. However, nearly equal percentages reported that the perpetrator was white (18.8 percent first generation versus 18.2 percent second generation and beyond). In addition, many respondents did not know the race of the perpetrator. About 25 percent of the first generation, primarily first-generation citizens, and about 37 percent of the second generation and beyond did not know the race of the perpetrator.

Another site where anecdotal evidence suggests that Latinos are vulnerable to mistreatment is on the job. Because a substantial number of Latinos in the LNS are first-generation residents of the United States, they are more likely to be in a situation where employers promise pay (in cash, on a daily or weekly basis). We asked whether they had "ever been paid less than you were promised, or not paid at all, for work you completed?" The vast majority of respondents were paid just what they were

Table 6.6. *Promised Pay, by Generation and Citizenship*
Category: Community, Crime/Discrimination

Response		First Generation			2+ Generation	
		Noncitizen	Citizen	Total	Citizen	Total
Paid less	Freq.	241	129	370	266	636
	Row%	65.14	34.86	58.18	41.82	100.00
	Col%	6.15	6.47	6.26	9.79	7.37
Not paid	Freq.	216	82	298	104	402
	Row%	72.48	27.52	74.13	25.87	100.00
	Col%	5.51	4.11	5.04	3.83	4.66
Both	Freq.	44	34	78	40	118
	Row%	56.41	43.59	66.10	33.90	100.00
	Col%	1.12	1.70	1.32	1.47	1.37
Neither	Freq.	3086	1576	4662	2112	6774
	Row%	66.19	33.81	68.82	31.18	100.00
	Col%	78.72	79.00	78.82	77.70	78.47
Don't know	Freq.	193	100	293	110	403
	Row%	65.87	34.13	72.70	27.30	100.00
	Col%	4.92	5.01	4.95	4.05	4.67
Refused or not	Freq.	140	74	214	86	300
applicable	Row%	46.67	24.67	71.33	28.67	100.00
	Col%	3.57	3.71	3.62	3.16	3.48
TOTAL	Freq.	3920	1995	5915	2718	8633
	Row%	66.27	33.73	68.52	31.48	100.00
	Col%	100.00	100.00	100.00	100.00	100.00

Note: First/2+ generation: (7 d.f.) 41.640 (P = 0.000). Citizen/noncitizen (first generation only): (7 d.f.) 75.140 (P = 0.000). Island-born Puerto Ricans are coded as first generation. Question wording: "Where you currently live, have you ever been paid less than you were promised, or not paid at all, for work you completed?"

promised: about 78 percent of first-generation respondents and about 77 percent of the second generation and beyond (see Table 6.6). There was a small percentage who had been not been paid (5.0 percent first generation versus 3.8 percent second generation and beyond) and who had been paid less or had not been paid (1.32 percent first generation versus 1.47 percent second generation and beyond). A slightly greater number of Latino respondents had been paid less than promised (6.26 percent first generation versus 9.79 percent second generation and beyond). But overall, more than 80 percent did not have such an experience.

We were also interested in the nature of the encounters between members of Latino communities and law enforcement personnel. Respondents were nearly evenly divided on whether the police in their community treated their racial-ethnic group fairly, with little difference based on

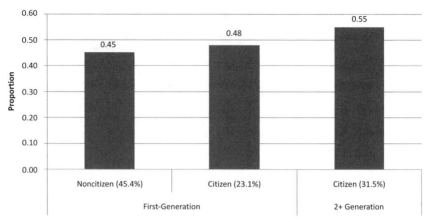

Figure 6.6. Racial-Ethnic Group Treated Unfairly by Police, by Generation and Citizenship

Question Wording: "Do you think the police in your community treat (answer to S4 = Latinos or Hispanics) fairly? 1 = Yes, 2 = No, 3 = Don't Know."

generation or citizenship status, as shown in Figure 6.6. Among the first generation, about 46 percent believe the police treated their racial-ethnic group fairly, whereas about 41 percent believe they do not. Similarly, among the second generation and beyond, roughly 55 percent responded that the police treat their racial-ethnic group fairly, whereas nearly 36 percent said they do not. Unfortunately, we are unable to determine whether these perceptions are based on actual contact with law enforcement or on perceptions from family members and/or friends.

Environmental Concerns and Exposure

Another form of inequality in American society involves differential exposure to toxic chemicals, waste, and the like. Often linked to struggles for environmental justice, the location of pollution in neighborhoods with low-income residents has become a hot-button issue in many cities. We asked respondents whether their neighborhood was affected by pollution, toxic waste, or landfills. Many respondents told us that their neighborhood was not affected by pollution, toxic, waste, or landfills (Table 6.7). Among the first generation, about 39 percent said their neighborhood was not affected at all, whereas about 30 percent of the second generation and beyond said the same. However, nearly similar percentages, across generations, said that their neighborhood was either not very affected or somewhat affected by pollution, toxic waste, or landfills. Among the

Table 6.7. *Impact on Neighborhood (Pollution, Toxic Waste, Landfills), by Generation and Citizenship*

Category: Community, Availability of Services

Response		First Generation			2+ Generation	
		Noncitizen	Citizen	Total	Citizen	Total
Impacted a lot	Freq.	145	100	245	150	395
	Row%	59.18	40.82	62.03	37.97	100.00
	Col%	7.49	10.10	8.37	11.07	9.22
Somewhat impacted	Freq.	408	187	595	327	922
	Row%	68.57	31.43	64.53	35.47	100.00
	Col%	21.06	18.89	20.33	24.13	21.53
Not very impacted	Freq.	501	245	746	414	1160
	Row%	67.16	32.84	64.31	35.69	100.00
	Col%	25.86	24.75	25.49	30.55	27.09
Not impacted at all	Freq.	757	413	1170	417	1587
	Row%	64.70	35.30	73.72	26.28	100.00
	Col%	39.08	41.72	39.97	30.77	37.06
Don't know	Freq.	126	45	171	47	218
	Row%	73.68	26.32	78.44	21.56	100.00
	Col%	6.50	4.55	5.84	3.47	5.09
TOTAL	Freq.	1937	990	2927	1355	4282
	Row%	66.18	33.82	68.36	31.64	100.00
	Col%	100.00	100.00	100.00	100.00	100.00

Note: First/2+ generation: (1 d.f.) 5.391 (P = 0.093). Citizen/noncitizen (first generation only): (1 d.f.) 3.895 (P = 0.144). Island-born Puerto Ricans are coded as first generation. Question wording: "Looking around at conditions in your neighborhood, how is your neighborhood today by pollution, toxic waste, landfills?"

first generation, about 25 percent said that their neighborhood was not very affected, whereas about 20 percent said it was somewhat affected. Among the second generation and beyond, about 30 percent said their neighborhood was not very affected, whereas about 24 percent said it was somewhat affected. More than 11 percent of the second generation and beyond said that their neighborhood was affected a lot by pollution, toxic waste, or landfills. Perhaps the residential overlap or distinctiveness between first- and second-generation Latinos could help clarify the extent to which residential location shapes the generational differences so that the second generation and beyond see themselves as more affected by the presence of environmental hazards.

Outside of our respondents' personal experiences, we were curious about their perception of the broader issues on this topic. We asked whether they agreed with the idea that minority neighborhoods are more

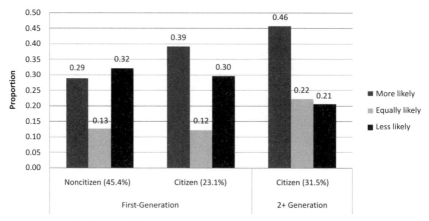

Figure 6.7. Likelihood of Pollution and Toxic Waste Being Located in Minority Neighborhoods, by Generation and Citizenship
Question Wording: "Do you believe that pollution, toxic waste etc. are less likely, more likely, or equally likely to be located in minority neighborhoods? 1 = More Likely, 2 = Equally Likely, 3 = Less Likely, 4 = DK/REF."

vulnerable to environmental waste and other pollutants than other neighborhoods. Respondents were fairly divided, as shown in Figure 6.7. Most believed that it is more likely, with about 32 percent of the first generation and about 45 percent of the second generation and beyond expressing this opinion.

However, an appreciable percentage thought that this was less likely, with about 31 percent of the first generation and about 20 percent of the second generation and beyond expressing skepticism toward the idea. Still, substantial percentages believe that pollution and toxic waste are equally likely to be located in minority neighborhoods as anywhere else, with about 12 percent of the first generation and about 22 percent of the second generation and beyond expressing this belief. Further dividing the responses, about 28 percent of the first generation and about 11 percent of the second generation and beyond said that they don't know the answer to this question. Again, the "do not know or no response" category is more common among the first generation. For respondents, length of residence in the United States and/or amount of time in their current place of residence could presumably be a contributing factor. In addition, the first generation could be evaluating the environmental quality of their life in the United States with the conditions of their residence in their country of origin. Although our presentation of important relationships has centered on dimensions of nativity, citizenship, generational status, and the like,

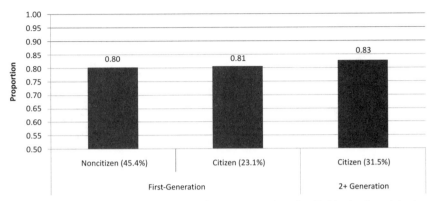

Figure 6.8. Government Services in Community Are Available in Spanish, by Generation and Citizenship

Question Wording: "Are the following government services available in Spanish in your community? Answer yes or no for each type of service. Social services including public health clinics or hospitals $1 = $ Yes, $2 = $ No, $3 = $ DK, $4 = $ REF/NA."

our findings illustrate the complexity of understanding and sorting the experiences and demographics of Latinos and their interface with the political system. There are statistically significant differences between the generations of Latinos with the measure of inter-group relations.

Governmental Service Availability and Latinos

One key to navigating life in the United States, especially for first-generation immigrants, is the availability of information and aid in their native language. Many respondents indicated that they primarily spoke Spanish and/or had limited English-language proficiency. We wanted to get a sense of the availability of information and services to Latinos in Spanish, and so we asked respondents whether governmental services in their area were provided in Spanish and in English. The majority said that police or law enforcement, as well as courts and legal representation, are available in Spanish in their community. Among the first generation, about 67 percent of respondents said these services are, in fact, available in Spanish, whereas about 77 percent of the second generation and beyond said the same, as indicated in Figures 6.8 and 6.9. There are, however, relatively large percentages of respondents who did not know whether these services were available in Spanish (12.5 percent of the first generation and 10.2 percent of the second generation and

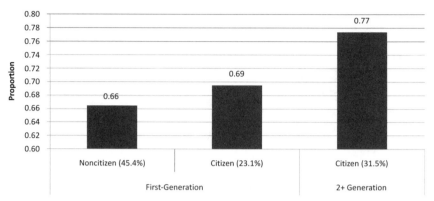

Figure 6.9. Police, Courts, and Legal Services in Community Are Available in Spanish, by Generation and Citizenship

Question Wording: "Are the following government services available in Spanish in your community? Answer yes or no for each type of service. Social services including public health clinics or hospitals 1 = Yes, 2 = No, 3 = DK, 4 = REF/NA."

beyond). The percentages were highest among first-generation nonciti-zens. Additional analyses might explore the length of time in the United States and need for such services, as well the respondents' legal and political status and these effects of relationship with governmental agen-cies. The extant research on political incorporation (Jones-Correa 2005) indicates that with longer periods of time living in the United States, immigrants become more familiar with U.S. socioeconomic and polit-ical institutions. This gained knowledge informs them as to availabil-ity of services and the fact that they have access to such services. In addition, other considerations may be fear or apprehension among some first-generation Latino immigrants about their visibility to governmental agencies or a sense that it is their own responsibility to meet their own needs.

Most respondents also said that information from public schools is available in Spanish in their community. Again, a not-insubstantial per-centage said they did not know whether the information was available in Spanish (9.13 percent of the first generation and 7.61 percent of the second generation and beyond; Table 6.8). Among the first generation, about 77 percent said the services are available in Spanish, whereas about 82 percent of the second generation and beyond said the same. It is worth noting that the percentage of Latino students in respondents' school districts could be a factor affecting whether Spanish services are available

Table 6.8. *Information from Public Schools in Spanish, by Generation and Citizenship*

Category: Community, Availability of Services

| Response | | First Generation | | | 2+ Generation | |
		Noncitizen	Citizen	Total	Citizen	Total
Yes	Freq.	3013	1578	4591	2241	6832
	Row%	65.63	34.37	67.20	32.80	100.00
	Col%	76.86	79.10	77.62	82.42	79.13
No	Freq.	519	199	718	226	944
	Row%	72.28	27.72	76.06	23.94	100.00
	Col%	13.24	9.97	12.14	8.31	10.93
Don't know	Freq.	349	191	540	207	747
	Row%	64.63	35.37	72.29	27.71	100.00
	Col%	8.90	9.57	9.13	7.61	8.65
Ref/NA	Freq.	39	27	66	45	111
	Row%	59.09	40.91	59.46	40.54	100.00
	Col%	0.99	1.35	1.12	1.66	1.29
TOTAL	Freq.	3920	1995	5915	2719	8634
	Row%	66.27	33.73	68.51	31.49	100.00
	Col%	100.00	100.00	100.00	100.00	100.00

Note: First/2+ generation: (3 d.f.) 4.720 (P = 0.040). Citizen/noncitizen (first generation only): (3 d.f.) 2.790 (P = 0.039). Island-born Puerto Ricans are coded as first generation. Question wording: "Are the following government services available in Spanish in your community? Information from public schools."

in that venue. It is not possible for us to discern whether immigration status (e.g., undocumented, permanent resident alien) affects persons' knowledge of governmental services. Although in the survey instrument we asked whether there were any children still living in respondents' country of origin, the question about governmental services refers to their experiences in their current community.

Intergroup Relations between Latinos and Other Groups in the United States

Living in the United States often places Latinos in contact with other racial-ethnic and socioeconomic groups. Although it is difficult to generalize about how Latinos as a whole feel about those other groups, it is important to see how their knowledge of these groups, both through contact and experiences with them and through information exchanges with other Latinos and the media, shapes their perceptions about them.

Table 6.9. *Latinos and African Americans Doing Well, by Generation and Citizenship*

Category: Community, Interethnic Relations

Response		First Generation			2+ Generation	
		Noncitizen	Citizen	Total	Citizen	Total
A lot	Freq.	1665	741	2406	602	3008
	Row%	69.20	30.80	79.99	20.01	100.00
	Col%	42.47	37.12	40.67	22.15	34.84
Some	Freq.	977	576	1553	831	2384
	Row%	62.91	37.09	65.14	34.86	100.00
	Col%	24.92	28.86	26.25	30.57	27.61
Little	Freq.	749	322	1071	606	1677
	Row%	69.93	30.07	63.86	36.14	100.00
	Col%	19.11	16.13	18.10	22.30	19.42
Nothing	Freq.	529	357	886	679	1565
	Row%	59.71	40.29	56.61	43.39	100.00
	Col%	13.49	17.89	14.98	24.98	18.13
TOTAL	Freq.	3920	1996	5916	2718	8634
	Row%	66.26	33.74	68.52	31.48	100.00
	Col%	100.00	100.00	100.00	100.00	100.00

Note: First/2+ generation: (1 d.f.) 99.987 (P = 0.000). Citizen/noncitizen (first generation only): (1 d.f.) 14.469 (P = 0.008). Island-born Puerto Ricans are coded as first generation. Question wording: "How much does Latinos' 'doing well' depend on African Americans also doing well?"

In the LNS, respondents were asked to describe their sense of three different racial-ethnic groups: Anglos (whites), African Americans, and Asian Americans.

We begin with African Americans and the question of whether respondents believe that their ability to succeed was tied to how well African Americans were doing, in economic terms. Many respondents, particularly in the first generation, responded that Latinos' doing well depends on African Americans doing well, with about 40 percent of the first generation and about 22 percent of the second generation and beyond expressing this belief, as shown in Table 6.9. An appreciable percentage believe that Latinos' doing well somewhat depends on African Americans doing well, with about 26 percent of the first generation expressing this belief and about 30 percent of the second generation and beyond in agreement. The remaining respondents are fairly evenly divided between those who believe that Latinos doing well depends little or not at all on African Americans doing well. It is worth noting that there is a statistically significant relationship between Latino generations on the issue of linked fate, as it is viewed more strongly among first-generation Latinos, especially noncitizens. The extant research literature would have predicted that second generation and beyond respondents would see themselves as an American minority and more like another minority group – African Americans. If Latino immigrants see themselves as more marginalized in American society, then their working knowledge of how race works in the United States might make a a connection that race and ethnicity can affect their "life chances" thus seeing a linked fate with African Americans.

This result compels researchers and activists to examine further the bases for common links between Latino immigrants and African Americans. Differential treatment and occupying a "subordinate" status may be some reasons for perceived linkages. At the same time, it is clear that this initial finding leads to greater scrutiny of the popular characterization in the mass media of tense "black-brown" relations. Their interactions may not be so dichotomous, and variation could be affected by their geographical context.

Our latest findings about some noticeable sense of "linked fate" between Latinos and African Americans moves our examination in the area of their socioeconomic status and that of African Americans. The next question posed was, "Thinking about issues like job opportunities, educational attainment, or income, how much do Latinos have in common with other racial groups in the United States today? Would you say Latinos have a lot in common, some in common, little in common, or nothing with African Americans?"

Although the first generation perceived a greater degree of linked fate with African Americans, when it comes to seeing similarities between the challenges facing the two groups, the sense of common fate and intertwined destiny does not translate to a view that the two groups face similar problems. Here, the members of the second generation perceive a close relationship between the two groups on the issues of education, jobs, and earnings. Overall, most respondents believe that Latinos have just some issues in common with African Americans in the United States (29.5 percent of the first generation versus 40.7 percent of the second generation and beyond; see Table 6.10). However, there are also relatively large percentages who believed that Latinos have a lot in common with African Americans, including about 17 percent of the first generation and about 28 percent of the second generation and beyond. Still, a notable percentage believe that Latinos have little in common with African Americans, most notably in the first generation – 24 percent of the first generation and about 18 percent of the second generation. A larger percentage (17.4 percent) of the first generation believe that Latinos have nothing in

Table 6.10. *What Latinos Have in Common with African Americans, by Generation and Citizenship*

Category: Community, Interethnic Relations

Response		First Generation			2+ Generation	
		Noncitizen	Citizen	Total	Citizen	Total
A lot	Freq.	618	400	1018	769	1787
	Row%	60.71	39.29	56.97	43.03	100.00
	Col%	15.77	20.05	17.21	28.28	20.70
Some	Freq.	1093	653	1746	1106	2852
	Row%	62.60	37.40	61.22	38.78	100.00
	Col%	27.88	32.73	29.52	40.68	33.03
Little	Freq.	943	471	1414	487	1901
	Row%	66.69	33.31	74.38	25.62	100.00
	Col%	24.06	23.61	23.91	17.91	22.02
Nothing	Freq.	749	281	1030	211	1241
	Row%	72.72	27.28	83.00	17.00	100.00
	Col%	19.11	14.09	17.41	7.76	14.37
Don't know or	Freq.	517	190	707	146	853
not applicable	Row%	73.13	26.87	82.88	17.12	100.00
	Col%	13.19	9.52	11.95	5.37	9.88
TOTAL	Freq.	3920	1995	5915	2719	8634
	Row%	66.27	33.73	68.51	31.49	100.00
	Col%	100.00	100.00	100.00	100.00	100.00

Note: First/2+ generation: (1 d.f.) 80.520 (P = 0.000). Citizen/noncitizen (first generation only): (1 d.f.) 47.244 (P = 0.000). Island-born Puerto Ricans are coded as first generation. Question wording: "Thinking about issues like job opportunities, educational attainment, or income, how much do Latinos have in common with other racial groups in the United States today? Would you say Latinos have a lot in common, some in common, little in common, or nothing?"

common with African Americans. The generational differences are statistically significant, as the second generation and beyond is more likely to see commonalities with African Americans on the issues of education, jobs, and earnings.

Further nuance can be added to our understanding of the relationship between Latinos and African Americans by attending to Latinos' perception of how much the two groups have in common when it comes to government services, employment, political power, and representation. The results are telling. As with the previous question, those in the second generation were more likely to consider the two groups in a similar boat, which can be seen in Table 6.11. It is worth pointing out, though, that less than one-half feel that the two groups have something

Table 6.11. *Political Issues in Common with African Americans, by Generation and Citizenship*

Category: Community, Interethnic Relations

Response		First Generation			2+ Generation	
		Noncitizen	Citizen	Total	Citizen	Total
A lot	Freq.	544	366	910	617	1527
	Row%	59.78	40.22	59.59	40.41	100.00
	Col%	13.88	18.34	15.38	22.70	17.69
Some	Freq.	1011	640	1651	1106	2757
	Row%	61.24	38.76	59.88	40.12	100.00
	Col%	25.79	32.06	27.91	40.69	31.93
Little	Freq.	1107	541	1648	627	2275
	Row%	67.17	32.83	72.44	27.56	100.00
	Col%	28.24	27.10	27.86	23.07	26.35
Nothing	Freq.	678	254	932	210	1142
	Row%	72.75	27.25	81.61	18.39	100.00
	Col%	17.30	12.73	15.75	7.73	13.23
Don't know or	Freq.	580	195	775	158	933
not applicable	Row%	74.84	25.16	83.07	16.93	100.00
	Col%	14.80	9.77	13.10	5.81	10.81
TOTAL	Freq.	3920	1996	5916	2718	8634
	Row%	66.26	33.74	68.52	31.48	100.00
	Col%	100.00	100.00	100.00	100.00	100.00

Note: First/2+ generation: (1 d.f.) 21.309 (P = 0.000). Citizen/noncitizen (first generation only): (1 d.f.) 23.623 (P = 0.000). Island-born Puerto Ricans are coded as first generation. Question wording: "Now I'd like you to think about the political situation of Latinos in society. Thinking about things like government services and employment, political power and representation, how much do Latinos have in common with African Americans?"

in common – but that picture changes dramatically when separated by generation. Most told us that Latinos have some or little in common with African Americans, with more than 25 percent of noncitizens, about 32 percent of first-generation citizens, and more than 40 percent of the second generation and beyond believing that Latinos have some political interests in common with African Americans. Twenty-eight percent of first-generation citizens and noncitizens and about 23 percent of the second generation and beyond responded that Latinos had little in common with African Americans. But significant percentages are more strongly divided, believing that Latinos have either a lot or nothing in common with African Americans. Almost 14 percent of noncitizens, more than 18 percent of first-generation citizens, and more than 22 percent of the second generation and beyond believe that Latinos do have a lot in common with African Americans. However, more than 17 percent of noncitizens, almost 13 percent of first-generation citizens, and nearly 8 percent of the second generation and beyond think that Latinos have nothing in common with African Americans. Again, many of the first generation (13.10 percent) indicated a "don't know." This particular item reveals statistically significant differences based both on generational status and on citizenship.

What about Latinos' perceptions of Anglos? When asked about issues they might have in common with white Americans, like job opportunities, educational attainment, or income, respondents were divided. The differences across generations were statistically significant, as the second generation and beyond was more likely to see commonalities with whites on these issues than their immigrant counterparts. About 38 percent of the second generation and beyond said that Latinos have some levels of commonalities with whites, whereas about 27 percent of the first generation did so. About 28 percent of the first generation believes that Latinos have little in common with whites, and about 29 percent of the second generation and beyond expressed this belief, as shown in Table 6.12.

But notable percentages of Latinos also occupy stronger, opposing positions. Roughly, 16 percent of the first-generation Latinos believed that Latinos have a lot in common with whites, whereas about 17 percent of the first generation believes that Latinos have nothing in common with whites. Similarly, among the second generation and beyond, about 14 percent believe that Latinos have a lot in common with whites, but about 13 percent believe that they have nothing in common with whites. It is worth noting that a sizable 10 percent of the first generation responded "do not know." Although there is a significant difference in the percentage of respondents who saw commonalities between the situation of whites and Latinos, there is little difference between those who indicated little or no such commonality. Again, the differences across generations are statistically significant, as the second generation and beyond is more likely to see commonalities with whites on these issues than are their immigrant counterparts.

When it comes to political issues, the responses were fairly similar across the generations. Most believe that Latinos have either some or little in common with whites. More than 25 percent of noncitizens, nearly 30 percent of first-generation citizens, and more than 30 percent of the second generation and beyond think that Latinos have some commonalities with whites (Table 6.13). Similarly, nearly 30 percent of noncitizens

Table 6.12. *What Latinos Have in Common with Whites, by Generation and Citizenship*

Category: Community, Interethnic Relations

Response		First Generation			2+ Generation	
		Noncitizen	Citizen	Total	Citizen	Total
A lot	Freq.	644	341	985	397	1382
	Row%	65.38	34.62	71.27	28.73	100.00
	Col%	16.42	17.08	16.65	14.60	16.00
Some	Freq.	989	609	1598	1039	2637
	Row%	61.89	38.11	60.60	39.40	100.00
	Col%	25.22	30.51	27.01	38.21	30.53
Little	Freq.	1137	558	1695	804	2499
	Row%	67.08	32.92	67.83	32.17	100.00
	Col%	29.00	27.96	28.65	29.57	28.94
Nothing	Freq.	702	314	1016	356	1372
	Row%	69.09	30.91	74.05	25.95	100.00
	Col%	17.90	15.73	17.17	13.09	15.89
Don't know or	Freq.	449	174	623	123	746
not applicable	Row%	72.07	27.93	83.51	16.49	100.00
	Col%	11.45	8.72	10.53	4.52	8.64
TOTAL	Freq.	3921	1996	5917	2719	8636
	Row%	66.27	33.73	68.52	31.48	100.00
	Col%	100.00	100.00	100.00	100.00	100.00

Note: First/2+ generation: (4 d.f.) 58.609 (P = 0.000). Citizen/noncitizen (first generation only): (4 d.f.) 13.869 (P = 0.094). Island-born Puerto Ricans are coded as first generation. Question wording: "Thinking about issues like job opportunities, educational attainment, or income, how much do Latinos have in common with other racial groups in the United States today? With Whites?"

and first-generation citizens, as well as about 35 percent of the second generation and beyond, believe that Latinos have little in common with whites.

There are fairly notable divides by generation and citizenship status among those with strong opinions, with more than 13 percent of noncitizens, more than 15 percent of first-generation citizens, and more than 12 percent of the second generation and beyond believing that Latinos have a lot in common with whites. In contrast, about 18 percent of noncitizens, more than 15 percent of first-generation citizens, and more than 16 percent of the second generation and beyond believe that Latinos have nothing in common with whites. In addition, about 12 percent of the first generation responded "don't know." Again, these were statistically significant differences based on both generational status and citizenship.

Table 6.13. *Political Issues in Common with Whites, by Generation and Citizenship*

Category: Community, Interethnic Relations

Response		First Generation			2+ Generation	
		Noncitizen	Citizen	Total	Citizen	Total
A lot	Freq.	529	310	839	338	1177
	Row%	63.05	36.95	71.28	28.72	100.00
	Col%	13.49	15.54	14.18	12.44	13.63
Some	Freq.	1003	589	1592	841	2433
	Row%	63.00	37.00	65.43	34.57	100.00
	Col%	25.59	29.52	26.91	30.94	28.18
Little	Freq.	1167	584	1751	959	2710
	Row%	66.65	33.35	64.61	35.39	100.00
	Col%	29.77	29.27	29.60	35.28	31.39
Nothing	Freq.	709	309	1018	451	1469
	Row%	69.65	30.35	69.30	30.70	100.00
	Col%	18.09	15.49	17.21	16.59	17.02
Don't know or	Freq.	512	203	715	129	844
not applicable	Row%	71.61	28.39	84.72	15.28	100.00
	Col%	13.06	10.18	12.09	4.75	9.78
TOTAL	Freq.	3920	1995	5915	2718	8633
	Row%	66.27	33.73	68.52	31.48	100.00
	Col%	100.00	100.00	100.00	100.00	100.00

Note: First/2+ generation: (5 d.f.) 7.440 (P = 0.000). Citizen/noncitizen (first generation only): (5 d.f.) 2.290 (P = 0.043). Island-born Puerto Ricans are coded as first generation. Question wording: "Thinking about things like government services and employment, political power and representation, how much do Latinos have in common with Whites?"

The first-generation citizens more so than noncitizens, and the second generation and beyond more so than the first generation, were likely to feel some political commonalities with whites.

Let us turn to a final comparison: Asian Americans. Respondents were asked, "Thinking about issues like job opportunities, educational attainment, or income, how much do Latinos have in common with other racial groups in the United States today? With Asians?" It should be noted that LNS respondents only in California, Texas, New York, and Illinois were asked about Asian Americans.

As with the other groups we asked about, respondents across generations were divided on whether Latinos have something in common with Asian Americans on these issues. Many believe that Latinos have nothing in common with Asian Americans, including about 30 percent of the first generation and about 22 percent of the second generation and beyond,

Table 6.14. *What Latinos Have in Common with Asians, by Generation and Citizenship*

Category: Community, Interethnic Relations

Response		First Generation			2+ Generation	
		Noncitizen	Citizen	Total	Citizen	Total
A lot	Freq.	163	100	263	161	424
	Row%	61.98	38.02	62.03	37.97	100.00
	Col%	10.02	10.68	10.27	11.14	10.58
Some	Freq.	267	198	465	418	883
	Row%	57.42	42.58	52.66	47.34	100.00
	Col%	16.42	21.15	18.15	28.93	22.04
Little	Freq.	386	240	626	423	1049
	Row%	61.66	38.34	59.68	40.32	100.00
	Col%	23.74	25.64	24.43	29.27	26.18
Nothing	Freq.	514	279	793	320	1113
	Row%	64.82	35.18	71.25	28.75	100.00
	Col%	31.61	29.81	30.95	22.15	27.78
Don't know or	Freq.	296	119	415	123	538
not applicable	Row%	71.33	28.67	77.14	22.86	100.00
	Col%	18.20	12.71	16.20	8.51	13.43
TOTAL	Freq.	1626	936	2562	1445	4007
	Row%	63.47	36.53	63.94	36.06	100.00
	Col%	100.00	100.00	100.00	100.00	100.00

Note: First/2+ generation: (1 d.f.) 2.579 (P = 0.170). Citizen/noncitizen (first generation only): (1 d.f.) 0.121 (P = 0.766). Island-born Puerto Ricans are coded as first generation. Question wording: "Thinking about issues like job opportunities, educational attainment, or income, how much do Latinos have in common with other racial groups in the United States today? With Asians?"

as documented in Table 6.14. Similar numbers believe that Latinos have little in common with Asians, with about 24 percent of the first generation and about 29 percent of the second generation and beyond expressing this belief. There are also noteworthy percentages of respondents who believe that Latinos have some level of commonality with Asians (18.15 percent of the first generation and 28.93 percent of the second generation and beyond) and that Latinos have a lot in common with Asians (10.27 percent of the first generation and 11.14 percent of the second generation and beyond). Further, fairly large percentages of respondents reported "do not know" on how much Latinos have in common with Asians (16.2 percent of the first generation and 8.5 percent of the second generation and beyond). Again, the generational differences are statistically significant, as the tendency to view commonalities on these issues was more prevalent among Latinos in the second generation and beyond. Even with the potential for contact among the LNS Latino respondents in the states in which there would be more Asian Americans, there appears to be limited familiarity with this community. One follow-up would be to compare LNS respondents in California with the rest of the LNS respondents, as numerically more Asian Americans live in that state than any other. In addition, because some geographic markers are available in the LNS, it would be possible to isolate Latinos in Los Angeles, New York City, and San Francisco to determine whether these integrated communities might increase perception about commonalities with the Asian American community. Clearly, among examinations of intergroup relations between Latinos and other groups, that between Latinos and Asian Americans is the most understudied.

When it comes to the similarity of political interests between Asian Americans and Latinos, the division among respondents is somewhat different from that for African Americans and whites. There is a tendency is to see fewer political commonalities with Asian Americans than with the other two groups. Although more than 20 percent of noncitizens, more than 23 percent of first-generation citizens, and more than 25 percent of the second generation and beyond believe that Latinos have some political interests in common with Asian Americans. Relatively small percentages believe that Latinos have a lot in common with Asian Americans, as is shown in Table 6.15. Similarly, nearly 22 percent of noncitizens, more than 26 percent of first-generation citizens, and almost 33 percent of the second generation and beyond believe that Latinos have little in common with Asian Americans. In addition, more than 30 percent of noncitizens, nearly 29 percent of first-generation citizens, and almost 22 percent of the second generation and beyond believe that Latinos have nothing in common with Asian Americans. Interestingly, large percentages responded that they don't know, with more than 19 percent of noncitizens, more than 12 percent of first-generation citizens, and nearly 10 percent of the second generation and beyond giving this response. The higher percentage of "don't know" responses among the first generation could be a function of limited contact with Asian Americans either in residential neighborhoods and/or as coworkers.

Do Latinos Feel Competition with African Americans?
There has been considerable discussion over the past decade of a sense of struggle or competition between Latinos and African Americans for jobs and political power. Our respondents were nearly evenly divided in

Table 6.15. *Political Issues in Common with Asian Americans, by Generation and Citizenship*

Category: Community, Interethnic Relations

Response		First Generation			2+ Generation	
		Noncitizen	Citizen	Total	Citizen	Total
A lot	Freq.	130	88	218	152	370
	Row%	59.63	40.37	58.92	41.08	100.00
	Col%	8.00	9.39	8.51	10.52	9.23
Some	Freq.	332	218	550	367	917
	Row%	60.36	39.64	59.98	40.02	100.00
	Col%	20.43	23.27	21.47	25.40	22.88
Little	Freq.	357	246	603	474	1077
	Row%	59.20	40.80	55.99	44.01	100.00
	Col%	21.97	26.25	23.54	32.80	26.88
Nothing	Freq.	496	269	765	317	1082
	Row%	64.84	35.16	70.70	29.30	100.00
	Col%	30.52	28.71	29.86	21.94	27.00
Don't know or	Freq.	310	116	426	135	561
not applicable	Row%	72.77	27.23	75.94	24.06	100.00
	Col%	19.08	12.38	16.63	9.34	14.00
TOTAL	Freq.	1625	937	2562	1445	4007
	Row%	63.43	36.57	63.94	36.06	100.00
	Col%	100.00	100.00	100.00	100.00	100.00

Note: First/2+ generation: (1 d.f.) 45.595 (P = 0.000). Citizen/noncitizen (first generation only): (1 d.f.) 3.464 (P = 0.187). Island-born Puerto Ricans are coded as first generation. Question wording: "Thinking about things like government services and employment, political power and representation, how much do Latinos have in common with Asian Americans?"

their beliefs on whether Latinos compete for jobs with African Americans, regardless of generation or citizenship status.

Among the first generation, about 33 percent believe that Latinos are in strong competition with African Americans, whereas about 32 percent of the second generation expressed this belief. Among the first generation, about 25 percent of respondents believe that Latinos have weak competition with African Americans, whereas about 30 percent of the second generation and beyond agreed with this. Many respondents believe that Latinos have no competition at all with African Americans in getting jobs, with about 40 percent of the first generation and about 37 percent of the second generation and beyond expressing this belief. Our findings, documented in Figure 6.9, suggest that there is no uniform consensus as to whether Latinos believe that they compete with African Americans for access to jobs.

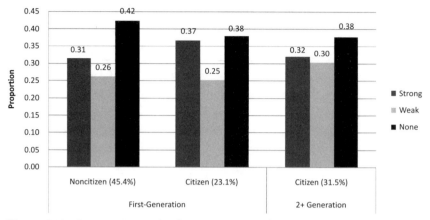

Figure 6.10. Competition with African Americans for City and State Government Jobs, by Generation and Citizenship

Question Wording: "Some have suggested that [Answer to B4] are in competition with other Latinos. After each of the next items, would you tell me if you believe there is strong competition, weak competition, or no competition at all with other Latinos... In getting jobs? 3 = Strong competition, 2 = Weak competition, 1 = No competition."

A principal area for potential competition in employment is access to jobs in city or state government. In the research literature on political incorporation, gains in local minority political representation and greater access is viewed as translating into governmental jobs (Eisinger 1983). A majority of respondents believe that Latinos are not in competition with African Americans getting government jobs. Among the first generation, almost 55 percent expressed this belief, whereas about 42 percent of the second generation and beyond agreed. The remaining respondents were evenly divided as to whether there is some competition or strong competition with African Americans in getting jobs, as shown in Figure 6.10.

When it comes to the question of having access to education and quality schools, nearly a majority of respondents believe that Latinos are not in competition at all with African Americans for access to education and quality schools, with about 48 percent of the first generation and about 41 percent of the second generation and beyond expressing this belief. The remaining respondents were evenly divided between believing that there was weak and strong competition with African Americans for access to education and quality schools (Figure 6.11). This finding may confirm the racial-ethnic resegregation of schools (Orfield 2007), in which school-age populations have been isolated by race and ethnicity.

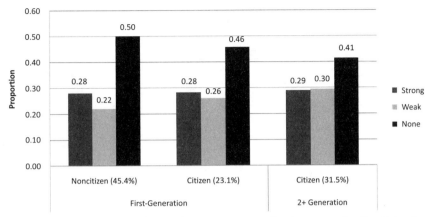

Figure 6.11. Competition with African Americans for Access to Quality Schools, by Generation and Citizenship
Question Wording: "Some have suggested that [Answer to B4] are in competition with other Latinos. After each of the next items, would you tell me if you believe there is strong competition, weak competition, or no competition at all with other Latinos...Having access to education and quality schools? 3 = Strong competition, 2 = Weak competition, 1 = No competition."

If Latino students attend Latino schools and African American students attend African American schools, then they are not likely to be in competition, except for schools that attract students districtwide, such as magnet schools.

Another area of potential competition with African Americans is in electing representatives of the same racial-ethnic group. Given the continued population growth of Latinos throughout the United States, there are more communities in which Latinos constitute a critical mass (that is, percentages that range from 15%–30%), in areas with established African American communities. In Figure 6.12, the respondents are divided on the question of whether Latinos are in competition with African Americans over racial-ethnic subgroup representatives in elected office. More than 36 percent of noncitizens, 39 percent of first-generation citizens, and more than 33 percent of the second generation and beyond believe that Latinos have strong competition from African Americans for racial-ethnic subgroup representatives in elected office, as recorded in Table 6.16. These levels are higher than the other areas of jobs and education.

In contrast, nearly 37 percent of noncitizens, more than 31 percent of first-generation citizens, and about 32 percent of the second generation and beyond believe that there is no competition at all. Falling in

Table 6.16. *Competition with African Americans on Ethnic Subgroup Representatives in Elected Office, by Generation and Citizenship*
Category: Community, Interethnic Relations

Response		First Generation			2+ Generation	
		Noncitizen	Citizen	Total	Citizen	Total
Strong competition	Freq.	1414	778	2192	899	3091
	Row%	64.51	35.49	70.92	29.08	100.00
	Col%	36.07	39.00	37.06	33.08	35.80
Weak competition	Freq.	1068	584	1652	947	2599
	Row%	64.65	35.35	63.56	36.44	100.00
	Col%	27.24	29.27	27.93	34.84	30.11
No competition	Freq.	1438	633	2071	872	2943
at all	Row%	69.44	30.56	70.37	29.63	100.00
	Col%	36.68	31.73	35.01	32.08	34.09
TOTAL	Freq.	3920	1995	5915	2718	8633
	Row%	66.27	33.73	68.52	31.48	100.00
	Col%	100.00	100.00	100.00	100.00	100.00

Note: First/2+ generation: (3 d.f.) 310.374 (P = 0.000). Citizen/noncitizen (first generation only): (3 d.f.) 60.358 (P = 0.000). Island-born Puerto Ricans are coded as first generation. Question wording: "Some people have suggested that Latinos or Hispanics are in competition with African Americans. After each of the next items, would you tell me if you believe there is strong competition, weak competition, or no competition at all with African Americans?"

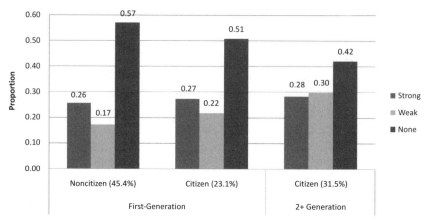

Figure 6.12. Competition with African Americans for Access to Quality Schools, by Generation and Citizenship
Question Wording: "Some have suggested that [Answer to B4] are in competition with other Latinos. After each of the next items, would you tell me if you believe there is strong competition, weak competition, or no competition at all with other Latinos...In getting jobs? 3 = Strong competition 2 = Weak competition 1 = No competition."

the middle are more than 27 percent of noncitizens, nearly 30 percent of first-generation citizens, and almost 35 percent of the second generation and beyond, who believe that there is weak competition with African Americans. These results might suggest a bifurcated view in the Latino community on the degree of electoral competition. The racial-ethnic composition of the communities in which Latino respondents reside could help explain these views.

Do Latinos Feel Welcomed in the United States?

In the LNS, more than three-fifths of respondents are foreign born. In Chapter 12, we discuss how the salience of immigration and current policies cut across nativity and generational status. Here, we seek to find the crux of intergroup relations: Latinos' perception of Americans' "general attitude as welcoming Latino immigrants or not."

The majority of respondents told us that the public in their state is either welcoming or somewhat welcoming toward Latino immigrants. The overall finding is that the second generation and beyond feels less welcomed than the first, and a majority of the second generation and beyond do not find Americans welcoming. Among the first generation, about 41 percent believe the public is welcoming toward Latino immigrants, whereas about 34 percent believe the public is somewhat unwelcoming. Among the second generation and beyond, about 31 percent believe the public is welcoming toward Latino immigrants, whereas about 41 percent believe the public is somewhat unwelcoming (Table 6.17).

Slightly more than one-half (54.0 percent) of first-generation Latinos and 42.6 percent of the second generation and beyond felt that the public was very welcoming of immigrants. In contrast, a sizable percentage believed that the public is very unwelcoming toward Latino immigrants (41.6 percent of the first generation and 52.4 percent of the second generation and beyond). These results indicate a statistically significant difference across generational status. That is, first-generation Latinos view the larger American society as more receptive toward Latino immigrants than does the second generation and beyond.

Conclusion

The results of our examination of LNS respondents' views about their life chances, experiences with discriminatory treatment, and intergroup relations produced some notable findings. Our survey responses by nativity

Table 6.17. *General Attitude of Public in Welcoming Latino Immigrants, by Generation and Citizenship*

Category: Community, Interethnic Relations

Response		First Generation			2+ Generation	
		Noncitizen	Citizen	Total	Citizen	Total
Very welcoming	Freq.	154	52	206	55	261
	Row%	74.76	25.24	78.93	21.07	100.00
	Col%	11.95	13.30	12.26	11.00	11.97
Welcoming	Freq.	537	163	700	158	858
	Row%	76.71	23.29	81.59	18.41	100.00
	Col%	41.66	41.69	41.67	31.60	39.36
Somewhat	Freq.	442	131	573	205	778
unwelcoming	Row%	77.14	22.86	73.65	26.35	100.00
	Col%	34.29	33.50	34.11	41.00	35.69
Very	Freq.	94	29	123	57	180
unwelcoming	Row%	76.42	23.58	68.33	31.67	100.00
	Col%	7.29	7.42	7.32	11.40	8.26
Don't know or	Freq.	62	16	78	25	103
no response	Row%	79.49	20.51	75.73	24.27	100.00
	Col%	4.81	4.09	4.64	5.00	4.72
TOTAL	Freq.	1289	391	1680	500	2180
	Row%	76.73	23.27	77.06	22.94	100.00
	Col%	100.00	100.00	100.00	100.00	100.00

Note: First/2+ generation: (3 d.f.) 90.789 (P = 0.000). Citizen/noncitizen (first generation only): (3 d.f.) 25.201 (P = 0.007). Island-born Puerto Ricans are coded as first generation. Question wording: "In general, how would you assess the general attitude of the public in your state towards Latino immigrants? Would you say it has been very welcoming, welcoming, somewhat unwelcoming, or very unwelcoming?"

and citizenship status proved meaningful. Clearly, the adjustment process for the foreign born requires gaining greater familiarity with the customs, language, and institutions of American society. Part of that process involves anchoring oneself in group identification terms – an immigrant, a Latino, by national origin, or by a variety of other possibilities. In addition, the act of becoming a naturalized citizen is a behavior that indicates attachment to the United States. The first battery of items dealt with Latinos' perception about the opportunity structure in America. Whether respondents evaluate the opportunity structure by relating as Latinos or as poor people, they have positive expectations. More than three-fourths of LNS respondents see opportunities for either category. This view of a positive opportunity structure is slightly higher when referencing all Latinos as oppose to the generl category of poor people. There are very slight differences based on nativity, with the first generation holding higher positive views.

Latinos' experiences with discriminatory treatment are affected by the context of such experiences, which varies by their situation (e.g., workplace, housing). The extent of actual discriminatory treatment is not pervasive, but we find that it occurs in all the situations described. In most cases, these negative experiences were more likely to be found among the second generation and beyond. This was more the case in dealing with law enforcement and courts, as well as restaurants. When asked about the reasons for such treatment, respondents most often attributed it to being Latino and an immigrant. Perceptions of mistreatment for being Latino were similar across generations and citizen status. Yet among the first generation, frequent causes cited for mistreatment were a persistent accent and being an immigrant. Among the second generation and beyond, the mention of skin color was noted almost two and a half times more often than among the first generation. Finally, when asked who the perpetrator was causing such treatment, the second generation and beyond was more likely than the first generation to indicate whites or Anglos. In contrast, the first generation was nearly twice as likely as the second generation and beyond to mention other Latinos. In addition, the first generation was more likely to indicate African Americans.

Another set of questions dealt with Latinos' knowledge of the availability of services in Spanish and English. The areas included the courts, law enforcement, schools, and social services. Overall, there was no difference in the perceptions of the availability of services, which we broadly identified as governmental services. At the same time, members of the second generation and beyond were more aware of these services dealing with schools and law enforcement. On the matter of crime, second generation and beyond respondents were three times more likely to have been a victim of a crime than their first-generation counterparts. Interestingly, the perpetrator of the crime differed by generational status. First-generation respondents were more likely to report other Latinos as perpetrators, whereas the second generation and beyond identified African Americans. Overall, many could not identify their perpetrator.

Regarding intergroup relations and competition, our first set of questions dealt with perception of commonalities between Latinos and whites, African Americans, and Asian Americans. Relatively speaking, respondents viewed some commonalities with both whites and African Americans (approaching more than half of respondents). Both first-generation respondents and those in the second generation and beyond exhibited comparable levels in the "a lot" category, whereas the second generation and beyond had a higher response for the "some" category. Combining the two positive categories (i.e., "a lot" and "some") demonstrated that the highest percentage was among the second generation and beyond. Citizenship plays a role in perceiving commonalities among Latinos and African Americans. That is, both the first generation and the second generation and beyond are more likely to respond affirmatively. Almost two-thirds of the second generation and beyond answered either "a lot" or "some." In the case of Asian Americans, there were low responses of perceived commonalities with Asian Americans from any Latino segment. Lack of contact and/or familiarity could be a factor.

When the focus shifted to specifically common political concerns, the patterns of perceived commonalities changed. That is, first-generation citizens, followed by first-generation noncitizens and then the second generation and beyond found common political concerns with whites or Anglos. Yet for perceived political commonalities with African Americans, the order was second generation and beyond, first-generation citizens, and then noncitizens. Among the second generation and beyond, there was a clear differentiation that greater political commonalities existed with African American than whites. At the same time, this battery was not constructed into an either-or format, so the degree of political commonalities is noticeable; that is, the questions asked about commonalities for each group, and not for comparisons between groups. Our discussion of the research literature acknowledges the situational nature of collective endeavors.

The last section focused specifically on possible competitive situations between Latinos and African Americans (e.g., jobs, education, public employment, political representation). In most settings, the modal response was the absence of direct competition (about two-fifths), yet almost one-fourth of respondents indicated a perception of strong competition. First-generation Latinos evidenced the response of no competition slightly more often than the other two segments. In the area of public-sector job competition, a slightly greater percentage indicated strong competition (about one-third). A similar distribution was also evident regarding political representation and competition for elective office. One can surmise that the common ground Latinos perceive does exist between Latinos and African Americans and whites, whereas the Asian American community appears to be more distant.

This important but limited examination of intergroup relations and Latinos' experiences in various realms of American society reveals a population that believes in the equal opportunity structures of American society. However, they do encounter obstacles in terms of receiving differential treatment in a variety of settings. When perceiving commonalities with other groups, Latinos differentiate between the major racial-ethnic groups in American society. Having minority status can facilitate cooperative endeavors with other minority groups but not necessarily at the expense of joint venture with whites or broader-based coalitions. These results also point researchers and policy makers to probe beyond the dimensions of nativity and citizenship.

Bibliography

Brodie, Mollyann, Roberto Suro, Annie Steffenson, Jaime Valdez, and Rebecca Levin. 2002. *National Survey of Latinos*. Menlo Park, CA: Henry J. Kaiser Family Foundation; Washington, D.C.: Pew Hispanic Center.

Browning, Rufus, Dale Rogers Marshall, and David H. Tabb. 1984. *Protest Is Not Enough: The Struggle of Blacks and Hispanics for Equality in Urban Politics*. Berkeley: University of California Press.

Browning, Rufus, Dale Rogers Marshall, and David H. Tabb. 1990. *Racial Politics in American Cities*. New York: Longman.

Carmichael, Stokely, and Charles Hamilton. 1967. *Black Power: Politics of Liberation in America*. New York: Vintage.

Danigelis, Nicholas L. 1977. "A Theory of Black Political Participation in the United States." *Social Forces* 56(1): 31–47.

De la Garza, Rodolfo, L. DeSipio, F. C. García, J. A. García, and A. Falcón. 1993. *Latino Voices: Mexican, Puerto Rican, and Cuban Perspectives on American Politics*. Boulder, CO: Westview.

De la Garza, Rodolfo Z., and David Vaughn. 1984. "The Political Socialization of Chicano Elites: A Generational Approach." *Social Science Quarterly* 65: 290–307.

Dyer, James, Arnold Vedlitz and David B. Hill. 1988. New Voters, Switchers, and Political Party Realignment in Texas *The Western Political Quarterly* Vol. 41, No. 1 (Mar.), pp. 155–67.

Eisinger, Peter. 1982. "A Black Employment in Municipal Jobs: The Impact of Black Political Power." *American Political Science Review* 76(June): 380–92.

Falcón, Angelo. 1988. "Black and Latino Politics in New York City." In *Latinos and the Political System*, ed. F. C. García. Notre Dame, IN: University of Notre Dame Press.

Fraga, Luis Ricardo, Kenneth J. Meier, and Robert E. England. 1986. "Hispanic Americans and Educational Policy: Limits to Equal Access." *Journal of Politics* 48(4): 850–76.

Fraga, Luis R., and Gary M. Segura. 2006. "Culture Clash? Contesting Notions of American Identity and the Effects of Latin American Immigration." *Perspectives on Politics* 4(2): 279–87.

Frankenberg, Erica, and Gary Orfield, eds. 2007. *Lessons in Integration: Realizing the Promise of Racial Diversity in American Schools*. Charlottesville: University of Virginia Press.

Garcia, John A. 2009. "Latino Public Opinion: Exploring Political Community and Policy Preferences." In *Understanding Public Opinion*, 3rd ed., ed. Barbara Norrander and Clyde Wilcox. Washington, D.C.: Congressional Quarterly Press.

Giles, Michael, and Arthur Evans. 1986. "The Power Approach to Intergroup Hostility." *Journal of Conflict Resolution* 30(3): 469–86.

Grenier, G. J., and M. Castro. 2001. "Blacks and Cubans in Miami: The Negative Consequences of the Cuban Enclave on Ethnic Relations." In *Governing American Cities*, ed. M. Jones-Correa, 137–57. New York: Russell Sage Foundation.

Henry, Charles, and Carlos Muñoz. 1991. "Ideology and Interest Linkage to California's Rainbow Coalition." In *Race and Ethnic Politics in California*, ed. B. Jackson and M. Preston. Berkeley: Institute for Governmental Research, University of California.

Hero, Rodney. 1992. *Latinos and the Political System*. Philadelphia: Temple University Press.

LARASA. 1989. *Survey on the Status of Hispanics in Colorado*. Denver: LARASA.

Lovrich, N. P., and O. Marenin. 1976. "Comparison of Black and Mexican American Voters in Denver: Assertive and Acquiescent Political Orientations and Voting Behavior in an Urban Electorate." *Western Political Quarterly* 29: 284–94.

McManus, S., and C. Cassel. 1982. "Mexican-Americans in City Politics: Participation, Representation, and Policy Preferences." *Urban Interest* 4: 57–69.

Marable, Manning. 1985. *Black American Politics: From the Washington Marches to Jesse Jackson*. London: Verso.

McClain, Paula D., and Albert K. Karnig. 1990. "Black and Hispanic Socioeconomic and Political Competition." *American Political Science Review* 84(2): 535–45.

Oliver, Melvin, and Charles Johnson. 1984. "Inter-Ethnic Conflict in an Urban Ghetto: The Case of Blacks and Latinos in Los Angeles." *Social Movement, Conflict, and Change* 6: 57–94.

Ong, Paul. 1994. *The New Asian Immigration in Los Angeles and Global Restructuring*. Philadelphia: Temple University Press.

Orfield, G. and Frankenberg, E. (Eds.) (2007). *Lessons in Integration: Realizing the Promise of Racial Diversity in America's Public Schools*. Charlottesville, VA: University of Virginia Press.

Pew Hispanic Center and Kaiser Family Foundation. 2002. *The 2002 National Survey of Latinos: Summary of Findings*. Washington, D.C.: Henry J. Kaiser Family Foundation and Pew Hispanic Center.

Pew Hispanic Center. 2004. Latinos in California, Texas, New York, Florida, and New Jersey (Survey Brief), Washington, D.C.

Ramakrishnan, S. Karthick, and Irene Bloemraad, eds. 2008. *Civic Hopes and Political Realities: Immigrants, Community Organizations, and Political Engagement*. New York: Russell Sage Foundation.

Robinson, Theodore, and Thomas R. Dye. 1978. "Reformism and Black Representation on City Councils." *Social Science Quarterly* 59: 153–61.
Schmidt, Ronald, Sr., Yvette M. Alex-Assensoh, Andrew L. Aoki, and Rodney E. Hero. 2009. *Newcomers, Outsiders, and Insiders: Immigrants and American Racial Politics in the Early Twenty-First Century.* Ann Arbor: University of Michigan Press.
Sniderman, Paul M., Philip E. Tetlock, and Edward G. Carmines. 1993. "Prejudice and Politics: An Introduction." In *Prejudice, Politics and the American Dilemma*, ed. Paul M. Sniderman, Philip E. Tetlock, and Edward G. Carmines, 1–31. Stanford, CA: Stanford University Press.
Sniderman, Paul M., Philip E. Tetlock, Edward G. Carmines, and Randall S. Peterson. 1993. "The Politics of the American Dilemma: Issue Pluralism." In *Prejudice, Politics and the American Dilemma*, ed. Paul M. Sniderman, Philip E. Tetlock, and Edward G. Carmines, 212–36. Stanford, CA: Stanford University Press.
Sonenshein, Raphael. 1990. "Bi-Racial Coalitions Politics in Los Angeles." In *Racial Politics in American Cities*, ed. R. Browning, D. Marshall, and D. Tabb. New York: Longman.
Sonenshein, Raphael. 1994. *Politics in Black and White.* Princeton, NJ: Princeton University Press.
Uhlaner, Carole. 1991. "Perceived Prejudiced and Coalitional Prospects among Black, Latinos, and Asian Americans." In *Ethnic and Racial Politics in California*, ed. Byron Jackson and Michael Preston, 339–71. Berkeley, CA: Institute for Governmental Studies.
Waldinger, Roger, and Mehdi Bozorgmehr, eds. 1996. *Ethnic Los Angeles.* New York: Russell Sage Foundation.
Warren, Christopher L., John G. Corbett, and John F. Stack Jr. 1990. "Hispanic Ascendancy and Tripartite Politics in Miami." In *Racial Politics in American Cities*, ed. Rufus Browning, Dale Rogers Marshall, and David Tabb. New York: Longman.
Yu, Eu, and Edward Chang. 1995. "Minorities Talking Coalition Building in Los Angeles." A two-day symposium.

7

Civic Engagement

Entering the Political Process

Over the past decade political scientists and sociologists have come to see the importance of people coming together for social or civic reasons. Whether through bridge clubs, food pantries, or political organizations, Americans benefit both individually and as a society when people leave their homes and become involved with others. This coming together, or civic engagement, also helps people develop civic skills that can carry over into other social arenas, including the electoral and political realms, such as voting, political party affiliation, interest groups, social movements, contacting, and others. Greater civic involvement has also been found to heighten interpersonal trust and sense of efficacy, and to give people the sense that they can have an impact on social issues affecting them as well as more generally to improve their attitudes toward the social and political realms, including government.

The term *civic engagement* has two key ideas associated with it: civic association and social capital. Social capital refers to "connections among individuals in social networks," and such social contacts, or "connected-ness," affect the well-being and "productivity of individuals and groups" (Putnam 2000, 19). Although the phenomena of social capital and civic engagement are associated in that they seem to go together with trust, reciprocity, and the like, the direction of causation (i.e., which leads to which) is not clear (see, e.g., Hero 2007). Some of the ways social capital contributes to democratic processes include the following:

"Associations and less formal networks of civic engagement instill in their members habits of cooperation and public-spiritedness, as well as the practical skills necessary to partake in public life" (Putnam 2000, 338; see also Verba, Schlozman, and Brady 1995).

"Political information flows through social networks, and in these networks public life is discussed" (Knack 2002, 774).

"Externally, voluntary associations...allow individuals to express their interests and demands on government and to protect themselves from abuses of power from political leaders." That is, extensive and nurturing social connections through civic association facilitate norms of reciprocity and social trust that deeply enrich a group and the larger society, thus leading to a host of salutary effects (Putnam 2000, 19).

Despite the considerable attention given to social capital and civic engagement in political science research over the past decade, rather little research has been done on the role of civic engagement among Latinos, nor have the implications of the idea been used to understand Latinos (and other racial groups) either as a group or within the larger society. Some time ago, Barrera (1985), demonstrated that during different historical periods, Mexican Americans formed their own associations and organizations (see Hero 1992). Chicano groups from the nineteenth century until around 1920 created groups that focused on "maintaining the physical and cultural integrity of the Mexican communities, which were under heavy pressure from the expansion of the American political economy into the Southwest... Beginning with the 1920s and continuing through the 1950s, there was an emphasis on 'egalitarian' ideals, which aimed at securing for Chicanos the *legal* statuses and privileges of the dominant, Anglo group" (Barrera 1985, 5). Hence, Barrera and others (see, e.g., Marquez 1993) have suggested that Latino civic associations have long existed and have often emphasized procedural equality and basic substantive concerns.

To systematically assess the impact of social capital, scholars have created and applied certain measures of participation and engagement. Putnam developed a social capital index (for 1990), with five components and fourteen specific variables. The components include measures of community volunteerism and organizational life, engagement in public affairs, informal sociability, and social trust (Putnam 2000). Most measures categorize forms of civic engagement as either bridging or bonding. Bridging social capital are those activities where groups reach out to other groups, have an external focus, and are more inclusive. In contrast, bonding organizations emphasize an internal focus, one that is not particularly conducive to engagement in other civic endeavors. The evidence we draw on here from the LNS considers issues of civic engagement among

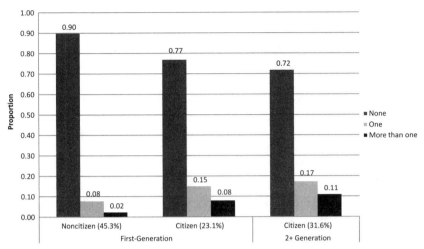

Figure 7.1. Participation in Social, Cultural, Civic, or Political Groups, by Generation and Citizenship
Question wording: "Do you participate in the activities of one social, cultural, or civic group, more than one such group, or do you not participate in the activities of any such groups?"

Latinos, as well as some related topics, including views of government. The central substantive issues, the responses to our questions, will serve as (what analysts call) dependent variables. A number of factors that may explain variation in the responses to the questions, what analysts call independent variables, will be considered; our focus here is on such potential explanatory factors as individuals' citizenship status and generation (first or second), as well as national origin, income, education, and gender. We also examine a number of questions having to do with trust in and views of government, which are commonly thought to be causes and/or consequences of civic engagement.

Participation in Social, Cultural, Civic, or Political Groups

The level of Latino civic engagement through social, cultural, civic, or political groups appears low, although the data point to the possibility that this will change over time. Citizenship and generation are associated with increasing rates of group participation, as can be seen in Figure 7.1. So, although there is lesser social and/or civic engagement among first-generation noncitizens, 10.1 percent of whom report some participation with such groups, first-generation citizens are more involved (23 percent). Similarly, the first generation participates less than the second generation

nd beyond (10 compared to 28 percent, respectively). Citizenship status,
en, has a greater effect on engagement than does change in generational
atus. These relationships between participation rates with both citizen-
ip and generational status are statistically significant.

The generally low levels of participation in social, cultural, civic, and
olitical groups aside, there is considerable variation by national origin
roup. These differences are documented in Table 7.1. Of the large Latino
roups participating in one or more civic and/or social groups, Cubans
nd Puerto Ricans are the most active, at 26 and 23 percent, respectively;
ther Latinos, at 43 percent, are actually the most likely to say they have
articipated in one or more civic and/or social groups, but other Latinos
ccount for less than 1 percent of the sample. Among what is far and away
e largest national origin group, those of Mexican descent (70 percent),
bout 18 percent say that they have participated in a civic and/or social
roup one or more times. Whether we can attribute these patterns to
xperiences in the home countries or countries of origin, or other factors,
ıch as experiences in the United States, individual socioeconomic status,
nd/or some other factors requires further exploration. In general, we
now that socioeconomic status is a consistently strong predictor of civic
ngagement in the population as a whole, and it would be expected
ɔ be important for Latinos as well, albeit not necessarily to the same
egree.

The evidence on the relationship between income levels and participa-
on in civic and/or social groups is strong and consistent. The percentage
f those who say they have participated in one, or more than one, civic
nd/or social group increases substantially from the lowest to the highest
icome levels, as seen in Figure 7.2. For example, about twice as many
espondents in the highest income level ($54,000 and more) say they
ave participated in one civic and/or social group, compared with those
t the lowest income level (less than $15,000), about 20 percent versus
percent, respectively. And the differences in participation rates are even
reater for those participating in more than one civic or social group. For
ese individuals, those at the highest income levels are about eight times
ore likely to participate in more than one civic and/or social group than
ose at the lowest income levels.

Another indicator of socioeconomic status, education, shows patterns
f involvement in civic and/or social groups that are roughly comparable
ɔ those noted for income levels. That is, there is a monotonic and sub-
antial increase in participation in either one or more than one group,
s levels of education increase, which echoes the increased participation
tes for those with higher incomes (Figure 7.3).

Table 7.1. *Participation in Social, Cultural, Civic, or Political Groups, by National Origin*

Response		Cuba	Dominican Republic	El Salvador	Mexico	Puerto Rico	Other Central America	Other South America	Other	Missing	Total
None	Freq.	238	257	349	4866	499	288	285	45	60	6887
	Row%	3.46	3.72	5.07	70.66	7.24	4.18	4.14	0.65	0.88	100.00
	Col%	73.97	83.88	86.33	82.13	76.39	84.37	76.70	57.04	76.06	81.21
Yes, one	Freq.	55	33	42	707	105	36	56	13	12	1057
	Row%	5.18	3.09	3.94	66.82	9.92	3.42	5.26	1.26	1.11	100.00
	Col%	17.01	10.67	10.30	11.93	16.06	10.60	14.97	17.03	14.81	12.47
Yes, more than one	Freq.	29	17	14	352	49	17	31	20	7	536
	Row%	5.42	3.11	2.54	65.62	9.20	3.20	5.77	3.78	1.35	100.00
	Col%	9.02	5.45	3.37	5.94	7.55	5.03	8.33	25.94	9.13	6.32
TOTAL	Freq.	322	306	405	5924	653	341	371	78	79	8480
	Row%	3.80	3.61	4.77	69.86	7.70	4.03	4.38	0.92	0.94	100.00
	Col%	100.00	100.00	100.00	100.00	100.00	100.00	100.00	100.00	100.00	100.00

Note: National origin: (16 d.f.) 98.0385 (P = 0.000). Question wording: "Do you participate in the activities of one social, cultural, civic or political group, more than one such group, or do you not participate in the activities of any such groups?"

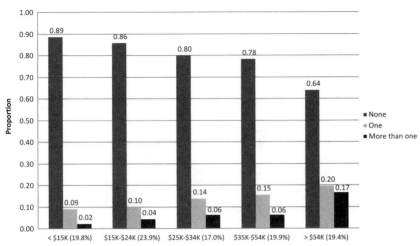

Figure 7.2. Participation in Social, Cultural, Civic, or Political Groups, by Income
Question wording: "Do you participate in the activities of one social, cultural, or civic group, more than one such group, or do you not participate in the activities of any such groups?"

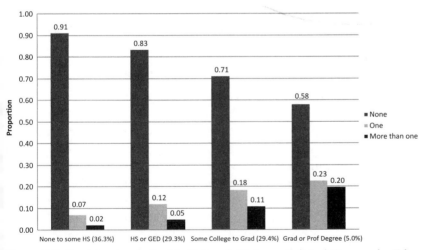

Figure 7.3. Participation in Social, Cultural, Civic, or Political Groups, by Education
Question wording: "Do you participate in the activities of one social, cultural, or civic group, more than one such group, or do you not participate in the activities of any such groups?"

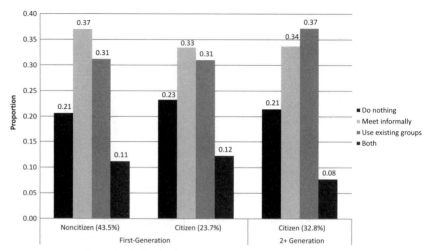

Figure 7.4. Preferred Method of Addressing Issues or Problems, by Generation and Citizenship
Question wording: "When an issue or problem needs to be addressed, would you work through existing groups or organizations to bring people together, would you get together informally, or would you do nothing to deal with this matter?"

Interestingly enough, the likelihood of participation in civic and/or social groups is unaffected by gender. The response patterns on this question are essentially identical for men and women (data not shown).

Addressing Issues or Problems

One way that political scientists think about civic engagement is what people do in times of need – do they try to solve problems on their own or look for help? Our survey found that when an issue or problem arises that needs to be addressed, about a third of our respondents, across citizenship status and generations, lean toward "getting together informally," as can be seen in Figure 7.4. Between the first and second generation there is an uptick of about 6 percent in the inclination to "use existing organizations" rather than to get together informally. The number of people who indicate doing both (i.e., getting together informally and using organizations) is between 7 percent to 12 percent, with the lower levels among the second generation and beyond. Roughly 20 percent of respondents indicate they "do nothing" when a problem arises; this seems to be equally true for both first-generation citizens and noncitizens, as well as for the first and second generation more generally.

There are no clear, distinctive patterns regarding whether and how issues or problems are addressed by national origin groups (Table 7.2). In all cases, the most common response is to "get together informally" and/or to "use existing organizations," but the preferred approach(es) are not necessarily consistent.

The impact of socioeconomic factors – specifically, income and education – as they affect addressing issues or problems is only modestly consistent and strong, as can be seen in Figures 7.5 and 7.6. It does seem, however, that the more affluent and the more educated use existing organizations more often than do others, which suggests that the better off may be more likely to be associated with organizations than are the less well off, which is also consistent with general patterns of participation in civic and/or social groups (as already suggested).

There are, in fact, notable gender differences with regard to addressing problems. Women are less likely to do nothing and more likely to use both informal and organized ways of addressing issues than are men, as indicated in Figure 7.7.

We now turn to the question of which groups are being joined by Latinos. Our focus is on the composition, essentially the racial-ethnic homogeneity or heterogeneity, of these groups. Figure 7.8 shows that among the first generation, and particularly among noncitizens, there is a strong tendency to be involved with social and cultural groups that are "mostly Latino." About half of first-generation noncitizens and 40 percent of first-generation citizens interact in mostly Latino groups. That pattern attenuates considerably, lessening by somewhere between a half and a third among the second generation; that is, about 42 percent say that their involvement is mostly with groups that are a "mix of Latinos and whites," and about 32 percent say that their groups are a "mix of all." If we assume that Latinos' activities with their fellows is a rough barometer of Putnam's notion of "bonding" social capital – social networks connecting individuals with similar demographic characteristics – then one can interpret these results as suggesting "bonding" activities taking place within ethnic groups decrease over time in the United States.

There are some striking differences when the demographic characteristics of social, cultural, civic, or political group participation are examined in terms of national origin. Among those from the Dominican Republic, almost two-thirds (64 percent) are involved in "mostly Latino" groups, as are more than half (53 percent) of those from El Salvador (note, however, that Dominicans and Salvadorans are not especially large proportions of the sample), as can be seen in Table 7.3. In contrast, barely more than

Table 7.2. *Addressing Issues or Problems, by National Origin*
Category: Political Participation, Civic Participation

Response		Cuba	Dominican Republic	El Salvador	Mexico	Puerto Rico	Other Central America	Other South America	Other	Missing	Total
Do nothing	Freq.	81	57	83	1087	134	76	63	14	18	1612
	Row%	5.03	3.55	5.12	67.40	8.31	4.72	3.88	0.86	1.12	100.00
	Col%	28.24	20.61	23.43	20.87	22.49	25.50	18.65	18.06	24.90	21.49
Get together informally	Freq.	103	106	104	1894	190	73	118	23	21	2631
	Row%	3.90	4.01	3.94	71.99	7.23	2.76	4.50	0.86	0.82	100.00
	Col%	35.66	37.93	29.45	36.38	31.92	24.35	35.27	29.36	29.60	35.06
Use existing organizations	Freq.	83	74	138	1693	204	115	118	30	30	2484
	Row%	3.36	2.99	5.57	68.13	8.19	4.63	4.74	1.20	1.20	100.00
	Col%	29.00	26.70	39.28	32.51	34.15	38.49	35.11	38.91	41.03	33.11
Both	Freq.	20	41	28	533	68	35	37	10	3	775
	Row%	2.63	5.30	3.56	68.71	8.79	4.49	4.75	1.35	0.42	100.00
	Col%	7.10	14.77	7.84	10.23	11.44	11.66	10.97	13.67	4.48	10.33
TOTAL	Freq.	287	278	352	5206	596	299	336	77	73	7502
	Row%	3.83	3.71	4.69	69.39	7.94	3.98	4.47	1.02	0.97	100.00
	Col%	100.00	100.00	100.00	100.00	100.00	100.00	100.00	100.00	100.00	100.00

Note: National origin: (24 d.f.) 61.0102 (P = 0.0062). Question wording: "When an issue or problem needs to be addressed, would you work through existing groups or organizations to bring people together, would you get together informally, or would you do nothing to deal with this matter?"

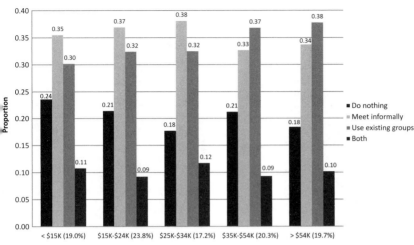

Figure 7.5. Preferred Method of Addressing Issues or Problems, by Income
Question wording: "When an issue or problem needs to be addressed, would you work through existing groups or organizations to bring people together, would you get together informally, or would you do nothing to deal with this matter?"

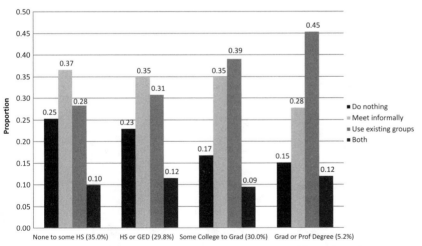

Figure 7.6. Preferred Method of Addressing Issues or Problems, by Education
Question wording: "When an issue or problem needs to be addressed, would you work through existing groups or organizations to bring people together, would you get together informally, or would you do nothing to deal with this matter?"

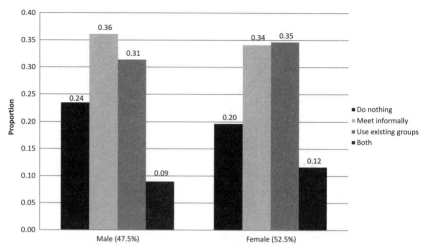

Figure 7.7. Preferred Method of Addressing Issues or Problems, by Gender
Question wording: "When an issue or problem needs to be addressed, would you work through existing groups or organizations to bring people together, would you get together informally, or would you do nothing to deal with this matter?"

a quarter (27 percent) of those of Puerto Rican background, and roughly a third of those of Mexican and of Cuban background, participate in mostly Latino groups. In other words, for Puerto Ricans, Mexicans, and Cubans, more than two-thirds of those who participate in civic and/or

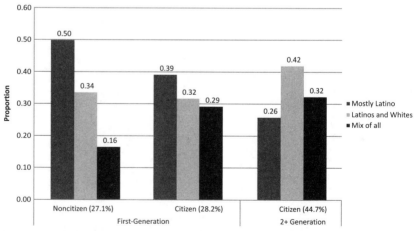

Figure 7.8. Demographic Characteristics of Social, Cultural, Civic, or Political Groups, by Generation and Citizenship
Question wording: "How would you describe these groups? Are they ... "

Table 7.3. *Demographic Characteristics of Social, Cultural, Civic, or Political Groups, by National Origin*

Category: Political Participation, Civic Participation

Response		Cuba	Dominican Republic	El Salvador	Mexico	Puerto Rico	Other Central America	Other South America	Other	Missing	Total
Mostly Latino	Freq.	22	25	28	307	31	18	23	4	3	460
	Row%	4.80	5.44	5.99	66.66	6.72	3.81	4.98	0.94	0.67	100.00
	Col%	31.62	63.92	53.31	35.77	27.02	47.87	38.63	19.40	22.42	36.39
Mix of Latinos and whites	Freq.	25	8	14	335	29	11	19	10	8	458
	Row%	5.51	1.70	3.03	73.10	6.29	2.37	4.08	2.15	1.79	100.00
	Col%	36.15	19.85	26.80	39.06	25.20	29.62	31.47	44.28	59.78	36.23
Mix of all	Freq.	23	6	10	216	55	8	18	8	2	346
	Row%	6.50	1.84	2.97	62.36	15.79	2.38	5.13	2.34	0.70	100.00
	Col%	32.22	16.23	19.88	25.17	47.78	22.51	29.90	36.32	17.80	27.38
TOTAL	Freq.	70	39	52	858	115	37	59	22	14	1265
	Row%	5.52	3.10	4.09	67.81	9.05	2.89	4.70	1.76	1.08	100.00
	Col%	100.00	100.00	100.00	100.00	100.00	100.00	100.00	100.00	100.00	100.00

Notes: National origin: (16 d.f.) 58.9050 (P = 0.0002). Question wording: "How would you describe these groups? Are they . . ."

199

social groups do so in groups that are a "mix of Latinos and whites" or a "mix of all." Clearly, for the Latinos in our survey at least, national heritage and, presumably, associated life experiences have a strong hand in shaping the type of groups they join.

Looking further at the racial-ethnic homogeneity or heterogeneity of the groups in which Latinos participate relative to their income, those with lower income are more likely to be involved in mostly Latino civic and/or social groups; those at higher income levels are less likely to participate in mostly Latino groups and more likely to participate in groups that are a "mix of Latinos and whites" or a "mix of all" (Figure 7.9). The pattern regarding income is echoed for levels of education, the data for which are found in Figure 7.9. For example, almost half (47 percent) of those with high school education or less participate in mostly Latino groups, whereas about 30 percent of those with some college and those holding graduate or professional degrees participate in mostly Latino groups.

Unlike socioeconomic status, gender seems to have little impact on the racial-ethnic homogeneity or heterogeneity of groups in which one participates, although there is a slight (though not statistically significant) tendency for women to participate in mixed civic and social groups (data not shown).

Contacting Officials

Civic engagement means various things. One important dimension is participating in the political system. This may be done in a number of ways, as we discuss in the pages that follow. A very basic way of recognizing and participating in the political system is to contact individuals in the formal institutions of government. This contact may suggest a number of things about the contactor, such as a perceived need for governmental assistance or a particular view of public policy. It also demonstrates that the contactor has some knowledge of government, as well as a certain level of comfort with, or willingness to approach, its officials or officers (see, e.g., Hero 1986). However, most respondents in our survey report that they have not contacted a government official, as shown in Figure 7.10. These findings are not surprising, considering that this is a less common form of political participation, one that requires more effort and resources. In addition, although this is a form of political participation technically open to all respondents, regardless of citizenship status, we would expect that newer noncitizens may feel less comfortable in making contact and might prefer to avoid government contact – and this is what we found. Citizenship status turns out to be an important predictor. Just about 17 percent

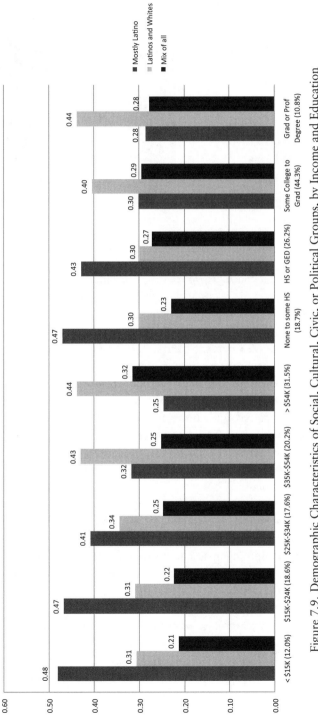

Figure 7.9. Demographic Characteristics of Social, Cultural, Civic, or Political Groups, by Income and Education **Question wording:** "How would you describe these groups? Are they . . ."

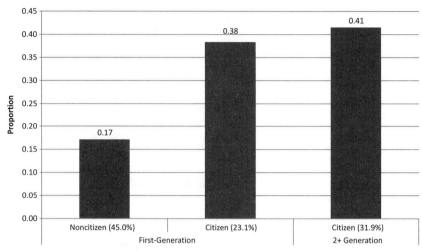

Figure 7.10. Contacted Government Official, by Generation and Citizenship
Question wording: "Have you ever tried to get government officials to pay attention to something that concerned you, either by calling, writing a letter, or going
to a meeting?"

of first-generation noncitizens report having contacted government officials, whereas about 38 percent of first-generation citizens and about 41
percent of second generation and beyond citizens report having done so.
Although citizenship has the largest statistical effect, generation has an
effect as well, and both are statistically significant. However, although
citizenship is associated with more frequent contacts with government
officials, generation is not. The data do not indicate the specific nature or
purpose of the contact, so there is no way to know whether the purpose of
the contact was broad and/or policy oriented rather than more particular
or personal in its focus.

Whether or not one contacts officials varies to some degree by national
origin, as can be seen in Table 7.4. Puerto Ricans and Cubans are far more
likely to indicate that they have contacted officials than are those of other
Latino national origin groups. The reasons for this are not immediately
clear, but it may be that local political processes, including more descriptive representation – that is, officials of similar heritage – among the
public officials in the locales in which Puerto Ricans and Cubans are concentrated facilitate greater ease of contact and, hence, greater likelihood
of contacting officials.

One of the debates in the broader literature on citizen contacting has
been whether higher individual socioeconomic status would lead to more

Table 7.4. *Contacting Officials, by National Origin*
Category: Political Participation, Civic Participation

Response		Cuba	Dominican Republic	El Salvador	Mexico	Puerto Rico	Other Central America	Other South America	Other	Missing	Total
Yes	Freq.	120	84	96	1724	266	61	114	39	25	2529
	Row%	4.75	3.34	3.79	68.16	10.52	2.40	4.51	1.53	1.01	100.00
	Col%	37.82	27.69	23.74	29.06	40.55	17.99	30.94	48.97	31.96	29.83
No	Freq.	197	220	308	4207	390	277	255	40	54	5948
	Row%	3.32	3.71	5.18	70.73	6.56	4.65	4.28	0.68	0.91	100.00
	Col%	62.18	72.31	76.26	70.94	59.45	82.01	69.06	51.03	68.04	70.17
TOTAL	Freq.	317	305	404	5931	656	337	369	79	80	8477
	Row%	3.74	3.60	4.76	69.96	7.74	3.98	4.35	0.93	0.94	100.00
	Col%	100.00	100.00	100.00	100.00	100.00	100.00	100.00	100.00	100.00	100.00

Notes: National origin: (8 d.f.) 91.9988 (P = 0.0000). Question wording: "Have you ever tried to get government officials to pay attention to something that concerned you, either by calling, writing a letter, or going to a meeting?"

or less contacting. On the one hand, lower socioeconomic circumstances might suggest a greater need to contact officials, because more basic problems or issues might arise for those less well off. At the same time, however, the political participation literature finds that the less well off generally participate less than better off; hence, we would expect the latter to participate most because they have more resources that predispose them to do so. On the other hand, precisely because they are better off, the more affluent and/or educated might have less need to contact. In short, there is a needs-versus-resources debate in the research literature, which ultimately suggests that those at the middle levels of needs and of resources are the most likely to contact. The findings here (see Figure 7.11), however, indicate that higher socioeconomic status – income and education – are emphatically associated with higher levels of contacting. Gender, though, has no impact on propensity to contact (data not shown)

Following on our brief consideration of descriptive representation, we were curious as to the ethnic background of the official contacted by our respondents. We found that immigrants were more likely to contact coethnic government officials than persons born in the United States (see Figure 7.12). Specifically, almost 60 percent of first-generation noncitizens reported their contact was with a Latino and/or Hispanic elected official, but far fewer first-generation citizens (41 percent) or second generation and beyond citizens (36 percent) did so. Factors such as the presence, and hence availability, of coethnic government officials and residential segregation may affect whether respondents can, and actually do, seek out Latino and/or Hispanic government officials. First-generation respondents are presumably more likely to live in areas where there are more coethnic officials; in contrast, second generation and beyond respondents are probably more likely to live in areas where coethnic government officials are not as common.

Of the five largest national origin groups listed, for two, Puerto Ricans and Dominicans, clear majorities (about 60 percent) said the official contacted was not Latino and/or Hispanic, as Table 7.5 shows. Those in the several other national origin groups (Cuban, Mexican, and Salvadoran) were roughly split regarding whether the official contacted was Latino and/or Hispanic. The number of groups and the complexity of findings make it difficult to make general observations on this issue.

The ethnic background of the individual contacted is strongly associated with respondents' income and education levels. Figure 7.13 indicates that those who have lower income and lower education levels are much more likely to have contacted Latino and/or Hispanic officials, whereas

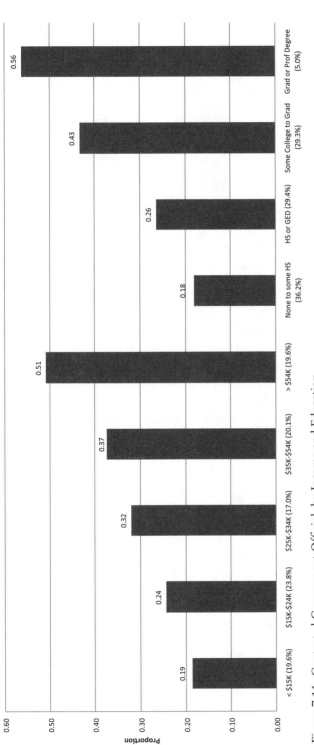

Figure 7.11. Contacted Government Official, by Income and Education

Question wording: "Have you ever tried to get government officials to pay attention to something that concerned you, either by calling, writing a letter, or going to a meeting?"

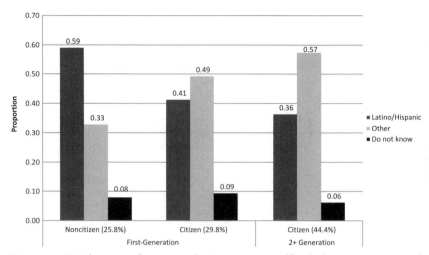

Figure 7.12. Ethnicity of Contacted Government Official, by Generation and Citizenship
Question wording: "Was the official you contacted a Latino or Hispanic?"

those of higher income and education levels are much less likely to have contacted Latino and/or Hispanic officials. For instance, well more than half (56 percent) of Latinos in the lowest income group ($15,000 or less) contacted Latino and/or Hispanic officials, whereas only slightly more than a third (35 percent) of the highest income group ($54,000 or more) had done so. The monotonic pattern across both income and education levels is similarly striking. We see no differences on this question with regard to gender (data not shown).

Interest in Public Affairs

As noted already, we don't know exactly why someone has chosen to contact a public official, so we are reticent to read too deeply into those responses for a sense of Latinos real level of interest or engagement with either the government or politics more generally. A second way of getting at the issue is to simply ask directly, "How interested are you in politics and public affairs?" We found that the plurality of first-generation citizens and noncitizens as well as second-generation citizens claim to be (at least) "somewhat interested" in politics and public affairs (Figure 7.14). The other quarter of citizens (whether first or second generation) say they are "very interested," with a slight but significant increase in the percentage who are "very interested" across generational status. Approximately

Table 7.5. *Ethnicity of Contacted Official, by National Origin*
Category: Political Participation, Civic Participation

Response		Cuba	Dominican Republic	El Salvador	Mexico	Puerto Rico	Other Central America	Other South America	Other	Missing	Total
Yes, Latino or Hispanic	Freq.	50	27	47	798	87	22	48	11	7	1097
	Row%	4.58	2.41	4.30	72.77	7.90	2.02	4.41	0.97	0.64	100.00
	Col%	42.13	31.62	49.42	46.69	32.76	36.79	42.37	27.70	27.41	43.69
No, other	Freq.	58	50	44	775	161	35	60	27	12	1221
	Row%	4.72	4.11	3.58	63.44	13.19	2.87	4.89	2.19	1.00	100.00
	Col%	48.34	59.89	45.79	45.32	60.94	58.32	52.40	69.44	48.18	48.64
Do not know	Freq.	11	7	5	137	17	3	6	1	6	193
	Row%	5.91	3.70	2.38	70.94	8.66	1.53	3.10	0.57	3.22	100.00
	Col%	9.53	8.49	4.79	7.99	6.30	4.89	5.23	2.86	24.41	7.67
TOTAL	Freq.	119	84	95	1709	264	60	114	39	25	2510
	Row%	4.75	3.34	3.80	68.09	10.53	2.40	4.54	1.54	1.01	100.00
	Col%	100.00	100.00	100.00	100.00	100.00	100.00	100.00	100.00	100.00	100.00

Notes: National origin: (16 d.f.) 57.2210 (P = 0.0001). Race-ethnicity of contacted official. Question wording: "Was the official you contacted Latino or Hispanic?"

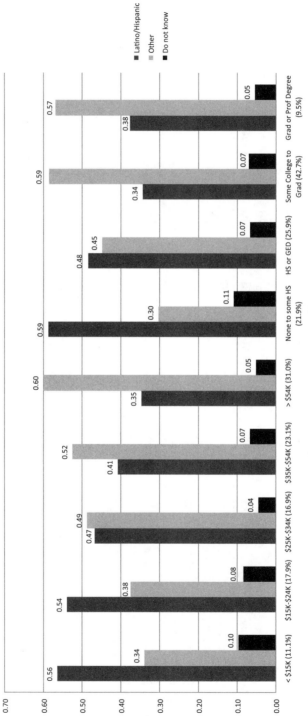

Figure 7.13. Ethnicity of Contacted Government Official, by Income and Education
Question wording: "Was the official you contacted a Latino or Hispanic?"

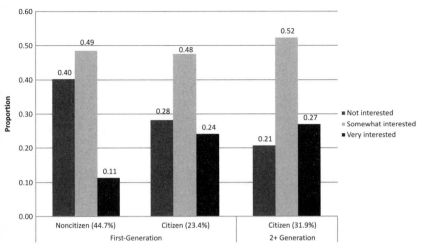

Figure 7.14. Interest in Politics and Public Affairs, by Generation and Citizenship
Question wording: "How interested are you in politics and public affairs? Would you say you are very interested, somewhat interested, or not at all interested?"

60 percent of first-generation noncitizens report being "somewhat interested" or "very interested," compared to almost 72 percent of naturalized citizens and more than three-quarters (79 percent) of those born in the mainland United States as citizens. There is a notable difference in interest level between citizens and noncitizens as well.

When broken down by national origin groups, our respondents showed some interesting differences. Cubans stand out as the most likely to say they are "very" interested and the least likely to say they are "not interested." These patterns are consistent with perceptions of Cubans' levels of interest, particularly regarding foreign affairs and especially U.S. relations with Cuba. For every group, more than a quarter say "not interested," ranging from 25 percent to 44 percent. The views and intensity of views held by the other national origin groups are shown in Table 7.6.

The impact of income and education on levels of interest in public affairs follows a pattern evident in other aspects of civic engagement addressed in other questions, and it is most apparent when comparing the lowest to the highest socioeconomic and education strata and certain response choices using the data in Figure 7.15. Those with the highest incomes and the most education are about three times less likely to say they are "not interested" in public affairs than are those with the lowest levels of income and education. Similarly, those with the highest incomes and the most education are about three to four times more likely to say

Table 7.6. *Interest in Politics and Public Affairs, by National Origin*
Category: Political Participation, Civic Participation

Response		Cuba	Dominican Republic	El Salvador	Mexico	Puerto Rico	Other Central America	Other South America	Other	Missing	Total
Not interested	Freq.	81	92	169	1778	182	143	105	7	23	2579
	Row%	3.13	3.55	6.56	68.92	7.05	5.54	4.06	0.28	0.91	100.00
	Col%	25.12	30.61	43.88	30.75	28.31	44.56	29.03	9.07	28.76	31.19
Somewhat interested	Freq.	124	139	153	2997	309	130	169	41	35	4097
	Row%	3.03	3.39	3.72	73.15	7.54	3.17	4.13	1.01	0.85	100.00
	Col%	38.58	46.44	39.53	51.84	48.13	40.51	46.85	52.79	43.13	49.53
Very interested	Freq.	117	69	64	1006	151	48	87	30	23	1595
	Row%	7.32	4.31	4.01	63.11	9.49	3.00	5.46	1.87	1.43	100.00
	Col%	36.30	22.95	16.59	17.41	23.56	14.93	24.12	38.13	28.12	19.28
TOTAL	Freq.	321	299	386	5781	642	321	361	78	81	8271
	Row%	3.89	3.62	4.67	69.90	7.76	3.88	4.36	0.95	0.98	100.00
	Col%	100.00	100.00	100.00	100.00	100.00	100.00	100.00	100.00	100.00	100.00

Notes: National origin: (16 d.f.) 179.7615 (P = 0.0000). Question wording: "How interested are you in politics and public affairs? Would you say you are interested, somewhat interested, or not at all interested?"

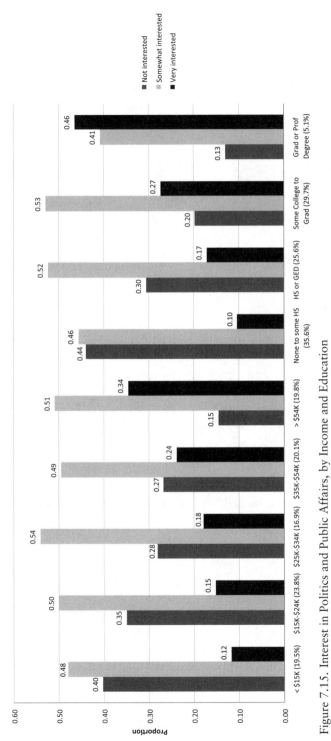

Figure 7.15. Interest in Politics and Public Affairs, by Income and Education

Question wording: "How interested are you in politics and public affairs? Would you say you are very interested, somewhat interested, or not at all interested?"

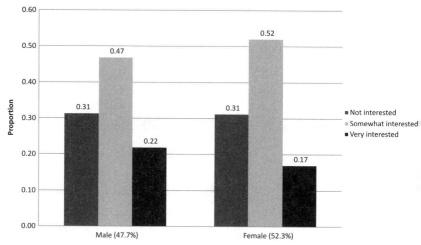

Figure 7.16. Interest in Politics and Public Affairs, by Gender
Question wording: "How interested are you in politics and public affairs? Would you say you are very interested, somewhat interested, or not at all interested?"

they are "very interested" in public affairs than are those with the lowest levels of income and education.

There is a modest difference between men and women regarding their interest in public affairs (Figure 7.16). The two genders are virtually identical in the degree of their "not interested" responses; however, men are a bit more likely than women to say they are "very interested" (22 versus 17 percent, respectively), whereas the reverse is the case for "somewhat" interested (47 percent for men, and 52 percent for women).

Perspectives (Political Views) on Government or Efficacy

Beyond civic engagement and interest in public affairs, the LNS allows us to assess several questions concerning how Latinos view the formal authoritative institutions of government in the United States. Some scholars refer to these views as suggesting more or less efficacy, that is, the degree to which people feel they can affect or influence government, as well as broader political and social relations. The evidence suggests strong reservations among Latinos on several dimensions. The respondents' perceptions of "which interests are served by government," and more specifically, whether government is run "by just a few big interests looking out for themselves, and not for the benefit of all" can be seen in Figure 7.17.

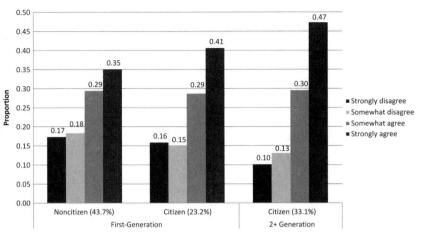

Figure 7.17. Government Is Run by a Few Big Interests for Their Own Benefit, by Generation and Citizenship
Question wording: "People have different ideas about government in the United States. Please tell me how strongly you agree or disagree. . . . Government is pretty much run by just a few big interests looking out for themselves, and not for the benefit of all people."

They are striking. More than two-thirds (69 percent) of first-generation citizens "strongly" or "somewhat" agree that government is run by a few big interests, and this increases to more than three-quarters (77 percent) among second-generation citizens; indeed, the largest proportion (47 percent) of the second generation overall "strongly agree."

Reservations about the openness of the political system are also evident, but there are notable differences about whether "government is pretty much run by just a few big interests," according to national origin (Table 7.7). For all the national origin groups, more than 60 percent, and usually much higher than that, believe that at least to some degree "government is pretty much run by just a few big interests." Cubans are the least likely (61 percent) to somewhat or strongly agree with the statement; among several of the other national origin groups (Mexican, Puerto Rican, and Dominican), 70 percent or more somewhat or strongly agree. Views on this question are also interesting to consider on the basis of respondents' socioeconomic status.

About two-thirds or more across all income levels somewhat or strongly agree that "government is pretty much run by just a few big interests." And those at the highest income levels are the most likely to feel this way, which is perhaps surprising given their somewhat higher

Table 7.7. *Perception of Which Interests Are Served by Government, by National Origin*

Category: Political Views, Role/View of Government

Response		Cuba	Dominican Republic	El Salvador	Mexico	Puerto Rico	Other Central America	Other South America	Other	Missing	Total
Strongly disagree	Freq.	54	46	60	785	73	37	56	10	11	1132
	Row%	4.74	4.08	5.31	69.31	6.44	3.28	4.98	0.91	0.95	100.00
	Col%	18.35	16.86	16.77	14.47	11.85	12.20	16.50	13.59	15.87	14.61
Somewhat disagree	Freq.	60	34	56	863	87	64	40	11	6	1222
	Row%	4.91	2.80	4.56	70.65	7.13	5.27	3.26	0.93	0.50	100.00
	Col%	20.49	12.49	15.52	15.92	14.15	21.17	11.65	15.01	9.08	15.76
Somewhat agree	Freq.	64	68	97	1614	180	105	93	32	19	2269
	Row%	2.80	2.98	4.25	71.12	7.93	4.61	4.10	1.39	0.82	100.00
	Col%	21.75	24.63	26.90	29.77	29.23	34.42	27.24	41.81	27.29	29.28
Strongly agree	Freq.	115	126	146	2159	276	98	152	22	32	3128
	Row%	3.69	4.03	4.68	69.04	8.81	3.13	4.87	0.71	1.04	100.00
	Col%	39.41	46.01	40.81	39.84	44.78	32.22	44.60	29.59	47.76	40.36
TOTAL	Freq.	293	274	359	5420	616	304	342	75	68	7750
	Row%	3.78	3.54	4.63	69.94	7.94	3.92	4.41	0.97	0.87	100.00
	Col%	100.00	100.00	100.00	100.00	100.00	100.00	100.00	100.00	100.00	100.00

Notes: National origin: (24 d.f.) 59.4406 (P = 0.0142). Question wording: "People have different ideas about the government in the United States. Please tell me how strongly you agree or disagree with this statement: 'Government is pretty much run by just a few big interests looking out for themselves, and not for the benefit of all the people.'"

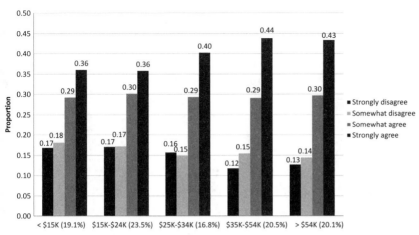

Figure 7.18. Government Is Run by a Few Big Interests for Their Own Benefit, by Income
Question wording: "People have different ideas about government in the United States. Please tell me how strongly you agree or disagree. . . . Government is pretty much run by just a few big interests looking out for themselves, and not for the benefit of all people."

social status; although higher status may also imply more information and knowledge on which to base opinions, and in this case, more information may be associated with more reservation, as described by the data summarized in Figure 7.18. The distribution of views according to levels of education (Figure 7.19) is fairly similar to that described concerning income; that is, the more educated are somewhat more likely than the less educated to think that "government is pretty much run by just a few big interests." Finally, women are somewhat more inclined than men to think that "government is pretty much run by just a few big interests," a trend covered in Figure 7.20.

Other data on trust in government reinforces the sense that Latinos have considerable reservations about their elected leaders. When asked "how much of the time" one trusts the government to do "what is right," about 17 to 20 percent of our respondents, across citizenship status and first and second generations, say "never," whereas roughly half indicate they "trust" government (only) "some of the time." This varies rather modestly (though statistically significantly) across citizenship status and generation (Figure 7.21). Fewer than a third indicate that they trust government "most of the time" or "just about always." Perhaps most notable,

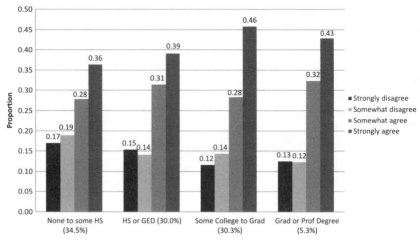

Figure 7.19. Government Is Run by a Few Big Interests for Their Own Benefit, by Education

Question wording: "People have different ideas about government in the United States. Please tell me how strongly you agree or disagree. . . . Government is pretty much run by just a few big interests looking out for themselves, and not for the benefit of all people."

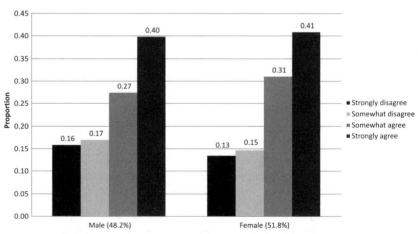

Figure 7.20. Government Is Run by a Few Big Interests for Their Own Benefit, by Gender

Question wording: "People have different ideas about government in the United States. Please tell me how strongly you agree or disagree. . . . Government is pretty much run by just a few big interests looking out for themselves, and not for the benefit of all people."

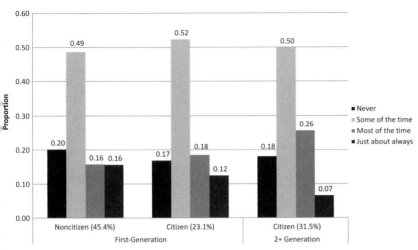

Figure 7.21. Government Can Be Trusted, by Generation and Citizenship
Question wording: "How much of the time do you trust the government to do what is right – just about always, most of the time, some of the time or never?"

only about 7 percent of the second generation and beyond says "just about always." These ostensibly very low levels of trust are remarkable.

All the national origin groups in the survey appear to share a high level of distrust of government; at least 60 percent (of Cubans) and as many as 71 percent (of Dominicans) "never" or (only) "some of the time" "trust government to do what is right."

As noted here and elsewhere, Cubans have the most positive views of government, though not by all that much, and even the level of trust among this group is not particularly favorable. Details of the responses of different national origin groups are found in Table 7.8.

The clear modal category on trust in government is "some of the time" across the levels of income and of education, and gender (Figures 7.22–7.24). Although those of higher income and education are somewhat more trusting (i.e., they are less likely to say they "never" trust government) the differences by income and education levels are, in general, not particularly dramatic. And echoing the pattern regarding interests served by government, women are somewhat less trusting of government than are men (although the differences are not quite statistically significant).

Latinos perceive of themselves as having a somewhat limited ability to influence government. Well more than half (55–59 percent) somewhat or strongly agreed that "people like me don't have any say in what the government does." Citizens are only slightly less likely to say this than

Table 7.8. *Trust in Government, by National Origin*
Category: Political Views, Role/View of Government

Response		Cuba	Dominican Republic	El Salvador	Mexico	Puerto Rico	Other Central America	Other South America	Other	Missing	Total
Never	Freq.	43	76	84	1109	119	73	72	8	26	1610
	Row%	2.66	4.73	5.23	68.88	7.39	4.55	4.46	0.49	1.61	100.00
	Col%	13.07	24.59	20.42	18.35	18.06	21.26	19.18	9.99	30.93	18.65
Some of the time	Freq.	154	143	206	3031	343	156	190	52	34	4308
	Row%	3.57	3.33	4.77	70.36	7.95	3.62	4.42	1.21	0.78	100.00
	Col%	47.00	46.21	49.81	50.14	52.00	45.22	50.85	65.91	40.27	49.89
Most of the time	Freq.	73	47	61	1192	141	60	71	16	19	1681
	Row%	4.35	2.80	3.63	70.93	8.41	3.56	4.23	0.94	1.16	100.00
	Col%	22.33	15.17	14.80	19.73	21.47	17.38	18.99	20.01	23.20	19.47
Just about always	Freq.	58	44	62	712	56	56	41	3	5	1035
	Row%	5.56	4.20	5.96	68.79	5.39	5.37	3.96	0.31	0.45	100.00
	Col%	17.60	14.04	14.96	11.78	8.47	16.14	10.97	4.09	5.61	11.99
TOTAL	Freq.	327	310	413	6045	659	344	374	79	84	8634
	Row%	3.79	3.59	4.78	70.01	7.63	3.99	4.33	0.91	0.97	100.00
	Col%	100.00	100.00	100.00	100.00	100.00	100.00	100.00	100.00	100.00	100.00

Notes: National origin: (24 d.f.) 76.8308 (P = 0.0002). Question wording: "How much of the time do you trust the government to do what is right – just about always, most of the time, some of the time, or never?"

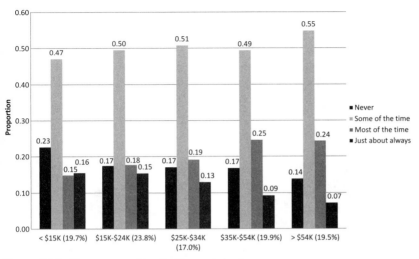

Figure 7.22. Government Can Be Trusted, by Income
Question wording: "How much of the time do you trust the government to do what is right – just about always, most of the time, some of the time or never?"

are noncitizens. Further, there is essentially no difference between first- and second-generation citizens on this question; about two-thirds agree somewhat or strongly on their limited ability to influence government (Figure 7.25).

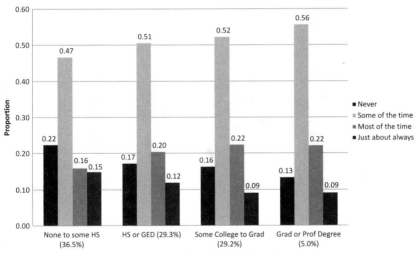

Figure 7.23. Government Can Be Trusted, by Education
Question wording: "How much of the time do you trust the government to do what is right – just about always, most of the time, some of the time, or never?"

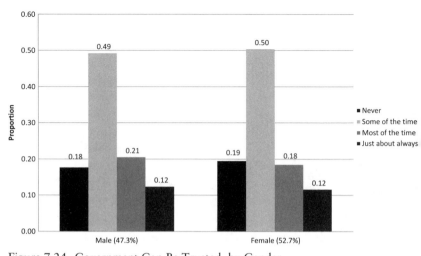

Figure 7.24. Government Can Be Trusted, by Gender
Question wording: "How much of the time do you trust the government to do what is right – just about always, most of the time, some of the time, or never?"

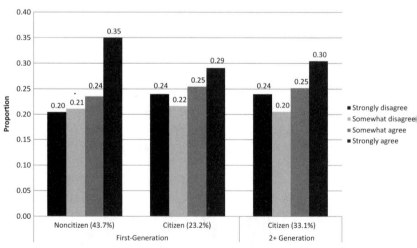

Figure 7.25. "People Like Me" Do Not Influence Government, by Generation and Citizenship
Question wording: "People have different ideas about government in the United States. Please tell me how strongly you agree or disagree.... People like me don't have any say in what the government does."

Table 7.9. *Perception of Ability to Influence Government, by National Origin*
Category: Political Views, Role/View of Government

Response		Cuba	Dominican Republic	El Salvador	Mexico	Puerto Rico	Other Central America	Other South America	Other	Missing	Total
Strongly disagree	Freq.	79	45	65	1250	144	65	74	18	18	1757
	Row%	4.48	2.54	3.69	71.14	8.18	3.71	4.19	1.04	1.03	100.00
	Col%	26.80	16.35	18.14	22.73	23.28	21.92	21.24	23.51	24.52	22.42
Somewhat disagree	Freq.	59	41	67	1184	125	64	72	24	8	1644
	Row%	3.59	2.48	4.09	72.03	7.58	3.90	4.38	1.49	0.46	100.00
	Col%	20.09	14.92	18.80	21.54	20.18	21.60	20.79	31.52	10.24	20.98
Somewhat agree	Freq.	61	68	102	1343	166	62	74	21	23	1918
	Row%	3.19	3.55	5.30	70.01	8.63	3.21	3.86	1.07	1.18	100.00
	Col%	20.85	24.91	28.45	24.42	26.82	20.70	21.38	26.44	30.80	24.48
Strongly agree	Freq.	95	120	124	1721	184	106	127	14	25	2516
	Row%	3.77	4.76	4.91	68.42	7.29	4.23	5.04	0.57	1.01	100.00
	Col%	32.27	43.81	34.61	31.31	29.72	35.78	36.59	18.54	34.45	32.11
TOTAL	Freq.	294	273	357	5498	618	297	347	78	73	7835
	Row%	3.75	3.49	4.56	70.18	7.88	3.79	4.42	0.99	0.94	100.00
	Col%	100.00	100.00	100.00	100.00	100.00	100.00	100.00	100.00	100.00	100.00

Notes: National origin: (24 d.f.) 57.4804 (P = 0.0157). Question wording: "People have different ideas about the government in the United States. Please tell me how strongly you agree or disagree with this statement: 'People like me don't have any say in what the government does.'"

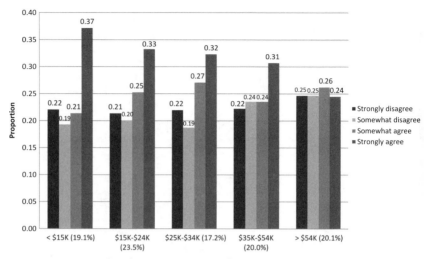

Figure 7.26. "People Like Me" Do Not Influence Government, by Income
Question wording: "People have different ideas about government in the United States. Please tell me how strongly you agree or disagree. . . . 'People like me don't have any say in what the government does.'"

Across the national origin groups, roughly a third strongly agree that "people like me don't have any say in what the government does;" indeed, "strongly agree" is the modal category for each of the national origin groups. This is described by the data in Table 7.9. When those who strongly agree are combined with those who somewhat agree, between half and two-thirds across the groups indicate some level of agreement. More specifically, roughly two-thirds of Dominicans and Salvadorans express such views, whereas more than half of Cubans, Mexicans, and Puerto Ricans agree at least somewhat.

For four of the five income levels examined, the most common response about whether "people like [them] having a say in what the government does" is "strongly agree"; for the other, the highest income level ($54,000 and more) "somewhat agree" is the modal response (26 percent), followed closely by "strongly agree" (25 percent), as shown in Figure 7.26. That said, there is still some variation by income, perhaps most evident in that those at the lowest income levels (less than $15,000) and the highest income levels ($54,000 and more) differ by about 13 percent (37 percent versus 24 percent). With modest exceptions, education affects perceptions about "having a say in what the government does" in ways that parallel those of income (Figure 7.27). Gender has no real impact on assessments of influencing "what the government does" (data not shown).

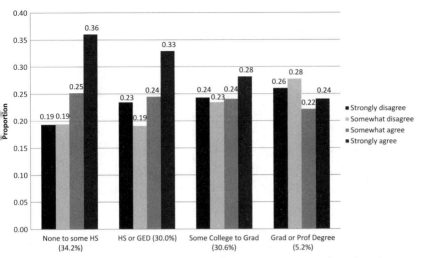

Figure 7.27. "People Like Me" Do Not Influence Government, by Education
Question wording: "People have different ideas about government in the United States. Please tell me how strongly you agree or disagree.... 'People like me don't have any say in what the government does.'"

On the face of it, our respondents' perceptions of their ability to understand politics and government seem somewhat like those concerning influencing government. For instance, more than a third of first-generation noncitizens and citizens strongly agree that "sometimes politics and government seem so complicated that a person like me can't really understand what's going on"; more than a quarter across all the groups somewhat agree. This can be seen in the data summarized in Figure 7.28. Although this sense of lack of understanding does seem to attenuate between the first generation and second generation, still more than 60 percent of the second generation strongly agrees about how complicated government appears to them. One point to note, though, is that the question reads that "sometimes" government may seem too complicated; how much of the time this is so cannot be directly ascertained from the question as posed. Nonetheless, the perceived lack of understanding seems high.

For all of the national origin groups, the clear plurality response is "strong" agreement that "government seems so complicated that a person like me can't really understand what's going on." There is only modest variation across the groups; perhaps the largest divergence among the groups regarding the various response choices is Cubans' strong disagreement with the statement (Table 7.10).

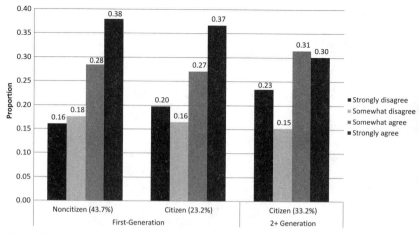

Figure 7.28. Politics Is Complicated and "a Person Like Me" Cannot Understand It, by Generation and Citizenship
Question wording: "People have different ideas about government in the United States. Please tell me how strongly you agree or disagree.... 'Sometimes politics and government seem so complicated that a person like me can't really understand what's going on.'"

For all but the highest income group, strong agreement with the view that "government seems so complicated that a person like me can't really understand what's going on" is the leading response, and more than half (53 percent) and up to 68 percent in each income group somewhat or strongly agree, as shown in Figure 7.29. At the same time, income shapes responses in ways that might be expected, albeit modestly. The starkest example is that fully 38 percent of those at the lowest income level and 22 percent of those at the highest income levels strongly agree that "sometimes politics and government seem so complicated that a person like me can't really understand what's going on."

The impact of education on these views is also most striking concerning the highest versus lowest levels and the "strongly disagree" versus "strongly agree" responses, shown in Figure 7.30. Clear majorities of both women and men somewhat or strongly agree that government sometimes seems too complicated (Figure 7.31); women are rather more likely to see government this way (67 percent and 60 percent, respectively).

Table 7.10. *Perception of Ability to Understand Government and Politics, by National Origin*

Category: Political Views, Role/View of Government

Response		Cuba	Dominican Republic	El Salvador	Mexico	Puerto Rico	Other Central America	Other South America	Other	Missing	Total
Strongly disagree	Freq.	77	53	63	1039	140	57	70	19	25	1544
	Row%	5.00	3.42	4.10	67.31	9.04	3.72	4.53	1.26	1.62	100.00
	Col%	25.61	18.30	17.30	18.59	21.93	18.69	19.89	25.03	32.26	19.31
Somewhat disagree	Freq.	47	51	69	909	92	57	73	13	11	1322
	Row%	3.59	3.85	5.20	68.72	6.98	4.34	5.53	0.95	0.83	100.00
	Col%	15.76	17.67	18.77	16.25	14.51	18.68	20.81	16.20	14.18	16.54
Somewhat agree	Freq.	71	79	106	1661	173	81	111	29	17	2327
	Row%	3.05	3.38	4.55	71.40	7.42	3.49	4.76	1.24	0.71	100.00
	Col%	23.58	27.26	28.94	29.72	27.12	26.49	31.50	37.17	21.34	29.10
Strongly agree	Freq.	106	106	128	1980	232	111	98	17	25	2802
	Row%	3.77	3.78	4.57	70.67	8.27	3.96	3.49	0.60	0.89	100.00
	Col%	35.05	36.77	35.00	35.43	36.44	36.13	27.80	21.60	32.22	35.05
TOTAL	Freq.	301	288	366	5589	636	307	352	78	78	7995
	Row%	3.77	3.61	4.58	69.91	7.96	3.84	4.40	0.97	0.97	100.00
	Col%	100.00	100.00	100.00	100.00	100.00	100.00	100.00	100.00	100.00	100.00

Notes: National origin: (24 d.f.) 47.3951 (P = 0.1073). Question wording: "People have different ideas about the government in the United States. Please tell me how strongly you agree or disagree with this statement: 'Sometimes politics and government seem so complicated that a person like me can't really understand what's going on.'"

225

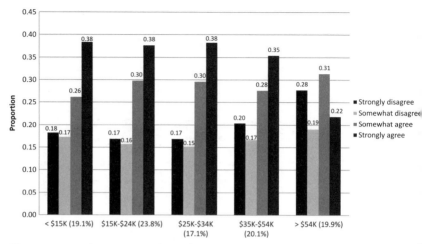

Figure 7.29. Politics Is Complicated and "a Person Like Me" Cannot Understand It, by Income

Question wording: "People have different ideas about government in the United States. Please tell me how strongly you agree or disagree. . . . 'Sometimes politics and government seem so complicated that a person like me can't really understand what's going on.'"

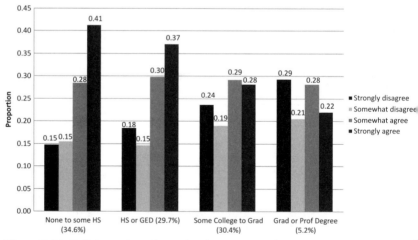

Figure 7.30. Politics Is Complicated and "a Person Like Me" Cannot Understand It, by Education

Question wording: "People have different ideas about government in the United States. Please tell me how strongly you agree or disagree. . . . 'Sometimes politics and government seem so complicated that a person like me can't really understand what's going on.'"

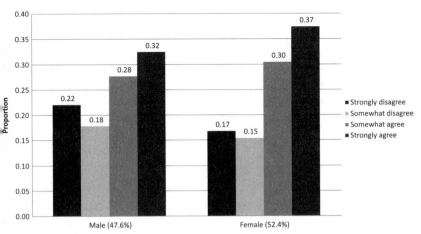

Figure 7.31. Politics Is Complicated and "a Person Like Me" Cannot Understand It, by Gender

Question wording: "People have different ideas about government in the United States. Please tell me how strongly you agree or disagree.... 'Sometimes politics and government seem so complicated that a person like me can't really understand what's going on.'"

Conclusion

Civic association and engagement are though to be important and beneficial to groups' and individuals' becoming part of a society and polity. Latinos' immersion in American civil society – the extent and depth, as well as ethnic composition of the associations, among other dimensions – has been the central topic of this chapter. Specifically, we explored Latinos' levels of such activity, their focus on and interest in various public affairs, and the social contexts of Latinos' interactions in civic arenas. In addition, we considered Latinos' views of government (i.e., their perceptions of its orientation and of their ability to influence, trust, and understand it).

In a nutshell, there are not high levels of civic engagement among Latinos. There is a limited sense of trust in government and an ability to influence and understand it. But our analysis also entailed a consideration of factors that may account for those patterns. We examined whether generation, citizenship status, national origin background, socioeconomic situation, or gender affects the views and assessments. In general, these variables (with the possible exception of gender) significantly affect most of the dimensions of civic engagement and attitudes about government.

This is important to remember because our survey respondents are disproportionately noncitizen, first generation, and of lower socioeconomic status; as those circumstances change, we might expect Latinos' civic engagement and outlooks on government to change as well. For the moment, we identify notable, broad conclusions that emerge from the complex array of findings presented here. We discuss the civic engagement issues and the views or assessments of government in turn.

On the whole, levels of civic engagement, as indicated by participation in groups, contacting officials, and interest in public affairs, seem very modest. Participation in social, cultural, civic, and political groups seems low. There is, however, some variation: in general participation increases with citizenship status, generation, and income and education; there are also differences associated with national origin. The social composition of the groups in which Latinos do participate varies somewhat by generation, with the first generation participating in mostly Latino groups and later generations most commonly being part of groups with a substantial mix of white and/or a broader racial-ethnic composition. National origin seems to matter considerably for the composition of groups to which Latinos belong. Puerto Ricans, Mexicans, and Cubans belong to mostly mixed groups; Dominicans and Salvadorans are much more likely to be involved in mostly Latino groups. Furthermore, lower socioeconomic status is also associated with involvement in mostly Latino groups.

The frequency of another type of participation, contacting public officials, is found to be quite low as well, although several factors increase this somewhat. Being a citizen, being of Puerto Rican or Cuban background, and being of higher socioeconomic status are each associated with greater likelihood of contacting. We also looked at the ethnic background of the officials contacted by our respondents and found that Puerto Ricans and Dominicans most often had contacted someone who is not Latino and/or Hispanic, whereas those of other national origin backgrounds were about evenly split, and that those of higher socioeconomic status had more frequently contacted non-Latino officials than had those of lower socioeconomic status.

Perhaps the broadest question in our survey regarding civic association asked respondents about how interested they are in politics and public affairs. On the one hand, a considerable portion responded "not interested," yet the most common response among the first generation (citizens and noncitizens) and the second generation is at least "somewhat interested." Furthermore, higher socioeconomic status appreciably increases the degree of interest. Women and men are equally likely to say they are not interested, but beyond that, no clear pattern by gender is readily discernible.

A second key set of questions examined in this chapter dealt with a sense of efficacy and trust in government. The findings on questions concerning what "interests are served by government," the level of trust in government, how much say one has in government, and the ability to understand government are quite consistent and generally striking, which indicates strong reservations about government's concern for the common good, its trustworthiness, and one's ability to influence or understand government. For example, large majorities believe government is "run by just a few big interests looking out for themselves, and not the benefit of all," a view that actually increases from the first to the second generation. There is some difference according to national origin (with Cubans being the most sanguine). Interestingly, higher levels of education and income seem to spur a stronger sense of government being mostly run by "just a few big interests." In this instance, women differed from men, with women more likely to hold a negative view of government.

Overall, levels of trust in government were very low; fewer than a third of all respondents say they trust government "most of the time" or "just about always"; this varies relatively little by generation. Cubans show slightly higher levels of trust than other national origin groups, as do those with more income and education. Women, however, are a bit less trusting than men. Respondents' views about how much say they have in government generally echo those regarding the interests served by and the degree of trust in government. Stated briefly, there is a sense of (only) limited influence on or say in government, although there is some variation by generation, citizenship, and socioeconomic factors, comparable to what was found in other responses evaluating government. It also is unsurprising, then, that respondents express roughly similar sentiments in believing that government is often very complex and difficult to understand.

Further research should consider possible causal connections between aspects of civic engagement, discussed in the first section of this chapter, and assessments of government, assessed in the second part of this chapter. There are plausible prima facie reasons and previous research that would suggest such a link. In addition, the relationship between issues discussed in this chapter with those considered in other chapters are intriguing and certainly worthy of exploration. For example, Latinos' positive and generally strong affinity with American core values, as discussed in Chapter 3 of this volume, seem to stand in clear contrast with most of the findings presented here. Assuming that is in fact the case, how and why this is so is another compelling and significant question. Yet the findings in this chapter are certainly notable in their own right.

Bibliography

Barrera, Mario. 1985. "The Historical Evolution of Chicano Ethnic Goals: A Bibliographic Essay," in *Sage Race Relations Abstracts* 10, 1: 1–48.
Hero, Rodney E. 2007. *Racial Diversity and Social Capital: Equality and Community in America*. New York: Cambridge University Press.
Knack, Stephen. 2002. "Social Capital and the Quality of Government: Evidence from the States." *American Journal of Political Science* 46, 4: 772–85.
Marquez, Benjamin. 1993. *LULAC: The Evolution of a Mexican American Organization*. Austin, TX: University of Texas Press.
Putnam, Robert D. 2000. *Bowling Alone: The Collapse and Revival of American Community*. New York: Simon and Schuster.
Verba, Sindey, Kay L. Schlozman, and Henry Brady. 1995. *Voice and Equality: Civic Voluntarism in American Politics*. Cambridge, MA: Harvard University Press.

8

Latino Media and Technology Usage

Another aspect of the Latino experience in the United States deals with acquiring information about the American political system and politics. This chapter focuses on media usage and news sources among Latinos, as well as their language of preference for those sources. In addition, what has been referred to as a digital divide among racial-ethnic and social-class grouping is examined briefly by exploring Latinos' access to the Internet. In essence, this chapter represents an introduction to the small but growing area of research and interest regarding Latinos and media use, as well as its application to the world of politics.

Political Knowledge and Media Usage

Gateways to the world of politics can be enhanced by becoming more knowledgeable about the political system, its institutions, and its leadership (Subvervi-Velez 2008). In addition, accounts of governmental actions, policy considerations and debates, and activities of political parties are important pieces of information that direct an individual's civic and political engagement (Johnson and Arceneaux 2010). A major source of that political knowledge comes from mass media outlets. Obviously, media outlets have been expanding in recent years with more nontraditional media (e.g., electronic news, magazines, blogs, social networks, international news media). For the most part, our introductory examination will focus on the two more traditional outlets – newspapers and television. Historically, mass media has been a source of both political facts or news and political expression or opinion on issues, candidates, and public policies (Johnson and Arceneaux 2010).

231

There is a relationship between an individual's level of political knowl
edge and use of mass media, although it is not always clear whether on
seeks out media to acquire political knowledge or whether, with level
of political knowledge through socialization, peers, and so on, one seek
out mass media sources. Media access and political interest have a simila
chicken-and-egg relationship: does having access to mass media generat
a person's political interests, or does having political interest motivate a
individual to look for media sources? In any event, in this chapter, we ar
not able to determine the ordering of political knowledge and politica
interest with mass media usage and effects. What we are able to do i
examine the extent of type of media usage, as well as preferred languag
of mass media, by critical characteristics of our Latino respondents (e.g.
nativity, citizenship status, age, gender; Salzman and Salzman 2010).

In addition, we examine respondents' level of political knowledge
political interest, and indicators of political participation with frequenc
of newspaper and television news usage. Finally, we look briefly at th
extent of access and/or usage of the Internet among Latinos. As we hav
indicated, there is a small but growing research literature that analyze
the patterns and effects of media on Latinos.

Extant Work on Latinos and News Media Usage

Our examination directly benefits from previous work that examined th
extent of Latinos' news media usage and its contributing factors (DeSipi
2003; Hale, Olsen, and Fowler 2009; Salzman and Aloisi 2009; Salzma
and Salzman 2010; Subvervi-Velez 2008). One of the main findings o
prior research is that factors predicting newspaper readership are dif
ferent from those predicting television news consumption. Overall, th
explanation for newspaper readership is much clearer than the puzzl
of television news (Salzman and Salzman 2010). Compared to televisio
news viewers, newspaper readers have been shown to have higher educa
tion levels, higher levels of political knowledge, higher levels of politica
interest, and a greater likelihood of contacting governmental agencie
and/or officials and being civically engaged than their television viewin
counterparts.

In general, consumption or usage of news media is primarily related t
individual-level characteristics, which can be divided into three broad set
of factors. These sets have been identified as ability, interest, and expec
tations (Salzman and Salzman 2010). Ability refers to an individual'
personal resources and access to media sources. Interest in the America

political system is characterized by expressed attitudes of interest, level of political knowledge, and participation in the political process broadly defined. Expectations are reflected in the desire to be more knowledgeable of or incorporated in the political system and efforts to be less or more assimilated and/or culturally distinct.

Ability resources include the level of educational attainment and other indicators of socioeconomic status, including wealth, income, employment status, occupation, and homeownership. Ability could also be the availability of free time and media possession, such as owning televisions and radios and having Internet service. Another potential determinant of an individual's ability to use news sources is English-language proficiency. In the United States, news information is available in a variety of languages, including Spanish. English-language media is, however, the most readily available in the United States, so an individual's level of English proficiency is also considered part of his or her ability to consume news. *Access ability* relates both to the outlets one typically uses to consume media (e.g., cable television, purchased media products, Internet access) and its availability in one's geographic area. Although not all ability factors were found to significantly influence media consumption, most ability factors appear to have the hypothesized positive effect. English proficiency, education, and income had significant and positive effects on newspaper consumption (Salzman and Salzman 2010).

The interest dimension is perhaps more easily understood and measured. As previously stated, political interest is directly measured by the individual's expressed level of interest in politics and political affairs. However, it can also be captured by an assessment of the individuals' level of political knowledge and his or her reported level of civic and political participation, including membership in civic-minded groups, contacting government officials, lobby and protest activities, and (for citizens only) registering and turning out to vote. Sadly, interest indicators were not much help in Salzman and Salzman's (2010) efforts to predict television-news viewing among Latinos. The level of expressed interest in politics was the only factor that had a significant effect. Interest factors were much more successful in the prediction of newspaper consumption. Overall, the individual's level of expressed interest, political knowledge, membership in civic organizations, and contacting officials were significant and positively related to the individual's frequency of newspaper consumption.

Information about the United States, especially knowledge of its politics and the workings of the political system, could reasonably be expected to be in short supply among new immigrants to this country. Immigrants' expectations of and/or need for information about politics in the United States and the "American way" should increase their consumption of media news. For the foreign born, the extent of freedom of the press in one's home country may also influence their expectation of media news reliability and thus influence their news media consumption. Age and time spent in the United States could ameliorate immigrant expectations of information from media news. Similarly, naturalized citizens and later generations may have lower or different expectations for media news and thus different levels of consumption from noncitizens. With no direct measures of expectation factors, Salzman and Salzman (2010) used the proxy measures of citizenship status and generation and press-freedom scores for Latin American countries published by Freedom House in 2004. They had little success explaining the frequency of television-news usage among Latinos with these proxy measures, but once again there was greater success explaining the frequency of newspaper consumption. Latinos born in the United States were significantly more likely to read newspapers than the foreign born. Newspaper consumption was also positively related to increased freedom of the press in immigrants' home counties.

Prior Research on Latinos and Preferred Language of News Consumption

Although the dimensions of ability interest and expectations are useful for understanding media usage and/or consumption, they may also help explain the preferred or primary language of media consumption. As ability factors increase the preference for English as the primary language for news, consumption is expected to increase. For example, the level of English-language proficiency will directly affect an individual's preference for using English-language media. Upper social mobility or the rise in socioeconomic status increases contact with native-born populations, especially non-Latinos, which also affects English media preference. For those most interested in gaining greater knowledge about the U.S. political system, it would be expected that they would seek out media sources with the broadest appeal, which more than likely are mainstream media and English sources (Salzman and Salzman 2010). Generational distance from the immigration experience for Latinos also has the effect of greater usage of English-language media (Hale et al. 2009; Salzman and Alois 2009).

Media language preference, however, is also affected by one's social identity. That is, those Latinos who identify with a pan-ethnic and/or national origin identity are more likely to prefer Spanish-language media

or use both language options equally. The desire for cultural maintenance with one's country of origin and traditions is also associated with
Spanish-language preference. Research shows that as Spanish-language
options have increased, so too has the tendency of Spanish speakers to
prefer Spanish-language programming (DiSipio 2003). That is true not
just of Spanish-only speakers but also of bilingual consumers (Associated
Press and Univision 2010). Overall, the American assimilation process
has been found to have a direct bearing on the primary language of
news consumption. More assimilated Latinos, as well as those wanting
to assimilate or blend in, were more likely to rely primarily on English-
language news sources, whereas those wanting to maintain their Spanish
and remain culturally distinct were more likely to prefer Spanish-language
news options (Salzman and Salzman 2010).

Latinos, Technology, and the Internet

Examination of the digital divide among racial and ethnic groups and
social class has been a subject of concern in the new millennium. The
expansion of new communication technology and products and the
World Wide Web have served to expand and facilitate greater communication for most people. Although our examination of access to the
Internet is quite limited, it is worthwhile to present some general information about access and use of technology among Latinos. The Pew
Hispanic Center (Livingston et al. 2009; Livingston 2010a, 2010b, 2011;
Lopez and Livingston 2010) has conducted a number of focused surveys
regarding the digital divide and communication technology.

Results from the Pew Hispanic Center (Livingston et al. 2009; Livingston 2011) surveys indicate lower levels of access to the Internet for
Latinos relative to other racial groups, especially in the home setting.
Between 2006 and 2008, Internet use among Latinos increased by 10
percent to 64 percent. At the same time, there remains a 13 percent gap
between Latinos and non-Latinos. There is a clear socioeconomic bias
with respect to access to the Internet, as Latinos with higher income and
educational levels are more likely to have Internet access. Although home
access is increasing, use of broadband connections continues to exhibit
a major gap between Latinos and non-Latinos. Other key distinctions
among Latinos are English-language proficiency (more people who are
English proficient have greater Internet access) and nativity status (more
native born have Internet access). Finally, age also differentiates Internet
users, as younger Latinos have greater use. If one controls for most of
the socioeconomic differences, differences in Internet access and usage

Table 8.1. *Frequency of Daily Newspaper Consumption, by Generation an*
Citizenship

Category: Identity/Assimilation, Latino Identity/Assimilation

Response		First generation			2+ generation	
		Noncitizen	Citizen	Total	Response	To
Daily	Freq.	338	418	756	791	1547
	Row%	44.71	55.29	48.87	51.13	100
	Col%	8.62	20.95	12.78	29.09	17
Most days	Freq.	157	146	303	278	581
	Row%	51.82	48.18	52.15	47.85	100
	Col%	4.01	7.32	5.12	10.22	6
Once or twice	Freq.	1131	563	1694	811	2505
weekly	Row%	66.77	33.23	67.62	32.38	100
	Col%	28.85	28.22	28.64	29.83	29
Almost never	Freq.	2294	868	3162	839	4001
	Row%	72.55	27.45	79.03	20.97	100
	Col%	58.52	43.51	53.46	30.86	46
TOTAL	Freq.	3920	1995	5915	2719	8634
	Row%	66.27	33.73	68.51	31.49	100
	Col%	100	100	100	100	100

Note: First/2+ generation: chi-square (4 d.f.) 554.550 (P = 0.000). Citizen/noncitizen (first
eration only): chi-square (4 d.f.) 353.930 (P = 0.000). Respondents born in Puerto Rico are c
as first generation. Question wording: "How often would you say you read a daily newspa
Would it be daily, most days, only once or twice a week, or almost never?"

between the Spanish dominant versus English-speaking and bilingua
Latinos essentially disappears (Lopez and Livingston 2010). With thi
background on media, technology, and Latinos, we present our results ir
this area.

LNS Respondents and Newspaper Usage

Given our previous discussion about the differences between newspaper readers and television viewers, we begin our examination by looking specifically at newspaper usage among LNS respondents. Wher
respondents were asked, "How often would you say you read a daily
newspaper? Would it be daily, most days, only once or twice a week
or almost never?" almost half (46 percent) reported that they almost
never read a newspaper (see Table 8.1). Noncitizens (72 percent) were
about three times more likely than naturalized (27 percent) or U.S.-
born citizens (21 percent) to report that they never read a newspaper.

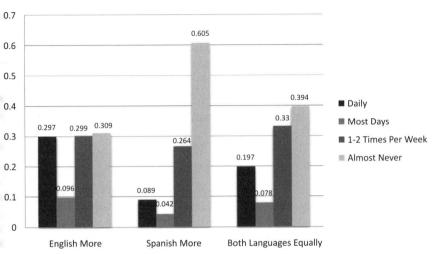

Figure 8.1. Frequency of Daily Newspaper Consumption, by Media Language Preference
Question wording: "How often would you say you read a daily newspaper? Would it be daily, most days, only once or twice a week, or almost never?" "For information about public affairs and politics, would you say you rely more heavily on Spanish-language television, radio, and newspapers or on English?"

Interestingly, there was minimal difference in the frequency of newspaper reading between those who were naturalized (first generation) and those who were born in the United States (second generation and beyond).

With this information in mind, it is not surprising to see that those preferring Spanish-language news sources were the most likely to report almost never reading a newspaper (see Figure 8.1). Those relying primarily on English-language news sources were considerably more likely to be daily or almost-daily newspaper readers. Those using news sources in both languages equally were roughly in the middle with respect to the frequency of newspaper readership.

Similar to the findings of previous research, LNS respondents who were daily newspaper readers demonstrated higher levels of political knowledge than those who read the newspaper less frequently (see Table 8.2). The lowest level of political knowledge was among those respondents who reported that they almost never read the newspaper. Daily newspaper readers were also more interested in politics and public affairs and more likely to report that they voted in the presidential election (data not shown).

Table 8.2. *Frequency of Daily Newspaper Consumption, by Summated Levels*
Political Knowledge

Category: Identity/Assimilation, Latino Identity/Assimilation

Response		None correct	One correct	Two correct	All correct	To
Daily	Freq.	272	381	437	457	154
	Row%	17.6	24.6	28.2	29.5	10
	Col%	8.8	15.9	23.9	34.3	1
Most days	Freq.	130	147	165	139	58
	Row%	17.6	24.6	28.2	29.5	10
	Col%	4.2	6.1	9	10.4	
Once or twice	Freq.	820	727	601	357	250
weekly	Row%	32.7	29	24	14.3	10
	Col%	26.6	30.4	32.9	26.8	2
Almost never	Freq.	1856	1140	623	381	400
	Row%	46.4	28.5	15.6	9.5	10
	Col%	60.3	47.6	34.1	28.6	4
TOTAL	**Freq.**	3078	2395	1826	1334	863
	Row%	35.7	27.7	21.2	15.5	10
	Col%	100	100	100	100	10

Note: Daily consumption of newspaper/summated political knowledge: chi-square (9 d.f.) 819.
(P = 0.00). Question wording: "How often would you say you read a daily newspaper? Would i
daily, most days, only once or twice a week, or almost never?" "Which political party, Demo
or Republican [alternate order], has a majority in the United States House of Representative
"In the United States, presidential elections are decided state-by-state. Can you tell me, in
election of 2004, which candidate, Bush or Kerry, won the most votes in [R's current state
residence]?" "Which one of the political parties is more conservative than the other at the natic
level, the Democrats or the Republicans?" "For information about public affairs and poli
would you say you rely more heavily on Spanish-language television, radio, and newspapers o
English?"

LNS Respondents and Television News Viewership

Similar to other subgroups in the U.S. population, there were many more
LNS respondents who were daily television-news viewers than daily newspaper readers (5,037 to 1547; data not shown).

Naturalized citizens were most likely to be daily viewers (62 percent),
and noncitizens were least likely (56 percent; see Table 8.3). The percentage of daily viewers among U.S. born or second generation and
beyond respondents was about right in the middle, at 59 percent. There
were essentially no differences in the frequency of television-news viewing by the language of media preference (see Figure 8.2). However,
and perhaps not surprisingly, the frequency of viewing television news
increased with the level of interest in politics and public affairs (data

Table 8.3. *Frequency of Watching Television News, by Generation and Citizenship*

Category: Identity/Assimilation, Latino Identity/Assimilation

ponse		First generation			2+ generation	
		Noncitizen	Citizen	Total	Citizen	Total
ly	Freq.	2185	1036	3321	1816	5037
	Row%	43.4	20.6	65.9	34.1	100
	Col%	55.9	62.3	59.5	59.5	17.92
st days	Freq.	568	199	767	403	1170
	Row%	51.82	48.18	65.5	34.5	100
	Col%	14.5	12	13.7	13.2	6.73
ce or twice	Freq.	801	295	1096	531	1627
eekly	Row%	66.77	33.23	67.4	32.6	100
	Col%	20.4	17.7	19.6	17.4	29.01
1ost never	Freq.	366	133	499	301	800
	Row%	72.55	27.45	62.4	37.6	100
	Col%	9.3	8	8.9	9.9	46.34
AL	Freq.	3920	1663	5583	3051	8634
	Row%	66.27	33.73	64.7	35.3	100
	Col%	100	100	100	100	100

e: First/2+ generation: chi-square (4 d.f.) 554.550 (P = 0.000). Citizen/noncitizen (first gen- ion only): chi-square (4 d.f.) 353.930 (P = 0.000). Respondents born in Puerto Rico are coded rst generation. Question wording: "How frequently would you say you watch television news? uld it be daily, most days, only once or twice a week, or almost never?" "For information about lic affairs and politics, would you say you rely more heavily on Spanish-language television, o, and newspapers or on English?"

not shown) and with the level of demonstrated political knowledge (see Table 8.4).

Media Language Preference, Political Knowledge, and Interest

Not surprisingly, given the level of Spanish-language dominance among Latino noncitizens, users of primarily Spanish media sources were far more likely to be noncitizens (see Table 8.5).

Naturalized citizens were more likely to use dual-language media equally, whereas a large majority of second generation and beyond respondents relied primarily on English-language media. Interestingly, there were noticeable differences in the level of political knowledge and interest by language of media preference. Respondents who relied primarily on English-language sources for their news information were able to answer more political knowledge questions correctly than those who

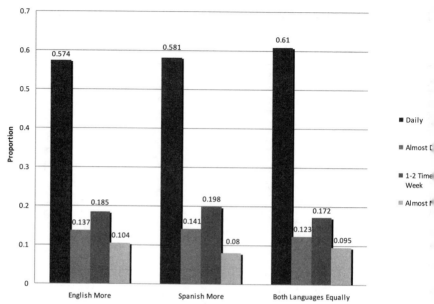

Figure 8.2. Frequency of TV News Watching, by Media Language Preference
Question wording: "How frequently would you say you watch television news? Would it be daily, most days, only once or twice a week, or almost never?" "For information about public affairs and politics, would you say you rely more heavily on Spanish-language television, radio, and newspapers or on English?"

received their news primarily in Spanish (see Figure 8.3). About 30 percent of the English-source users answered all the questions correctly, compared to just 6 percent of the Spanish-source users. Respondents who used both English- and Spanish-language sources for their news were somewhere in the middle; about 14 percent answered all the political knowledge questions correctly.

Respondents with Spanish media preferences were clearly less interested in politics and political affairs than those with English-language media preference. About 38 percent of Spanish media users said they were not interested in politics, compared to only 19 percent of the English media users (see Figure 8.4). Again, dual-language media users were in the middle, with 28 percent expressing no interest.

Internet Access

Prior research suggests lower Internet usage among Latinos than non-Latinos, which is then exacerbated by socioeconomic status, age, and

Table 8.4. *Frequency of Watching Television News, by Summated Levels of Political Knowledge*

Category: Identity/Assimilation, Latino Identity/Assimilation

;ponse		None correct	One correct	Two correct	All correct	Total
ily	Freq.	1660	1411	11132	835	5038
	Row%	32.9	28	22.5	16.6	100
	Col%	53.9	58.9	61.9	62.5	58.3
st days	Freq.	422	325	226	197	1170
	Row%	36.1	27.8	19.3	16.8	100
	Col%	13.7	13.6	12.4	14.8	13.5
ce or twice	Freq.	674	464	307	182	1627
veekly	Row%	41.4	28.5	18.9	11.2	100
	Col%	21.9	19.4	16.8	13.6	18.8
most never	Freq.	321	196	163	121	801
	Row%	40.1	24.5	20.3	15.1	100
	Col%	10.4	8.2	8.9	9.1	9.3
AL	Freq.	3077	2396	1828	1335	8636
	Row%	35.6	27.7	21.2	15.5	100
	Col%	100	100	100	100	100

te: Daily consumption of newspaper/summated political knowledge: chi-square (9 d.f.) 82.361 = 0.00). Questions wording: "How frequently would you say you watch television news? uld it be daily, most days, only once or twice a week, or almost never?" "Which political ty, Democrat or Republican [alternate order], has a majority in the United States House of presentatives?" "In the United States, presidential elections are decided state-by-state. Can you me, in the election of 2004, which candidate, Bush or Kerry, won the most votes in [R's rent state of residence]?" "Which one of the political parties is more conservative than the er at the national level, the Democrats or the Republicans?" "For information about public airs and politics, would you say you rely more heavily on Spanish-language television, radio, l newspapers or on English?"

other immigrant factors (Livingson 2010a). Tables 8.6 and 8.7 provide some support for these findings. About half of the LNS respondents report having no Internet access at all (49 percent; see Table 8.6). Noncitizens are most likely to report having no access (69 percent), compared to only 25 percent of U.S.-born Latinos who report no access. Second generation and beyond Latinos are most likely to report having Internet in their homes (54 percent), compared to only 25 percent of noncitizens. Naturalized citizens report more sources of access to the Internet than noncitizens, but they do not have as much access as second generation and beyond respondents.

Age appears to have some bearing on Internet access but is less pronounced than might be expected (see Table 8.7). Seniors (older than

Table 8.5. *Media Language Preference, by Generation and Citizenship*
Category: Identity/Assimilation, Latino Identity/Assimilation

Response		First generation			2+ generation	
		Noncitizen	Citizen	Total	Citizen	Tot
English more	Freq.	291	534	825	1808	2633
	Row%	35.27	64.73	31.33	68.67	100
	Col%	7.49	27.05	14.08	67.11	30
Both equally	Freq.	851	631	1482	642	2124
	Row%	57.42	42.58	69.77	30.23	100
	Col%	21.89	31.97	25.29	23.83	24
Spanish more	Freq.	2745	809	3554	244	3798
	Row%	77.24	22.76	93.58	6.42	100
	Col%	70.62	40.98	60.64	9.06	44
TOTAL	Freq.	3887	1974	5861	2694	8555
	Row%	66.32	33.68	68.51	31.49	100
	Col%	100.00	100.00	100.00	100.00	100

Note: First/2+ generation: chi-square (3 d.f.) 2794.610 (P = 0.000). Citizen/noncitizen (first g
eration only): chi-square (3 d.f.) 873.410 (P = 0.000). Respondents born in Puerto Rico
coded as first generation. Question wording: "For information about public affairs and poli
would you say you rely more heavily on Spanish-language television, radio, and newspapers
on English-language TV, radio, and newspapers?"

fifty-five years) are the least likely to have Internet access and are the
least likely to have it in their homes. The youngest age group (between
eight and twenty-four) is somewhat more likely to have Internet access
someplace other than homes. Other differences across the age groups are
marginal. Interestingly, Table 8.8 shows no differences by gender, which
refutes the findings of previous research.

Conclusion

Our brief introductory examination of media use by Latinos in the LNS
serves as a preliminary profile of the extent of media consumption, the
primary language of media used, and some demographic and politically
relevant relationships. More specifically, we identified the frequency of
newspaper reading and watching television news in relation to nativity,
citizenship status, and generational status. Our results indicate that daily
newspaper readers tend to be more knowledgeable (three to one daily versus never reading newspaper) in answering all of the political knowledge
items correctly. In addition, daily reading of newspapers in English versus

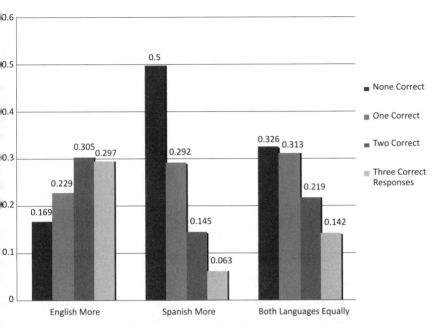

Figure 8.3. Summed Political Knowledge, by Media Language Preference

Question wording: "For information about public affairs and politics, would you say you rely more heavily on Spanish-language television, radio, and newspapers or on English?" "Which political party, Democrat or Republican [alternate order], has a majority in the United States House of Representatives?" "In the United States, presidential elections are decided state-by-state. Can you tell me, in the election of 2004, which candidate, Bush or Kerry, won the most votes in [R's current state of residence]?" "Which one of the political parties is more conservative than the other at the national level, the Democrats or the Republicans?"

Spanish makes a positive difference in levels of political knowledge. The combination of regular consumption of primarily English newspapers seems to have complementary associations with levels of political interest as well. This medium clearly differentiates the Latino adult population.

Interestingly, such a trend is not prevalent among Latinos who regularly watch television-news programming. Another noticeable pattern is that significantly more Latinos (i.e., citizens, noncitizens, and second generation and beyond) watch television news. The biggest difference is the language of the medium. First-generation noncitizens disproportionately watch Spanish-language news programming. Overall, more than 90 percent of first-generation Latinos (citizens and noncitizens) are consumers of Spanish-language news. For those who watch English-language instead

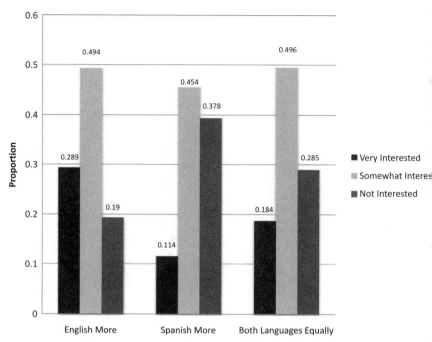

Figure 8.4. Interest in Politics and Public Affairs, by Media Language Preference **Question wording**: "For information about public affairs and politics, would you say you rely more heavily on Spanish-language television, radio, and newspapers or on English?" "How interested are you in politics and public affairs? Would you say you are very interested, somewhat interested, or not at all interested?"

of Spanish-language television news, there are also some differences. In terms of political knowledge, infrequent English-language television-news watchers are three times less likely than daily watchers to correctly answer all the political knowledge items. Conversely, Spanish-language viewers are five times more likely than daily watchers to answer none of the items correctly. Latinos who use media in both languages are closer in political attitudes and behaviors to Latinos who use English-language media.

As is evident in other sections of this work, it is important to differentiate Latinos by nativity, citizenship, and generational status. For example, noncitizens are three times more likely than their naturalized citizen counterparts to never read the newspaper. Naturalized citizens watch television news more than their noncitizen counterparts. When we add the language of news programming, then citizens are four times

Table 8.6. *Internet Access, By Generation and Citizenship*
Category: Identity/Assimilation, Latino Identity/Assimilation

ponse		First generation			2+ generation	
		Noncitizen	Citizen	Total	Citizen	Total
at all	Freq.	2691	823	3514	689	4203
	Row%	76.58	23.42	83.61	16.39	100.00
	Col%	68.65	41.25	59.41	25.35	48.69
where	Freq.	192	113	305	300	605
	Row%	62.95	37.05	50.41	49.59	100.00
	Col%	4.90	5.66	5.16	11.04	7.01
ne	Freq.	966	942	1908	1458	3366
	Row%	50.63	49.37	56.68	43.32	100.00
	Col%	24.64	47.22	32.26	53.64	38.99
h	Freq.	71	117	188	271	459
	Row%	37.77	62.23	40.96	59.04	100.00
	Col%	1.81	5.86	3.18	9.97	5.32
AL	Freq.	3920	1995	5915	2718	8633
	Row%	66.27	33.73	68.52	31.48	100.00
	Col%	100.00	100.00	100.00	100.00	100.00

e: First/2+ generation: chi-square (4 d.f.) 915.750 (P = 0.000) Citizen/noncitizen (first gener-
1 only): chi-square (4 d.f.) 650.100 (P = 0.000). Respondents born in Puerto Rico are coded
rst generation. Question wording: "Do you have regular Internet access at home, somewhere
, or not at all?"

more likely to use English news sources than noncitizens, and the ratio
is much greater between the second generation and noncitizens. With
Spanish-language media receiving greater attention from political parties
and candidates, then the role, content, and impact of this language
medium on Latinos becomes an important development to examine.

Our limited query of access and/or use of the Internet reinforces the
general understanding of a digital divide between Latinos' access relative to that of other groups in America. In the Latino community, this
divide is more pronounced among noncitizens, especially in the home. If
the Internet is not available in the home, there is a low probability that
Latinos will get access elsewhere. The age group of twenty-four to forty-
four years has the highest level of access, and there is little gender difference in terms of Internet access. Again noncitizens are two and a half times
more likely not to have access at all relative to their naturalized citizen
counterparts. Given the greater use of the Internet and growing pervasive-
ness of social networks for sociopolitical purpose, how Latinos access and

Table 8.7. *Internet Access, by Age Group*
Category: Identity/Assimilation, Latino Identity/Assimilation

Response		18–24	25–34	35–44	45–54	55+	To
Home	Freq.	516	728	861	593	498	31!
	Row%	16.1	22.8	26.9	18.6	15.6	1(
	Col%	41.1	35.1	45.8	44.7	31	3
Somewhere else	Freq.	132	127	94	69	46	4(
	Row%	28.2	27.1	20.1	14.7	9.8	1(
	Col%	10.5	6.1	5	5.2	2.9	
Both	Freq.	77	108	102	89	66	44
	Row%	17.4	24.4	23.1	20.1	14.9	1(
	Col%	6.1	5.2	5.4	6.7	4.1	
Not at all	Freq.	529	1112	823	576	995	403
	Row%	13.1	27.6	20.4	14.3	24.7	1(
	Col%	42.2	53.6	43.8	43.4	62	4
TOTAL	Freq.	1254	2075	1880	1327	1605	814
	Row%	15.4	25.5	23.1	16.3	19.7	1(
	Col%	100	100	100	100	100	1(

Note: Daily consumption of newspaper/summated political knowledge: chi-square (12 d.f.) 24! (P = 0.00). Question wording: "Do you have regular Internet access at home, somewhere else not at all?"

Table 8.8. *Internet Access, by Gender*
Category: Identity/Assimilation, Latino Identity/Assimilation

Response		Latino Males	Latina Females	Total
Home	Freq.	1615	1752	3367
	Row%	48	52	100
	Col%	39.5	38.5	39
Somewhere else	Freq.	293	312	390
	Row%	48.4	51.6	100
	Col%	7.2	6.9	7
Both	Freq.	212	247	459
	Row%	46.2	53.8	100
	Col%	5.2	5.4	5.3
Not at all	Freq.	1766	2337	4203
	Row%	46.8	53.2	100
	Col%	48.1	49.2	48.7
TOTAL	Freq.	4086	4548	8634
	Row%	47.3	52.7	100
	Col%	100	100	100

Note: Daily consumption of newspaper/summated political knowledge; chi-square (3 d.f.) 10.009 (P = 0.00). Question wording: "Do you have regular Internet access at home, somewhere else, or not at all?"

make use of such developments will be important considerations for their future political development. The future impact of the language of media and content and exposure to politics and public policies are discussed in the Chapter 14.

References

Associated Press and Univision. 2010. *Associated Press–Univision Poll.* http://surveys.ap.org/data/NORC/AP-Univision%20Topline_posting.pdf.

DeSipio, Louis. 2003. *Bilingual Television Viewers and the Language Choices They Make.* Claremont, CA: Tomás Rivera Policy Institute.

Hale, M., T. Olsen, and E. F. Fowler. 2009. "A Matter of Language or Culture: Coverage of the 2004 U.S. Elections on Spanish and English Language Television." *Mass Communication and Society* 12(1): 26–51.

Johnson, M., and K. Arceneaux. 2010. "Who Watches Political Talk? Revisiting Political Television Reception with Behavioral Measures." Paper presented at the 2010 meeting of the Southwestern Political Science Association, Houston, TX.

Livingston, Gretchen. 2010a. *The Latino Digital Divide: The Native Born versus the Foreign Born.* Washington D.C.: Pew Hispanic Center.

Livingston, Gretchen. 2010b. *Latinos and Digital Technology.* Washington D.C.: Pew Hispanic Center.

Livingston, Gretchen. 2011. *Latinos and the Digital Divide.* Washington D.C.: Pew Hispanic Center.

Livingston, Gretchen, Kim Parker, and Susannah Fox. 2009. *Latinos Online, 2006–2008: Narrowing the Gap.* Washington D.C.: Pew Hispanic Center.

Lopez, Mark Hugo, and Gretchen Livingston. 2010. *How Young Latinos Communicate with Friends in the Digital Age.* Washington, D.C.: Pew Hispanic Center.

Salzman, Ryan, and Catherine Salzman. 2010. "Understanding News Media Consumption among Latinos in the United States." Paper prepared for the Spanish Language Media 2010 conference, Denton, TX, November 11–13.

Salzman, Ryan, and Rosa Aloisi. 2009. "News Media Consumption and Political Participation in Central America: Causation and Explanation" *Journal of Spanish Language Media* 2: 46–75.

Subvervi-Velez, F. A. 2008. *The Mass Media and Latino Politics: Studies of U.S. Media Content, Campaign Strategies and Survey Research, 1984–2004.* New York: Routledge.

9

Voter Registration, Turnout, and Choice

Voting in a meaningful election is the defining act of democratic citizenship. Voting is a unique form of political participation in that it is widely engaged in, generally of low cost, and enjoys widespread support as a behavioral norm. Although there are many other forms of political action – ranging from simple conversations to revolutionary violence, and more generally including contacting elected officials, joining civic groups, attending a meeting or donating money – none is as frequently engaged in as registration and voting.

Despite the centrality of the vote to democratic citizenship, voting has often not been an easy undertaking for Latinos. For Latino citizens, voting often involved overcoming vote suppression tactics; low levels of political information; resource disadvantages, including poor education and low income; and in many instances, language barriers that foreclosed participation and that jurisdictions were not motivated to redress. On top of those obstacles to voting, once a Latino voter gained access to the ballot box, there were often poor choices of candidates and few or none from the community itself. Latinos elected to public office, outside of New Mexico at least, were exceedingly rare.

The Voting Rights Act of 1965, and particularly the extension of the act to "language minorities" in 1975, did a great deal to tear down the functional obstacles to voting. Ballot materials prepared in Spanish – at least where the population criteria provided for such a requirement – along with the abolition of poll taxes and shady registration practices, created greater opportunities for Latino citizens to vote if they chose to do so. Moreover, the amendments to section 2 of the act in 1982 and their subsequent judicial interpretation provided many potential Latino voters with a chance to actually vote for first-choice candidates who had any prayer of winning. The creation of majority-minority districts, along with federal court intervention to stop practices of minority vote dilution, dramatically increased the representation of Latino elected officials at every level of government in the 1980s and 1990s.

These legal changes, however, are not alone sufficient to redress the relative disadvantages Latinos have in the electoral arena, particularly in terms of voter turnout. Specifically, Latino participation lags Latinos' population share for four critical reasons: the immigration process and its delays, continued resource disadvantages, their relatively young age, and a painful lack of outreach.

Because so many Latinos are foreign born, they must undergo naturalization as a first step to full participation. This process is unavailable to the undocumented, of course, but even for documented immigrants, naturalization is a time-consuming and costly process that must be completed before having an electoral voice, and this process (not surprisingly) suppresses the available pool of eligible voters. Moreover, because foreign-born citizens often lack the necessary socialization into the U.S. political system, there is a long history of low voter turnout among newly naturalized citizens (DeSipio 1996), and the evidence shows a monotonic and nearly linear increase in vote propensity across generations (Santoro and Segura 2011). In contrast, the recent politicization of Latino identity and immigration appears to have reversed this trend, and there is good evidence that newly naturalized voters and their offspring vote at rates higher than those of U.S.-born Latinos, precisely because they naturalized for political purposes (Pantoja, Ramirez, and Segura 2001).

Second, notwithstanding the mobilizing potential of anti-immigrant rhetoric and action, Latinos remain poorer and less educated than other Americans. With few exceptions, income and education are rock-solid predictors of all forms of political behavior (Verba, Scholzman, and Brady 1995). Political participation requires both time and attention, and it can demand some level of cognitive resource to decipher what is at stake, what candidates believe, and the like. Politics, in short, is a luxury.

Third, Latinos are young. At 27.4 years, the median age of Latinos (Census Bureau, 2011) in the United States is almost a decade younger than the rest of the society, at 36.8 years (Statistical Abstract of the United States: 2011). Although 87 percent of Latinos younger than eighteen are U.S.-born citizens and will be immediately eligible to vote when they reach adulthood, only 60 percent of Latino adults are citizens, and many of those are among the young, another group with historically low participation.

Finally, outreach is a major concern. Although there is good evidence (Michelson 2006; Michelson, Garcia-Bedolla, and Green 2008) that asking Latinos to vote significantly enhances mobilization, there is a history of poor outreach to Latino communities. This is true, in part, because parties and candidates see these voters are low propensity and hard to mobilize. Hence the expenditure of resources is less likely to yield significant vote increase. And, for all but South Florida Cubans, party outreach to Latinos is done by one and only one political party. But a second reason, suggested by Frymer (1999), is that outreach to minority voters can plausibly demobilize white voters if race or ethnicity is a salient consideration in a community, district, or state, thereby costing the party and/or candidate more votes than are gained. As a consequence of these two dynamics, outreach to minority voters is often weaker than toward whites, with significant effect.

The Latino National Survey probed several aspects of electoral participation. Because of our very large sample size, we were able to explore questions of registration and turnout among the citizen-only subsample and still have adequate numbers for analysis.

Voter Registration

Among the complications in assessing both registration and turnout is the substantial documented overreporting. As a consequence of the social desirability bias, survey respondents are often unwilling to provide survey answers that would be accurate but embarrassing, that is, inconsistent with social norms. This is why we have low incidence of admission by survey respondents that they cheat on their taxes, hold hostile views of particular social groups, or engage in specific sexual practices. In the case of registration and voting, the broadly held norm that these activities are inherently good, something that is the duty of a citizen in a democratic society, reduces the willingness of respondents to admit that they are either not registered to vote or did not turn out on election day.

As a consequence, surveys systematically overreport both registration and turnout, and the Latino National Survey is no exception. Both of these two phenomena, and registration in particular, also suffer from the simple problem that people may not actually remember behavior two years past with accuracy or may not even know. Although it sounds odd, the registration requirements are often unfamiliar to people. Voters are

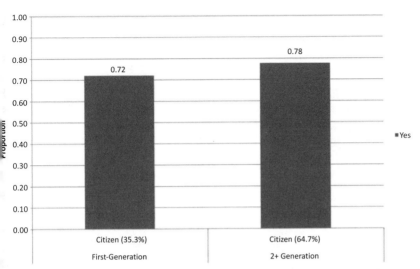

Figure 9.1. Self-Report as Registered to Vote, by Generation and Citizenship
Question wording: "Are you currently registered to vote in the U.S.?"

required to report changes of address to remain registered, something few
know. Some number of Americans believes themselves to be registered
when they are not, for example.

Figure 9.1 reports respondents' self-reported registration by generation. Unlike the other tables in this volume, noncitizens are excluded from
the tables on registration and voting. Large majorities of those eligible
to register to vote self-report as registered with a statistically significant
increase in voter registration (self-reported) across generational status.
Seventy-two percent of first-generation citizens and almost 78 percent of
second generation and beyond citizens self-report as registered to vote.
These numbers are certainly inflated by overreporting.

If we examine registration by socioeconomic status, familiar patterns again appear. Figures 9.2 and 9.3 show that income and education are both positively associated with self-reporting as registered to
vote. Although a majority of respondents self-report as registered to vote
regardless of income or education, we find the highest percentages of self-
reporting for those with the highest income and education. The effect on
income is not monotonic, but the trend is upward, and the effect statistically significant. Table 9.1 tabulates registration by gender, and there
is no discernible effect. Women and men appear to report registration
at approximately the same rates. Large majorities of all national origin
groups self-report as registered to vote, as reported in Table 9.2. Some

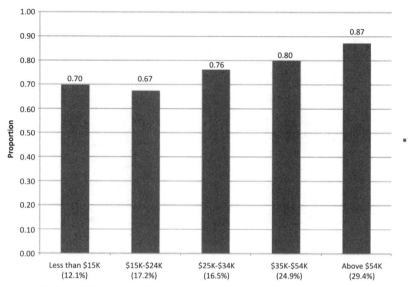

Figure 9.2. Self-Report as Registered to Vote, by Income
Question wording: "Are you currently registered to vote in the U.S.?"

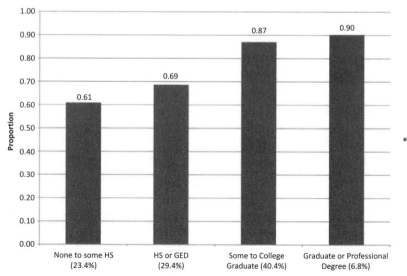

Figure 9.3. Self-Report as Registered to Vote, by Education
Question wording: "Are you currently registered to vote in the U.S.?"

Table 9.1. *Self-Report as Registered to Vote, by Gender*
Category: Political Participation, Electoral Participation

Response		Male	Female	Total
Yes	Freq.	1578	1947	3525
	Row%	44.76	55.24	100.00
	Col%	74.39	76.87	75.74
No	Freq.	543	586	1129
	Row%	48.10	51.90	100.00
	Col%	25.61	23.13	24.26
TOTAL	Freq.	2121	2533	4655
	Row%	45.57	54.43	100.00
	Col%	100.00	100.00	100.00

Note: Gender: (1 d.f.) 3.9280 (P = 0.1542). Asked of U.S. citizens. Question wording: "Are you currently registered to vote in the U.S.?"

regional variation exists as we go from a high of 92 percent of Cubans self-reporting as registered to vote to a low of 72 percent of Mexicans self-reporting as registered to vote.

Although we are concerned with overreporting, and the numbers here clearly reflect this, we have confidence in the trends we observe. That is, although overreporting is an issue, the between-group differences of interest likely reflect the underlying realities.

Turnout

Like registration, turnout is generally overreported in surveys. To minimize the size of this effect, we employ a question wording first tested by Belli et al. (1999) to reduce the social costs of honestly admitting to not voting and, by extension, to reduce the rate of overreport. The question stem offers respondents a variety of reasons they might have legitimately not voted without running afoul of norms of responsible democratic citizenship. The question wording employed is included in Figure 9.4, along with the results by generational status.

There appears to be a slight increase in the propensity to self-report voter turnout across the two groups. Just shy of 55 percent of foreign-born respondents, naturalized to citizenship, report turning out in 2004, compared with almost 59 percent of the U.S. born. This increase is in the

Table 9.2. *Self-Report as Registered to Vote, by National Origin*
Category: Political Participation, Electoral Participation

Response		Cuba	Dominican Republic	El Salvador	Mexico	Puerto Rico	Other Central America	Other South America	Other	Missing	Total
Yes	Freq.	221	138	119	2201	502	86	147	56	57	3525
	Row%	6.28	3.90	3.37	62.42	14.24	2.43	4.16	1.59	1.61	100.00
	Col%	92.27	78.71	73.85	72.32	82.82	72.38	82.36	85.15	83.86	75.74
No	Freq.	19	37	42	842	104	33	31	10	11	1129
	Row%	1.64	3.33	3.73	74.61	9.22	2.89	2.78	0.87	0.97	100.00
	Col%	7.73	21.29	26.15	27.68	17.18	27.62	17.64	14.85	16.14	24.26
TOTAL	Freq.	240	175	161	3043	606	118	178	66	68	4655
	Row%	5.15	3.76	3.46	65.38	13.02	2.54	3.83	1.41	1.45	100.00
	Col%	100.00	100.00	100.00	100.00	100.00	100.00	100.00	100.00	100.00	100.00

Note: National origin: (8 d.f.) 84.9533 (P = 0.0000). Asked of U.S. citizens. Question wording: "Are you currently registered to vote in the U.S.?"

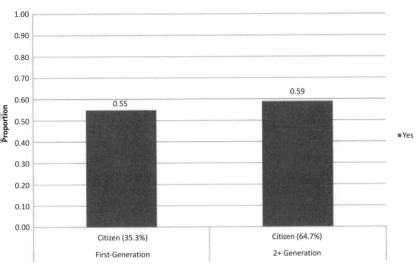

Figure 9.4. Self-Report as Voted in 2004 Election, by Generation and Citizenship
Question wording: "In talking to people about elections, we often find that a lot
of people were not able to vote because they weren't registered, they were sick,
or they just didn't have time. How about you – did you vote in the presidential
election last November?"

expected direction but not particularly sizable and only bordering on significance ($p = 0.063$). Although these turnout percentages are inflated in
comparison to other benchmarks, there appears to be somewhat less overreporting than one might have expected. Income and education (reported
in Figures 9.5 and 9.6) are positively associated with self-reporting as
having voted in the 2004 presidential election, with those in the highest
response categories reporting turnout at substantially higher rates than
those in the lowest. The effect is monotonic for education and nearly so
for income. There are no meaningful gender differences in propensity to
report turnout, as illustrated in Table 9.3.

Just as in the reports of voter registration, self-reported turnout has
visible variation by national origin, as shown in Table 9.4. Cubans self-
report the highest level of participation in the 2004 presidential election,
at 78 percent, whereas Salvadorans self-report the lowest level of participation, at 49 percent. Participation among Puerto Ricans is at 68 percent;
Dominicans, at 66 percent, and Mexicans, at 52 percent.

Again, we are certain that these numbers are significantly inflated by
the overreporting of respondents, but the patterns of difference likely
reflect genuine underlying distinctions.

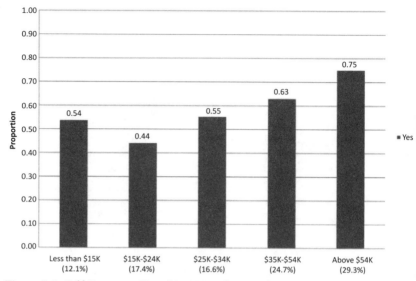

Figure 9.5. Self-Report as Voted in 2004 Election, by Income
Question wording: "In talking to people about elections, we often find that a lot of people were not able to vote because they weren't registered, they were sick, or they just didn't have time. How about you – did you vote in the presidential election last November?"

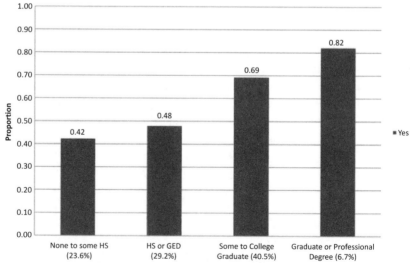

Figure 9.6. Self-Report as Voted in 2004 Election, by Education
Question wording: "In talking to people about elections, we often find that a lot of people were not able to vote because they weren't registered, they were sick, or they just didn't have time. How about you – did you vote in the presidential election last November?"

Table 9.3. *Self-Report as Voted in 2004 Election, by Gender*
Category: Political Participation, Electoral Participation

Response		Male	Female	Total
Yes	Freq.	1212	1499	2711
	Row%	44.70	55.30	100.00
	Col%	56.29	58.54	57.51
No	Freq.	914	1035	1948
	Row%	46.89	53.11	100.00
	Col%	42.44	40.40	41.33
Don't know or refused	Freq.	27	27	55
	Row%	50.23	49.77	100.00
	Col%	1.27	1.06	1.16
TOTAL	Freq.	2153	2561	4714
	Row%	45.67	54.33	100.00
	Col%	100.00	100.00	100.00

Note: Gender: (2 d.f.) 2.7108 (P = 0.4510). Asked of U.S. citizens. Question wording: "In talking to people about elections, we often find that a lot of people were not able to vote because they weren't registered, they were sick, or they just didn't have time. How about you – did you vote in the presidential election last November?"

Contact by Candidates and Campaigns

It is a truism of American politics that being asked to vote is an important indicator of turnout likelihood. Latino eligible voters, along with other minority citizens, are often undermobilized, either because the cost of doing so is perceived as prohibitive or because their perception as low-propensity voters discourage parties, candidates, and groups from investing in their turnout. There is good evidence, however, to suggest that contact yields results, so this undermobilization likely has meaningful electoral costs.

We asked eligible citizens whether each had been contacted for the purposes of voter mobilization or to raise money, by either a candidate or a party. Overall, only 30 percent of the citizen respondents to the LNS had received any mobilization contact, and there are discernible patterns in who did and did not receive a call.

Figure 9.7 reports respondent recall of contact by a party or candidate across naturalized and native citizen cohorts. A majority of foreign-born citizens, though eligible voters, self-report no contact from candidates to solicit either a vote or a financial contribution, as do a majority of native-born citizens. The improvement from naturalized citizens (23.5 percent)

Table 9.4. *Self-Report as Voted in 2004 Election, by National Origin*
Category: Political Participation, Electoral Participation

Response		Cuba	Dominican Republic	El Salvador	Mexico	Puerto Rico	Other Central America	Other South America	Other	Missing	Total
Yes	Freq.	193	116	83	1613	413	70	127	48	48	2711
	Row%	7.11	4.29	3.05	59.49	15.24	2.57	4.70	1.77	1.79	100.00
	Col%	78.48	66.47	49.12	52.43	67.89	57.05	71.20	70.19	68.09	57.51
No	Freq.	48	59	84	1425	189	51	51	20	21	1948
	Row%	2.49	3.01	4.32	73.13	9.71	2.60	2.61	1.04	1.09	100.00
	Col%	19.73	33.53	50.09	46.32	31.07	41.40	28.41	29.81	29.76	41.33
Don't know or refused	Freq.	4	0	1	38	6	2	1	0	2	55
	Row%	8.04	0.00	2.41	70.41	11.60	3.47	1.28	0.00	2.79	100.00
	Col%	1.79	0.00	0.78	1.25	1.04	1.55	0.39	0.00	2.14	1.16
TOTAL	Freq.	246	175	168	3076	609	122	179	68	71	4714
	Row%	5.21	3.71	3.57	65.26	12.91	2.59	3.79	1.45	1.51	100.00
	Col%	100.00	100.00	100.00	100.00	100.00	100.00	100.00	100.00	100.00	100.00

Note: National origin: (16 d.f.) 144.9192 (P = 0.0000). Asked of U.S. citizens. Question wording: "In talking to people about elections, we often find that a lot of people were not able to vote because they weren't registered, they were sick, or they just didn't have time. How about you – did you vote in the presidential election last November?"

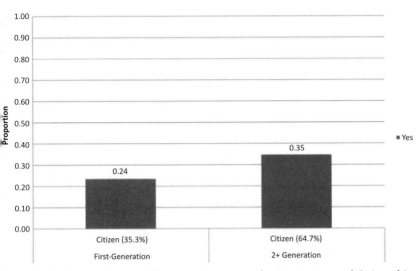

Figure 9.7. Contacts by Candidates or Campaigns, by Generation and Citizenship
Question wording: "In the 2004 elections, were you ever contacted to vote for or
contribute money to a candidate or political campaign?"

to native born (about 34.5 percent) is a modest 11 percent, although this
is a significant difference.

Those in the highest income and education categories are more likely
to report having been contacted, and the effect (visible in Figures 9.8 and
9.9) is both monotonic and significant. Moving from the lowest to highest
income group increases the likelihood of contact by more than 30 percentage points, whereas a similar movement across education categories
increases the likelihood by more than 37 percentage points. Party recruit-
ment and mobilization strategies are clearly structured with a significant
socioeconomic status bias, as these citizens are higher propensity voters.
Of course, the irony is that those reporting contact are among the most
likely to vote and, hence, those least in need of contact. The presence of
the "give money" element of the stem raises the possibility that some of
this socioeconomic effect is driven by the logical decision of the parties
and candidates to ask for money more from those most able to give.

Curiously, there does appear to be a slight gender effect, where men
report greater contact than women (Table 9.5). Because men and women
are more or less evenly distributed in society (and, if anything, Latina
women increasingly have greater educational attainment than men),
this finding is odd. It may reflect differential recall or a gender pattern in answering the phone when strangers call – in this case, party

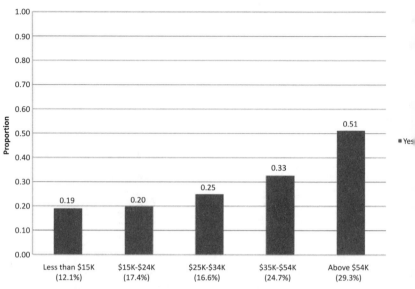

Figure 9.8. Contacts by Candidates or Campaigns, by Income
Question wording: "In the 2004 elections, were you ever contacted to vote for or contribute money to a candidate or political campaign?"

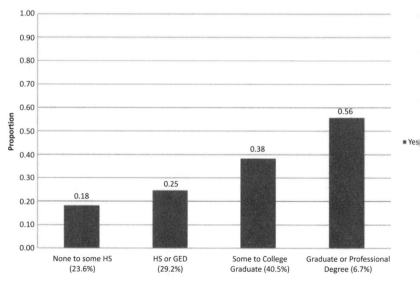

Figure 9.9. Contacts by Candidates or Campaigns, by Education
Question wording: "In the 2004 elections, were you ever contacted to vote for or contribute money to a candidate or political campaign?"

Table 9.5. *Contacts by Candidates or Campaigns, by Gender*
Category: Political Participation, Electoral Participation

Response		Male	Female	Total
Yes	Freq.	721	728	1449
	Row%	49.73	50.27	100.00
	Col%	33.47	28.44	30.74
No	Freq.	1373	1761	3134
	Row%	43.80	56.20	100.00
	Col%	63.76	68.76	66.48
Don't know	Freq.	60	72	131
	Row%	45.38	54.62	100.00
	Col%	2.77	2.80	2.79
TOTAL	Freq.	2153	2561	4714
	Row%	45.67	54.33	100.00
	Col%	100.00	100.00	100.00

Note: Gender: (2 d.f.) 14.2653 (P = 0.0105). Asked of U.S. citizens. Question wording: "In the 2004 elections, were you ever contacted to vote for or contribute money to a candidate or political campaign?"

and campaign workers. Nevertheless, this modest 5 percent difference is significant and curious. Regardless of national origin, there is little contact overall for any group, reported in Table 9.6. However, at about 35 percent, Cubans report the highest levels of contact, followed by Mexicans and Puerto Ricans, at 31 percent. An incredible 73 percent of Salvadorans report no contact by a candidate or campaigns. Patterns across national origin groups are not statistically significant.

Overall, the results demonstrate the relatively weak mobilization of Latino voters and a considerable missed opportunity.

Knowledge of How to Register

At least one obstacle to voter registration and participation is citizens' familiarity with the process (or lack thereof). This problem is exacerbated by a large percentage of foreign-born citizens who often lack extensive political socialization in the United States and the relatively transient nature of the population, requiring repeated reregistration. Like any economically disadvantaged group, Latinos move more frequently than others who are not disadvantaged and are hence more likely to be purged from the voter rolls or to not even know whether they are

Table 9.6. *Contacts by Candidates or Campaigns, by National Origin*
Category: Political Participation, Electoral Participation

Response		Cuba	Dominican Republic	El Salvador	Mexico	Puerto Rico	Other Central America	Other South America	Other	Missing	Total
Yes	Freq.	86	45	41	948	191	32	52	30	24	1449
	Row%	5.91	3.11	2.84	65.45	13.15	2.22	3.60	2.08	1.62	100.00
	Col%	34.90	25.78	24.52	30.83	31.29	26.34	29.20	44.16	33.08	30.74
No	Freq.	150	127	123	2047	394	86	125	37	45	3134
	Row%	4.79	4.04	3.92	65.33	12.57	2.75	3.98	1.18	1.44	100.00
	Col%	61.19	72.45	73.02	66.55	64.70	70.54	69.75	53.99	63.23	66.48
Don't Know	Freq.	10	3	4	81	24	4	2	1	3	131
	Row%	7.32	2.35	3.15	61.29	18.58	2.90	1.44	0.96	0.20	100.00
	Col%	3.91	1.77	2.46	2.62	4.01	3.12	1.06	1.85	3.70	2.79
TOTAL	Freq.	246	175	168	3076	609	122	179	68	71	4714
	Row%	5.21	3.71	3.57	65.26	12.91	2.59	3.79	1.45	1.51	100.00
	Col%	100.00	100.00	100.00	100.00	100.00	100.00	100.00	100.00	100.00	100.00

Note: National origin: (16 d.f.) 23.8677 (P = 0.3878). Asked of U.S. citizens. Question wording: "In the 2006 elections, were you ever contacted to vote for or contribute money to a candidate or political campaign?"

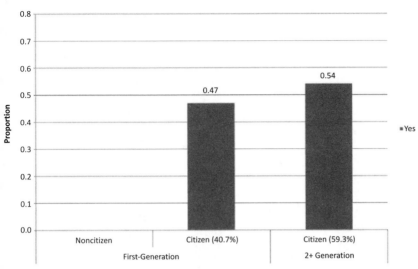

Figure 9.10. Know How to Register to Vote, by Generation and Citizenship
Question wording: "Do you know how and where to register to vote?"

registered (a point we raised earlier). That frequency of relocation adds to the information demands of voter registration. Participation requires that respondents know where, in their new place of residence, voter registration is easily accomplished. In the hierarchy of urgent demands on relocation, reregistering to vote is often low on the priority list.

We asked citizen respondents who reported not being registered whether they knew how – and perhaps more important, where – to register to vote. Looking first at nativity, reported in Figure 9.10, a somewhat larger share of foreign-born citizens report lacking the necessary knowledge, but the differences are not statistically significant. Because many naturalized citizens are afforded the opportunity to register at the time of naturalization, this is perhaps not surprising.

The effects on income and education are significant, and the size of the effect is substantial. Examining the first columns of Figures 9.11 and 9.12, we see that more than half of those respondents in the lowest income category and with the lowest educational attainment report not knowing where and how to register. By contrast, around two-thirds of the highest income and educational attainment groups have the necessary knowledge.

The implications of this finding are curious. It suggests that better distribution of information and access to registration might conceivably add a considerable number of voters from low-socioeconomic-status cohorts

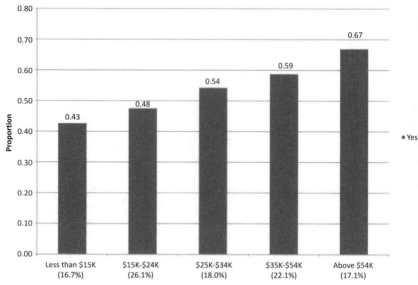

Figure 9.11. Know How to Register to Vote, by Income
Question wording: "Do you know how and where to register to vote?"

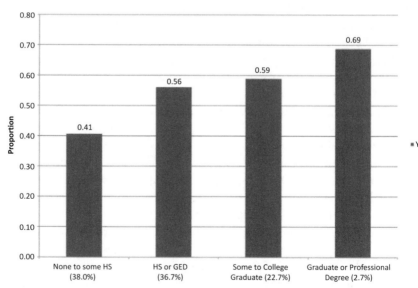

Figure 9.12. Know How to Register to Vote, by Education
Question wording: "Do you know how and where to register to vote?"

Table 9.7. *Know How to Register to Vote, by Gender*
Category: Political Participation, Electoral Participation

Response		Male	Female	Total
Yes	Freq.	297	312	609
	Row%	48.71	51.29	100.00
	Col%	51.61	50.89	51.24
No	Freq.	241	272	514
	Row%	46.94	53.06	100.00
	Col%	41.94	44.40	43.21
Don't know	Freq.	37	29	66
	Row%	56.19	43.81	100.00
	Col%	6.45	4.71	5.55
TOTAL	Freq.	575	614	1188
	Row%	48.36	51.64	100.00
	Col%	100.00	100.00	100.00

Note: Gender: (2 d.f.) 1.5899 (P = 0.5985). Asked of citizens, if not yet registered. Question wording: "Do you know how and where to register to vote?"

to the electorate. By contrast, nonvoters among the most well-off and middle-class cohorts have the information to register and, for one reason or another, have failed to do so. Of course, the plurality of respondents among Latino nonregistered citizens are in those lower-socioeconomic-status groups, and thus efforts at registration and mobilization through information sharing are likely to have significant payoff.

There are no discernible gender effects in Table 9.7, and little systematic variation by national origin group in Table 9.8. That said, a surprising 56 percent of nonregistered Cubans report a lack of knowledge about how to register to vote, as do Dominicans and other Central Americans. In contrast, Salvadorans, Mexicans, and especially Puerto Ricans report knowledge of the voter registration process. This difference does not reach significance because of small cell sizes, but we find the result both unexpected and remarkable.

Vote Choice in 2004

Much has been written about the two-party vote choice of Latinos in the 2004 elections. Media reports and exit polls suggested only a 53 percent vote for Kerry, with as much as 44 percent for Bush, and the

Table 9.8. *Know How to Register to Vote, by National Origin*

Category: Political Participation, Electoral Participation

Response		Cuba	Dominican Republic	El Salvador	Mexico	Puerto Rico	Other Central America	Other South America	Other	Missing	Total
Yes	Freq.	10	16	26	446	69	14	19	8	2	609
	Row%	1.64	2.66	4.24	73.16	11.30	2.31	3.06	1.28	0.34	100.00
	Col%	41.22	43.48	52.52	50.89	64.38	38.29	57.93	63.75	14.57	51.24
No	Freq.	14	17	22	381	32	20	13	4	11	514
	Row%	2.67	3.38	4.26	74.13	6.27	3.80	2.49	0.86	2.13	100.00
	Col%	56.42	46.58	44.50	43.48	30.14	53.25	36.69	36.25	76.11	43.21
Don't know	Freq.	1	4	1	49	6	3	1	0	1	66
	Row%	0.87	5.61	2.22	74.53	8.88	4.70	1.16	0.00	2.03	100.00
	Col%	2.36	9.94	2.98	5.62	5.49	8.47	2.38	0.00	9.32	5.55
TOTAL	Freq.	24	37	49	875	107	37	32	12	14	1188
	Row%	2.04	3.13	4.14	73.66	8.99	3.09	2.71	1.03	1.21	100.00
	Col%	100.00	100.00	100.00	100.00	100.00	100.00	100.00	100.00	100.00	100.00

Note: National origin: (16 d.f.) 19.0678 (P = 0.5235). Asked of citizens, if not yet registered. Question wording: "Do you know how and where to register to vote?"

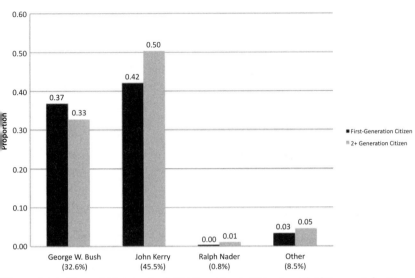

Figure 9.13. Voters' Pick in the 2004 Presidential Election (Self-Report), by Generation and Citizenship
Question wording: "Who did you vote for in the past presidential election of 2004?"

rest for third parties. This estimation has encountered significant criticism, however, driven largely by documented shortcomings in exit-poll methodology with respect to capturing the preferences of nonrandomly distributed subpopulations (see Barreto et al. 2006; Pedraza and Barreto 2008). Effectively, because exit polls attempt to represent national or state-level outcomes, there is no specific effort to ensure that subpopulations are represented accurately, which leads to a skew in those subpopulations toward more assimilated members living primarily among whites.

Our data appear to bear this out. Overall, 81.6 percent of respondents in Figure 9.13 reported voting for Bush or Kerry, and among those, 58.1 percent of respondents reported supporting Kerry, and 41.9 percent supporting Bush. These poll results are consistent with the claims made by critics of the exit polls that a split of 53 percent to 44 percent was unlikely and driven by the sample skew. The preference for Kerry over Bush was significantly greater among the U.S. born than among the foreign born. This result is suggestive of two potentially important implications. First, Democratic identification and vote choice are learned and/or socialized behavior. New citizens are not necessarily predisposed to Democratic

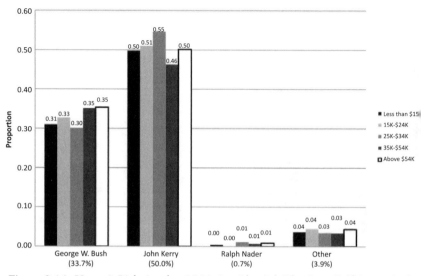

Figure 9.14. Voters' Pick in the 2004 Presidential Election (Self-Report), by Income
Question wording: "Who did you vote for in the past presidential election of 2004?"

identification, which appears to become stronger across generation. Second, the rapid incorporation of large waves of new immigrants into the electorate is not as likely to create a significant pro-Democratic shift, as some in the Democratic Party hope and the GOP fear. Rather, the end point of that process remains an open question, endogenous to the behavior of each party and its candidates. It is worth noting that a significant share of those surveyed report voting for someone else or not recalling for whom they voted. This is unlikely. Respondents who answer with "don't know" or as having voted for "other" are likely nonvoters, and these responses most likely reflect overreporting, which decreases across generational status.

Curiously, there is no consistent or significant effect demonstrated by income in Figure 9.14. The trends across income groups are nonmonotonic. By contrast, although Kerry wins the plurality of votes across all educational categories, there is a systematic variation. In Figure 9.15, we see that Kerry did better across better-educated respondents, whereas George W. Bush's support (self-reported) was highest among those with the least education. This finding is consistent with the one on nativity, thus suggesting that fuller incorporation into society is associated with stronger Democratic partisan preference.

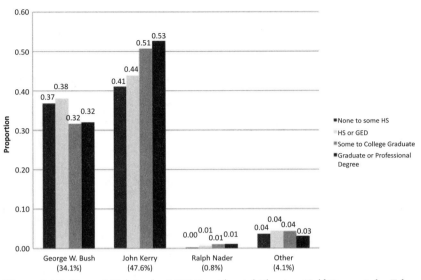

Figure 9.15. Voters' Pick in the 2004 Presidential Election (Self-Report), by Education

Question wording: "Who did you vote for in the past presidential election of 2004?"

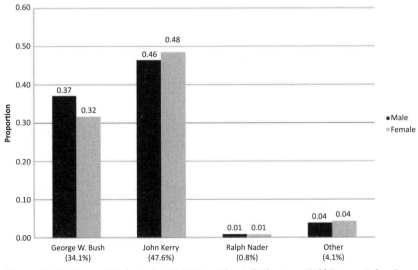

Figure 9.16. Voters' Pick in the 2004 Presidential Election (Self-Report), by Gender

Question wording: "Who did you vote for in the past presidential election of 2004?"

Table 9.9. *Voters' Pick in the 2004 Presidential Election (Self-Report), by National Origin*

Category: Political Participation, Electoral Participation

Response		Cuba	Dominican Republic	El Salvador	Mexico	Puerto Rico	Other Central America	Other South America	Other	Missing	Total
George W. Bush	Freq.	113	20	22	547	135	25	31	18	13	925
	Row%	12.22	2.20	2.38	59.13	14.62	2.76	3.31	1.92	1.46	100.00
	Col%	58.62	17.48	26.68	33.90	32.71	36.53	24.04	37.13	27.78	34.10
John Kerry	Freq.	55	67	46	778	199	31	67	22	26	1290
	Row%	4.25	5.16	3.58	60.27	15.40	2.43	5.22	1.68	1.99	100.00
	Col%	28.44	57.29	55.86	48.21	48.08	45.02	52.90	45.31	53.12	47.58
Ralph Nader	Freq.	2	2	0	11	8	0	1	0	0	23
	Row%	6.82	8.38	0.00	46.86	35.72	0.00	2.22	0.00	0.00	100.00
	Col%	0.80	1.64	0.00	0.66	1.96	0.00	0.40	0.00	0.00	0.84
Other	Freq.	3	7	1	63	17	3	11	3	2	111
	Row%	2.70	6.54	1.24	56.18	15.66	3.07	10.01	2.57	2.03	100.00
	Col%	1.56	6.28	1.67	3.88	4.22	4.91	8.76	5.97	4.66	4.11
Don't know	Freq.	20	20	13	216	54	9	18	6	7	363
	Row%	5.62	5.55	3.60	59.44	14.85	2.60	4.88	1.53	1.93	100.00
	Col%	10.57	17.32	15.78	13.36	13.03	13.53	13.90	11.59	14.43	13.37
TOTAL	Freq.	193	116	83	1613	413	70	127	48	48	2711
	Row%	7.11	4.29	3.05	59.49	15.24	2.57	4.70	1.77	1.79	100.00
	Col%	100.00	100.00	100.00	100.00	100.00	100.00	100.00	100.00	100.00	100.00

Note: National origin: (32 d.f.) 112.5779 (P = 0.0000). Asked of U.S. citizens who self-reported as voters. Question wording: "Who did you vote for in the past presidential election of 2004?"

ble 9.10. *Nonvoters' Choice in the 2004 Presidential Election (Self-Report), by Generation and Citizenship*

Category: Political Participation, Electoral Participation

sponse		First Generation			2+ Generation	
		Noncitizen	Citizen	Total	Citizen	Total
orge W. Bush	Freq.	818	204	1022	298	1320
	Row%	80.08	19.92	77.43	22.57	100.00
	Col%	21.01	27.16	22.01	23.76	22.38
n Kerry	Freq.	1230	220	1450	500	1950
	Row%	84.85	15.15	74.36	25.64	100.00
	Col%	31.59	29.32	31.22	39.87	33.06
lph Nader	Freq.	33	6	38	23	62
	Row%	85.40	14.60	62.21	37.79	100.00
	Col%	0.84	0.75	0.83	1.86	1.04
her	Freq.	280	68	348	127	474
	Row%	80.53	19.47	73.29	26.71	100.00
	Col%	7.19	9.03	7.49	10.11	8.04
n't know	Freq.	1533	253	1786	306	2092
	Row%	85.84	14.16	85.38	14.62	100.00
	Col%	39.37	33.74	38.46	24.40	35.47
AL	Freq.	3894	749	4643	1254	5897
	Row%	83.86	16.14	78.74	21.26	100.00
	Col%	100.00	100.00	100.00	100.00	100.00

te: First/2+ generation: (5 d.f.) 88.9056 (P = 0.0000). Citizen/noncitizen (first generation only): .d.f.) 23.1374 (P = 0.000). Asked of nonvoters and noncitizen respondents. Island-born Puerto ans are coded as 2+ generation. Question wording: "Whom did you favor or prefer for president his past 2004 election?"

Similarly, there does appear to be a modest, albeit nearly significant, effect of gender on vote preference. In Figure 9.16, it appears that Latinas offered greater levels of support to Kerry than did Latino males, although Kerry won handily in both groups.

Table 9.9 reports vote by national origin groups. The preference for Kerry was consistent across all groups, with one important caveat. Cubans stand out as the exception, as about 59 percent of Cubans self-report as having voted for George W. Bush in the 2004 election, that is, more than 67 percent of those voting for one of the two major-party candidates. For all other national origin groups, John Kerry was the candidate of choice. Kerry gained the highest support (self-report) from Dominicans, at 58 percent, followed by Salvadorans, at 56 percent.

Table 9.11. *Nonvoters' Choice in the 2004 Presidential Election (Self-Report*
by Income

Category: Political Participation, Electoral Participation

Response		Less than $15K	$15K–$24K	$25K–$34K	$35K–$54K	More than $54K	Tot
George	Freq.	239	327	229	169	96	1060
	Row%	22.49	30.85	21.60	15.98	9.08	100
	Col%	22.33	25.25	29.08	22.97	20.62	24
John	Freq.	342	451	271	310	187	1561
Kerry	Row%	21.92	28.90	17.33	19.88	11.96	100
	Col%	32.04	34.81	34.33	42.07	40.00	35
Ralph	Freq.	10	15	5	9	14	52
Nader	Row%	18.42	28.11	9.93	17.39	26.16	100
	Col%	0.90	1.14	0.66	1.24	2.94	1
Other	Freq.	77	99	72	60	43	352
	Row%	21.92	28.29	20.37	17.21	12.21	100
	Col%	7.21	7.67	9.09	8.20	9.20	8
Don't	Freq.	401	403	211	188	127	1331
know	Row%	30.11	30.31	15.88	14.14	9.55	100
	Col%	37.51	31.13	26.83	25.51	27.24	30
TOTAL	Freq.	1068	1296	788	738	467	4356
	Row%	24.52	29.75	18.08	16.93	10.71	100
	Col%	100.00	100.00	100.00	100.00	100.00	100

Note: Income: (16 d.f.) 69.6861 (P = 0.0003). Asked of nonvoters and noncitizen respondents. Question word: "Whom did you favor or prefer for president in this past 2004 election?"

About one-third of Mexicans and Puerto Ricans self-report as having voted for George W. Bush, or around 40 percent of the two-party vote.

Vote Preference by Noncitizens and Nonvoters in 2004

To assess whether those voting were meaningfully distinct from those not voting or ineligible, we asked nonvoters their presidential preference as well. The results are largely, though not entirely, consistent with those for those who actually cast ballots.

All respondents are more likely to self-report as preferring the Democratic candidate, with an increase in Democratic preference with a change in generational status reported in Table 9.10. This, again, suggests that their Democratic identity is socialized after the immigration and naturalization stage and is not the "automatic" identity of new Latino Americans. Overall, about 55 percent of nonvoters self-report a preference for one of these two candidates, with 40.2 percent reporting a preference for

able 9.12. *Nonvoters' Choice in the 2004 Presidential Election (Self-Report), by Education*

Category: Political Participation, Electoral Participation

ponse		None to Some HS	HS or GED	Some to College Graduate	Graduate or Professional Degree	Total
rge W. Bush	Freq.	599	452	223	46	1320
	Row%	45.41	34.24	16.87	3.48	100.00
	Col%	22.44	24.17	18.69	27.80	22.38
n Kerry	Freq.	776	660	459	55	1950
	Row%	39.81	33.85	23.54	2.80	100.00
	Col%	29.06	35.31	38.50	33.11	33.06
ph Nader	Freq.	26	14	18	4	62
	Row%	41.41	23.13	29.53	5.93	100.00
	Col%	0.96	0.76	1.53	2.21	1.04
er	Freq.	186	152	130	7	474
	Row%	39.15	32.01	27.39	1.44	100.00
	Col%	6.95	8.12	10.90	4.14	8.04
n't know	Freq.	1084	591	362	54	2091
	Row%	51.83	28.28	17.31	2.58	100.00
	Col%	40.59	31.64	30.38	32.74	35.47
AL	Freq.	2670	1869	1192	165	5896
	Row%	45.29	31.70	20.21	2.80	100.00
	Col%	100.00	100.00	100.00	100.00	100.00

e: Education: (12 d.f.) 92.1880 (P = 0.0000). Asked of nonvoters and noncitizen respon- ts. Question wording: "Whom did you favor or prefer for president in this past 2004 tion?"

Bush and 59.6 percent reporting a preference for Kerry. These marginals are not significantly different from those among the self-reported voters.

Education has less of an effect among nonvoters. Although there is a significant decline in the "don't know" category, there is not a monotonic trend toward (or away from) either candidate across categories. By contrast, income matters more than it did for voters, with higher-income respondents reporting a significantly greater preference for Kerry. The numbers in Tables 9.11 and 9.12 are not an exact replication of those in Figures 9.14 and 9.15, but the overall trends and lessons remain the same. Improved social location, security, and status are generally associated with stronger Democratic share of preferences.

Table 9.13. *Nonvoters' Choice in the 2004 Presidential Election (Self-Report), by Gender*

Category: Political Participation, Electoral Participation

Response		Male	Female	Total
George W. Bush	Freq.	682	638	1320
	Row%	51.67	48.33	100.00
	Col%	23.79	21.04	22.38
John Kerry	Freq.	1047	903	1950
	Row%	53.70	46.30	100.00
	Col%	36.53	29.78	33.06
Ralph Nader	Freq.	34	28	62
	Row%	55.06	44.94	100.00
	Col%	1.18	0.91	1.04
Other	Freq.	232	243	474
	Row%	48.85	51.15	100.00
	Col%	8.08	8.00	8.04
Don't know	Freq.	871	1220	2091
	Row%	41.67	58.33	100.00
	Col%	30.41	40.26	35.47
TOTAL	**Freq.**	**2866**	**3031**	**5896**
	Row%	**48.60**	**51.40**	**100.00**
	Col%	**100.00**	**100.00**	**100.00**

Note: Gender: (4 d.f.) 60.9633 (P = 0.0000). Asked of nonvoters and noncitizen respondents. Question wording: "Whom did you favor or prefer for president in this past 2004 election?"

By contrast, the gender effect (Table 9.13) among nonvoters is exactly the reverse of that found for self-reported voters. Although both women and men report a stronger preference for Kerry, here it is the men for whom Democratic plurality is greater. Effects on national origin (Table 9.14) are very consistent with those reported earlier, with Cubans being more Republican than other nationality groups. Dominicans, Mexicans, Puerto Ricans, and South Americans offered the most pro-Democratic responses.

The overall take on these results is one of essential stability. Nonvoters, across the dimensions we identify here, look a great deal like voters. The additional of a substantially greater share of the Latino population to the participating electorate is unlikely, in the extreme, to significantly reshape the distribution of partisan preferences or the patterns across important covariates.

Table 9.14. *Nonvoters' Choice in the 2004 Presidential Election (Self-Report), by National Origin*

Category: Political Participation, Electoral Participation

Response		Cuba	Dominican Republic	El Salvador	Mexico	Puerto Rico	Other Central America	Other South America	Other	Missing	Total
George W. Bush	Freq.	45	25	76	980	54	76	40	15	9	1320
	Row%	3.38	1.88	5.79	74.24	4.06	5.77	3.07	1.14	0.68	100.00
	Col%	33.29	12.82	23.15	22.11	24.23	27.71	16.41	48.62	26.47	22.38
John Kerry	Freq.	29	78	95	1483	69	78	105	8	4	1950
	Row%	1.50	3.98	4.89	76.08	3.52	4.00	5.40	0.40	0.23	100.00
	Col%	21.84	40.08	28.89	33.47	31.03	28.41	42.70	25.28	13.14	33.06
Ralph Nader	Freq.	0	0	5	42	7	1	6	1	0	61
	Row%	0.64	0.00	8.52	68.35	11.30	0.82	9.22	1.15	0.00	100.00
	Col%	0.29	0.00	1.59	0.95	3.15	0.18	2.30	2.29	0.00	1.04
Other	Freq.	7	11	14	374	26	19	15	4	5	474
	Row%	1.50	2.36	3.00	78.85	5.47	4.01	3.11	0.75	0.96	100.00
	Col%	5.32	5.78	4.31	8.44	11.74	6.92	5.97	11.52	13.40	8.04
Don't know	Freq.	53	80	139	1553	66	101	80	4	16	2091
	Row%	2.51	3.83	6.64	74.25	3.15	4.83	3.85	0.18	0.77	100.00
	Col%	39.25	41.32	42.06	35.04	29.85	36.78	32.62	12.29	46.99	35.47
TOTAL	Freq.	134	194	330	4432	221	275	247	31	34	5896
	Row%	2.27	3.29	5.60	75.16	3.75	4.66	4.18	0.52	0.58	100.00
	Col%	100.00	100.00	100.00	100.00	100.00	100.00	100.00	100.00	100.00	100.00

Note: National origin: (32 d.f.) 98.7257 (P = 0.0001). Asked of nonvoters and noncitizen respondents. Question wording: "Whom did you favor or prefer for president in this past 2004 election?"

Bibliography

Barreto, Matt, Fernando Guerra, Mara Marks, Stephen Nuño, and Nathan Woods. 2006. "Controversies in Exit Polling: Implementing a Racially Stratified Homogenous Precinct Approach." *PS: Political Science and Politics* 39(3): 477–83.

Belli, Robert F., Michael Traugott, Margaret Yong, and Katherine McGonagle. 1999. "Reducing Vote Overreporting in Surveys: Social Desirability, Memory Failure, and Source Monitoring." *Public Opinion Quarterly* 63: 90–108.

DeSipio, Louis. 1996. *Counting on the Latino Vote: Latinos as a New Electorate.* Charlottesville: University of Virginia Press.

Frymer, Paul. 1999. *Uneasy Alliances.* Princeton, NJ: Princeton University Press.

Michelson, Melissa R. 2006. "Mobilizing the Latino Youth Vote: Some Experimental Results." *Social Science Quarterly* 87(5): 1188–1206.

Michelson, Melissa R., Lisa Garcia-Bedolla, and Donald Phillip Green. 2008. "New Experiments in Minority Voter Mobilization." http://class.csueastbay.edu/faculty/mmichelson/CVI%202008.pdf.

Pantoja, Adrian D., Ricardo Ramirez, and Gary M. Segura. 2001. "Citizens by Choice, Voters by Necessity: Patterns in Political Mobilization by Naturalized Latinos." *Political Research Quarterly* 54(4): 729–50.

Pedraza, Francisco, and Matt Barreto. 2008. "Exit Polls and Ethnic Diversity: How to Improve Estimates and Reduce Bias among Minority Voters." In *Elections and Exit Polling*, ed. Wendy Alvey and Fritz Scheuren. Hoboken, NJ: Wiley and Sons.

Santoro, Wayne A., and Gary Segura. 2011. "Generational Status and Mexican American Political Participation: The Benefits and Limitations of Assimilation." *Political Research Quarterly* 64(1): 172–84.

Statistical Abstract of the United States: 2011. United States Bureau of the Census. http://www.census.gov/prod/2011pubs/11statab/pop.pdf.

Verba, Sidney, Kay Lehman Schlozman, and Henry Brady. 1995. *Voice and Equality: Civic Voluntarism in American Politics.* Cambridge, MA: Harvard University Press.

10

Evolving Patterns and Preferences in Latino Partisanship

Among the areas in which there has been much speculation about the growth and especially increased political participation of Latinos is their patterns of partisan identification, registration, and voting. It is well accepted that current Latino party identification favors Democrats, with the consistent exception of those Latinos of Cuban origin (DeSipio 1996; de la Garza, DeSipio, Garcia, Garcia, and Falcon 1992). However, significant speculation exists as to how stable this Democratic advantage is, how deeply these patterns hold, what the value foundations are of Latino partisan preferences, and whether the growing size and diversity of the Latino electorate present new opportunities and challenges for political parties to garner significant Latino voter support (Fraga and Ramírez 2003–2004; Fraga and Leal 2004).

We examine several aspects of Latino partisanship in this chapter, beginning with a summary of social science research regarding Latino partisanship. We then break down partisan identification by generation and citizenship, national origin, income, and education. This is followed by a discussion of the patterns of reported party registration by the same categories. We then provide data on important correlates of partisan identification, including recent changes in attitudes toward parties, ideology, coethnic candidates, and political knowledge. The chapter concludes with a consideration of what we learn about patterns of Latino partisanship from the LNS.

Understanding Latino Partisanship

Most accepted theories of partisanship in the United States have omitted serious consideration of how general patterns of identification and registration for the national population are applicable to African American, Latino, and other nonwhite voters (Campbell et al. 1960; Markus and Converse 1979; Fiorina 1981; McKuen Erikson, and Stimson 1989; Miller 1991). No doubt this has been, in part, because the data sets most often used to study national partisanship, such as the American National Election Study (ANES), have not included representative samples of ethnic and racial minority voters. As a result, it has been unclear how distinct experiences of being Latino in the United States affect how Latinos relate to the two major political parties. In other words, when it comes to partisanship, does it make a difference whether one is U.S. born, foreign-born, or becoming naturalized as a citizen? Moreover, it is also unclear whether the traditional explanations grounded in theories of political socialization, retrospective assessment, or policy preferences hold for Latinos, even if they are reasonably accurate for large segments of the population and are driven by understandings of family tradition, ideology, income, and education. This lack of consistent study of Latino partisanship has made it difficult to gauge the stability of Latino partisan preferences over time.

Nonetheless, a few studies of Latino partisanship have been conducted over the past twenty-five years. Using a sample drawn from California in the mid-1980s, Cain, Kiewiet, and Uhlaner (1991) found that Latinos become more likely to identify with the Democratic Party and have stronger partisan preferences as their time of residence in the United States grows, thus giving them more exposure to and related familiarity with U.S. politics. They also showed that the patterns increase across generations. Using data from the Latino National Political Survey (LNPS) gathered in 1989, Uhlaner and Garcia (2001) similarly found that among national samples of Latinos of Mexican, Puerto Rican, and Cuban origin, increased identification with the Democratic Party occurred with more years in the United States. This even occurred for respondents of Cuban origin, although Cubans were distinct from Mexicans and Puerto Ricans in that they preferred the Republican Party over the Democratic Party.

With data drawn from a national survey of Latino "likely" citizen voters in 2000, Alvarez and Garcia Bedolla (2003) reported that 56.6 percent of respondents identified as Democrats, 24.5 percent as Republicans, and

13 percent as independents. More time in the United States was again associated with greater identification with the Democratic Party for Latinos of Mexican and Puerto Rican origin, but with stronger identification with the Republican Party for those of Cuban origin. They also found that the alignment of issue positions of voters and parties drives partisan identification. They speculate that future shifts in partisan preferences of Latinos are unlikely unless the two major parties shift their positions on issues considerably.

Hajnal and Lee (2004), again using data from the LNPS, found that patterns of partisanship among Latinos, especially for those who identify as independents, is best explained not by how many years they are in the United States but by what degree of acculturation, both social and more explicitly political, that they experience in the time that they are in the United States. By focusing on political independents, the authors suggested that traditional models of partisan identification compensate for the ways that the processes of party attachment may be far more complex for Latinos than for others in the United States. These studies make clear that an understanding of Latino partisan identification will require great care in sampling design and question wording. Sampling only citizens and likely voters, for example, may miss important elements of the processes through which important subgroups of Latinos, especially the foreign born, come to identify with a political party.

Patterns of Latino Partisan Identification

Overall, respondents are far more likely to report identifying as Democrat than Republican, from a 2:1 ratio for first-generation citizens to a 3:1 Democratic advantage for first-generation noncitizens and second generation and beyond citizens, but important variations exist, as is shown in Figure 10.1. A change in citizenship status is associated with a noticeable shift in party identification. Although only about 12 percent of first-generation noncitizens identify as "strong Democrats," almost 28 percent of first-generation citizens do so. There is a modest increase in identification, to about 29 percent, for second generation and beyond citizens. In addition, changes in citizenship and generational status seem to be associated with the adoption of any party identification (a logical outcome, as noncitizens cannot vote): whereas 50 percent of first-generation noncitizens did not identify with either party, only 22 percent of first-generation citizens and 16 percent of second generation and beyond citizens did so.

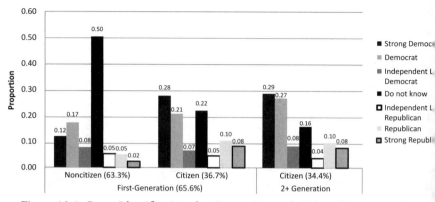

Figure 10.1. Party Identification, by Generation and Citizenship. *Note:* Seven-point scale constructed from responses to questions about party identification and strength of party identification. Island-born Puerto Ricans are coded as first generation.

Question wording: "Generally speaking, do you usually consider yourself a Democrat, a Republican, an Independent, some other party, or what?"

The Democratic advantage in partisan identification holds among all Latino national origin subgroups by very substantial margins, ranging from the lowest 2.5:1 margin among those from other Central American countries to an overwhelming 7.6:1 among Dominicans (Table 10.1). The lone exception is for those Latinos of Cuban origin. On a seven-point scale that measures respondents' party identification, Dominicans, Mexicans, and Puerto Ricans show the highest levels of identification as Democrats, at 64 percent, 50 percent, and 66 percent, respectively. Cubans report the highest percentage of identification as Republicans: overall, about 48 percent of Cubans consider themselves Republicans, and of those, almost 27 percent identify as "strong Republicans." Interestingly, slightly more than one-third of all Cuban-origin respondents identify with the Democratic Party.

We find that respondents with higher income and higher education are more likely to report identification with a political party, which perhaps reflects a relationship between resources and political knowledge, as is shown in Tables 10.2 and 10.3. Approximately 42 percent of those earning less than $15,000 in 2004 report that they "do not know" with which party they identify, whereas only about 15 percent of those earning more than $54,000 report the same. For education, about 44 percent of respondents with less than a high school education report "do not know," whereas only about 15 percent of those with education beyond graduate

Response		Cuba	Dominican Republic	El Salvador	Mexico	Puerto Rico	Other Central America	Other South America	Other	Missing	Total
Strong Democrat	Freq.	56	86	67	917	170	51	74	21	22	1463
	Row%	3.81	5.87	4.61	62.66	11.63	3.47	5.07	1.40	1.48	100.00
	Col%	19.80	35.05	20.88	19.60	30.37	18.30	23.29	28.66	31.62	21.44
Democrat	Freq.	26	56	74	1014	153	44	70	11	11	1460
	Row%	1.80	3.86	5.07	69.45	10.46	3.04	4.82	0.76	0.75	100.00
	Col%	9.33	22.98	22.89	21.67	27.26	15.98	22.10	15.43	16.00	21.39
Independent Lean Democrat	Freq.	15	15	18	351	52	26	37	5	4	524
	Row%	2.81	2.90	3.36	66.99	10.00	5.02	7.16	0.94	0.83	100.00
	Col%	5.22	6.21	5.45	7.50	9.34	9.47	11.77	6.85	6.35	7.67
Do not know	Freq.	49	67	124	1618	76	109	91	9	17	2160
	Row%	2.29	3.10	5.74	74.91	3.50	5.03	4.20	0.43	0.80	100.00
	Col%	17.53	27.35	38.37	34.59	13.49	39.12	28.51	12.89	25.34	31.65
Independent Lean Republican	Freq.	20	6	11	234	12	5	10	5	1	304
	Row%	6.53	1.93	3.71	76.95	4.03	1.78	3.21	1.70	0.17	100.00
	Col%	7.04	2.39	3.49	4.99	2.18	1.94	3.06	7.22	0.73	4.45
Republican	Freq.	41	8	21	357	55	20	22	8	7	538
	Row%	7.57	1.50	3.83	66.34	10.17	3.75	4.03	1.55	1.27	100.00
	Col%	14.45	3.29	6.38	7.63	9.77	7.27	6.81	11.62	9.97	7.88
Strong Republican	Freq.	75	7	8	188	43	22	14	12	7	376
	Row%	19.96	1.78	2.18	50.04	11.31	5.84	3.77	3.30	1.82	100.00
	Col%	26.65	2.74	2.54	4.02	7.59	7.92	4.46	17.33	9.99	5.51
TOTAL	Freq.	282	245	323	4678	560	278	318	72	69	6825
	Row%	4.13	3.59	4.73	68.55	8.21	4.07	4.66	1.05	1.00	100.00
	Col%	100.00	100.00	100.00	100.00	100.00	100.00	100.00	100.00	100.00	100.00

Note: National origin: (48 d.f.) 560.8556 (P = 0.0000). Seven-point scale constructed from responses to questions about party identification and strength of party identification. Question wording: "Generally speaking, do you usually consider yourself a Democrat, a Republican, an Independent, some other party, or what?"

Table 10.2. *Party Identification, by Income*
Category: Political Views, Party/Ideology

Response		Less than $15K	$15K–$24K	$25K–$34K	$35K–$54K	More than $54K	Total
Strong Democrat	Freq.	198	238	183	273	339	1231
	Row%	16.04	19.37	14.86	22.17	27.56	100.00
	Col%	19.35	18.89	19.70	23.90	29.64	22.39
Democrat	Freq.	183	275	227	286	248	1218
	Row%	15.00	22.55	18.60	23.45	20.39	100.00
	Col%	17.91	21.77	24.39	25.02	21.70	22.16
Independent Lean Democrat	Freq.	73	85	84	102	100	443
	Row%	16.42	19.18	18.98	22.97	22.45	100.00
	Col%	7.13	6.74	9.06	8.92	8.69	8.06
Do not know	Freq.	426	453	290	254	167	1589
	Row%	26.80	28.49	18.22	16.00	10.48	100.00
	Col%	41.72	35.88	31.17	22.27	14.55	28.90
Independent Lean Republican	Freq.	59	69	40	43	45	256
	Row%	23.23	26.92	15.50	16.67	17.68	100.00
	Col%	5.82	5.45	4.27	3.73	3.95	4.65
Republican	Freq.	54	95	69	120	116	453
	Row%	11.82	20.91	15.14	26.49	25.64	100.00
	Col%	5.25	7.51	7.38	10.52	10.15	8.24
Strong Republican	Freq.	29	47	38	64	130	308
	Row%	9.38	15.42	12.19	20.92	42.09	100.00
	Col%	2.83	3.76	4.04	5.64	11.31	5.59
TOTAL	Freq.	1021	1262	929	1142	1145	5499
	Row%	18.57	22.95	16.90	20.77	20.82	100.00
	Col%	100.00	100.00	100.00	100.00	100.00	100.00

Note: Income: (24 d.f.) 380.4510 (P = 0.0000). Seven-point scale constructed from responses to questions about party identification and strength

Table 10.3. *Party Identification, by Education*
Category: Political Views, Party/Ideology

sponse		None to Some HS	HS or GED	Some to College Graduate	Graduate or Professional Degree	Total
ong Democrat	Freq.	413	392	524	135	1463
	Row%	28.24	26.79	35.78	9.19	100.00
	Col%	18.03	19.60	24.38	34.85	21.44
mocrat	Freq.	383	447	554	76	1460
	Row%	26.20	30.64	37.96	5.20	100.00
	Col%	16.69	22.37	25.82	19.66	21.39
lependent Lean Democrat	Freq.	166	170	160	29	524
	Row%	31.61	32.39	30.45	5.55	100.00
	Col%	7.22	8.48	7.43	7.53	7.67
not know	Freq.	1004	634	464	58	2160
	Row%	46.48	29.34	21.48	2.70	100.00
	Col%	43.81	31.68	21.61	15.14	31.65
lependent Lean Republican	Freq.	110	93	80	20	304
	Row%	36.30	30.79	26.24	6.67	100.00
	Col%	4.81	4.67	3.71	5.25	4.45
publican	Freq.	119	168	212	39	538
	Row%	22.18	31.17	39.48	7.17	100.00
	Col%	5.21	8.38	9.89	9.99	7.88
ong Republican	Freq.	97	96	154	29	376
	Row%	25.77	25.60	40.85	7.78	100.00
	Col%	4.23	4.81	7.16	7.58	5.51
TAL	Freq.	2292	2000	2147	386	6825
	Row%	33.58	29.31	31.46	5.66	100.00
	Col%	100.00	100.00	100.00	100.00	100.00

te: Education: (18 d.f.) 377.4692 (P = 0.0000). Seven-point scale constructed from responses
questions about party identification and strength of party identification. Question wording:
enerally speaking, do you usually consider yourself a Democrat, a Republican, an Independent,
ne other party, or what?"

school report the same. Finally, those with higher income and higher
education both identify as Democrats, a fundamental disconnect from the
usual assumptions about income identification with the Republican Party.

Latino Party Registration

We asked those citizen respondents who indicated that they were registered to vote whether they were registered as Democrats or Republicans.

Latinos in the New Millennium

Table 10.4. *Party Registration, by Generation and Citizenship*
Category: Political Participation, Electoral Participation

Response		First Generation		2+ Generation	
		Citizen	Total	Citizen	Tot
Democrat	Freq.	488	488	1219	1707
	Row%	100.00	28.58	70.67	100
	Col%	41.21	41.21	52.07	48
Republican	Freq.	238	238	365	603
	Row%	100.00	39.49	59.84	100
	Col%	20.12	20.12	15.59	17
Independent	Freq.	136	136	268	404.
	Row%	100.00	33.68	65.61	100
	Col%	11.5	11.5	11.45	11
Some other party	Freq.	32	32	59	91.
	Row%	100.00	35.09	63.98	100.
	Col%	2.70	2.70	2.53	2.
No state requirement	Freq.	73	73	166	238
	Row%	100.00	30.69	68.96	100
	Col%	6.19	6.19	7.07	6
Do not know	Freq.	216	216.4	264	480.
	Row%	100.00	450.4	53.92	100
	Col%	18.28	18.28	11.28	13
TOTAL	Freq.	1184	1184	2341	3525
	Row%	100.0	33.59	65.65	100.
	Col%	100.00	100.00	100.00	100.

Note: First/2+ generation: (6 d.f.) 65.7099 (P = 0.0000). Citizen/noncitizen (first generat
only): (6 d.f.) 4.8496 (P = 0.0000). Asked of registered voters. Order of items rotated. Isla
born Puerto Ricans are coded as 2+ generation. Question wording: "Are you registered as..
Respondents born in the United States (second generation and beyond) are significantly m
Democratic than first-generation citizens, which supports the idea that Democratic identity for
during socialization.

As revealed in Table 10.4, 41 percent of all naturalized citizens who registered were Democrats. This represents a Democratic advantage of slightly
more than a 2:1 ratio over those naturalized citizens who were registered
as Republicans. Interestingly, only 11 percent of respondents indicated
that they were registered as independents. The patterns of Democratic
advantage are even more apparent among those in the second generation
and beyond who reported being registered. Approximately 52 percent

were registered as Democrats; only 16 percent were registered as Republicans, and, as among first-generation citizens, 11 percent were registered as independents.

Recall that we asked respondents who indicated that they were U.S. citizens and registered to vote about their party registration. Table 10.5 displays reported party registration by national origin group. All Latino subgroups are much more likely to be registered as Democrats than as Republicans, with the lone exception of Cuban Americans. The Democratic advantage ranges from slightly less than 50 percent for Latinos from Mexico, Central America, and "other" Latin American origin to a high of more than 60 percent for those Latinos of Dominican origin, followed closely by Puerto Ricans and Salvadorans. Just less than 50 percent of those of Cuban origin report being registered as Republicans. Interestingly, one-quarter of Cubans report being registered as Democrats, and a full 17 percent report being registered as independents.

Similarly, regardless of income, respondents self-report as registered Democrats, as displayed in Table 10.6. Lower-income respondents have the highest levels of being registered as Democrats, at 57 percent. Those respondents with incomes greater than $54,000 per year report being registered as Democrats at slightly less than 50 percent. There is more variation by income among those who are registered as Republicans. Those earning more than $54,000 are almost twice as likely to register as Republican than are those earning less than $15,000.

Respondents were also much more likely to report being registered as Democrats than as Republicans, regardless of their level of formal education. As revealed in Table 10.7, slightly less than 50 percent of respondents with no to some high school, a high school diploma or GED, or some college to college graduate are registered as Democrats. More than half of those with a graduate or professional degree, 56 percent, are registered as Democrats. The largest group of those registered as Republicans, 20 percent, is among those who have a graduate or professional degree.

Changed Feelings toward Democrat and Republican Parties

The presidential campaigns of George W. Bush in 2000 and 2004 clearly made a significant attempt to emphasize his relationship to Latino voters. This was an important component of his electoral strategy (de la Garza and DeSipio 2004; Fraga and Leal 2004). By most estimates, Bush

Table 10.5. *Party Registration, by National Origin*
Category: Political Participation, Electoral Participation

Response		Cuba	Dominican Republic	El Salvador	Mexico	Puerto Rico	Other Central America	Other South America	Other	Missing	Total
Democrat	Freq.	57	84	64	1048	281	41	76	27	30	1707
	Row%	3.36	4.91	3.77	61.38	16.45	2.37	4.44	1.57	1.76	100.00
	Col%	25.90	60.92	54.10	47.62	55.97	47.35	51.63	47.75	52.86	48.43
Republican	Freq.	105	11	9	340	76	20	19	12	12	603
	Row%	17.45	1.81	1.56	56.30	12.54	3.35	3.08	1.93	1.98	100.00
	Col%	47.58	7.92	7.91	15.43	15.07	23.64	12.65	20.73	21.10	17.11
Independent	Freq.	38	7	15	255	47	8	21	7	8	404
	Row%	9.30	1.77	3.60	63.10	11.54	2.03	5.10	1.62	1.93	100.00
	Col%	17.00	5.21	12.24	11.59	9.30	9.59	14.05	11.67	13.73	11.47
Some other party	Freq.	5	2	6	54	16	1	8	0	1	91
	Row%	5.12	1.95	6.16	58.70	17.65	0.67	8.45	0.00	1.31	100.00
	Col%	2.11	1.29	4.72	2.43	3.21	0.71	5.25	0.00	2.11	2.59
No state requirement	Freq.	5	5	8	168	30	5	9	7	2	239
	Row%	1.92	2.30	3.41	70.22	12.57	2.15	3.76	3.01	0.67	100.00
	Col%	2.08	3.99	6.84	7.62	5.98	6.01	6.12	12.82	2.83	6.78
Do not know	Freq.	12	28	17	337	53	11	15	4	4	481
	Row%	2.46	5.92	3.51	70.09	10.94	2.26	3.14	0.82	0.87	100.00
	Col%	5.33	20.66	14.18	15.30	10.47	12.69	10.30	7.03	7.37	13.63
TOTAL	Freq.	221	138	119	2201	502	86	147	56	57	3525
	Row%	6.28	3.90	3.37	62.42	14.24	2.43	4.16	1.59	1.61	100.00
	Col%	100.00	100.00	100.00	100.00	100.00	100.00	100.00	100.00	100.00	100.00

Table 10.6. *Party Registration, by Income*

Category: Political Participation, Electoral Participation

Response		Less than $15K	$15K–$24K	$25K–$34K	$35K–$54K	More than $54K	Total
Democrat	Freq.	179	205	217	372	476	1449
	Row%	12.37	14.15	14.99	25.64	32.85	100.00
	Col%	57.02	47.47	46.19	50.07	49.71	49.69
Republican	Freq.	35	69	74	134	206	517
	Row%	6.72	13.28	14.26	25.89	39.86	100.00
	Col%	11.04	15.89	15.67	18.03	21.51	17.72
Independent	Freq.	17	48	81	81	117	345
	Row%	5.03	13.89	23.58	23.52	33.98	100.00
	Col%	5.52	11.10	17.30	10.93	12.24	11.83
Some other party	Freq.	9	9	12	18	36	84
	Row%	10.80	10.60	14.44	20.82	43.33	100.00
	Col%	2.89	2.07	2.58	2.36	3.81	2.89
No state requirement	Freq.	11	41	30	51	61	194
	Row%	5.89	21.09	15.49	26.31	31.21	100.00
	Col%	3.63	9.47	6.39	6.88	6.32	6.65
Do not know	Freq.	63	60	56	87	61	327
	Row%	19.11	18.48	17.05	26.61	18.75	100.00
	Col%	19.89	14.00	11.87	11.73	6.41	11.22
TOTAL	Freq.	314	432	470	742	958	2916
	Row%	10.78	14.81	16.13	25.45	32.84	100.00
	Col%	100.00	100.00	100.00	100.00	100.00	100.00

Note: Income: (20 d.f.) 115.7953 (P = 0.0000). Asked of registered voters. Order of items rotated. Question wording: "Are you registered as…?"

287

Table 10.7. *Party Registration, by Education*
Category: Political Participation, Electoral Participation

Response		None to Some HS	HS or GED	Some to College Graduate	Graduate or Professional Degree	Tot
Democrat	Freq.	318	444	785	160	1707
	Row%	18.64	26.02	45.95	9.39	100
	Col%	47.98	47.31	47.91	56.13	48
Republican	Freq.	83	164	301	56	603
	Row%	13.70	27.20	49.83	9.27	100
	Col%	12.46	17.47	18.36	19.58	17
Independent	Freq.	71	108	194	32	404
	Row%	17.53	26.76	47.90	7.81	100
	Col%	10.68	11.52	11.82	11.05	11
Some other party	Freq.	14	29	44	4	91
	Row%	15.88	31.95	48.16	4.01	100
	Col%	2.18	3.10	2.68	1.28	2
No state requirement	Freq.	39	45	142	13	239
	Row%	16.29	18.89	59.35	5.48	100
	Col%	5.87	4.81	8.66	4.58	6
Do not know	Freq.	138	148	173	21	481
	Row%	28.73	30.87	36.02	4.38	100
	Col%	20.82	15.80	10.57	7.37	13
TOTAL	Freq.	663	939	1637	286	3525
	Row%	18.81	26.64	46.45	8.10	100
	Col%	100.00	100.00	100.00	100.00	100

Note: Education: (15 d.f.) 91.5684 (P = 0.0000). Asked of registered voters. Question word
"Are you registered as . . . ?"

received approximately 35 percent of the Latino national vote in 2000
and a full 40 percent in 2004 (van der Linden 2004). It was argued that
this increased Republican support signaled a new shift by a significant
number of Latino voters toward the Republican Party. Clearly, the elections of 2006, and especially 2008, reveal that the support Bush received
could not be sustained. New candidates and changing issues undermined
the gains made across two presidential elections and showed that the shift
in Latino voter preferences was not permanent.

To consider these elements of Latino partisan preferences, we asked
a question about whether Latino attitudes toward the Democratic and
Republican parties had changed in recent years. Again, we provide

Table 10.8. *Change in Feelings toward Democratic and Republican Parties,*
by Generation and Citizenship
Category: Political Views, Party/Ideology

sponse		First Generation			2+ Generation		
		Noncitizen	Citizen	Total	Citizen	Total	
el much closer to	Freq.	104	109	214	145	359	
he Republicans	Row%	48.76	51.24	59.54	40.46	100.00	
han I used to	Col%	4.08	6.96	5.18	6.25	5.56	
el somewhat	Freq.	169	140	309	175	483	
loser to the	Row%	54.72	45.28	63.83	36.17	100.00	
Republicans than	Col%	6.62	8.89	7.48	7.52	7.50	
used to							
y feelings have	Freq.	1723	851	2574	1266	3840	
ot changed	Row%	66.95	33.05	67.03	32.97	100.00	
	Col%	67.56	54.14	62.44	54.49	59.58	
el somewhat	Freq.	267	187	455	393	847	
loser to the	Row%	58.77	41.23	53.65	46.35	100.00	
Democrats than	Col%	10.47	11.93	11.03	16.90	13.14	
used to							
el much closer to	Freq.	287	284	572	345	916	
he Democrats	Row%	50.29	49.71	62.37	37.63	100.00	
han I used to	Col%	11.27	18.08	13.87	14.84	14.22	
TAL	Freq.	2550	1571	4122	2323	6445	
	Row%	61.88	38.12	63.95	36.05	100.00	
	Col%	100.00	100.00	100.00	100.00	100.00	

te: First/2+ generation: chi-square (5 d.f.) 58.597 (P = 0.000). Citizen/noncitizen (first gener-
on only): chi-square (5 d.f.) 132.010 (P = 0.000). Island-born Puerto Ricans are coded as first
eration. Question wording: "Which of the following best describes how your feelings about the
ties have changed in recent years?"

these responses by citizenship, generation, education, and income for
all respondents. Table 10.8 reveals that respondents' feelings toward the
Democratic and Republican parties seem to be stable, as clear and consistent majorities of respondents report that their feelings toward the parties
have not changed in recent years. In addition, an appreciably higher percentage of respondents report being "much closer" or even "somewhat
closer" to the Democratic Party than those reporting being "much closer"
or "somewhat closer" to the Republican Party. This pattern is strongest
among second generation and beyond citizens.

Most respondents, regardless of national origin, report "no change" in their feelings toward the political parties, as is shown in Table 10.9. Clear and consistent majorities report no change, except for those of "other" origin. For those who have feelings of being closer or somewhat closer to one of the two parties, the Democratic Party fares far better than the Republican Party. For example, 38 percent of Dominicans report feeling much closer or somewhat closer to the Democratic Party, whereas only 11 percent of the same group report the same changed feelings toward the Republican Party. Most interestingly, 24.6 percent of those of Cuban origin report feeling closer or somewhat closer to the Republican Party. An almost equal 23.4 percent of Cuban respondents, however, report feeling closer to the Democratic Party.

The data in Tables 10.10 and 10.11 reveal that, when one looks at responses by income and education, the same pattern of overall stability in feelings exists. Although across all income groups most respondents say that their feelings haven't changed toward either political party, of those who do feel close, more feel closer to Democrats. The same pattern occurs across all income groups. In addition, those with higher incomes and education are more likely to report a change in feelings toward one party or the other.

Ideology

One attitude that shapes partisan identification is a respondent's ideology. Interestingly, although most respondents identify with the Democratic Party, slightly less than 50 percent of noncitizens and those who are naturalized identify as either leaning conservative, conservative, or strongly conservative, as indicated in Figure 10.2. Those in the second generation and beyond display a more bifurcated pattern. Among those respondents, 39.3 percent indicate that they lean liberal, are liberal, or are strong liberals. A slightly smaller percentage, 35.7 percent, classify themselves as leaning conservative, conservative, or strong conservatives. Between one-fifth and one-quarter of all respondents, regardless of citizenship or generation, consider themselves middle of the road.

Our seven-point scale measuring respondents' ideology also reveals that the plurality of respondents identify as conservatives regardless of country of origin, as is shown in Table 10.12. Cubans and Salvadorans report the highest percentages of those with a conservative ideology: 57 percent and 61 percent, respectively. At least a third of Dominicans,

Table 10.9. *Change in Feelings toward Democratic and Republican Parties, by National Origin*

Category: Political Views, Party/Ideology

Response		Cuba	Dominican Republic	El Salvador	Mexico	Puerto Rico	Other Central America	Other South America	Other	Missing	Total
I feel much closer to the Republicans than I used to	Freq.	46	15	12	221	34	10	10	5	6	359
	Row%	12.70	4.28	3.34	61.56	9.50	2.91	2.70	1.29	1.72	100.00
	Col%	17.26	6.85	4.08	4.97	6.44	4.09	3.25	4.49	9.39	5.56
I feel somewhat closer to the Republicans than I used to	Freq.	19	9	26	343	30	18	19	17	3	483
	Row%	4.01	1.77	5.39	71.05	6.13	3.67	3.87	3.57	0.53	100.00
	Col%	7.35	3.83	8.87	7.73	5.59	6.96	6.27	24.22	3.92	7.50
My feelings have not changed	Freq.	137	116	192	2705	303	154	164	30	37	3839
	Row%	3.57	3.02	5.01	70.46	7.90	4.01	4.27	0.79	0.96	100.00
	Col%	52.03	51.79	65.42	60.87	57.32	60.47	54.96	42.47	56.29	59.57
I feel somewhat closer to the Democrats than I used to	Freq.	27	29	31	575	69	36	59	9	12	847
	Row%	3.18	3.43	3.63	67.84	8.14	4.30	6.98	1.03	1.46	100.00
	Col%	10.23	12.96	10.46	12.93	13.04	14.29	19.83	12.28	18.95	13.15
I feel much closer to the Democrats than I used to	Freq.	35	55	33	600	93	36	47	10	8	916
	Row%	3.78	6.01	3.58	65.46	10.17	3.94	5.11	1.13	0.82	100.00
	Col%	13.13	24.58	11.17	13.50	17.61	14.19	15.68	14.54	11.45	14.22
TOTAL	Freq.	264	224	294	4444	529	255	298	71	66	6445
	Row%	4.09	3.48	4.56	68.69	8.21	3.95	4.63	1.10	1.02	100.00
	Col%	100.00	100.00	100.00	100.00	100.00	100.00	100.00	100.00	100.00	100.00

Note: National origin: (32 d.f.) 165.6586 (P = 0.0000). Question wording: "Which of the following best describes how your feelings about the parties have changed in recent years?"

291

Table 10.10. *Change in Feelings toward Democratic and Republican Parties, by Income*

Category: Political Views, Party/Ideology

Response		Less than $15K	$15K–$24K	$25K–$34K	$35K–$54K	More than $54K	Total
I feel much closer to the	Freq.	36	58	39	55	101	289
Republicans than I used to	Row%	12.30	20.27	13.37	19.09	34.97	100.00
	Col%	3.74	4.73	4.20	5.01	9.10	5.43
I feel somewhat closer to the	Freq.	53	93	78	86	105	415
Republicans than I used to	Row%	12.81	22.36	18.88	20.64	25.32	100.00
	Col%	5.60	7.50	8.53	7.79	9.47	7.81
My feelings have not changed	Freq.	650	767	545	636	531	3129
	Row%	20.79	24.51	17.40	20.32	16.98	100.00
	Col%	68.52	61.96	59.29	57.85	47.92	58.89
I feel somewhat closer to the	Freq.	103	150	124	160	186	723
Democrats than I used to	Row%	14.28	20.79	17.13	22.10	25.71	100.00
	Col%	10.87	12.15	13.48	14.54	16.76	13.61
I feel much closer to the	Freq.	107	169	133	163	186	758
Democrats than I used to	Row%	14.13	22.33	17.57	21.47	24.50	100.00
	Col%	11.27	13.67	14.50	14.80	16.74	14.26
TOTAL	Freq.	949	1237	918	1099	1109	5312
	Row%	17.87	23.29	17.29	20.68	20.87	100.00
	Col%	100.00	100.00	100.00	100.00	100.00	100.00

Note: Income: (16 d.f.) 116.3172 (P = 0.0000). Question wording: "Which of the following best describes how your feelings about the parties have changed in recent years?"

Table 10.11. *Change in Feelings toward Democratic and Republican Parties, by Education*
Category: Political Views, Party/Ideology

Response		None to Some HS	HS or GED	Some to College Graduate	Graduate or Professional Degree	Total
I feel much closer to the Republicans than I used to	Freq.	115	91	121	32	359
	Row%	31.93	25.27	33.76	9.04	100.00
	Col%	5.46	4.77	5.83	8.77	5.56
I feel somewhat closer to the Republicans than I used to	Freq.	115	161	179	29	483
	Row%	23.68	33.30	37.01	6.01	100.00
	Col%	5.46	8.47	8.61	7.86	7.50
My feelings have not changed	Freq.	1375	1168	1119	117	3839
	Row%	35.81	30.42	29.16	4.62	100.00
	Col%	65.58	61.44	53.86	47.99	59.57
I feel somewhat closer to the Democrats than I used to	Freq.	200	250	337	61	847
	Row%	23.58	29.54	39.71	7.16	100.00
	Col%	9.53	13.17	16.19	16.42	13.15
I feel much closer to the Democrats than I used to	Freq.	293	231	323	70	916
	Row%	31.94	25.22	35.20	7.65	100.00
	Col%	13.96	12.16	15.52	18.96	14.22
TOTAL	Freq.	2096	1901	2078	370	6445
	Row%	32.52	29.49	32.25	5.74	100.00
	Col%	100.00	100.00	100.00	100.00	100.00

Note: Education: (12 d.f.) 112.4809 (P = 0.0000). Question wording: "Which of the following best describes how your feelings about the parties have changed in recent years?"

293

Table 10.12. *Ideology, by National Origin*
Category: Political Views, Party/Ideology

Response		Cuba	Dominican Republic	El Salvador	Mexico	Puerto Rico	Other Central America	Other South America	Other	Missing	Total
Strong Liberal	Freq.	22	30	20	400	65	37	47	8	2	631
	Row%	3.46	4.72	3.16	63.38	10.34	5.87	7.52	1.20	0.34	100.00
	Col%	11.83	19.97	9.36	13.74	18.35	22.19	24.77	15.27	6.18	14.82
Liberal	Freq.	15	10	16	390	36	23	29	8	7	533
	Row%	2.76	1.94	3.07	73.05	6.80	4.27	5.37	1.42	1.32	100.00
	Col%	7.97	6.91	7.68	13.38	10.19	13.64	14.95	15.29	19.91	12.52
Liberal leaning	Freq.	5	8	4	165	20	11	6	4	2	225
	Row%	2.12	3.62	1.70	73.52	8.75	5.05	2.72	1.58	0.95	100.00
	Col%	2.58	5.46	1.79	5.68	5.53	6.80	3.20	7.14	6.06	5.28
Middle of the road	Freq.	39	31	41	718	79	31	39	6	7	990
	Row%	3.91	3.15	4.10	72.55	7.97	3.08	3.92	0.58	0.74	100.00
	Col%	20.95	20.90	19.03	24.66	22.17	18.28	20.24	11.57	20.76	23.25
Conservative leaning	Freq.	12	7	9	142	7	8	6	3	0	194
	Row%	6.28	3.66	4.82	73.10	3.76	4.21	2.87	1.30	0.00	100.00
	Col%	6.59	4.75	4.38	4.87	2.05	4.89	2.91	5.09	0.00	4.55
Conservative	Freq.	29	31	65	514	46	19	36	10	5	754
	Row%	3.83	4.05	8.62	68.17	6.09	2.52	4.76	1.34	0.61	100.00
	Col%	15.64	20.47	30.49	17.66	12.92	11.38	18.76	20.41	13.11	17.71
Strong Conservative	Freq.	64	32	58	583	102	38	29	13	12	931
	Row%	6.84	3.45	6.25	62.61	11.00	4.09	3.12	1.35	1.29	100.00
	Col%	34.44	21.54	27.27	20.01	28.78	22.82	15.17	25.23	33.99	21.86
TOTAL	Freq.	185	149	213	2912	356	167	192	50	35	4258
	Row%	4.34	3.51	5.01	68.38	8.36	3.92	4.50	1.17	0.83	100.00
	Col%	100.00	100.00	100.00	100.00	100.00	100.00	100.00	100.00	100.00	100.00

Note: National origin: (48 d.f.) 151.2707 (P = 0.0000). Note: Seven-point scale constructed from responses to questions about ideological identification and strength of

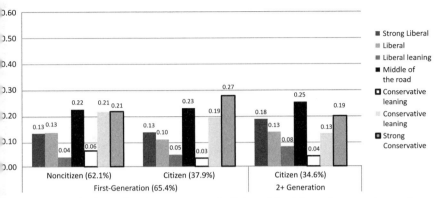

Figure 10.2. Ideology, by Generation and Citizenship. *Note:* Seven-point scale constructed from responses to questions about ideological identification and strength of ideological identification. Island-born Puerto Ricans coded as first generation.

Question wording: "Generally speaking, in politics do you consider yourself as conservative, liberal, middle-of-the-road, or don't you think of yourself in these terms?"

Mexicans, Puerto Ricans, "other" Central Americans, and "other" South Americans identify as leaning liberal, liberal, or strongly liberal.

Interestingly enough, there are no major shifts in ideology by income (Table 10.13). It is the case, however, that slightly less than one-quarter of those earning less than $15,000 per year identify as strong conservative and just less than one-fifth of those earning more than $54,000 per year identify as strong liberals.

Similarly, the data in Table 10.14 indicate that there is no major shift in propensity to identify as liberal or conservative according to formal education. However, the plurality of respondents who have a high school education or less identify as conservative or strong conservative, whereas one-fifth of those with graduate or professional degrees identify as strong liberals.

Importance of Coethnic Candidates

We were curious as to whether a candidate's ethnicity mattered to our respondents. A clear majority of respondents who are Dominican, Salvadoran, Mexican, from other central American countries, and from other South American countries indicate that it is very important to them that a candidate is Latino or Hispanic, details of which are shown in

Table 10.13. *Ideology, by Income*
Category: Political Views, Party/Ideology

Response		Less than $15K	$15K-$24K	$25K-$34K	$35K-$54K	More than $54K	Total
Strong Liberal	Freq.	98	90	93	94	152	527
	Row%	18.59	17.06	17.74	17.75	28.86	100.00
	Col%	16.19	11.21	15.05	12.81	18.29	14.68
Liberal	Freq.	64	95	78	99	94	430
	Row%	14.90	22.16	18.16	22.97	21.81	100.00
	Col%	10.59	11.88	12.58	13.52	11.28	11.98
Liberal leaning	Freq.	29	39	34	37	67	206
	Row%	14.18	19.06	16.39	18.03	32.35	100.00
	Col%	4.84	4.90	5.45	5.09	8.03	5.75
Middle of the road	Freq.	117	203	137	179	201	837
	Row%	14.01	24.24	16.36	21.38	24.02	100.00
	Col%	19.39	25.31	22.07	24.51	24.19	23.33
Conservative leaning	Freq.	35	42	29	28	30	163
	Row%	21.15	25.75	17.50	17.27	18.32	100.00
	Col%	5.71	5.24	4.60	3.86	3.60	4.55
Conservative	Freq.	111	167	136	123	106	643
	Row%	17.32	25.90	21.14	19.11	16.53	100.00
	Col%	18.42	20.79	21.91	16.84	12.79	17.93
Strong conservative	Freq.	150	166	114	171	181	782
	Row%	19.23	21.19	14.56	21.82	23.19	100.00
	Col%	24.86	20.67	18.34	23.37	21.82	21.79
TOTAL	Freq.	605	802	621	730	831	3589
	Row%	16.85	22.34	17.30	20.35	23.16	100.00
	Col%	100.00	100.00	100.00	100.00	100.00	100.00

Note: Income: (24 d.f.) 73.4898 (P = 0.0079). Note: Seven-point scale constructed from responses to questions about ideological identification and strength

296

Table 10.14. *Ideology, by Education*
Category: Political Views, Party/Ideology

sponse		None to Some HS	HS or GED	Some to College Graduate	Graduate or Professional Degree	Total
ong liberal	Freq.	160	165	248	58	631
	Row%	25.41	26.14	39.35	9.11	100.00
	Col%	12.39	13.52	17.14	19.53	14.82
ɔeral	Freq.	170	150	179	35	533
	Row%	31.86	28.17	33.48	6.50	100.00
	Col%	13.13	12.31	12.32	11.76	12.52
ɔeral leaning	Freq.	45	65	96	19	225
	Row%	19.78	29.06	42.64	8.52	100.00
	Col%	3.44	5.36	6.62	6.51	5.28
iddle of the road	Freq.	283	264	371	72	990
	Row%	28.60	26.66	37.50	7.24	100.00
	Col%	21.87	21.62	25.61	24.34	23.25
ɔnservative leaning	Freq.	86	48	48	13	194
	Row%	44.22	24.66	24.68	6.44	100.00
	Col%	6.63	3.92	3.30	4.24	4.55
ɔnservative	Freq.	243	262	215	34	754
	Row%	32.23	34.76	28.49	4.52	100.00
	Col%	18.78	21.49	14.83	11.58	17.71
ʳong conservative	Freq.	308	266	292	65	931
	Row%	33.03	28.57	31.42	6.98	100.00
	Col%	23.76	21.79	20.18	22.05	21.86
TAL	Freq.	1294	1220	1449	295	4258
	Row%	30.39	28.66	34.03	6.92	100.00
	Col%	100.00	100.00	100.00	100.00	100.00

ɔte: Education: (18 d.f.) 84.9950 (P = 0.0000). Note: Seven-point scale constructed from ponses to questions about ideological identification and strength of ideological identification. estion wording: "Generally speaking, in politics do you consider yourself as conservative, lib-ˌl, middle-of-the-road, or don't you think of yourself in these terms?"

Figure 10.3. Just more than a third of those with origins in Cuba and Puerto Rico indicate that this is important, although just more than 40 percent of each of these two groups indicate that it is not important at all.

The importance of whether a candidate is Latino declines substantially as respondents' income increases and their education advances (Tables 10.15 and 10.16). In both cases, from one-fifth to one-quarter of respondents indicate that it remains somewhat important regardless of income and education.

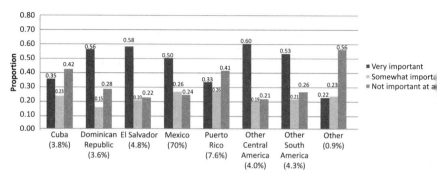

Figure 10.3. Importance of Candidate Being Latino or Hispanic, by National Origin.
Question wording: "People can prefer a candidate for a variety of different reasons. How important is it for you that a candidate is Latino/Hispanic?"

The importance of a candidate being Latino and/or Hispanic is approximately the same for Latinas and for Latino men. For both groups, slightly less than half responded that it is very important, less than a quarter said that it is somewhat important, and slightly more than a quarter noted that it is not important at all. This is all documented in Table 10.17.

Importance of Candidate Speaking Spanish

A substantial majority of respondents with origins in the Dominican Republic, El Salvador, Mexico, other Central American countries, and other South American countries reported that it is very important to them that a candidate be able to speak Spanish, as reflected in Figure 10.4. It is only among those with origins in Cuba and Puerto Rico that the pattern is distinct. Among respondents from these two groups, 45 percent of Cubans and 47 percent of Puerto Ricans, the plurality of respondents in each group, think that it is important for a candidate to be able to speak Spanish. When one combines the percentage of respondents who think that it is somewhat important with those who think that it is very important, a sizable majority values a candidate's ability to speak Spanish.

The importance of a candidate's ability to speak Spanish is very significant across all income groups, except for those in the highest group, which earns more than $54,000 per year (Table 10.18). For example, three-quarters of all respondents whose income is less than $15,000 per year indicate that ability to speak Spanish is very important, slightly less than 70 percent of those who earn between $15,000 and $24,000,

Table 10.15. *Importance of Candidate Being Latino or Hispanic, by Income*
Category: Political Participation, Civic Participation

Response		Less than $15K	$15K–$24K	$25K–$34K	$35K–$54K	More than $54K	Total
Not important at all	Freq.	229	280	268	415	633	1825
	Row%	12.54	15.35	14.69	22.71	34.70	100.00
	Col%	17.37	17.62	23.62	31.22	48.74	27.36
Somewhat important	Freq.	260	361	280	359	356	1615
	Row%	16.09	22.36	17.35	22.19	22.01	100.00
	Col%	19.72	22.71	24.69	27.00	27.36	24.22
Very important	Freq.	829	949	587	555	311	3230
	Row%	25.66	29.38	18.17	17.18	9.62	100.00
	Col%	62.90	59.66	51.69	41.79	23.90	48.42
TOTAL	Freq.	1317	1590	1135	1328	1300	6670
	Row%	19.75	23.84	17.02	19.91	19.48	100.00
	Col%	100.00	100.00	100.00	100.00	100.00	100.00

Note: Income: (8 d.f.) 645.2226 (P = 0.0000). Question wording: "People can prefer a candidate for a variety of different reasons. How important is it for you that a candidate is Latino/Hispanic?"

Table 10.16. *Importance of Candidate Being Latino or Hispanic, by Educatio*
Category: Political Participation, Civic Participation

Response		None to Some HS	HS or GED	Some to College Graduate	Graduate or Professional Degree	Tota
Not important at all	Freq.	535	657	941	179	2311
	Row%	23.15	28.41	40.71	7.73	100.
	Col%	16.99	25.91	37.31	41.65	26.
Somewhat important	Freq.	675	629	682	114	2101
	Row%	32.13	29.96	32.46	5.45	100.
	Col%	21.43	24.84	27.04	26.66	24.
Very important	Freq.	1939	1248	899	136	4222
	Row%	45.93	29.56	21.29	3.22	100.
	Col%	61.58	49.25	35.65	31.69	48.
TOTAL	Freq.	3149	2534	2522	429	8634
	Row%	36.47	29.35	29.21	4.97	100.
	Col%	100.00	100.00	100.00	100.00	100.

Note: Education: (6 d.f.) 493.2794 (P = 0.0000). Question wording: "People can prefer candidate for a variety of different reasons. How important is it for you that a candidate Latino/Hispanic?"

Table 10.17. *Importance of Candidate Being Latino or Hispanic,*
by Gender
Category: Political Participation, Civic Participation

Response		Male	Female	Total
Not important at all	Freq.	1113	1198	2311
	Row%	48.16	51.84	100.00
	Col%	27.24	26.35	26.77
Somewhat important	Freq.	1001	1100	2101
	Row%	47.65	52.35	100.00
	Col%	24.49	24.18	24.33
Very important	Freq.	1972	2250	4222
	Row%	46.72	53.28	100.00
	Col%	48.27	49.47	48.90
TOTAL	Freq.	4087	4547	8634
	Row%	47.33	52.67	100.00
	Col%	100.00	100.00	100.00

Note: Gender: (2 d.f.) 1.3630 (P = 0.6596). Question wording: "People can prefer a candidate for a variety of different reasons. How important is it for you that a candidate is Latino/Hispanic?"

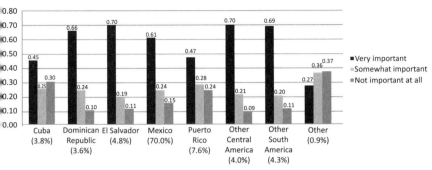

Figure 10.4. Importance of Candidate Speaking Spanish, by National Origin. Question wording: "People can prefer a candidate for a variety of different reasons. How important is it for you that a candidate speaks Spanish?"

61 percent of those who earn between $25,000 and $34,000, and 53 percent of those who earn between $35,000 and $54,000. By contrast, only one-third of respondents with incomes more than $54,000 do so.

A similar pattern is revealed by a respondent's educational level in Table 10.19. Slightly less than three-quarters of those who are not high school graduates believe that a candidate's ability to speak Spanish is very important in their preference for a candidate, 60 percent of those who are high school graduates or have a GED, and 46 percent of those with some college or who are college graduates. By comparison, only 39 percent of those with graduate or professional degrees think that it is important. Interestingly, clear majorities of all educational groups think that it is either somewhat or very important that a candidate speak Spanish.

Majorities of both male and female respondents indicated that a candidate's ability to speak Spanish was important in determining which candidate they might prefer (Table 10.20). Less than one-fifth of both of these groups responded that it was not important at all.

Political Knowledge

It is well known that an important contributor to partisan preferences is political knowledge. The more knowledgeable respondents are about important aspects of politics, the more likely it is that their preferences are well informed and therefore less subject to manipulation by candidates and parties during campaigns. We asked respondents three separate questions to determine their political knowledge: (1) "Which political party is more conservative at the national level?" (2) "Which political party had a majority in the House of Representatives in 2006?" and (3) "Which

Table 10.18. *Importance of Candidate Speaking Spanish, by Income*
Category: Political Views, Party/Ideology

Response		Less than $15K	$15K–$24K	$25K–$34K	$35K–$54K	More than $54K	Total
Not important at all	Freq.	105	140	136	252	466	1099
	Row%	9.53	12.76	12.40	22.92	42.39	100.00
	Col%	7.95	8.82	12.01	18.98	35.86	16.48
Somewhat important	Freq.	225	350	304	370	402	1652
	Row%	13.64	21.21	18.41	22.42	24.32	100.00
	Col%	17.10	22.03	26.79	27.89	30.92	24.76
Very important	Freq.	987	1100	695	706	432	3919
	Row%	25.19	28.06	17.73	18.00	11.01	100.00
	Col%	74.95	69.15	61.20	53.13	33.22	58.75
TOTAL	Freq.	1317	1590	1135	1328	1300	6670
	Row%	19.75	23.84	17.02	19.91	19.48	100.00
	Col%	100.00	100.00	100.00	100.00	100.00	100.00

Note: Income: (8 d.f.) 751.2360 (P = 0.0000). Question wording: "People can prefer a candidate for a variety of different reasons. How important is it for you that a candidate speaks Spanish?"

Table 10.19. *Importance of Candidate Speaking Spanish, by Education*
Category: Political Views, Party/Ideology

sponse		None to Some HS	HS or GED	Some to College Graduate	Graduate or Professional Degree	Total
t important at all	Freq.	238	376	634	130	1378
	Row%	17.26	27.25	46.04	9.44	100.00
	Col%	7.55	14.82	25.16	30.33	15.96
mewhat important	Freq.	567	647	720	130	2064
	Row%	27.48	31.33	34.87	6.32	100.00
	Col%	18.01	25.51	28.54	30.40	23.90
ry important	Freq.	2344	1512	1168	169	5192
	Row%	45.14	29.12	22.49	3.25	100.00
	Col%	74.44	59.67	46.30	39.28	60.14
TAL	Freq.	3149	2534	2522	429	8634
	Row%	36.47	29.35	29.21	4.97	100.00
	Col%	100.00	100.00	100.00	100.00	100.00

te: Education: (6 d.f.) 627.8215 (P = 0.0000). Question wording: "People can prefer a can-
ate for a variety of different reasons. How important is it for you that a candidate speaks
anish?"

Table 10.20. *Importance of Candidate Speaking Spanish, by Gender*
Category: Political Views, Party/Ideology

Response		Male	Female	Total
Not important at all	Freq.	709	669	1378
	Row%	51.44	48.56	100.00
	Col%	17.35	14.71	15.96
Somewhat important	Freq.	1054	1010	2064
	Row%	51.07	48.93	100.00
	Col%	25.79	22.21	23.90
Very important	Freq.	2324	2868	5192
	Row%	44.75	55.25	100.00
	Col%	56.86	63.08	60.14
TOTAL	Freq.	4087	4547	8634
	Row%	47.33	52.67	100.00
	Col%	100.00	100.00	100.00

Note: Gender: (2 d.f.) 34.7557 (P = 0.0000). Question wording: "People can prefer a
candidate for a variety of different reasons. How important is it for you that a candidate
speaks Spanish?"

Table 10.21. *Political Knowledge: Which National Party Is More Conservativ*
by Generation and Citizenship
Category: Political Views, Party/Ideology

Response		First Generation			2+ Generation	
		Noncitizen	Citizen	Total	Citizen	Tota
Democratic	Freq.	1000	534	1534	722	2257
	Row%	65.17	34.83	67.99	32.01	100.
	Col%	25.50	26.78	25.93	26.57	26.
Republican	Freq.	968	825	1793	1340	3133
	Row%	53.97	46.03	57.23	42.77	100.
	Col%	24.68	41.37	30.31	49.29	36.
Do not know	Freq.	1953	636	2589	656	3245
	Row%	75.44	24.56	79.78	20.22	100.
	Col%	49.81	31.86	43.76	24.14	37.
TOTAL	Freq.	3921	1995	5916	2719	8635
	Row%	66.27	33.73	68.52	31.48	100.
	Col%	100.00	100.00	100.00	100.00	100.

Note: First/2+ generation: (3 d.f.) 375.8778 (P = 0.0000). Citizen/noncitizen (first generati
only): (3 d.f.) 320.4678 (P = 0.000). Island-born Puerto Ricans are coded as first generati
Question wording: "Which one of the political parties is more conservative than the other at
national level, the Democrats or the Republicans?"

presidential candidate won their current state of residence in the 2004
presidential election?"

Only a quarter of noncitizens were able to answer correctly which
national party was more conservative, as indicated in Table 10.22. However, a noticeably higher 41 percent of naturalized citizens were able to
do so, as were 49 percent of those in the second generation and beyond.
Moreover, slightly less than half of all noncitizens indicated that they did
not know, slightly less than a third of foreign-born citizens, and slightly
less than a quarter of the second generation and beyond. Interestingly,
about a quarter of all respondents, regardless of citizenship or generation,
incorrectly responded that the Democratic Party was more conservative.

Table 10.21 reveals responses to the same question by country of
origin. The only cases where a majority of respondents answered correctly
was for those of Cuban origin and those from "other" origins, as can be
seen in the data on variations in responses to this question by national
origin group (Table 10.22). Just less than half of those from other South
American countries answered this question correctly. Sizable percentages
of respondents from all groups, except for those from "other" origins,
responded that they did not know.

Table 10.22. *Political Knowledge: Which National Party Is More Conservative, by National Origin*

Category: Political Views, Party/Ideology

Response		Cuba	Dominican Republic	El Salvador	Mexico	Puerto Rico	Other Central America	Other South America	Other	Missing	Total
Democratic	Freq.	59	108	131	1557	193	105	79	10	15	2257
	Row%	2.62	4.78	5.82	68.99	8.55	4.64	3.51	0.44	0.65	100.00
	Col%	18.04	34.77	31.86	25.76	29.29	30.41	21.20	12.62	17.40	26.14
Republican	Freq.	178	93	118	2084	261	120	180	54	44	3133
	Row%	5.67	2.98	3.77	66.53	8.34	3.82	5.76	1.72	1.41	100.00
	Col%	54.30	30.14	28.66	34.49	39.68	34.72	48.24	68.24	52.48	36.29
Do not know	Freq.	91	109	163	2403	204	120	114	15	25	3244
	Row%	2.79	3.35	5.02	74.07	6.30	3.70	3.52	0.46	0.78	100.00
	Col%	27.66	35.09	39.48	39.76	31.03	34.87	30.56	19.13	30.12	37.58
TOTAL	Freq.	327	310	413	6045	659	344	374	79	84	8634
	Row%	3.79	3.59	4.78	70.01	7.63	3.99	4.33	0.91	0.97	100.00
	Col%	100.00	100.00	100.00	100.00	100.00	100.00	100.00	100.00	100.00	100.00

Note: National origin: (16 d.f.) 167.2954 (P = 0.0000). Question wording: "Which one of the political parties is more conservative than the other at the national level, the Democrats or the Republicans?"

As income and education increase, greater percentages of respondents correctly answer which political party is more conservative in national politics (Tables 10.23 and 10.24). That said, just less than 20 percent of respondents in the highest categories of income and education still respond that they do not know.

Once again, it is naturalized citizens and those in the second generation and beyond who are more likely to know that the Republican Party was in control of the House of Representatives during the time we conducted the interviews. Table 10.25 indicates that only 24 percent of noncitizens correctly answered this question, compared with 48 percent of naturalized citizens and 53 percent of the second generation and beyond. Sizable percentages of respondents indicated that they did not know which party controlled the House of Representatives. Of noncitizens, naturalized citizens, and second generation and beyond citizens, 62 percent, 39 percent, and 31 percent, respectively, responded in this way.

Similar to responses to the first question about which political party is more conservative at the national level, it was only among respondents of Cuban origin and those from "other" origins that majorities knew which party controlled the House of Representatives, as displayed in Table 10.26. More than 60 percent of these groups correctly answered this question. Slightly less than a majority of those from Puerto Rico and those from other South American countries did so as well. Again, sizable percentages of respondents from all countries responded that they did not know. This was especially the case for those respondents from Mexico, other Central American countries, El Salvador, and the Dominican Republic.

Much like the responses to the previous question, a significantly greater percentage of respondents answered the question correctly as income and education increased. Although only about 26 percent of those who reported earning less than $15,000 in 2004 correctly answered the question, about 63 percent of those who reported earning more than $54,000 did so, as indicated in Table 10.27. Higher-income respondents were also half as likely to report that they did not know. Moreover, as indicated in Table 10.28, 24 percent of those without a high school diploma correctly identify the Republican Party as the party in control of the House of Representatives at the time of the interview, whereas 63 percent of those with advanced college degrees do so. More than a quarter of those with advanced degrees responded that they do not know the answer.

The final question examining political knowledge asked which presidential candidate won the respondent's current state of residence in the

Table 10.23. *Political Knowledge: Which National Party Is More Conservative, by Income*

Category: Political Views, Party/Ideology

Response		Less than $15K	$15K–$24K	$25K–$34K	$35K–$54K	More than $54K	Total
Democratic	Freq.	377	508	357	368	262	1871
	Row%	20.14	27.15	19.06	19.67	13.98	100.00
	Col%	28.60	31.94	31.41	27.70	20.12	28.04
Republican	Freq.	358	505	415	591	810	2678
	Row%	13.36	18.86	15.48	22.07	30.23	100.00
	Col%	27.16	31.76	36.54	44.51	62.31	40.16
Do not know	Freq.	583	577	364	369	228	2121
	Row%	27.47	27.21	17.15	17.39	10.76	100.00
	Col%	44.24	36.30	32.05	27.78	17.57	31.80
TOTAL	Freq.	1317	1590	1135	1328	1300	6670
	Row%	19.75	23.84	17.02	19.91	19.48	100.00
	Col%	100.00	100.00	100.00	100.00	100.00	100.00

Note: Income: (8 d.f.) 469.4158 (P = 0.0000). Question wording: "Which one of the political parties is more conservative than the other at the national level, the Democrats or the Republicans?"

Table 10.24. *Political Knowledge: Which National Party Is More Conservativ*
by Education
Category: Political Views, Party/Ideology

Response		None to Some HS	HS or GED	Some to College Graduate	Graduate or Professional Degree	Tot
Democratic	Freq.	808	748	620	81	2257
	Row%	35.81	33.12	27.48	3.58	100
	Col%	25.67	29.49	24.60	18.81	26
Republican	Freq.	711	857	1289	277	3133
	Row%	22.69	27.34	41.14	8.83	100
	Col%	22.58	33.80	51.11	64.47	36
Do not know	Freq.	1630	930	613	72	3244
	Row%	50.24	28.67	18.88	2.21	100
	Col%	51.76	36.71	24.29	16.72	37
TOTAL	Freq.	3149	2534	2522	429	8634
	Row%	36.47	29.35	29.21	4.97	100
	Col%	100.00	100.00	100.00	100.00	100

Note: Education: (6 d.f.) 773.6586 (P = 0.0000). Question wording: "Which one of the polit
parties is more conservative than the other at the national level, the Democrats or the Republican

Table 10.25. *Political Knowledge: Control of the U.S. House of Representativ*
by Generation and Citizenship
Category: Political Views, Party/Ideology

| Response | | First Generation | | | 2+ Generation | |
		Noncitizen	Citizen	Total	Citizen	Tot.
Democratic	Freq.	547	268	816	417	1233
	Row%	67.10	32.90	66.17	33.83	100.
	Col%	13.96	13.45	13.79	15.34	14
Republican	Freq.	932	957	1889	1453	3342
	Row%	49.33	50.67	56.52	43.48	100.
	Col%	23.77	47.96	31.93	53.45	38.
Do not know	Freq.	2441	770	3211	849	4060
	Row%	76.02	23.98	79.10	20.90	100.
	Col%	62.27	38.59	54.28	31.21	47.
TOTAL	Freq.	3920	1995	5915	2719	8634
	Row%	66.27	33.73	68.51	31.49	100.
	Col%	100.00	100.00	100.00	100.00	100.

Note: First/2+ generation: (3 d.f.) 436.6369 (P = 0.000). Citizen/noncitizen (first generation on
(3 d.f) 553.5707 (P = 0.000). Island-born Puerto Ricans are coded as first generation. Quest
wording: "Which political party, Democrat or Republican (alternate order), has a majority in
United States House of Representatives?"

Table 10.26. *Political Knowledge: Control of the U.S. House of Representatives, by National Origin*

Category: Political Views, Party/Ideology

Response		Cuba	Dominican Republic	El Salvador	Mexico	Puerto Rico	Other Central America	Other South America	Other	Missing	Total
Democratic	Freq.	36	48	53	878	90	53	58	7	10	1233
	Row%	2.90	3.92	4.26	71.19	7.34	4.28	4.74	0.53	0.84	100.00
	Col%	10.93	15.59	12.73	14.52	13.74	15.31	15.62	8.30	12.38	14.28
Republican	Freq.	200	120	156	2147	329	120	178	55	37	3341
	Row%	5.99	3.60	4.67	64.25	9.83	3.59	5.33	1.63	1.11	100.00
	Col%	61.13	38.79	37.82	35.52	49.88	34.87	47.61	69.24	44.18	38.70
Do not know	Freq.	91	141	204	3020	240	172	138	18	36	4060
	Row%	2.25	3.48	5.02	74.39	5.90	4.23	3.39	0.44	0.90	100.00
	Col%	27.95	45.62	49.45	49.96	36.38	49.82	36.78	22.46	43.44	47.02
TOTAL	Freq.	327	310	413	6045	659	344	374	79	84	8634
	Row%	3.79	3.59	4.78	70.01	7.63	3.99	4.33	0.91	0.97	100.00
	Col%	100.00	100.00	100.00	100.00	100.00	100.00	100.00	100.00	100.00	100.00

Note: National origin: (16 d.f.) 187.4513 (P = 0.0000). Question wording: "Which political party, Democrat or Republican (alternate order), has a majority in the United States House of Representatives?"

Table 10.27. *Political Knowledge: Control of the U.S. House of Representatives, by Income*

Category: Political Views, Party/Ideology

Response		Less than $15K	$15K-$24K	$25K-$34K	$35K-$54K	More than $54K	Total
Democratic	Freq.	218	242	166	233	164	1023
	Row%	21.30	23.66	16.26	22.73	16.05	100.00
	Col%	16.54	15.22	14.65	17.51	12.63	15.33
Republican	Freq.	341	563	454	666	814	2838
	Row%	12.00	19.85	16.00	23.48	28.67	100.00
	Col%	25.85	35.42	39.99	50.18	62.61	42.54
Do not know	Freq.	759	785	515	429	322	2810
	Row%	27.01	27.94	18.32	15.27	11.45	100.00
	Col%	57.61	49.37	45.36	32.32	24.76	42.13
TOTAL	Freq.	1317	1590	1135	1328	1300	6670
	Row%	19.75	23.84	17.02	19.91	19.48	100.00
	Col%	100.00	100.00	100.00	100.00	100.00	100.00

Note: Income: (8 d.f.) 492.9228 (P = 0.0000). Question wording: "Which political party, Democrat or Republican (alternate order), has a majority in the United States House of Representatives?"

ıble 10.28. *Political Knowledge: Control of the U.S. House of Representatives,*
by Education

Category: Political Views, Party/Ideology

sponse		None to Some HS	HS or GED	Some to College Graduate	Graduate or Professional Degree	Total
mocratic	Freq.	469	400	317	47	1233
	Row%	38.08	32.41	25.69	3.82	100.00
	Col%	14.91	15.77	12.56	10.97	14.28
publican	Freq.	766	953	1353	269	3341
	Row%	22.93	28.52	40.50	8.05	100.00
	Col%	24.33	37.60	53.66	62.71	38.70
ɔ not know	Freq.	1913	1182	852	113	4060
	Row%	47.13	29.11	20.98	2.78	100.00
	Col%	60.76	46.63	33.78	26.32	47.02
TAL	Freq.	3149	2534	2522	429	8634
	Row%	36.47	29.35	29.21	4.97	100.00
	Col%	100.00	100.00	100.00	100.00	100.00

te: Education: (6 d.f.) 651.5471 (P = 0.0000). Question wording: "Which political party, mocrat or Republican (alternate order), has a majority in the United States House of presentatives?"

2004 election. Because responses varied by each state, we categorized them as correct and incorrect. Although only a minority of noncitizens, 30 percent, correctly reported the presidential candidate who won their state, just less than a majority of first-generation citizens, 48 percent, and almost 60 percent of second generation and beyond citizens correctly reported which presidential candidate won the election in the respondent's state of residence, as indicated in Table 10.29. Consistent with the pattern of previous responses, the group that reported the largest number of "don't know" responses, 52 percent, was first-generation noncitizens. By contrast, only 24 percent of the second generation and beyond answered "don't know."

We find variation among national origin groups with respect to this measure of political knowledge (Table 10.30). Cubans and Puerto Ricans perform strongly, with about 70 percent of Cubans and about 50 percent of Puerto Ricans correctly identifying the candidate who won the state in which they reside. Only about 40 percent of Dominicans, 38 percent of Salvadorans, and 40 percent of Mexicans, by contrast, correctly identified the candidate who won the state in which they reside.

Tables 10.31 and 10.32 reveal that as income and education increase, the propensity of respondents to answer correctly increases as well.

Table 10.29. *Political Knowledge: Which Presidential Candidate Won in Respondent's State of Residence, by Generation and Citizenship* **Category:** Political Views, Party/Ideology

| Response | | First Generation | | 2+ Generation | | |
		Noncitizen	Citizen	Total	Citizen	Tota
Correct	Freq.	1085	1048	2133	1478	3611
	Row%	30.05	29.02	59.07	40.93	100.
	Col%	30.09	47.77	36.78	59.00	43
Incorrect	Freq.	646	406	1052	419	1471
	Row%	43.92	27.60	71.52	28.48	100.
	Col%	17.91	18.51	18.14	16.73	17.
Do not know	Freq.	1875	740	2615	547	3162
	Row%	59.30	23.40	82.70	17.30	100
	Col%	52.00	33.73	45.09	24.27	38.
TOTAL	Freq.	3606	2194	5800	2444	8244
	Row%	43.74	26.61	70.35	29.66	100.
	Col%	100.00	100.00	100.00	100.00	100.

Note: First/2+ generation: (3 d.f.) 406.7503 (P = 0.000). Citizen/non-citizen (first generat only): (3 d.f.) 331.4718 (P = 0.000). Island-born Puerto Ricans coded as first generation. Quest wording: "In the United States, presidential elections are decided state-by-state. Can you tell ¤ in the election of 2004, which candidate, Bush or Kerry, won the most votes in [R's current st of residence]?"

For example, 31 percent of those who earned less than $15,000 per year answered correctly, whereas 67 percent of those with incomes of more than $54,000 answered correctly. Similarly, 30 percent of those with less that a high school education correctly identified which presidential candidate won their respective states, whereas 67 percent of those with graduate or professional degrees did so. Not surprisingly, just more than a majority of those with less than a high school education answered "don't know."

Partisanship in the Latino National Survey

It is, of course, necessary to again acknowledge that these data provide descriptive statistics, which only begin to outline variations in patterns of Latino partisanship and underlying factors that affect those patterns. Only multivariate analysis can reveal underlying causal frameworks to explain many of the patterns in the data revealed in this chapter. However, we suggest a few important conclusions.

First, Latino partisan identification strongly favors the Democratic Party. Although gains may have been made for the Republican Party

Table 10.30. *Political Knowledge (Which Presidential Candidate Won in Respondent's State of Residence), by National Origin*

Category: Political Views, Party/Ideology

Response		Cuba	Dominican Republic	El Salvador	Mexico	Puerto Rico	Other Central America	Other South America	Other	Missing	Total
Incorrect	Freq.	40	76	76	966	170	45	77	11	10	1471
	Row%	2.72	5.17	5.17	65.67	11.56	3.06	5.23	0.75	0.68	100.00
	Col%	9.80	23.97	19.19	17.84	21.30	14.33	19.20	10.58	12.82	17.05
Correct	Freq.	285	128	152	2211	392	139	190	72	42	3611
	Row%	7.89	3.54	4.21	61.23	10.86	3.85	5.26	1.20	1.16	100.00
	Col%	69.85	40.38	38.38	40.83	49.12	44.27	47.38	69.23	53.85	41.85
Do not know	Freq.	83	113	168	2238	236	130	134	21	26	3149
	Row%	2.64	3.59	5.34	71.07	7.49	4.13	4.26	0.67	0.83	100.00
	Col%	20.34	35.65	42.42	41.33	29.57	41.40	33.42	20.19	33.33	41.11
TOTAL	Freq.	408	317	396	5415	798	314	401	104	78	8231
	Row%	4.96	3.85	4.81	65.79	9.70	3.81	4.87	1.26	0.95	100.00
	Col%	100.00	100.00	100.00	100.00	100.00	100.00	100.00	100.00	100.00	100.00

Note: National origin: (8 d.f.) 160.4799 (P = 0.0000). Question wording: "In the United States, presidential elections are decided state-by-state. Can you tell me, in the election of 2004, which candidate, Bush or Kerry, won the most votes in [R's current state of residence]?"

Table 10.31. *Political Knowledge: Which Presidential Candidate Won in Respondent's State of Residence, by Income*

Category: Political Views, Party/Ideology

Response		Less than $15K	$15K–$24K	$25K–$34K	$35K–$54K	More than $54K	Total
Incorrect	Freq.	238	301	219	246	213	1217
	Row%	19.56	24.73	18.00	20.21	17.50	100.00
	Col%	19.64	20.41	19.11	17.84	15.18	18.40
Correct	Freq.	372	530	503	725	946	3076
	Row%	12.09	17.23	16.35	23.57	30.75	100.00
	Col%	30.69	35.93	43.89	52.57	67.43	46.50
Do not know	Freq.	602	644	424	408	244	2322
	Row%	25.93	27.73	18.26	17.57	10.51	100.00
	Col%	49.67	43.66	37.00	29.59	17.39	35.10
TOTAL	Freq.	1212	1475	1146	1379	1403	6615
	Row%	18.32	22.30	17.32	20.84	21.21	100.00
	Col%	100.00	100.00	100.00	100.00	100.00	100.00

Note: Income: (4 d.f.) 375.4738 (P = 0.0000). Question wording: "In the United States, presidential elections are decided state-by-state. Can you tell me, in the election of 2004, which candidate, Bush or Kerry, won the most votes in [R's current state of residence]?"

Table 10.32. *Political Knowledge: Which Presidential Candidate Won in Respondent's State of Residence, by Education*
Category: Political Views, Party/Ideology

ponse		None to Some HS	HS or GED	Some to College Graduate	Graduate or Professional Degree	Total
orrect	Freq.	562	441	383	85	1471
	Row%	38.21	29.80	26.04	5.78	100.00
	Col%	18.86	19.18	16.01	14.83	17.84
rrect	Freq.	893	951	1385	382	3611
	Row%	24.73	26.34	38.36	10.58	100.00
	Col%	29.97	41.37	57.90	66.67	43.80
not know	Freq.	1525	907	624	106	3162
	Row%	48.23	28.68	19.73	3.35	100.00
	Col%	51.17	39.45	26.09	18.50	38.36
AL	Freq.	2980	2299	2392	573	8244
	Row%	36.15	27.89	29.03	6.95	100.00
	Col%	100.00	100.00	100.00	100.00	100.00

e: Education: (3 d.f.) 505.9396 (P = 0.0000). Question wording: "In the United States, pres-
itial elections are decided state-by-state. Can you tell me, in the election of 2004, which
didate, Bush or Kerry, won the most votes in [R's current state of residence]?"

during the two Bush presidential campaigns of 2000 and 2004, those
gains are not grounded in an underlying shift in Latino preferences away
from the Democratic Party. This applies to party registration as well.
Most important, identification with the Democratic Party increases with
citizenship, generation, income, and more years of formal education. It
also applies broadly across country of origin. The same applies for party
registration. Latinos of Cuban origin remain distinct in both these regards.
Moreover, to the extent that feelings toward the two parties have changed
in recent years, the Democratic Party stands in a much better position with
Latinos than does the Republican Party. This also generally applies across
variations in citizenship, generation, income, and education. Democratic
gains made among Latino voters in the 2006 congressional elections and
the 2008 presidential election reflect an underlying pattern of partisan
preferences, which presents great challenges to any possibility of future
Republican gains.

Second, Latinos tend to identify themselves as middle of the road, conservative, or strongly conservative, regardless of citizenship and generation. Those with lower income and less education identify most as strong
conservatives, and those with more education are more likely to identify

themselves as strong liberals. Thus, those who assume that Latinos' propensity to identify as conservative leaves them open to appeals from the social conservative wing of the Republican Party could be making a grave mistake, because ideology and party identification do not coincide for Latinos in ways that they may for other segments of the American population. Similarly, Democrats should not assume that Latinos easily identify with the term *liberal*. No doubt, positions on issues, discussed in other segments of this volume, carry significant weight in Latino partisan preferences.

Third, Latino respondents indicate strong preferences for Latino candidates and for those candidates who speak Spanish. This applies broadly, though not perfectly, regardless of citizenship, generation, and country of origin. The importance of coethnic and bilingual candidates declines, however, with increasing income and years of education. These data suggest that the political party that can nominate the greatest number of Latino candidates and candidates who speak Spanish has a strong advantage among substantial segments of the Latino population.

Fourth, levels of political knowledge among Latino voters are lowest for noncitizens but are still substantially lower for foreign-born citizens and those in the second generation and beyond. Although some variation exists by country of origin, overall, a pattern of limited political knowledge is apparent. The only clear exceptions to this are for those in the highest categories of income and education. This is a pattern apparent in the American public as a whole. However, it is one that may leave many Latino voters particularly vulnerable to manipulation during campaigns. It may be that Latino community leaders should better educate their communities in the intricacies of American politics.

Bibliography

Alvarez, R. Michael, and Lisa García Bedolla. 2003. "The Foundations of Latino Voter Partisanship: Evidence from the 2000 Election." *Journal of Politics* 65(1): 31–49.

Barreto, M. A., M. Villarreal, and N. D. Woods. 2005. "Metropolitan Latino Political Behavior: Voter Turnout and Candidate Preference in Los Angeles." *Journal of Urban Affairs* 27: 71–91.

Bowler, S., S. P. Nicholson, and G. M. Segura. 2006. "Earthquakes and Aftershocks: Race, Direct Democracy, and Partisan Change." *American Journal of Political Science* 50: 146–59.

Broder, J. M. 2007. "Outgoing Chief Warns G.O.P. on Outlook for 2008 Races." *New York Times*, January 29. http://select.nytimes.com/search/restricted/article?res=F20B11FC35540C7A8DDDA80894DF404482.

Cain, B. E., D. R. Kiewiet, and C. J. Uhlaner. 1991. "The Acquisition of Partisanship by Latinos and Asian Americans." *American Journal of Political Science* 35(2): 390–422.

Campbell, Angus, Philip E. Converse, Warren E. Miller, and Donald E. Stokes. 1960. *The American Voter*. New York: John Wiley and Sons.

de la Garza, Rodolfo O., and Louis DeSipio, eds. 2004. *Muted Voices: Latinos and the 2000 Elections*. Lanham, MD: Rowman and Littlefield Publishers, Inc.

de la Garza, Rodolfo O., Louis DeSipio, F. Chris Garcia, John Garcia, and Angelo Falcon. 1992. *Latino Voices: Mexican, Puerto Rican, and Cuban Perspectives on American Politics*. Boulder, CO: Westview Press.

DeSipio, Louis. 1996. *Counting on the Latino Vote: Latinos as a New Electorate*. Charlottesville, VA: University of Virginia Press.

Fiorina, Morris. 1981. *Retrospective Voting in American National Elections*. New Haven, CT: Yale University Press.

Fraga, Luis Ricardo, John A. Garcia, Rodney E. Hero, Michael Jones-Correa, Valerie Martinez-Ebers, and Gary M. Segura. 2006. "*Su casa es nuestra casa*: Latino Politics Research and the Development of American Political Science." *American Political Science Review* 100(4): 515–21.

Fraga, Luis Ricardo, and David Leal. 2004. "Playing the 'Latino Card': Race, Ethnicity, and National Party Politics." *Du Bois Review* 1(2): 297–317.

Fraga, Luis Ricardo, and Ricardo Ramírez. 2003. "Latino Political Incorporation in California, 1990–2000." In *Latinos and Public Policy in California: An Agenda for Opportunity*, ed. David Lopez and Andrés Jiménez, 301–35. Berkeley: Berkeley Public Policy Press, Institute of Governmental Studies, University of California, Berkeley.

Fraga, Luis Ricardo, and Ricardo Ramírez. 2003–2004. "Demography and Political Influence: Disentangling the Latino Vote." *Harvard Journal of Hispanic Policy* 16: 69–96.

Hajnal, Zoltan, and Taeku Lee. 2004. "Beyond the Middle: Latinos and the Multiple Dimensions of Political Independents." Paper presented at the conference "A Nation of Immigrants: Ethnic Identity and Political Incorporation," University of California at Berkeley.

Jobling, Ian. 2004. "Did Hispanics Elect Bush?" *American Renaissance*, December 8. http://www.amren.com/mtnews/archives/2004/12/did_hispanics_e.php.

Markus, Gregory B., and Philip E. Converse. 1979. "A Dynamic Simultaneous Equation Model of Electoral Choice." *American Political Science Review* 73(4): 1055–70.

Marrero, Pilar. 2004. "America's New Soccer Moms: Latinos a Swing Vote in 2004." *Pacific News Service*, January 28. http://news.pacificnews.org/news/view_article.html?article_id=9972f40038aa19afd64b00d7adccf497.

McKuen, Michael B., Robert S. Erikson, and James A. Stimson. 1989. "Macropartisanship." *American Political Science Review* 73(4): 1125–42.

Miller, Warren E. 1991. "Party Identification, Realignment and Party Voting: Back to the Basics." *American Political Science Review* 85(2): 557–68.

Ohlemacher, Stephen. 2007. "Hispanics Swing to Dems but Maybe Not for Long: Voters also Supported Republicans in November." *Associated Press*,

January 12. http://www.dailycamera.com/news/2007/jan/12/hispanics-swing-to-dems-but-maybe-not-for-long/.

Pew Hispanic Center. 2006a. "Fact Sheet," November 27. http://pewhispanic.org/files/factsheets/26.pdf.

Pew Hispanic Center. 2006b. "Immigration Reform in 2006: Not So Fast," December 20, MSNBC, http://www.msnbc.msn.com/id/16206163/.

Uhlaner, Carole J., and F. Chris García. 2001. "Learning Which Party Fits: Experience, Ethnic Identity, and the Demographic Foundations of Latino Partisan Identification." Paper presented at the Minority Representation: Institutions, Behavior and Identity Conference, Claremont Graduate University.

van der Linden, Page. 2004. "NBC corrects exit polls on Latino support for Bush." *Daily Kos*. December 3. Available at http://www.dailykos.com/story/2004/12/03/77583/-NBC-corrects-exit-polls-on-Latino-support-for-Bush.

11

Latinos and Gender Role Attitudes

The attitudes that people hold with regard to gender roles often have a significant influence on their life experiences, including most aspects of marital and family relationships. They can help continue or can help bring to an end gender-differentiated opportunities and accomplishments in education, employment, and politics. This chapter explores what the LNS respondents regard as proper gender roles, as well as their gender-related attitudes.

Gender roles are sometimes viewed as the division of labor by gender, but feminist scholars argue that this is a simplistic approach that ignores the power relationships that exist between men and women (DeBiaggi 2002; Ridgeway and Correll 2004; McCabe 2005). We use DeBiaggi's (2002, 39) definition of gender roles as "an individual's endorsement of personal characteristics, occupations and behaviors considered appropriate for women and men in a particular culture." Attitudes toward gender roles range from very traditional ideas to extremely egalitarian views.

Parson and Bales' (1951, 1955) theory of the nuclear family lays out an extreme version of the traditional view, with a strict division of normative beliefs, expectations, and responsibilities: men should be more educated because they are expected to hold a job with sufficient income to provide for the family; women require less education and are expected to remain at home with primary responsibility for child rearing and housekeeping. As head of the family, the husband or father is the final decision maker in all matters of importance. As a subordinate family member, the woman is expected to obey the decisions of her husband or father. As an extension of their function in the family, men represent their families to the outside world and are expected to be more active and competent in the public domain, whereas women, in their function as child bearers and caretakers of the family, are best suited to remain in the private domain. Later scholars also assigned masculine and feminine traits within the traditional view: men are strong, aggressive, and logical, whereas women are gentle, nurturing, and emotional (Conover and Gray 1983; Gerson 1993).

In contrast to this traditional view, the egalitarian view of gender roles espouses an equal distribution of labor market participation and household and child-care responsibilities. Other indicators of egalitarian attitudes include the recognition of the importance (not just the necessity) of women obtaining a college education and having careers; support for the right of women to plan their families, including the right to choose not to have children; and refutation of the assertion that men alone should make important family decisions. Finally, men and women are perceived as equally qualified to participate and excel in the public domain. Personality traits are considered malleable and non–gender specific (McCabe 2005; Gerson 1993; Fox and Lawless 2003).

Previous Research Findings

Different cultures impose different expectations on the men and women who live in that culture. Latin American cultures are generally considered patriarchal societies in which men and women hold very traditional gender-related views, but scholars have found both egalitarian attitudes and behaviors in Latin American countries becoming more evident over time, especially among younger women and the better educated (Dore 1997; Schild 1998). Research on Latino gender-related attitudes in the United States is limited but has consistently found more traditional gender-role attitudes among Latinos than among whites or African Americans (Gonzalez 1982; Wilkie 1993; Harris and Firestone 1998; Kane 2000).

In studies focusing only on Latinos, the findings are mixed. Vasquez-Nuttall, Romero-Garcia, and De Leon (1987) emphasize the importance of recognizing heterogeneity within the Hispanic population and urge caution in making group generalizations. Similarly, Montoya (1996) finds that Cuban Americans hold significantly more traditional gender-related attitudes than do Mexican Americans or Puerto Ricans, and she concludes that the amount of variation across national origin groups is sufficient to discourage scholars from reaching any conclusion regarding the group as a whole. In contrast, Harris and Firestone (1998) find too little variation among the three main subgroups to warrant disaggregation.

Other predictors of gender-related attitudes among Latinos previously examined in the literature include the acculturation process that occurs from increased exposure to American culture, social class location or income, Latinas' level of education, and Latinas' participation in the work force (Vasquez-Nuttall et al.1987; Kane 2000). Positive relationships have been found between these variables and more egalitarian attitudes (Bejarano and Martinez-Ebers 2008; Leaper and Valin 1996; Wilkie 1993; Williams 1988; Jones-Correa 1998).

LNS Findings

At least four questions were asked of all LNS respondents that can be used to identify their gender-role attitudes.[1] The ordering of the specific questions was randomized using the following question wording:

People frequently have different opinions on the status of women in society, including the nature of relationships between men and women. Please tell me if you strongly agree, somewhat agree, somewhat disagree, strongly disagree, or have no opinion about the following statements:

Women should have easy access to birth control/contraception.
Men and women should get equal pay when they are in the same job.
Men are better qualified to be political leaders than women.
Mothers should be more responsible for caring for their children than fathers.

Egalitarian gender-role views are indicated by the respondent's agreement with the statements on birth control and contraception and equal pay, and disagreement with the statements on political leadership and caring for children. In contrast, traditional gender-role views are indicated by disagreement with the statements on birth control and contraception and equal pay, and agreement with the statements on political leadership and caring for children. We first examine the variables that may explain child-care perspectives.

Attitudes Regarding Child Care

The process of acculturation has been found to be an explanation for the diminishing traditional gender-role attitudes among Latinos (Vasquez-Nuttall et al. 1987; Leaper and Valin 1996). Proxy measures for acculturation used in this analysis include the citizenship status of first-generation

---

[1] An additional question measuring respondents support for legalized abortion could be viewed as tapping into gender-related attitudes, but for our purposes, the analysis of this is included in the discussion of public opinion. All five questions in some form have been used in prior studies of feminist attitudes, but they do not represent the full range of indicators identified as necessary to assess feminist ideology (McCabe 2005).

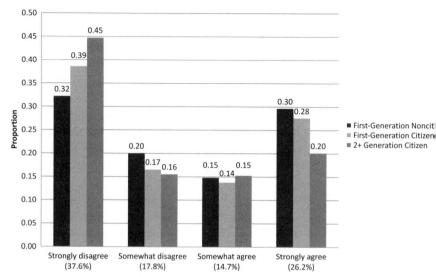

Figure 11.1. Support for (Agreement with) Mothers' Responsibility for Child Care, by Generation and Citizenship
Note: Island-born Puerto Ricans coded as first generation. **Question wording:** "People frequently have different opinions on the status of women in society, including the nature of relationships between men and women. Please tell me if you strongly agree, somewhat agree, somewhat disagree, strongly disagree, or have no opinion about the following statement: 'Mothers should be more responsible for caring for their children than fathers.'"

respondents and the number of generations (limited to first-generation and second generation and beyond comparisons). Figures 11.1 and 11.2 and Tables 11.1 to 11.3 display the respondents' level of agreement or disagreement with the position that mothers should bear greater responsibility for child-care duties. Although the majority of respondents, irrespective of their generation or citizenship status, are egalitarian in their reported attitude toward child care, we find that a sizable minority of respondents still hold traditional attitudes regarding which parent should be more involved in child care (see Figure 11.1). Still, the process of acculturation appears to positively relate to increasingly egalitarian views. For example, noncitizens are almost equally divided on whether they strongly disagree or strongly agree with holding mothers primarily responsible for child care, 32 percent to 30 percent, respectively. Citizens, however, are significantly less supportive of mothers as primary child caregivers: among first-generation citizens, 39 percent strongly disagree, and 28 percent strongly agree. The gap is greater among second-generation citizens:

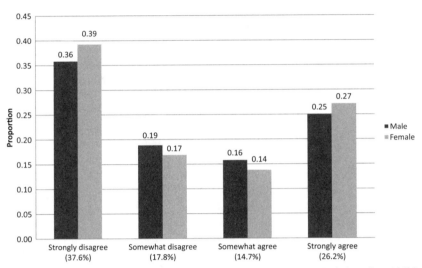

Figure 11.2. Support for (Agreement with) Mothers' Responsibility for Child Care, by Gender
Question wording: "People frequently have different opinions on the status of women in society, including the nature of relationships between men and women. Please tell me if you strongly agree, somewhat agree, somewhat disagree, strongly disagree, or have no opinion about the following statement: 'Mothers should be more responsible for caring for their children than fathers.'"

45 percent strongly disagree with the appropriateness of the traditional role of greater maternal responsibility for child-care duties, compared with only 20 percent who strongly agree.

Interestingly, there are no major differences by gender on this issue (see Figure 11.2), but Latinas' views are seemingly stronger and more polarized. Latinas are more likely than Latino men to say that they strongly disagree with the view that mothers should be more responsible for child care (39 percent to 36 percent). Latinas are also more likely than Latino men to say that they strongly agree with this traditional view (27 percent to 25 percent). About 5 percent of the men have no opinion on the topic, compared with only 2 percent of the women (data not shown).

The answers of the LNS survey respondents also support the conclusions of previous research that education and income are positively associated with egalitarian gender-role attitudes (Williams 1988; Leaper and Valin 1996). Those with the least education are the most likely to express the strongest agreement with the position that child care is the mother's responsibility, whereas those with professional or graduate degrees are

Table 11.1. *Support for (Agreement with) Mothers' Responsibility for Child Care, by Education*

Category: Political Views, Specific Issues/Views

Response		None to Some HS	HS or GED	Some to College Graduate	Graduate or Professional Degree	Total
Strongly	Freq.	880	965	1163	217	3225
disagree	Row%	27.30	29.92	36.06	6.72	100.00
	Col%	28.27	38.15	46.46	51.19	37.63
Somewhat	Freq.	519	464	467	74	1524
disagree	Row%	34.06	30.44	30.61	4.88	100.00
	Col%	16.67	18.34	18.63	17.57	17.78
No opinion	Freq.	148	83	86	2	318
	Row%	46.56	25.98	26.94	0.52	100.00
	Col%	4.75	3.27	3.42	0.39	3.71
Somewhat	Freq.	467	386	349	60	1262
agree	Row%	37.01	30.55	27.66	4.77	100.00
	Col%	15.00	15.24	13.94	14.21	14.72
Strongly	Freq.	1100	632	439	70	2242
agree	Row%	49.06	28.21	19.59	3.14	100.00
	Col%	35.31	25.00	17.55	16.63	26.16
TOTAL	Freq.	3114	2529	2503	424	8570
	Row%	36.34	29.51	29.21	4.94	100.00
	Col%	100.00	100.00	100.00	100.00	100.00

Note: Education: (12 d.f.) 360.7445 (P = 0.0000). Question wording: "People frequently have different opinions on the status of women in society, including the nature of relationships between men and women. Please tell me if you strongly agree, somewhat agree, somewhat disagree, strongly disagree, or have no opinion about the following statement: 'Mothers should be more responsible for caring for their children than fathers.'"

the most likely to strongly disagree (see Table 11.1). Likewise, those who make less than $15,000 are found to constitute the highest percentage of those who strongly agree with the traditional view, and those in the top income category constitute the highest percentage of those in strong disagreement (see Table 11.2).

There are no major differences across national origin groups. With the exception of a small number of respondents whose national origin is reported as "other" or "missing," majorities from every county disagree with the traditional view (see Table 11.3). Interesting, within the small range of variation, those with Cuban origins are the most egalitarian, which contrasts with Montoya's (1996) earlier findings. Respondents

Table 11.2. *Support for (Agreement with) Mothers' Responsibility for Child Care, by Income*

Category: Political Views, Specific Issues/Views

Response		Less than $15K	$15K–$24K	$25K–$34K	$35K–$54K	More than $54K	Total
Strongly disagree	Freq.	404	521	428	556	641	2550
	Row%	15.85	20.43	16.77	21.80	25.15	100.00
	Col%	30.77	32.92	37.86	42.40	49.73	38.48
Somewhat disagree	Freq.	213	306	238	242	208	1207
	Row%	17.67	25.39	19.70	20.02	17.21	100.00
	Col%	16.24	19.36	21.05	18.43	16.10	18.21
No opinion	Freq.	48	46	34	62	43	233
	Row%	20.49	19.93	14.58	26.45	18.56	100.00
	Col%	3.64	2.93	3.01	4.70	3.35	3.52
Somewhat agree	Freq.	201	262	139	189	173	963
	Row%	20.82	27.17	14.44	19.58	17.98	100.00
	Col%	15.27	16.54	12.31	14.38	13.43	14.54
Strongly agree	Freq.	448	447	291	263	224	1673
	Row%	26.75	26.70	17.40	15.74	13.40	100.00
	Col%	34.08	28.24	25.77	20.09	17.39	25.25
TOTAL	Freq.	1313	1582	1129	1311	1290	6625
	Row%	19.82	23.88	17.05	19.79	19.46	100.00
	Col%	100.00	100.00	100.00	100.00	100.00	100.00

Note: Income: (16 d.f.) 206.9882 (P = 0.0000). Question wording: "People frequently have different opinions on the status of women in society, including the nature of relationships between men and women. Please tell me if you strongly agree, somewhat agree, somewhat disagree, strongly disagree, or have no opinion about the following statement: 'Mothers should be more responsible for caring for their children than fathers.'"

325

Table 11.3. *Support for (Agreement with) Mothers' Responsibility for Child Care, by National Origin*

Category: Political Views, Specific Issues/Views

Response		Cuba	Dominican Republic	El Salvador	Mexico	Puerto Rico	Other Central America	Other South America	Other	Missing	Total
Strongly disagree	Freq.	130	112	133	2278	267	111	134	27	32	3225
	Row%	4.04	3.46	4.14	70.65	8.28	3.45	4.14	0.84	0.99	100.00
	Col%	39.95	36.08	32.82	37.98	40.99	32.49	35.72	34.47	38.83	37.63
Somewhat disagree	Freq.	60	54	71	1068	103	69	79	10	9	1524
	Row%	3.93	3.54	4.65	70.11	6.76	4.55	5.20	0.67	0.60	100.00
	Col%	18.33	17.45	17.45	17.81	15.80	20.25	21.17	12.90	11.00	17.78
No opinion	Freq.	7	8	13	242	12	17	11	4	4	318
	Row%	2.14	2.54	4.09	75.93	3.90	5.25	3.52	1.34	1.30	100.00
	Col%	2.08	2.61	3.20	4.02	1.90	4.88	2.99	5.41	5.02	3.71
Somewhat agree	Freq.	42	37	63	890	95	47	45	28	14	1262
	Row%	3.34	2.95	4.97	70.57	7.55	3.68	3.57	2.24	1.14	100.00
	Col%	12.90	12.03	15.43	14.84	14.62	13.56	12.03	35.82	17.42	14.72
Strongly agree	Freq.	87	98	126	1520	174	99	105	9	23	2242
	Row%	3.89	4.39	5.64	67.82	7.76	4.40	4.69	0.40	1.02	100.00
	Col%	26.74	31.83	31.10	25.34	26.68	28.81	28.09	11.40	27.73	26.16
TOTAL	Freq.	327	309	406	5999	652	342	374	39	83	8570
	Row%	3.81	3.61	4.74	70.00	7.60	3.99	4.36	0.92	0.96	100.00
	Col%	100.00	100.00	100.00	100.00	100.00	100.00	100.00	100.00	100.00	100.00

Note: National origin: (32 d.f.) 76.48851 (P = 0.0135). Question wording: "People frequently have different opinions on the status of women in society, including the nature of relationships between men and women. Please tell me if you strongly agree, somewhat agree, somewhat disagree, strongly disagree, or have no opinion about the following statement: 'Mothers should be more responsible for caring for their children than fathers.'"

326

Table 11.4. *Support for Easy Access to Contraception, by Generation and Citizenship*

Category: Political Views, Specific Issues/Views

Response		First Generation Noncitizen	Citizen	Total	2+ Generation Citizen	Total
Strongly	Freq.	169	114	283	146	429
disagree	Row%	59.84	40.16	65.96	34.04	100.00
	Col%	4.50	5.83	4.95	5.46	5.11
Somewhat	Freq.	205	88	294	119	413
disagree	Row%	69.87	30.13	71.15	28.85	100.00
	Col%	5.45	4.54	5.14	4.45	4.92
No opinion	Freq.	451	213	664	196	860
	Row%	67.90	32.10	77.23	22.77	100.00
	Col%	11.98	10.93	11.62	7.32	10.25
Somewhat	Freq.	837	371	1208	404	1613
agree	Row%	69.28	30.72	74.92	25.08	100.00
	Col%	22.25	19.04	21.16	15.12	19.23
Strongly	Freq.	2099	1163	3262	1810	5072
agree	Row%	64.35	35.65	64.31	35.69	100.00
	Col%	55.81	59.66	57.12	67.66	60.49
TOTAL	Freq.	3761	1949	5710	2675	8385
	Row%	65.86	34.14	68.10	31.90	100.00
	Col%	100.00	100.00	100.00	100.00	100.00

Note: First/2+ generation: chi-square (5 d.f.) 103.721 (P = 0.000). Citizen/noncitizen (first generation only): chi-square (5 d.f.) 25.733 (P = 0.016). Island-born Puerto Ricans are coded as first generation. Question wording: "People frequently have different opinions on the status of women in society, including the nature of relationships between men and women. Please tell me if you strongly agree, somewhat agree, somewhat disagree, strongly disagree, or have no opinion about the following statement: 'Women should have easy access to birth control/contraception.'"

with origins in El Salvador, who constitute the third-largest subgroup in our sample, appear to be slightly more traditional in their attitudes regarding child care than those in other subgroups.

Attitudes on Artificial Birth Control

Artificial birth control methods have facilitated women's independence by giving them greater control over what happens to their bodies. Egalitarian gender-role attitudes favor family planning and the right for women to choose not to have children. Opposition to easy access to birth control, specifically the use of contraception, is a reflection of traditional gender-role attitudes. Table 11.4 shows the level of support or

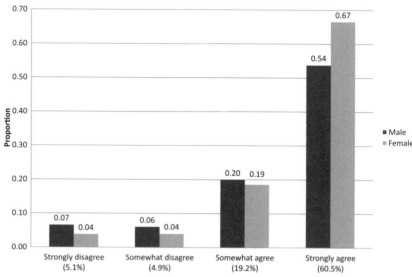

Figure 11.3. Support for Easy Access to Contraception, by Gender
Question wording: "People frequently have different opinions on the status of
women in society, including the nature of relationships between men and women.
Please tell me if you strongly agree, somewhat agree, somewhat disagree, strongly
disagree, or have no opinion about the following statement: 'Women should have
easy access to birth control/contraception.'"

opposition among LNS respondents by generation and citizenship status. There are no major differences: overwhelming large majorities in
every category strongly support the idea of easy access to contraception.
However, immigrants (first generation) are somewhat more likely than
U.S.-born Latinos (second generation and beyond) to express no opinion
on this issue, 12 percent to 7 percent (data not shown).

Majorities of both men and women support easy access to contraceptives (see Figure 11.3). However, women are more likely to hold this
egalitarian view (86 percent of women to 73 percent of men) and their
level of support is stronger (67 percent to 54 percent).

Surprisingly, religion seems to play a minor role in Latino attitudes
toward birth control. Although the Catholic Church has taken a strong
position against contraceptives, a comfortable majority of Catholic LNS
respondents (58 percent) strongly support contraceptive availability (see
Table 11.5). More than two-thirds of those from every religious affiliation
(including Latinos who report "none" or no religious affiliation), say they
somewhat agree or strongly agree that women should have easy access

Table 11.5. *Support for Contraception Availability, by Religious Affiliation*

Category: Political Views, Specific Issue Views

Response		Jehovah's Witness	Catholic	Assemblies of God	Southern Baptist	Pentecostal	Other Protestant	Other	None	Total
Strongly disagree	Freq.	12	285	16	14	30	23	31	18	429
	Row%	2.80	66.43	3.73	3.26	6.99	5.35	7.23	4.20	100.00
	Col%	5.53	4.77	10.46	7.91	9.09	5.41	5.27	3.50	5.12
Somewhat disagree	Freq.	8	269	12	8	18	15	26	18	374
	Row%	2.14	71.93	3.21	2.14	4.81	4.01	6.95	4.81	100.00
	Col%	3.69	4.50	7.84	4.52	5.45	3.53	4.42	3.50	4.46
No opinion	Freq.	26	619	15	18	34	45	62	40	859
	Row%	3.03	72.06	1.75	2.10	3.96	5.24	7.22	4.66	100.00
	Col%	11.98	10.36	9.80	10.17	10.30	10.59	10.54	7.78	10.25
Somewhat agree	Freq.	38	1151	33	27	78	78	87	74	1566
	Row%	2.43	73.50	2.11	1.72	4.98	4.98	5.56	4.73	100.00
	Col%	17.51	19.26	21.57	15.25	23.64	18.35	14.80	14.40	18.69
Strongly agree	Freq.	133	3653	77	110	170	264	382	364	5153
	Row%	2.58	70.89	1.49	2.13	3.30	5.12	7.41	7.06	100.00
	Col%	61.29	61.12	50.33	62.15	51.52	62.12	64.97	70.82	61.48
TOTAL	Freq.	217	5977	153	177	330	425	588	514	8361
	Row%	2.59	71.32	1.83	2.11	3.94	5.07	7.02	5.13	100.00
	Col%	100.00	100.00	100.00	100.00	100.00	100.00	100.00	100.00	100.00

Note: Gender: (28 d.f.) 70.5727 (P = 0.0000). Question wording: "People frequently have different opinions on the status of women in society, including the nature of relationships between men and women. Please tell me if you strongly agree, somewhat agree, somewhat disagree, strongly disagree, or have no opinion about the following statement: 'Women should have easy access to birth control/contraception.'"

Table 11.6. *Support for Easy Access to Contraception, by Education*
Category: Political Views, Specific Issues/Views

Response		None to Some HS	HS or GED	Some to College Graduate	Graduate or Professional Degree	Tot:
Strongly disagree	Freq.	164	120	122	22	429
	Row%	38.33	28.05	28.38	5.24	100.
	Col%	5.50	4.83	4.90	5.33	5.
Somewhat disagree	Freq.	166	109	124	13	413
	Row%	40.34	26.31	30.11	3.24	100.
	Col%	5.57	4.36	5.00	3.17	4.
No opinion	Freq.	396	254	183	26	860
	Row%	46.05	29.58	21.31	3.07	100.
	Col%	13.24	10.20	7.38	6.25	10.
Somewhat agree	Freq.	648	519	386	60	1612
	Row%	40.17	32.20	23.91	3.73	100.
	Col%	21.67	20.84	15.53	14.24	19.
Strongly agree	Freq.	1615	1489	1668	300	5072
	Row%	31.84	29.36	32.89	5.91	100.
	Col%	54.02	59.77	67.19	71.01	60.
TOTAL	Freq.	2989	2491	2483	422	8385
	Row%	35.65	29.71	29.61	5.03	100.
	Col%	100.00	100.00	100.00	100.00	100.

Note: Education: (12 d.f.) 143.7633 (P = 0.0000). Question wording: "People frequently ha different opinions on the status of women in society, including the nature of relationships betwe men and women. Please tell me if you strongly agree, somewhat agree, somewhat disagr strongly disagree, or have no opinion about the following statement: 'Women should have e: access to birth control/contraception.'"

to birth control and contraceptives. The highest opposition (including somewhat and strong disagreement) to easy contraception availability is among Pentecostals and the Assemblies of God, at 13 percent and 20 percent, respectively.

As education and income increases, support or agreement for easy access to contraception also increases (see Tables 11.6 and 11.7). The number of people having no opinion consistently decreases with advanced education.

There is some variation across national origin groups regarding attitudes toward the availability of contraception (see Table 11.8). Support or agreement for easy access ranges from 75 percent (El Salvador) to 86 percent (Puerto Rico).

Table 11.7. *Support for Easy Access to Contraception, by Income*
Category: Political Views, Specific Issues/Views

Response		Less than $15K	$15K–$24K	$25K–$34K	$35K–$54K	More than $54K	Total
Strongly disagree	Freq.	59	70	55	71	73	328
	Row%	18.06	21.24	16.80	21.62	22.29	100.00
	Col%	4.62	4.50	4.95	5.41	5.72	5.02
Somewhat disagree	Freq.	65	82	42	67	70	325
	Row%	19.88	25.12	12.92	20.44	21.64	100.00
	Col%	5.04	5.28	3.77	5.07	5.50	4.98
No opinion	Freq.	127	160	95	130	70	582
	Row%	21.80	27.40	16.38	22.34	12.08	100.00
	Col%	9.89	10.30	8.56	9.91	5.50	8.91
Somewhat agree	Freq.	252	330	229	248	166	1224
	Row%	20.62	26.92	18.70	20.22	13.54	100.00
	Col%	19.68	21.28	20.55	18.86	12.96	18.73
Strongly agree	Freq.	780	908	693	797	900	4077
	Row%	19.12	22.27	16.99	19.55	22.06	100.00
	Col%	60.77	58.64	62.16	60.75	70.32	62.37
TOTAL	Freq.	1283	1548	1114	1312	1279	6537
	Row%	19.63	23.69	17.04	20.07	19.57	100.00
	Col%	100.00	100.00	100.00	100.00	100.00	100.00

Note: Income: (16 d.f.) 80.3977 (P = 0.0000). Question wording: "People frequently have different opinions on the status of women in society, including the nature of relationships between men and women. Please tell me if you strongly agree, somewhat agree, somewhat disagree, strongly disagree, or have no opinion about the following statement: 'Women should have easy access to birth control/contraception.'"

Table 11.8. *Support for Easy Access to Contraception, by National Origin*
Category: Political Views, Specific Issues/Views

Response		Cuba	Dominican Republic	El Salvador	Mexico	Puerto Rico	Other Central America	Other South America	Other	Missing	Total
Strongly disagree	Freq.	10	18	27	293	34	20	16	5	7	429
	Row%	2.26	4.09	6.34	68.25	7.98	4.62	3.67	1.09	1.69	100.00
	Col%	3.03	5.92	6.79	5.00	5.29	5.96	4.29	6.04	8.79	5.11
Somewhat disagree	Freq.	14	15	14	291	23	24	22	3	7	413
	Row%	3.36	3.71	3.30	70.55	5.62	5.71	5.39	0.63	1.73	100.00
	Col%	4.31	5.17	3.40	4.97	3.56	7.08	6.06	3.38	8.64	4.92
No opinion	Freq.	25	37	62	622	35	36	25	8	10	860
	Row%	2.94	4.26	7.21	72.41	4.02	4.15	2.96	0.89	1.15	100.00
	Col%	7.86	12.38	15.49	10.63	5.30	10.71	6.93	9.91	12.02	10.25
Somewhat agree	Freq.	46	49	75	1192	87	75	70	10	8	1612
	Row%	2.88	3.06	4.66	73.90	5.39	4.68	4.31	0.62	0.49	100.00
	Col%	14.46	16.70	18.76	20.35	13.36	22.67	18.92	12.96	9.66	19.23
Strongly agree	Freq.	226	177	222	3459	472	178	234	52	50	5072
	Row%	4.45	3.49	4.38	68.20	9.31	3.52	4.62	1.03	0.99	100.00
	Col%	70.33	59.83	55.56	59.06	72.52	53.58	63.81	67.71	60.88	60.48
TOTAL	Freq.	321	296	400	5857	651	333	367	77	82	8385
	Row%	3.83	3.53	4.77	69.85	7.77	3.97	4.38	0.92	0.98	100.00
	Col%	100.00	100.00	100.00	100.00	100.00	100.00	100.00	100.00	100.00	100.00

Note: National origin: (32 d.f.) 110.7543 (P = 0.0000). Question wording: "People frequently have different opinions on the status of women in society, including the nature of relationships between men and women. Please tell me if you strongly agree, somewhat agree, somewhat disagree, strongly disagree, or have no opinion about the following statement: 'Women should have easy access to birth control/contraception.'"

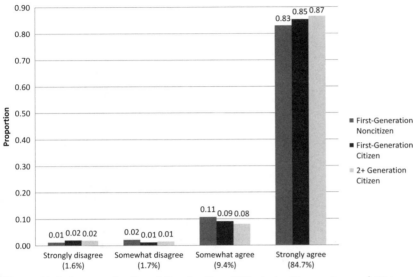

Figure 11.4. Support for Equal Pay for Equal Work, by Generation and Citizenship
Question wording: "People frequently have different opinions on the status of women in society, including the nature of relationships between men and women. Please tell me if you strongly agree, somewhat agree, somewhat disagree, strongly disagree, or have no opinion about the following statement: 'Men and women should get equal pay when they are in the same jobs.'"

Attitudes on Equal Pay for Equal Work

The LNS respondents overwhelming support the egalitarian idea of equal pay for men and women in the same job (approximately 94 percent either agree or strongly agree with equal pay). There is minimal variation in respondents' support or the intensity of their support across generation and citizenship status (see Figure 11.4).

Although the majority of both men and women support equal pay for equal work, women are more likely than men to have strong opinions on this matter. Eighty-eight percent of women strongly support equal pay for equal work, compared with 80 percent of men (see Figure 11.5).

Across all levels of education, support for equal pay for equal work is high. However, respondents become stronger in their support for equal pay as their level of education increases, from 83 percent of those with less than a high school education to 88.5 percent among graduates and professional (see Table 11.9). The same pattern occurs with income (see

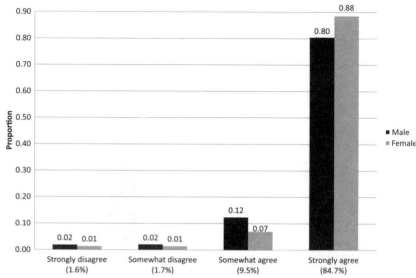

Figure 11.5. Support for Equal Pay for Equal Work, by Gender
Question wording: "People frequently have different opinions on the status of women in society, including the nature of relationships between men and women. Please tell me if you strongly agree, somewhat agree, somewhat disagree, strongly disagree, or have no opinion about the following statement: 'Men and women should get equal pay when they are in the same jobs.'"

Table 11.10). Large majorities favor equal wages across income categories, and the proportion expressing strong agreement grows as income increases, from 81 percent to 89 percent.

There are no major differences across national origin groups (see Table 11.11). All groups overwhelmingly agree with equal pay for equal work. Within the small range of variation, respondents with Cuban origins are most egalitarian, as measured by the 96 percent who say that they agree with men and women receiving equal pay and the 90 percent who say that they strongly agree with this view. Salvadorans are less egalitarian: 89 percent support equal pay and 79 percent strongly support it.

Attitudes on Men versus Women as Better Qualified for Political Leadership

When asked whether they agreed with the statement "Men are better qualified to be political leaders than women," the majority of LNS respondents sided with the egalitarian viewpoint: they disagreed. However, the

Table 11.9. *Support for Equal Pay for Equal Work, by Education*
Category: Political Views, Specific Issues/Views

Response		None to Some HS	HS or GED	Some to College Graduate	Graduate or Professional Degree	Total
Strongly	Freq.	48	41	45	3	137
disagree	Row%	35.03	29.81	32.94	2.22	100.00
	Col%	1.55	1.62	1.79	0.71	1.60
Somewhat	Freq.	51	54	29	12	146
disagree	Row%	34.86	36.84	20.09	8.21	100.00
	Col%	1.64	2.13	1.16	2.79	1.70
No opinion	Freq.	108	67	35	4	216
	Row%	50.29	31.27	16.41	2.02	100.00
	Col%	3.51	2.68	1.41	1.02	2.52
Somewhat	Freq.	329	251	201	30	810
agree	Row%	40.56	30.94	24.80	3.70	100.00
	Col%	10.63	9.95	8.00	7.00	9.48
Strongly	Freq.	2556	2106	2202	379	7243
agree	Row%	35.29	29.08	30.40	5.23	100.00
	Col%	82.67	83.62	87.64	88.48	84.70
TOTAL	Freq.	3092	2519	2512	428	8551
	Row%	36.16	29.46	29.38	5.01	100.00
	Col%	100.00	100.00	100.00	100.00	100.00

Note: Education: (12 d.f.) 59.7832 (P = 0.0005). Question wording: "People frequently have different opinions on the status of women in society, including the nature of relationships between men and women. Please tell me if you strongly agree, somewhat agree, somewhat disagree, strongly disagree, or have no opinion about the following statement: 'Men and women should get equal pay when they are in the same jobs.'"

positive influence of acculturation on egalitarian gender-role attitudes is clear when responses are examined by generation and citizenship. Table 11.12 shows that the level of support and strength of that opinion increases across categories of noncitizens, naturalized citizens, and U.S.-born citizens (which serve as proxy measures of the acculturation process). For example, 59 percent of noncitizens say that they disagree with the statement, whereas 67 percent of naturalized citizens disagree and 74 percent of U.S.-born citizens. Similarly, those saying that they strongly disagree steadily increases from 37 percent to 45 percent to 56 percent among noncitizens, naturalized citizens, and U.S.-born citizens, respectively.

Although large majorities of both male and female respondents disagree with the traditional view that men are more qualified for political

Table 11.10. *Support for Equal Pay for Equal Work, by Income*

Category: Political Views, Specific Issues/Views

Response		Less than $15K	$15K–$24K	$25K–$34K	$35K–$54K	More than $54K	Total
Strongly disagree	Freq.	18	24	16	25	21	105
	Row%	16.77	23.25	15.30	24.27	20.41	100.00
	Col%	1.35	1.54	1.41	1.92	1.65	1.58
Somewhat disagree	Freq.	35	17	26	17	19	114
	Row%	31.22	14.74	22.69	14.97	16.38	100.00
	Col%	2.73	1.06	2.27	1.29	1.44	1.71
No opinion	Freq.	29	38	25	41	21	155
	Row%	18.70	24.58	16.06	26.76	13.89	100.00
	Col%	2.22	2.41	2.19	3.13	1.66	2.33
Somewhat agree	Freq.	161	175	117	123	83	659
	Row%	24.40	26.51	17.79	18.72	12.59	100.00
	Col%	12.35	11.08	10.34	9.34	6.41	9.94
Strongly agree	Freq.	1059	1322	950	1113	1150	5593
	Row%	18.93	23.64	16.98	19.89	20.55	100.00
	Col%	81.36	83.91	83.79	84.32	88.85	84.44
TOTAL	Freq.	1301	1576	1133	1320	1294	6624
	Row%	19.64	23.79	17.11	19.92	19.53	100.00
	Col%	100.00	100.00	100.00	100.00	100.00	100.00

Note: Income: (16 d.f.) 56.1957 (P = 0.0043). Question wording: "People frequently have different opinions on the status of women in society, including the nature of relationships between men and women. Please tell me if you strongly agree, somewhat agree, somewhat disagree, strongly disagree, or have no opinion about the following statement: 'Men and women should get equal pay when they are in the same jobs.'"

Table 11.11. *Support for Equal Pay for Equal Work, by National Origin*

Category: Political Views, Specific Issues/Views

Response		Cuba	Dominican Republic	El Salvador	Mexico	Puerto Rico	Other Central America	Other South America	Other	Missing	Total
Strongly disagree	Freq.	3	4	14	84	19	4	5	1	1	137
	Row%	2.38	2.98	10.52	61.76	14.03	3.06	3.96	0.51	0.81	100.00
	Col%	0.99	1.32	3.50	1.41	2.93	1.23	1.49	0.89	1.34	1.60
Somewhat disagree	Freq.	4	6	6	92	19	11	6	1	1	146
	Row%	2.92	4.17	4.26	63.14	12.76	7.48	4.46	0.39	0.42	100.00
	Col%	1.30	1.97	1.51	1.54	2.84	3.21	1.75	0.72	0.74	1.70
No opinion	Freq.	5	5	23	151	11	8	8	3	2	216
	Row%	2.20	2.16	10.44	69.91	5.33	3.85	3.54	1.59	0.98	100.00
	Col%	1.45	1.51	5.48	2.52	1.76	2.45	2.06	4.35	2.56	2.52
Somewhat agree	Freq.	19	26	44	589	43	38	40	7	4	810
	Row%	2.38	3.26	5.40	72.73	5.27	4.71	4.93	0.82	0.50	100.00
	Col%	5.91	8.59	10.66	9.85	6.53	11.27	10.79	8.43	4.96	9.48
Strongly agree	Freq.	295	266	324	5066	561	277	311	67	75	7243
	Row%	4.07	3.68	4.47	69.95	7.75	3.83	4.29	0.93	1.03	100.00
	Col%	90.35	86.60	78.86	84.68	85.93	81.83	83.93	85.62	90.40	84.70
TOTAL	Freq.	327	308	411	5983	653	339	370	79	83	8551
	Row%	3.82	3.60	4.80	69.96	7.64	3.96	4.33	0.92	0.97	100.00
	Col%	100.00	100.00	100.00	100.00	100.00	100.00	100.00	100.00	100.00	100.00

Note: National origin: (32 d.f.) 70.7809 (P = 0.0173). Question wording: "People frequently have different opinions on the status of women in society, including the nature of relationships between men and women. Please tell me if you strongly agree, somewhat agree, somewhat disagree, strongly disagree, or have no opinion about the following statement: 'Men and women should get equal pay when they are in the same jobs.'"

337

Table 11.12. *Support for Men Being More Qualified for Political Leadership, by Generation and Citizenship*
Category: Political Views, Specific Issues/Views

Response		First Generation			2+ Generation	
		Noncitizen	Citizen	Total	Citizen	Total
Strongly	Freq.	1420	916	2336	1513	3849
disagree	Row%	60.79	39.21	60.69	39.31	100.00
	Col%	37.26	46.97	40.55	56.29	45.56
Somewhat	Freq.	821	392	1213	477	1690
disagree	Row%	67.70	32.30	71.78	28.22	100.00
	Col%	21.55	20.08	21.05	17.74	20.00
No opinion	Freq.	328	135	464	148	612
	Row%	70.82	29.18	75.81	24.19	100.00
	Col%	8.62	6.94	8.05	5.51	7.24
Somewhat	Freq.	603	228	831	275	1106
agree	Row%	72.56	27.44	75.11	24.89	100.00
	Col%	15.81	11.68	14.42	10.24	13.09
Strongly	Freq.	639	280	918	275	1193
agree	Row%	69.55	30.45	76.96	23.04	100.00
	Col%	16.76	14.33	15.94	10.23	14.12
TOTAL	Freq.	3811	1951	5761	2688	8449
	Row%	66.14	33.86	68.19	31.81	100.00
	Col%	100.00	100.00	100.00	100.00	100.00

Note: First/2+ generation: chi-square (5 d.f.) 192.762 (P = 0.000). Citizen/noncitizen (first generation only): chi-square (5 d.f.) 81.814 (P = 0.000). Island-born Puerto Ricans coded as first generation. Question wording: "People frequently have different opinions on the status of women in society, including the nature of relationships between men and women. Please tell me if you strongly agree, somewhat agree, somewhat disagree, strongly disagree, or have no opinion about the following statement: 'Men are better qualified to be political leaders than women.'"

leadership (Table 11.13), females come out stronger in support for equal qualifications. Fifty-three percent of females strongly disagree, compared with 38 percent of males.

Income and education are both positively associated with viewing men and women as equally qualified to be political leaders (see Tables 11.14 and 11.15). Across all levels of education, majorities disagree with the traditional view of men as more qualified. However, respondents feel more strongly on the issue as their level of education increases, from 32 percent of those with less than a high school education to 63 percent among graduates and professionals. The same pattern occurs with income. Across all income categories, large majorities reject the view that men are more

Table 11.13. *Support for Men Being More Qualified for
Political Leadership, by Gender*
Category: Political Views, Specific Issues/Views

Response		Male	Female	Total
Strongly disagree	Freq.	1508	2341	3849
	Row%	39.19	60.81	100.00
	Col%	37.72	52.59	45.56
Somewhat disagree	Freq.	878	811	1690
	Row%	51.99	48.01	100.00
	Col%	21.97	18.23	20.00
No opinion	Freq.	354	258	612
	Row%	57.79	42.21	100.00
	Col%	8.84	5.80	7.24
Somewhat agree	Freq.	623	483	1106
	Row%	56.32	43.68	100.00
	Col%	15.58	10.85	13.09
Strongly agree	Freq.	635	558	1193
	Row%	53.25	46.75	100.00
	Col%	15.89	12.53	14.12
TOTAL	Freq.	3998	4451	8449
	Row%	47.32	52.68	100.00
	Col%	100.00	100.00	100.00

Note: Gender: (4 d.f.) 196.4697 (P = 0.0000). Question wording: "People frequently have different opinions on the status of women in society, including the nature of relationships between men and women. Please tell me if you strongly agree, somewhat agree, somewhat disagree, strongly disagree, or have no opinion about the following statement: 'Men are better qualified to be political leaders than women.'"

qualified to be political leaders, and the proportion expressing strong disagreement grows as income increases, from 40 percent to 61.5 percent.

Interesting, the greatest variation among national origin groups regarding gender-role attitudes is found on this particular question, even though majorities across all groups disagree with the traditional view that men are more qualified to be political leaders. Table 11.16 shows that support for the egalitarian view is lower and less intense among those from El Salvador, with 58 percent disagreeing and only 39 percent strongly disagreeing. Egalitarian gender-role attitudes are significantly stronger among Cubans and Puerto Ricans. Approximately 72 percent of those with Cuban origins disagree with the traditional view, and 52 percent feel very strongly against it. Similarly, 73 percent of Puerto Ricans disagree, and about 57 percent disagree strongly.

Table 11.14. *Support for Men Being More Qualified for Political
Leadership, by Education*
Category: Political Views, Specific Issues/Views

Response		None to Some HS	HS or GED	Some to College Graduate	Graduate or Professional Degree	Total
Strongly	Freq.	973	1126	1479	271	3849
disagree	Row%	25.28	29.26	38.43	7.04	100.00
	Col%	32.13	45.27	59.01	63.37	45.56
Somewhat	Freq.	640	509	474	67	1690
disagree	Row%	37.89	30.13	28.03	3.94	100.00
	Col%	21.14	20.47	18.90	15.57	20.00
No opinion	Freq.	336	154	99	23	612
	Row%	54.89	25.11	16.26	3.75	100.00
	Col%	11.09	6.18	3.97	5.36	7.24
Somewhat	Freq.	507	334	226	39	1106
agree	Row%	45.88	30.19	20.42	3.52	100.00
	Col%	16.75	13.42	9.01	9.10	13.09
Strongly	Freq.	572	365	228	28	1193
agree	Row%	47.93	30.56	19.15	2.36	100.00
	Col%	18.88	14.66	9.12	6.59	14.12
TOTAL	Freq.	3028	2487	2506	427	8449
	Row%	35.84	29.44	29.66	5.06	100.00
	Col%	100.00	100.00	100.00	100.00	100.00

Note: Education: (12 d.f.) 540.8630 (P = 0.0000). Question wording: "People frequently have different opinions on the status of women in society, including the nature of relationships between men and women. Please tell me if you strongly agree, somewhat agree, somewhat disagree, strongly disagree, or have no opinion about the following statement: 'Men are better qualified to be political leaders than women.'"

Conclusion

Overall, LNS respondents appear to be considerably more egalitarian than traditional in their gender-role views. These findings are very interesting, because they contradict stereotypical cultural characterizations of Latinos as patriarchal and suggest a far stronger egalitarian view of gender matters among Latino men than is usually assumed. For every gender-role question asked on the survey, the majority of respondents supported the egalitarian position. In fact, large majorities said they strongly supported equal pay for men and women (84.70 percent) and easy access to birth control and contraception (60 percent). Pluralities said that they strongly disagree with the notion that men are better qualified for political

Table 11.15. *Support for Men Being More Qualified for Political Leadership, by Income*

Category: Political Views, Specific Issues/Views

Response		Less than $15K	$15K–$24K	$25K–$34K	$35K–$54K	More than $54K	Total
Strongly disagree	Freq.	509	620	488	631	793	3041
	Row%	16.74	20.40	16.05	20.74	26.08	100.00
	Col%	39.61	39.68	43.53	47.97	61.50	46.26
Somewhat disagree	Freq.	256	325	236	272	219	1307
	Row%	19.57	24.85	18.03	20.83	16.73	100.00
	Col%	19.99	20.78	21.02	20.71	16.95	19.88
No opinion	Freq.	85	110	71	93	56	415
	Row%	20.54	26.45	17.15	22.37	13.49	100.00
	Col%	6.62	7.01	6.34	7.05	4.34	6.30
Somewhat agree	Freq.	203	230	168	154	113	868
	Row%	23.40	26.45	19.38	17.74	13.03	100.00
	Col%	15.79	14.68	14.99	11.71	8.76	13.20
Strongly agree	Freq.	232	279	158	165	109	944
	Row%	24.61	29.57	16.78	17.48	11.55	100.00
	Col%	18.07	17.85	14.13	12.55	8.45	14.36
TOTAL	Freq.	1285	1563	1121	1315	1290	6574
	Row%	19.55	23.78	17.06	19.99	19.62	100.00
	Col%	100.00	100.00	100.00	100.00	100.00	100.00

Note: Income: (16 d.f.) 210.4966 (P = 0.0000). Question wording: "People frequently have different opinions on the status of women in society, including the nature of relationships between men and women. Please tell me if you strongly agree, somewhat agree, somewhat disagree, strongly disagree, or have no opinion about the following statement: 'Men are better qualified to be political leaders than women.'"

Table 11.16. *Support for Men Being More Qualified for Political Leadership, by National Origin*

Category: Political Views, Specific Issues/Views

Response		Cuba	Dominican Republic	El Salvador	Mexico	Puerto Rico	Other Central America	Other South America	Other	Missing	Total
Strongly disagree	Freq.	169	136	158	2623	369	118	197	45	34	3849
	Row%	4.39	3.52	4.12	68.15	9.58	3.07	5.12	1.17	0.89	100.00
	Col%	52.35	44.62	39.22	44.48	56.93	34.76	52.82	57.79	40.99	45.56
Somewhat disagree	Freq.	66	55	77	1206	107	66	75	15	21	1690
	Row%	3.93	3.26	4.56	71.40	6.35	3.92	4.44	0.89	1.24	100.00
	Col%	20.60	18.14	19.07	20.46	16.56	19.48	20.11	19.43	25.21	20.00
No opinion	Freq.	21	16	40	426	43	32	20	3	11	612
	Row%	3.39	2.69	6.48	69.61	7.01	5.25	3.25	0.55	1.78	100.00
	Col%	6.42	5.41	9.81	7.22	6.62	9.45	5.33	4.31	13.13	7.24
Somewhat agree	Freq.	29	50	56	810	59	50	36	7	10	1106
	Row%	2.58	4.53	5.02	73.25	5.36	4.54	3.23	0.62	0.87	100.00
	Col%	8.86	16.46	13.75	13.74	9.16	14.76	9.57	8.77	11.52	13.09
Strongly agree	Freq.	38	47	73	832	70	73	45	8	8	1193
	Row%	3.19	3.92	6.15	69.70	5.83	6.13	3.81	0.63	0.64	100.00
	Col%	11.80	15.37	18.16	14.10	10.73	21.53	12.18	9.70	9.15	14.12
TOTAL	Freq.	323	304	404	5897	648	340	373	78	83	8449
	Row%	3.82	3.60	4.78	69.79	7.66	4.02	4.42	0.92	0.98	100.00
	Col%	100.00	100.00	100.00	100.00	100.00	100.00	100.00	100.00	100.00	100.00

Note: National origin: (32 d.f.) 114.2384 (P = 0.0000). Question wording: "People frequently have different opinions on the status of women in society, including the nature of relationships between men and women. Please tell me if you strongly agree, somewhat agree, somewhat disagree, strongly disagree, or have no opinion about the following statement: 'Men are better suited emotionally for politics than are most women.'"

342

eadership (45.56 percent) and that mothers should be more responsible or child care (37.63 percent). However, the bimodal distribution, or polarization, of respondents' answers to the child-care question should also be noted. Interestingly, Latinas are more likely than Latino men to either strongly agree or strongly disagree on whether women should have the primary role as child caregiver. Still, the presence of a sizable minority regardless of gender (26.16 percent) who strongly supported the view that women should be more responsible when it comes to caring for children lends support to the theory that women shoulder a double burden in terms of gender, even as attitudes become more egalitarian with respect to education and employment (Verba, Burns, and Schlozman 1997; Ridgeway and Correll 2004).

Bibliography

Bejarano, Christina, and Valerie Martinez-Ebers. 2008. "The Influence of Progressive Role Attitudes on Latinas' Civic and Political Behavior." Paper presented at the annual meeting of the Western Political Science Association, San Diego, CA, March 21.

Conover, Pamela Johnson, and Virginia Gray. 1983. *Feminism and the New Right: Conflict over the American Family.* New York: Praeger.

DeBiaggi, Sylvia Duarte Dantas. 2002. *Changing Gender Roles: Brazilian Immigrant Families in the U.S.* New York: LFB Scholarly Publishing.

Dore, Elizabeth, ed. 1997. *Gender Politics in Latin America: Debates in Theory and Practice.* New York: Monthly Review Press.

Fox, Richard, and Jennifer L. Lawless. 2003. "Family and Structure, Sex-Role Socialization and the Decision to Run for Office." *Women and Politics* 24: 19–48.

Gerson, Kathleen. 1993. *No Man's Land: Men's Changing Commitments to Family and Work.* New York: Basic Books.

Gonzalez, Alex. 1982. "Sex Roles of the Traditional Mexican American Family." *Journal of Cross-Cultural Psychology* 13(3): 330–39.

Harris, Richard J., and Juanita M. Firestone. 1998. "Changes in Predictors of Gender Role Ideologies among Women: A Multivariate Analysis." *Sex Roles* 38: 239–52.

Jones-Correa, Michael. 1998. "Different Paths: Gender, Immigration and Political Participation." *International Migration Review* 32: 326–49.

Kane, Emily W. 2000. "Racial and Ethnic Variations in Gender-Related Attitudes." *Annual Review of Sociology* 26: 419–39.

Leaper, Campbell, and Dena Valin. 1996. "Predictors of Mexican American Mothers' and Fathers' Attitudes towards Gender Equality." *Hispanic Journal of Behavioral Science* 18(3): 675–88.

McCabe, Janice. 2005. "What's in a Label? The Relationship between Feminist Self-Identification and 'Feminist' Attitudes among U.S. Women and Men.' *Gender and Society* 19(4): 480–505.

Montoya, Lisa J. 1996. "Latino Gender Differences in Public Opinion." *Hispanic Journal of Behavioral Science* 18(2): 255–76.

Parsons, Talcott. 1951. *The Social System*. New York: Free Press.

Parsons, Talcott and Robert Bales. 1955. *Family, Socialization and Interaction Process*. Glencoe, IL: Free Press.

Ridgeway, Cecilia L., and Shelley J. Correll. 2004. "Unpacking the Gender System: A Theoretical Perspective on Cultural Beliefs and Social Relations." *Gender and Society* 18(4): 510–31.

Schild, Veronica. 1998. "New Subjects of Rights? Women's Movements and the Construction of Citizenship in the 'New Democracies.' In *Cultures of Politics/Politics of Cultures: Re-visioning Latin American Social Movements*, ed. S. Alvarez, A. Escobar, and E. Dagnino, 24–49. Boulder, CO: Westview Press.

Vasquez-Nuttall, Ena, Irasema Romero-Garcia, and Brunilda De Leon. 1987. "Sex Roles and Perceptions of Femininity and Masculinity of Hispanic Women: A Review of the Literature." *Psychology of Women Quarterly* 11(4): 409–25.

Verba, Sidney, Nancy Burns, and Kay Lehman Schlozman. 1997. "Knowing and Caring about Politics: Gender and Political Engagement." *Journal of Politics* 59: 1051–72.

Wilkie, Jane Riblett. 1993. "Changes in U.S. Men's Attitudes toward the Family Provider Role, 1972–1989." *Gender and Society* 7: 261–79.

Williams, Norma. 1988. "Role Making among Married Mexican American Women: Issues of Class and Identity." *Journal of Applied Behavioral Science* 24: 203–17.

12

Latino Issues and Policy Preferences

It is not surprising that the unique place of Latinos in American society – as well as the variation within the group on many dimensions – serves to structure Latino opinion on important policy concerns. The Latino National Survey explored Latino opinion on several important policy dimensions.

Over the past two decades, scholars examining Latino public opinion have consistently found certain response patterns on issues of public importance (see, e.g., Welch and Sigelman 1993; Branton 2007; Nicholson and Segura 2005; Branton 2007). Education, economic concerns, and crime have historically been considered the most important problems facing the nation and the most important problem confronting the Latino community specifically. Indeed, the California politician Cruz Bustamante, who was elected California's first Latino assembly speaker in the late 1990s and went on to two terms as lieutenant governor and an ill-fated run for governor, frequently articulated that the Latino agenda is "the American agenda," ostensibly to emphasize Latinos' common concerns with these bread-and-butter political issues.

The Latino National Survey offers results largely consistent with Bustamante's claim, with the notable (and timely) exception of the Iraq War. Table 12.1 reports the percentage of respondents identifying each issue area as the most important facing the country. In 2006, the consensus answer was the Iraq War. More than 31 percent of respondents felt that this was the most critical issue facing the country. After the war, however, the hands-down winner was the economy and jobs, together for more than 18 percent of respondents, and immigration, identified by 11.4 percent, as the most pressing issue.

Table 12.1. *Most Important Problem Facing Nation, Open-Ended Responses Categorized, Latino National Survey*

Issue Category	Percent of Respondents
The economy	13.6
Unemployment/jobs	4.5
Education/public schools	2.7
Crime	2.2
Drugs	1.7
Health care	0.9
Race relations	2.6
Values/family values/morality	0.8
Budget deficit	0.5
Social security/care for the elderly	0.4
Illegal immigration	11.4
Affirmative action	0.1
Welfare/welfare reform	0.2
Environment	0.3
Political system/corruption/scandal	1.5
Foreign policy/international concerns/national defense	2.0
Abortion	0.1
Something else	9.7
Don't know/refused	13.4
Iraq War	31.5

By contrast, when asked about the most pressing issue facing Latinos specifically, the results shift noticeably. These results are reported in Table 12.2. The war fades in importance, which suggests that Latinos did not see Iraq through a specifically ethnic lens. Instead, the issue of immigration has the attention of almost 30 percent of respondents, with another 4.5 percent identifying race relations (Lopez and Pantoja 2004), a subject logically associated with the immigration question and broadly grouped under civil rights as an issue area. In the context of nationwide marches and protests over the status of immigrants, as well as the congressional consideration of comprehensive immigration reform legislation, the relative salience of civil rights and immigration is not surprising. The economy and jobs were important for almost 19 percent of respondents, although there is a curious and notable emphasis on jobs specifically in the response to the question regarding Latinos' most important problem that was absent in the definition of the national problem. Education is next at 9.1 percent, with crime and drugs – together 3.8 percent – rounding out the most common responses.

Table 12.2. *Most Important Problem Facing Latinos, Open-Ended Responses Categorized, Latino National Survey*

Issue Category	Percent of Respondents
The economy	6.8
Unemployment/jobs	12.1
Education/public schools	9.1
Crime	1.9
Drugs	1.9
Health care	0.8
Race relations	4.5
Values/family values/morality	0.7
Budget deficit	0.2
Social security/care for the elderly	0.2
Illegal immigration	29.8
Affirmative action	0.3
Welfare/welfare reform	0.2
Environment	0.1
Political system/corruption/scandal	0.6
Foreign policy/international concerns/national defense	0.3
Abortion	0.0
Something else	11.5
Don't know/refused	17.5
Iraq War	1.6

It is worth noting that social issues surrounding questions of morality, often identified as a potential source of GOP inroads to the traditionally Democratic group, hardly register. Abortion and values together are identified by only 0.9 percent as the nation's most pressing problem, and by 0.7 percent as Latinos' most pressing problem. Nevertheless, it is these social issues on which Republicans have historically rested their hopes of attracting Latino voters.

With the results in Tables 12.1 and 12.2 in mind, and setting aside the exception of the Iraq War, there are four policy dimensions that we think are most appropriate for a more detailed examination. First, given the relative economic disadvantages of the Latino population and the frequency with which they cite economic concerns, we asked respondents about their views on two important social welfare issues, income support and health care. Second, the oft-identified and GOP-emphasized social issues are examined. Third, we explore several aspects of the immigration issue, this being the most explicitly identified with Latinos specifically and most easily understood as an "ethnic" issue. Elsewhere, in Chapter 11, we offer a detailed examination of the fourth area, education. It is worth noting that, among the most salient issues, we devoted comparatively less attention to the issues of crime and drugs in our survey, although they received some attention (which we report elsewhere in this volume). Though interesting in terms of salience, there is relatively little variation in opinion on many aspects of this issue area and a conflation of these issues with the far more complex relationship between Latinos and law enforcement. For these reasons, we devote little attention to this in our survey and here.

We begin our discussion of Latinos' views of the varying policy issues in public discourses by examining Latino support for a social safety net. First and foremost, with so many Latino families living in the lowest-income segments of the society, we might expect questions of income guarantees to be salient. Almost 30 percent of respondents indicated that they had, at one time or another, relied on a form of public assistance. In our study, we asked whether government should "provide income support to those who need it." Not surprisingly, there was considerable enthusiasm for this proposition. Almost 88 percent of our respondents supported or strongly supported this assertion. However, support decreases slightly across generations and with movement toward citizenship. As illustrated in Table 12.3, more than 53 percent of foreign-born noncitizens strongly support this policy, 48 percent of foreign-born citizens strongly support it, and just less than 44 percent of native-born Latinos strongly support it. These differences by generation and citizenship status are statistically significant, but we don't want to overstate them. Even among born citizens, more than 84 percent generally favor the proposition.

Figures 12.1 and 12.2, and Tables 12.4 and 12.5, examine this same question of income support by income, education, gender, and national origin group. Across national origin groups, income, gender, and education, we find that the majority of respondents in all categories either support or strongly support a policy of the government providing income for those who need it. Not surprisingly, some predictable and significant patterns emerge. Income provision is more strongly favored by the poor, less educated respondents, and women. Although all national origin groups generally hold favorable opinions of government-provided income, that support is slightly (though significantly) less enthusiastic among Cubans and the category "other South Americans." This is not surprising given the relatively advantaged economic circumstances of Latinos from these national origin groups and the partisan identities

Table 12.3. *Support for Government Income Support, by Generation and Citizenship*

Category: Political Views, Specific Issue Views

ponse		First Generation			2+ Generation	
		Noncitizen	Citizen	Total	Citizen	Total
ngly oppose	Freq.	137	117	253	156	410
	Row%	53.99	46.01	61.85	38.15	100.00
	Col%	3.83	6.37	4.69	6.12	5.15
pose	Freq.	161	154	315	252	568
	Row%	51.11	48.89	55.58	44.42	100.00
	Col%	4.52	8.42	5.84	9.87	7.13
port	Freq.	1370	680	2050	1033	3083
	Row%	66.84	33.16	66.49	33.51	100.00
	Col%	38.38	37.11	37.95	40.42	38.74
ngly support	Freq.	1902	881	2783	1114	3897
	Row%	68.34	31.66	71.41	28.59	100.00
	Col%	53.28	48.11	51.52	43.59	48.98
AL	Freq.	3570	1832	5402	2555	7957
	Row%	66.09	33.91	67.88	32.12	100.00
	Col%	100.00	100.00	100.00	100.00	100.00

e: First/2+ generation: chi-square (4 d.f.) 70.468 (P = 0.000). Citizen/noncitizen (first gener-
n only): chi-square (4 d.f.) 80.099 (P = 0.000). Puerto Ricans are coded as first generation.
stion wording: "I'm going to ask you about some policy issues. Please tell me know strongly
support or oppose the following policy. Your response can be: strongly support, support,
ose, or strongly oppose. If you are not sure how you feel or don't know, feel free to say so.
v about... 'Government should provide income support to those who need it.'"

associated with them. Nevertheless, the key observation is that groups are more alike than different, and support for a social safety net among all Latinos, across generations, socioeconomic status, gender, and national origin groups, is extremely high.

Health care is a concern for all Americans in the beginning of the twenty-first century. According to a report from the U.S. Census Bureau based on the 2004 American Community Survey, approximately 15.7 percent of Americans were without any form of health insurance. Not surprisingly, however, there was considerable variation by race and ethnicity. For non-Hispanic whites, the rate was 10.8 percent; for African Americans, 19.1 percent; and for Asian Americans, 17.6 percent. For Hispanics, the comparable number was an eye-popping 30.7 percent (DeNavas-Walt, Proctor, and Smith 2009).

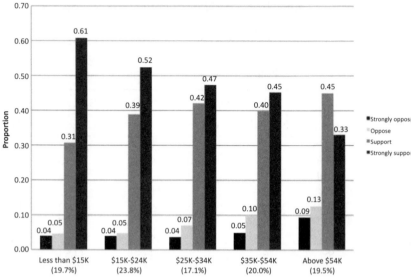

Figure 12.1. Support for Government Income Support, by Income
Question wording: "I'm going to ask you about some policy issues. Please tell me
know strongly you support or oppose the following policy. Your response can be
strongly support, support, oppose, or strongly oppose. If you are not sure how
you feel or don't know, feel free to say so. How about... 'Government should
provide income support to those who need it'."

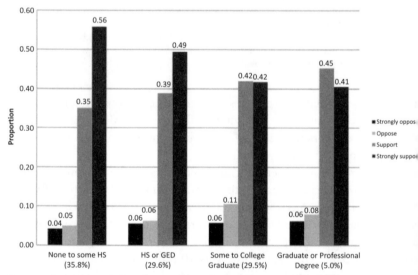

Figure 12.2. Support for Government Income Support, by Education
Question wording: "I'm going to ask you about some policy issues. Please tell me
know strongly you support or oppose the following policy. Your response can be
strongly support, support, oppose, or strongly oppose. If you are not sure how
you feel or don't know, feel free to say so. How about... 'Government should
provide income support to those who need it'."

Table 12.4. *Support for Government Income Support, by Gender*
Category: Political Views, Specific Issue Views

Response		Male	Female	Total
trongly oppose	Freq.	244	165	410
	Row%	59.63	40.37	100.00
	Col%	6.46	3.96	5.15
)ppose	Freq.	291	277	568
	Row%	51.24	48.76	100.00
	Col%	7.69	6.63	7.13
upport	Freq.	1444	1639	3082
	Row%	46.84	53.16	100.00
	Col%	38.17	39.25	38.73
trongly support	Freq.	1803	2094	3898
	Row%	46.27	53.73	100.00
	Col%	47.68	50.16	48.98
OTAL	**Freq.**	**3782**	**4175**	**7957**
	Row%	**47.53**	**52.47**	**100.00**
	Col%	**100.00**	**100.00**	**100.00**

Note: Gender: (3 d.f.) 29.9519 (P = 0.0002). Question wording: "I'm going to ask you bout some policy issues. Please tell me know strongly you support or oppose the following policy. Your response can be: strongly support, support, oppose, or strongly oppose. If you re not sure how you feel or don't know, feel free to say so. How about... 'Government hould provide income support to those who need it'."

Health insurance reform has been, and continues to be, an important political and electoral issue, and it ranks among the central policy dis-utes between political parties. As such, to gain perspective on the policy dimensions that may be shaping Latino partisan identity and electoral behavior, we felt it was necessary to ascertain Latino opinion on this ssue. We asked respondents how strongly they support or oppose the ollowing statement: "The current health care system needs government intervention to improve access and reduce costs." Responses are reported by citizenship status and generation in Table 12.6.

There is overwhelming support for government intervention in health are. The majority of all cohorts strongly support it, although support decreases slightly with change in citizenship status and across genera-ions (and opposition slightly increases). Likewise, across national origin groups, income, education, and gender (reported in Tables 12.7–12.10) we find that the majority of respondents either support or strongly sup-ort government intervention in health care. There is modest variation in

Table 12.5. *Support for Government Income Support, by National Origin*

Category: Political Views, Specific Issue Views

Response		Cuba	Dominican Republic	El Salvador	Mexico	Puerto Rico	Other Central America	Other South America	Other	Missing	Total
Strongly oppose	Freq.	21	15	8	298	22	12	20	7	6	410
	Row%	5.20	3.76	1.99	72.63	5.39	2.85	4.94	1.71	1.54	100.00
	Col%	7.00	5.22	2.18	5.35	3.60	3.71	5.83	9.59	8.96	5.15
Oppose	Freq.	28	12	27	390	41	19	27	15	9	568
	Row%	5.00	2.09	4.69	68.79	7.28	3.32	4.76	2.57	1.50	100.00
	Col%	9.32	4.01	7.13	7.01	6.74	6.00	7.80	20.00	12.10	7.13
Support	Freq.	117	102	122	2194	210	122	157	28	32	3082
	Row%	3.79	3.31	3.96	71.18	6.81	3.94	5.08	0.90	1.03	100.00
	Col%	38.43	34.56	32.65	39.41	34.22	38.66	45.15	38.05	45.04	38.73
Strongly support	Freq.	138	166	217	2685	340	162	143	24	24	3898
	Row%	3.53	4.26	5.56	68.88	8.72	4.16	3.67	0.61	0.61	100.00
	Col%	45.24	56.21	58.04	48.23	55.44	51.62	41.22	32.36	33.91	48.98
TOTAL	Freq.	304	295	373	5567	613	314	347	73	70	7957
	Row%	3.82	3.71	4.69	69.96	7.71	3.95	4.36	0.92	0.89	100.00
	Col%	100.00	100.00	100.00	100.00	100.00	100.00	100.00	100.00	100.00	100.00

Note: National origin: (24 d.f.) 85.0547 (P = 0.0001). Question wording: "I'm going to ask you about some policy issues. Please tell me know strongly you support or oppose the following policy. Your response can be: strongly support, support, oppose, or strongly oppose. If you are not sure how you feel or don't know, feel free to say so. How about… 'Government should provide income support to those who need it'."

le 12.6. *Support for Government Intervention in Health Care, by Generation and Citizenship*

Category: Political Views, Specific Issue Views

›onse		First Generation			2+ Generation	
		Noncitizen	Citizen	Total	Citizen	Total
ngly oppose	Freq.	98	74	172	125	297
	Row%	56.97	43.03	58.02	41.98	100.00
	Col%	2.51	3.72	2.92	4.59	3.44
›ose	Freq.	145	89	233	180	414
	Row%	61.89	38.11	56.45	43.55	100.00
	Col%	3.69	4.46	3.95	6.62	4.79
sure	Freq.	381	156	537	244	781
	Row%	70.87	29.13	68.73	31.27	100.00
	Col%	9.71	7.84	9.08	8.99	9.05
›ort	Freq.	1143	540	1683	803	2486
	Row%	67.92	32.08	67.69	32.31	100.00
	Col%	29.16	27.06	28.45	29.55	28.79
ngly support	Freq.	2154	1136	3290	1366	4656
	Row%	65.47	34.53	70.66	29.34	100.00
	Col%	54.95	56.93	55.61	50.25	53.92
↓L	Freq.	3920	1995	5916	2719	8634
	Row%	66.27	33.73	68.51	31.49	100.00
	Col%	100.00	100.00	100.00	100.00	100.00

›: First/2+ generation: chi-square (5 d.f.) 53.744 (P = 0.000). Citizen/noncitizen (first gener-↓ only): chi-square (5 d.f.) 24.447 (P = 0.019). Puerto Ricans are coded as first generation. stion wording: "I'm going to ask you about some policy issues. Please tell me know strongly support or oppose the following policy. Your response can be: strongly support, support, ›se, or strongly oppose. If you are not sure how you feel or don't know, feel free to say so. ↓ about... 'The current health care system needs government intervention to improve access ↓educe costs'."

nthusiasm across nationalities, but all are extremely supportive. Support ncreases slightly with education and decreases slightly with income, and ›omen are slightly more supportive than men. Support for government ntervention in the health care system is, by any measure, universally high mong our respondents.

Immigration – Latino-Specific Policy Concern

)f all the policy issues shaping electoral politics in recent years, few have ▮he direct resonance among and connection to Latinos as immigration.

Table 12.7. *Support for Government Intervention in Health Care, by Incom(e)* **Category:** Political Views, Specific Issue Views

Response		Less than $15K	$15K–$24K	$25K–$34K	$35K–$54K	More than $54K	To(tal)
Strongly	Freq.	31	48	37	44	73	23(
oppose	Row%	13.43	20.38	16.03	18.92	31.23	10(
	Col%	2.38	2.99	3.30	3.33	5.61	
Oppose	Freq.	38	77	47	76	73	31
	Row%	12.22	24.86	15.08	24.30	23.54	10(
	Col%	2.89	4.87	4.14	5.70	5.64	(
Not sure	Freq.	106	112	70	65	78	43(
	Row%	24.57	25.96	16.23	15.15	18.10	10(
	Col%	8.02	7.02	6.15	4.90	5.99	(
Support	Freq.	365	488	342	415	379	198(
	Row%	18.33	24.53	17.18	20.88	19.07	10(
	Col%	27.68	30.69	30.11	31.28	29.19	2(
Strongly	Freq.	778	866	639	728	696	370(
support	Row%	20.98	23.36	17.24	19.63	18.78	10(
	Col%	59.03	54.43	56.30	54.79	53.56	5(
TOTAL	**Freq.**	**1317**	**1590**	**1135**	**1328**	**1300**	**667(**
	Row%	**19.75**	**23.84**	**17.02**	**19.91**	**19.48**	**10(**
	Col%	**100.00**	**100.00**	**100.00**	**100.00**	**100.00**	**10(**

Note: Income: (16 d.f.) 58.8310 (P = 0.0017). Question wording: "I'm going to ask you a(bout) some policy issues. Please tell me know strongly you support or oppose the following policy. (The) response can be: strongly support, support, oppose, or strongly oppose. If you are not sure (how) you feel or don't know, feel free to say so. How about... 'The current health care system n(eeds) government intervention to improve access and reduce costs'."

The Latino population in the United States is overwhelmingly connecte(d) to the immigration experience. Something in excess of 85 percent o(f) all Latinos have at least one foreign-born grandparent, and a majorit(y) of Latino adults were born outside of the United States. This varies b(y) state and national origin group, of course, but there are relatively fe(w) Latinos in the United States who feel no connection to the immigratio(n) experience.

Immigration laws, however, have uneven effects across national origi(n) groups. The federal policy providing special status to Cuban asylum seek(-) ers, the so-called dry-feet policy, provides for nearly automatic residenc(y) to any Cuban national who makes it to the U.S. mainland. Puerto Ricans(,) as born U.S. citizens, similarly have little direct concern with immigratio(n) policy, although the issues and concerns remain of people living outsid(e)

Table 12.8. *Support for Government Intervention in Health Care, by Education* **Category:** Political Views, Specific Issue Views

.esponse		None to Some HS	HS or GED	Some to College Graduate	Graduate or Professional Degree	Total
trongly oppose	Freq.	95	88	89	25	297
	Row%	31.88	29.69	30.00	8.44	100.00
	Col%	3.01	3.48	3.54	5.84	3.44
)ppose	Freq.	110	131	155	18	414
	Row%	26.64	31.78	37.35	4.24	100.00
	Col%	3.50	5.19	6.13	4.08	4.79
Jot sure	Freq.	370	215	173	23	781
	Row%	47.36	27.55	22.09	3.00	100.00
	Col%	11.75	8.49	6.84	5.46	9.05
upport	Freq.	885	740	731	130	2486
	Row%	35.58	29.78	29.40	5.25	100.00
	Col%	28.09	29.22	28.99	30.40	28.80
trongly support	Freq.	1689	1359	1375	233	4655
	Row%	36.29	29.19	29.52	5.00	100.00
	Col%	53.65	53.62	54.51	54.22	53.92
OTAL	Freq.	3149	2534	2522	429	8643
	Row%	36.47	29.35	29.21	4.97	100.00
	Col%	100.00	100.00	100.00	100.00	100.00

Iote: Education: (12 d.f.) 77.8894 (P = 0.0000). Question wording: "I'm going to ask you bout some policy issues. Please tell me know strongly you support or oppose the follow ig policy. Your response can be: strongly support, support, oppose, or strongly oppose. : you are not sure how you feel or don't know, feel free to say so. How about… 'The urrent health care system needs government intervention to improve access and reduce osts'."

their born cultural context or those who have recent familial experiences with migration. The rest of the national origin groups have some collec tive understanding of immigration to the United States and its personal, cultural, and familial consequences.

Not surprisingly, we asked respondents a fair number of questions related to the general topic of immigration and to the specific policy issues that have arisen in recent years as the United States has attempted to cope with rapidly increasing immigrant populations and their needs. We asked two general questions to assess respondents' overall attitudes regarding immigration. The first asked respondents whether immigrants "strengthen our country" or "are a burden."

Table 12.9. *Support for Government Intervention in Health Care,*
by Gender

Category: Political Views, Specific Issue Views

Response		Male	Female	Total
Strongly oppose	Freq.	166	132	297
	Row%	55.69	44.31	100.00
	Col%	4.05	2.90	3.44
Oppose	Freq.	223	191	414
	Row%	53.92	46.08	100.00
	Col%	5.46	4.19	4.79
Not sure	Freq.	353	428	781
	Row%	45.16	54.84	100.00
	Col%	8.63	9.42	9.05
Support	Freq.	1169	1317	2486
	Row%	47.02	52.98	100.00
	Col%	28.61	28.97	28.80
Strongly support	Freq.	2176	2479	4655
	Row%	46.75	53.25	100.00
	Col%	53.25	54.52	53.92
TOTAL	Freq.	4087	4547	8634
	Row%	47.33	52.67	100.00
	Col%	100.00	100.00	100.00

Note: Gender: (4 d.f.) 17.7611 (P = 0.0255). Question wording: "I'm going to ask you about some policy issues. Please tell me know strongly you support or oppose the following policy. Your response can be: strongly support, support, oppose, or strongly oppose. If you are not sure how you feel or don't know, feel free to say so. How about... 'The current health care system needs government intervention to improve access and reduce costs'."

The overwhelming majority of every subgroup, national origin group, and category believe that immigrants have a positive impact on the United States. Looking first at generation and citizenship status, reported in Table 12.11, we see that support for "strengthen our country" decreases significantly among U.S.-born citizens, but it still strong at nearly 83 percent.

Tables 12.12–12.14 report results by income, education, and gender. Although across income and education groups the vast majority of respondents also agree on the benefits provided by immigrants, respondents with the highest income and education levels are slightly less supportive of immigrants. There is no discernible gender difference.

We have indicated that national origin groups differ in their strategic situation vis-à-vis the U.S. immigration regime, and this is somewhat

Table 12.13. *View of Impact of Immigrants on the United States, by Education*
Category: Political Views, Specific Issue Views

Response		None to Some HS	HS or GED	Some to College Graduate	Graduate or Professional Degree	Total
Immigrants today strengthen our country because of their hard work and talents	Freq.	2932	2302	2252	385	7871
	Row%	37.25	29.25	28.61	4.89	100.00
	Col%	93.10	90.85	89.30	89.75	91.17
Immigrants today are a burden on our country because they take our jobs, housing, and health care	Freq.	217	232	270	44	763
	Row%	28.47	30.40	35.37	5.77	100.00
	Col%	6.90	9.15	10.70	10.25	8.83
TOTAL	Freq.	3149	2534	2522	429	8634
	Row%	36.47	29.35	29.21	4.97	100.00
	Col%	100.00	100.00	100.00	100.00	100.00

Note: Education: (3 d.f.) 26.9432 (P = 0.0007). Question wording: "Which comes closer to your own views?"

reflected in opinion by nationality, reported in Table 12.15. Across national origin groups, the vast majority of respondents still agree that immigrants are beneficial to the United States. Though still high, support for the contention that immigration is a net benefit for the United States

Table 12.14. *View of Impact of Immigrants on the United States, by Gender*
Category: Political Views, Specific Issue Views

Response		Male	Female	Total
Immigrants today strengthen our country because of their hard work and talents	Freq.	3721	4150	7871
	Row%	47.27	52.73	100.00
	Col%	91.05	91.27	91.17
Immigrants today are a burden on our country because they take our jobs, housing, and health care	Freq.	366	397	763
	Row%	47.95	52.05	100.00
	Col%	8.95	8.73	8.83
TOTAL	Freq.	4087	4547	8634
	Row%	47.33	52.67	100.00
	Col%	100.00	100.00	100.00

Note: Gender: (1 d.f.) 0.1265 (P = 0.7747). Question wording: "Which comes closer to your own views?"

Table 12.15. *View of Impact of Immigrants on the United States, by National Origin*
Category: Political Views, Specific Issue Views

Response		Cuba	Dominican Republic	El Salvador	Mexico	Puerto Rico	Other Central America	Other South America	Other	Missing	Total
Immigrants today strengthen our country because of their hard work and talents	Freq.	299	285	383	5558	549	327	343	67	59	7871
	Row%	3.80	3.62	4.86	70.62	6.98	4.15	4.36	0.86	0.75	100.00
	Col%	91.35	91.97	92.81	91.96	83.37	94.97	91.83	85.45	70.32	91.17
Immigrants today are a burden on our country because they take our jobs, housing, and health care	Freq.	28	25	30	486	110	17	31	11	25	763
	Row%	3.71	3.26	3.89	63.74	14.36	2.27	4.01	1.50	3.26	100.00
	Col%	8.65	8.03	7.19	8.04	16.63	5.03	8.17	14.55	29.68	8.83
TOTAL	Freq.	327	310	413	6045	659	344	374	79	84	8634
	Row%	3.79	3.59	4.78	70.01	7.63	3.99	4.33	0.91	0.97	100.00
	Col%	100.00	100.00	100.00	100.00	100.00	100.00	100.00	100.00	100.00	100.00

Note: National origin: (8 d.f.) 110.8617 (P = 0.0000). Question wording: "Which comes closer to your own views?"

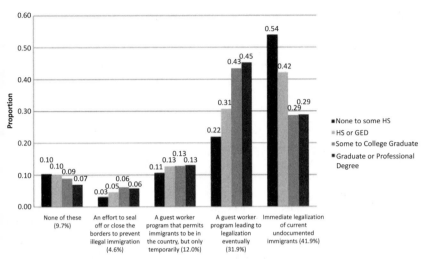

Figure 12.5. Preferred Policy on Undocumented or Illegal Immigration, by Education

Question wording: "What is your preferred policy on undocumented or illegal immigration? Should there be . . . immediate legalization of current undocumented immigrants; a guest worker program leading to legalization eventually; a guest worker program that permits immigrants to be in the country but only temporarily; an effort to seal or close off the border to stop illegal immigration; or none of these?"

are important patterns worth noting. As we move from the lowest levels of education and income to the highest, support for a blanket amnesty drops, whereas support for earned adjustment grows considerably. These trends are statistically significant and reflect a repeated pattern observed elsewhere in the data. Again, we don't want to make more of these distinctions than is warranted. Approximately 70 percent or more in every income group and education level favor one of the two policies that would eventually lead to citizenship. Gender is significant as well, with women being somewhat more generous than men on how undocumented persons should be handled.

The effects of national origin differences are reported in Table 12.17. Puerto Ricans, not surprisingly, are the least supportive of either a blanket amnesty or an earned adjustment, although even among this group, support for either of the two outcomes exceeds 60 percent. For the remaining groups, the support level again hovers at or greater than 70 percent.[1]

---

[1] The reader may note the outlier status of the group marked "other." It is worth noting that the cells are very small, and we cannot know for sure exactly how these respondents identify themselves, apart from self-identifying as in the sample frame.

Table 12.16. *Preferred Policy on Undocumented or Illegal Immigration,*
by Gender
Category: Political Views, Specific Issue Views

Response		Male	Female	Total
None of these	Freq.	377	457	834
	Row%	45.23	54.77	100.00
	Col%	9.23	10.05	9.66
An effort to seal off or close	Freq.	210	185	395
the borders to prevent	Row%	53.10	46.90	100.00
illegal immigration	Col%	5.14	4.08	4.58
A guest worker program	Freq.	558	478	1035
that permits immigrants	Row%	53.87	46.13	100.00
to be in the country but	Col%	13.65	10.50	11.99
only temporarily				
A guest worker program	Freq.	1318	1438	2756
leading to legalization	Row%	47.84	52.16	100.00
eventually	Col%	32.26	31.62	31.92
Immediate legalization of	Freq.	1623	1990	3613
current undocumented	Row%	44.93	55.07	100.00
immigrants	Col%	39.72	43.76	41.85
TOTAL	Freq.	4087	4547	8634
	Row%	47.33	52.67	100.00
	Col%	100.00	100.00	100.00

Note: Gender: (4 d.f.) 33.2035 (P = 0.0004). Question wording: "What is your preferred
policy on undocumented or illegal immigration? Should there be: immediate legalization of
current undocumented immigrants; a guest worker program leading to legalization eventually; a guest worker program that permits immigrants to be in the country but only
temporarily; an effort to seal or close off the border to stop illegal immigration; or none of
these?"

In the expansive debate on immigration, considerable attention has
been directed to the plight of juveniles who entered the country without permission. On the one hand, their status is the same as their adult
parents. On the other hand, having been brought into the United States
as juveniles undermines a claim to interpret their presence as "transgres-
sive," since American jurisprudence has never held children responsible
for acts committed by their parents (even if they are present). Owing to
this status, a number of efforts have emerged to lessen the impact of their
immigration status on their life chances. One such effort is with respect to
college tuition. Many states charge undocumented aliens the out-of-state
tuition rate, even if they have lived in the state for most of their lives and
graduated from a high school in the state. Other states have moved to
eliminate this provision.

Category: Political Views, Specific Issue Views

Response		Cuba	Dominican Republic	El Salvador	Mexico	Puerto Rico	Other Central America	Other South America	Other	Missing	Total
None of these	Freq.	39	30	45	522	105	30	33	10	19	834
	Row%	4.70	3.61	5.44	62.64	12.54	3.56	3.96	1.22	2.33	100.00
	Col%	11.99	9.72	10.99	8.64	15.87	8.61	8.84	12.93	23.21	9.66
An effort to seal off or close the borders to prevent illegal immigration	Freq.	27	19	15	215	62	8	25	9	16	395
	Row%	6.70	4.90	3.86	54.40	15.60	1.93	6.27	2.22	4.11	100.00
	Col%	8.10	6.25	3.70	3.56	9.36	2.22	6.63	11.12	19.38	4.58
A guest worker program that permits immigrants to be in the country, but only temporarily	Freq.	28	26	38	759	94	29	38	18	6	1035
	Row%	2.69	2.48	3.65	73.26	9.03	2.84	3.70	1.76	0.60	100.00
	Col%	8.50	8.27	9.16	12.55	14.20	8.54	10.25	23.09	7.42	11.99
A guest worker program leading to legalization eventually	Freq.	114	102	109	1873	262	119	120	32	25	2756
	Row%	4.12	3.68	3.95	67.97	9.52	4.32	4.36	1.18	0.91	100.00
	Col%	34.70	32.75	26.36	30.99	39.83	34.54	32.13	41.13	30.01	31.92
Immediate legalization of current undocumented immigrants	Freq.	120	133	205	2675	137	159	158	9	17	3613
	Row%	3.33	3.69	5.68	74.04	3.78	4.39	4.36	0.26	0.46	100.00
	Col%	36.71	43.01	49.79	44.26	20.74	46.09	42.15	11.73	19.98	41.85
TOTAL	Freq.	327	310	413	6045	659	344	374	79	84	8634
	Row%	3.79	3.59	4.78	70.01	7.63	3.99	4.33	0.91	0.97	100.00
	Col%	100.00	100.00	100.00	100.00	100.00	100.00	100.00	100.00	100.00	100.00

Note: National origin: (32 d.f.) 331.2382 (P = 0.0000). Question wording: "What is your preferred policy on undocumented or illegal immigration? Should there be: immediate legalization of current undocumented immigrants; a guest worker program leading to legalization eventually; a guest worker program that permits immigrants to be in the country but only temporarily; an effort to seal or close off the border to stop illegal immigration; or none of these?"

365

Table 12.18. *Support for Denying Undocumented Immigrants Tuition Benefits*
by Generation and Citizenship

Category: Political Views, Specific Issue Views

Response		First Generation			2+ Generation	
		Noncitizen	Citizen	Total	Citizen	Tota
Strongly oppose	Freq.	2375	1161	3536	1372	4908
	Row%	67.17	32.83	72.05	27.95	100.(
	Col%	60.58	58.19	59.78	50.47	56.{
Oppose	Freq.	827	437	1264	659	1923
	Row%	65.41	34.59	65.73	34.27	100.(
	Col%	21.09	21.91	21.36	24.24	22.;
Not sure	Freq.	294	133	427	168	595
	Row%	68.84	31.16	71.72	28.28	100.(
	Col%	7.49	6.67	7.21	6.19	6.{
Support	Freq.	234	130	365	246	610
	Row%	64.31	35.69	59.71	40.29	100.(
	Col%	5.98	6.52	6.16	9.05	7.(
Strongly support	Freq.	190	134	324	273	598
	Row%	58.66	41.34	54.28	45.72	100.(
	Col%	4.85	6.72	5.48	10.05	6.!
TOTAL	Freq.	3920	1995	5916	2718	8634
	Row%	66.27	33.73	68.51	31.49	100.(
	Col%	100.00	100.00	100.00	100.00	100.(

Note: First/2+ generation: chi-square (5 d.f.) 116.151 (P = 0.000). Citizen/noncitizen (first ge
eration only): chi-square (5 d.f.) 17.468 (P = 0.072). Puerto Ricans are coded as first generatio
Question wording: "I'm going to ask you about some policy issues. Please tell me how strongly y
support or oppose the following policy. Your response can be: strongly support, support, oppos
or strongly oppose. If you are not sure how you feel or don't know, feel free to say so. Ho
about... 'Undocumented immigrants attending college should be charged a higher tuition rate
state colleges and universities, even if they grew up and graduated high-school in the state'."

We asked our respondents about policies that charge undocumented
students the higher tuition rate (as compared to treating them as in-state
students). Imposing this penalty on undocumented students was wildly
unpopular with our respondents, the vast majority of whom felt that
charging in-state tuition rates was the preferable policy. More than
75 percent of U.S.-born respondents and more than 80 percent of
foreign-born respondents opposed or strongly opposed this practice, as
shown in Table 12.18. Although this does demonstrate a statistically
significant difference between the two groups, the 75 percent figure for
U.S.-born citizens clearly reflects the connectedness of most Latinos to

Table 12.19. *Support for Denying Undocumented Immigrants Tuition Benefits, by Income*

Category: Political Views, Specific Issue Views

Response		Less than $15K	$15K–$24K	$25K–$34K	$35K–$54K	More than $54K	Total
Strongly oppose	Freq.	766	918	685	739	729	3837
	Row%	19.96	23.92	17.86	19.26	18.99	100.00
	Col%	58.14	57.72	60.39	55.66	56.07	57.52
Oppose	Freq.	295	394	260	340	273	1563
	Row%	18.89	25.22	16.66	21.78	17.46	100.00
	Col%	22.40	24.78	22.93	25.63	20.99	23.43
Not sure	Freq.	85	85	51	47	63	332
	Row%	25.70	25.65	15.50	14.29	18.86	100.00
	Col%	6.48	5.35	4.53	3.57	4.82	4.98
Support	Freq.	80	96	64	98	118	457
	Row%	17.50	21.08	14.07	21.46	25.89	100.00
	Col%	6.07	6.05	5.66	7.38	9.10	6.85
Strongly support	Freq.	91	97	74	103	117	482
	Row%	18.91	20.10	15.30	21.37	24.33	100.00
	Col%	6.92	6.09	6.49	7.75	9.02	7.22
TOTAL	Freq.	1317	1590	1135	1328	1300	6670
	Row%	19.75	23.84	17.02	19.91	19.48	100.00
	Col%	100.00	100.00	100.00	100.00	100.00	100.00

Note: Income: (16 d.f.) 49.6815 (P = 0.0089). Question wording: "I'm going to ask you about some policy issues. Please tell me how strongly you support or oppose the following policy. Your response can be: strongly support, support, oppose, or strongly oppose. If you are not sure how you feel or don't know, feel free to say so. How about... 'Undocumented immigrants attending college should be charged a higher tuition rate at state colleges and universities, even if they grew up and graduated high-school in the state'."

the immigration experience and, by extension, their sympathies with those youths caught up in the issue.

Across income and education groups, the vast majority of respondents oppose higher tuition, as reported in Tables 12.19 and 12.20. Respondents with the highest level of income and education are slightly less opposed to charging undocumented immigrants higher tuition, but even for the highest income and highest education cohorts, opposition (or strong opposition) is at 77 percent and 76 percent, respectively. Even among the most assimilated and economically successful, the punitive policy of differential tuition rates has little support.

Table 12.20. *Support for Denying Undocumented Immigrants Tuition Benefits*
by Education
Category: Political Views, Specific Issue Views

Response		None to Some HS	HS or GED	Some to College Graduate	Graduate or Professional Degree	Tota
Strongly oppose	Freq.	1735	1497	1449	228	4908
	Row%	35.34	30.50	29.52	4.65	100.0
	Col%	55.08	59.07	57.46	53.14	56.8
Oppose	Freq.	684	546	595	98	1923
	Row%	35.60	28.37	30.93	5.10	100.0
	Col%	21.74	21.53	23.59	22.87	22.2
Not sure	Freq.	288	153	129	25	595
	Row%	48.40	25.72	21.68	4.20	100.0
	Col%	9.15	6.04	5.12	5.83	6.8
Support	Freq.	221	177	176	37	610
	Row%	36.19	28.97	28.79	6.04	100.0
	Col%	7.01	6.98	6.97	8.59	7.0
Strongly support	Freq.	221	162	173	41	598
	Row%	37.02	27.11	29.00	6.87	100.0
	Col%	7.02	6.39	6.87	9.57	6.9
TOTAL	Freq.	3149	2534	2522	429	8643
	Row%	36.47	29.35	29.21	4.97	100.0
	Col%	100.00	100.00	100.00	100.00	100.0

Note: Education: (12 d.f.) 53.2421 (P = 0.0003). Question wording: "I'm going to ask you abo
some policy issues. Please tell me how strongly you support or oppose the following policy. Yo
response can be: strongly support, support, oppose, or strongly oppose. If you are not sure ho
you feel or don't know, feel free to say so. How about... 'Undocumented immigrants attendi
college should be charged a higher tuition rate at state colleges and universities, even if they gre
up and graduated high-school in the state'."

The majority of both men and women opposes charging higher tuition
to undocumented immigrants, although men show slightly more support
for higher tuition, at 16 percent, compared with 13 percent for women
(Table 12.21).

Across national origin groups the vast majority of respondents opposes
or strongly opposes proposals to charge undocumented immigrants out-
of-state tuition at state colleges. The figures in Table 12.22 indicate that
Cubans and Puerto Ricans are somewhat less strong in these beliefs. In the
case of each, the category "strongly opposed" is significantly smaller than
among other groups and the category "opposed" is bigger. This somewhat
less strident view is certainly a consequence of the special status each
group has with respect to the entire immigration issue (Puerto Ricans as

Table 12.21. *Support for Denying Undocumented Immigrants Tuition Benefits, by Gender*

Category: Political Views, Specific Issue Views

Response		Male	Female	Total
Strongly oppose	Freq.	2233	2676	4908
	Row%	45.49	54.51	100.00
	Col%	54.63	58.84	56.85
Oppose	Freq.	927	996	1923
	Row%	48.22	51.78	100.00
	Col%	22.69	21.90	22.27
Not sure	Freq.	302	293	595
	Row%	50.68	49.32	100.00
	Col%	7.38	6.45	6.89
Support	Freq.	312	299	610
	Row%	51.06	48.94	100.00
	Col%	7.63	6.57	7.07
Strongly support	Freq.	314	284	598
	Row%	52.49	47.51	100.00
	Col%	7.68	6.24	6.92
TOTAL	Freq.	4087	4547	8634
	Row%	47.33	52.67	100.00
	Col%	100.00	100.00	100.00

Note: Gender: (4 d.f.) 19.7666 (P = 0.0131). Question wording: "I'm going to ask you about some policy issues. Please tell me how strongly you support or oppose the following policy. Your response can be: strongly support, support, oppose, or strongly oppose. If you are not sure how you feel or don't know, feel free to say so. How about ... 'Undocumented immigrants attending college should be charged a higher tuition rate at state colleges and universities, even if they grew up and graduated high-school in the state'."

born U.S. citizens and Cubans with a fast-track immigration process and asylum status). Nevertheless, even for these two groups, supermajorities – often in excess of 70 percent – are opposed to the policy.

Undocumented immigrants face persistent problems navigating everyday life, as a consequence of the absence of government identification. The simple act of opening a bank account, for example, is essentially impossible. In response to this difficulty, the Mexican government began lobbying in 2002, to have the *matrícula consular* document, issued by consulates to Mexican nationals living abroad, recognized as an identification card by state governments, banks, and other entities in the United States. Other Latin American nations have engaged in a similar process. This was and is a controversial practice, attracting the attention of anti-immigrant activists and politicians alike.

Table 12.22. *Support for Denying Undocumented Immigrants Tuition Benefits, by National Origin*

Category: Political Views, Specific Issue Views

Response		Cuba	Dominican Republic	El Salvador	Mexico	Puerto Rico	Other Central America	Other South America	Other	Missing	Total
Strongly oppose	Freq.	158	186	257	3488	326	197	238	35	24	4908
	Row%	3.21	3.79	5.23	71.07	6.65	4.01	4.84	0.72	0.48	100.00
	Col%	48.14	60.06	62.22	57.71	49.55	57.17	63.51	44.98	28.15	56.85
Oppose	Freq.	98	60	89	1322	155	73	77	20	28	1923
	Row%	5.12	3.14	4.61	68.74	8.08	3.81	3.99	1.04	1.46	100.00
	Col%	30.09	19.47	21.51	21.87	23.57	21.28	20.54	25.37	33.51	22.27
Not sure	Freq.	34	17	22	406	51	23	20	7	16	595
	Row%	5.65	2.91	3.64	68.14	8.51	3.93	3.29	1.25	2.68	100.00
	Col%	10.26	5.58	5.26	6.71	7.69	6.79	5.23	9.41	19.03	6.89
Support	Freq.	17	22	21	437	56	22	22	6	7	610
	Row%	2.84	3.62	3.36	71.62	9.13	3.61	3.53	1.06	1.21	100.00
	Col%	5.29	7.13	4.98	7.23	8.46	6.40	5.77	8.23	8.82	7.07
Strongly support	Freq.	20	24	25	392	71	29	19	9	9	598
	Row%	3.40	4.03	4.16	65.61	11.82	4.81	3.10	1.58	1.47	100.00
	Col%	6.22	7.77	6.03	6.49	10.73	8.35	4.95	12.01	10.49	6.92
TOTAL	Freq.	327	310	413	6045	659	344	374	79	84	8634
	Row%	3.79	3.59	4.78	70.01	7.63	3.99	4.33	0.91	0.97	100.00
	Col%	100.00	100.00	100.00	100.00	100.00	100.00	100.00	100.00	100.00	100.00

Note: National origin: (32 d.f.) 108.4555 (P = 0.0000). Question wording: "I'm going to ask you about some policy issues. Please tell me how strongly you support or oppose the following policy. Your response can be: strongly support, support, oppose, or strongly oppose. If you are not sure how you feel or don't know, feel free to say so. How about ... 'Undocumented immigrants attending college should be charged a higher tuition rate at state colleges and universities, even if they grew up and graduated high-school in the state'."

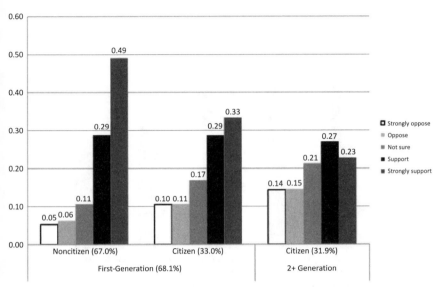

Figure 12.6. Support for Use of *Matrícula Consular* as ID in the United States, by Generation and Citizenship

Question wording: "I'm going to ask you about some policy issues. Please tell me how strongly you support or oppose the following policies. Your response can be: strongly support, support, oppose or strongly oppose. If you are not sure how you feel or don't know, feel free to say so. How about... 'Use of *matrícula consular* – an ID issued by foreign countries – is an acceptable form of identification for immigrants in the U.S.'"

We asked LNS respondents what they thought of the *matrícula consular* and its recognition by U.S. institutions as legitimate identification. In no case do we find majorities opposed to the use of the *matrícula consular*, but we do find considerable variation in levels of support. Perhaps not surprising, the differences of opinion on this issue were considerably more pronounced than on some other aspects of the immigration debate. These are shown through the data in Figures 12.6 to 12.8 and Tables 12.23 and 12.24. Almost 78 percent of noncitizens supported or strongly supported the practice, compared with only 73 percent of naturalized citizens and only about half of U.S.-born citizens, a substantial decline. Similarly, both income and education exert negative effects on support, with only 55 percent and 57 percent of those in the highest income and education cohorts, respectively, favoring the practice, compared with 73 percent and 74 percent of the those in the lowest income and education categories, respectively. There are no significant gender differences on this measure.

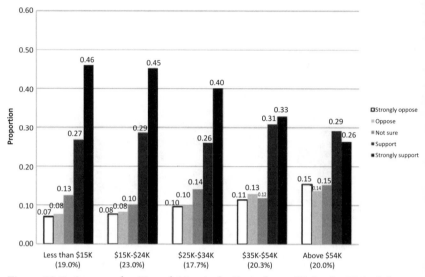

Figure 12.7. Support for Use of *Matrícula Consular* as ID in the United States, by Income

Question wording: "I'm going to ask you about some policy issues. Please tell me how strongly you support or oppose the following policies. Your response can be: strongly support, support, oppose or strongly oppose. If you are not sure how you feel or don't know, feel free to say so. How about... 'Use of *matrícula consular* – an ID issued by foreign countries – is an acceptable form of identification for immigrants in the U.S.'"

With the exception of Cubans and Puerto Ricans (neither of whom have real use for the *matrícula consular*), the majority of respondents from each national origin group supports the use and recognition of the *matrícula consular* (Table 12.24). Only 41 percent of Cubans and 45 percent of Puerto Ricans report support or strong support, again a clear result of their historical and institutional distance from the problems of undocumented migrants. Even for these groups, opposition remains low, with "don't know" a particularly large category.

Moral Issues and the GOP Strategy

As we suggested in the introduction to this chapter, the GOP strategy for attracting Latino votes has relied largely on appeals to "values" issues, with a specific emphasis on religious observance as it relates to the hot-button social issues of abortion and gay rights. Many GOP strategists have rightly observed – and previous opinion and exit polls on ballot initiatives

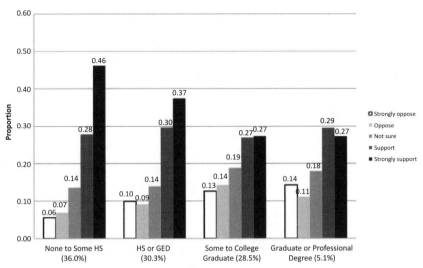

Figure 12.8. Support for Use of *Matrícula Consular* as ID in the United States, by Education

Question wording: "I'm going to ask you about some policy issues. Please tell me how strongly you support or oppose the following policies. Your response can be: strongly support, support, oppose or strongly oppose. If you are not sure how you feel or don't know, feel free to say so. How about . . . 'Use of *matrícula consular* – an ID issued by foreign countries – is an acceptable form of identification for immigrants in the U.S.'"

seem to confirm – that Latinos are among society's most conservative groups with respect to these morality-framed issues. That these issues have not, yet, served as important vote determinants among Latinos does not preclude the possibility that, at some future point, they may become increasingly salient such that they would pay greater electoral dividends for Republican candidates. And at least some Latinos find these issues important in their considerations of parties and candidates.

For these reasons, we asked our respondents about both issues. We might have asked any number of questions on lesbian, gay, bisexual, and transgender antidiscrimination protections; divorce laws; premarital sex; contraception; and the like – but we chose instead to focus on two: support and opposition to same-sex marriage, and support or opposition to legalized abortion.

We had good reason to expect considerable skepticism regarding same-sex marriage rights among respondents. In 2000, *Los Angeles Times* exit polls showed Latinos providing the largest margin of victory for Proposition 22, a so-called defense-of-marriage statute designed to prohibit state

Table 12.23. *Support for Use of* Matrícula Consular *as ID in the United States, by Gender*

Category: Political Views, Specific Issue Views

Response		Male	Female	Total
Strongly oppose	Freq.	207	189	396
	Row%	52.22	47.78	100.00
	Col%	10.14	8.58	9.33
Oppose	Freq.	202	216	418
	Row%	48.38	51.62	100.00
	Col%	9.94	9.80	9.87
Not sure	Freq.	286	368	654
	Row%	43.80	56.20	100.00
	Col%	14.06	16.68	15.43
Support	Freq.	573	624	1196
	Row%	47.87	52.13	100.00
	Col%	28.12	28.31	28.22
Strongly support	Freq.	769	807	1575
	Row%	48.78	51.22	100.00
	Col%	37.74	36.63	37.16
TOTAL	Freq.	2037	2203	4240
	Row%	48.04	51.96	100.00
	Col%	100.00	100.00	100.00

Note: Gender: (4 d.f.) 7.9334 (P = 0.2893). Split sample item in which one-half of respondents were asked the question. Question wording: "I'm going to ask you about some policy issues. Please tell me how strongly you support or oppose the following policies. Your response can be: strongly support, support, oppose or strongly oppose. If you are not sure how you feel or don't know, feel free to say so. How about... 'Use of *matrícula consular* – an ID issued by foreign countries – is an acceptable form of identification for immigrants in the U.S.'"

recognition of gay marriages performed in California and elsewhere. Our results here are broadly consistent with the result then. In our question, respondents were offered three potential outcomes: no legal recognition at all, a civil union, or legal marriage. Overall, more than half of respondents favored no legal recognition for gay and lesbian unions at all, as is made clear in Figure 12.9. There was, however, some significant variation across cohorts. Among U.S.-born citizens, almost 45 percent favored full marriage equality, something of a surprise. By contrast, although outright prohibition was favored by more than 57 percent of the foreign born, only 41.5 percent of the U.S. born favored such a prohibition, thus reflecting a clear moderating effect across generations. And more recent analysis surrounding California's adoption of Proposition 8, which

Table 12.24. *Support for Use of Matricula Consular as ID in the United States, by National Origin*

Category: Political Views, Specific Issue Views

Response		Cuba	Dominican Republic	El Salvador	Mexico	Puerto Rico	Other Central America	Other South America	Other	Missing	Total
Strongly oppose	Freq.	23	22	18	237	51	17	22	3	3	396
	Row%	5.78	5.61	4.57	59.80	12.90	4.33	5.45	0.84	0.71	100.00
	Col%	14.71	14.06	9.00	7.93	16.65	9.80	12.33	7.24	6.80	9.33
Oppose	Freq.	26	15	25	260	41	14	22	10	7	418
	Row%	6.15	3.47	5.99	62.15	9.76	3.26	5.31	2.29	1.63	100.00
	Col%	16.54	9.19	12.47	8.72	13.33	7.81	12.73	20.79	16.54	9.87
Not sure	Freq.	42	26	31	395	74	34	28	16	9	654
	Row%	6.37	4.00	4.69	60.46	11.28	5.15	4.30	2.37	1.39	100.00
	Col%	26.78	16.58	15.26	13.26	24.06	19.30	16.10	33.70	22.02	15.43
Support	Freq.	29	48	50	871	78	40	52	9	19	1196
	Row%	2.41	4.05	4.20	72.78	6.53	3.37	4.38	0.73	1.55	100.00
	Col%	18.51	30.70	25.01	29.19	25.49	23.11	30.00	18.96	45.21	28.22
Strongly support	Freq.	36	47	77	1220	63	70	50	9	4	1575
	Row%	2.32	2.95	4.88	77.43	3.99	4.43	3.20	0.56	0.25	100.00
	Col%	23.47	29.47	38.27	40.90	20.48	39.98	28.83	19.31	9.43	37.16
TOTAL	Freq.	156	158	201	2982	307	175	175	46	41	4240
	Row%	3.67	3.72	4.74	70.35	7.23	4.12	4.12	1.09	0.97	100.00
	Col%	100.00	100.00	100.00	100.00	100.00	100.00	100.00	100.00	100.00	100.00

Note: National origin: (32 d.f.) 188.3308 (P = 0.0000). Split sample item in which one-half of respondents were asked the question. Question wording: "I'm going to ask you about some policy issues. Please tell me how strongly you support or oppose the following policies. Your response can be: strongly support, support, oppose or strongly oppose. If you are not sure how you feel or don't know, feel free to say so. How about. . . . 'Use of *matricula consular* – an ID issued by foreign countries – is an acceptable form of identification for immigrants in the U.S.'"

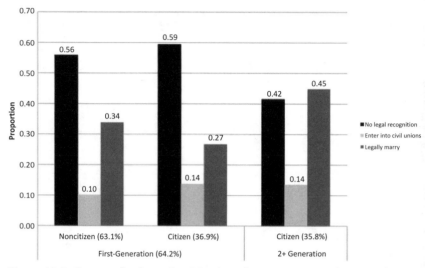

Figure 12.9. Support for Same-Sex Marriage, by Generation and Citizenship
Question wording: "What is your view about same-sex couples? Should they be permitted to legally marry, enter into civil union, or receive no legal recognition?"

overturned a court ruling opening marriage to gays and lesbians, as well as data from the 2008 American National Election Study, suggest that Latinos are nearly indistinguishable from non-Hispanic whites on this issue (Segura and Aylward 2010).

Income and education are curiously distinct on this question. Although there are differences across income groups, no clearly discernible pattern emerges from the data in Table 12.25. Marriage attracts the most support among the lowest and highest income groups, and the second-highest income group is among the least supportive. It is hard to interpret this bivariate relationship as anything other than not meaningful, and preliminary multivariate estimation does not change the result.[2] Education, however, shows a clearly discernible trend, where support for same-sex marriage equality increases and opposition to all legal recognition decreases monotonically across increasing levels of education. Education clearly has a moderating effect on the general opposition to same-sex unions among Latinos (Figure 12.10).

Gender clearly plays a role, with women significantly more likely to support marriage and to oppose a complete absence of recognition.

---

[2] Even in the presence of religious, generational, and other demographic variables, the effect of income on feelings about same-sex marriage remains insignificantly different from zero.

Table 12.25. *Support for Same-Sex Marriage, by Income*
Category: Political Views, Specific Issue Views

esponse		Less than $15K	$15K–$24K	$25K–$34K	$35K–$54K	More than $54K	Total
o legal	Freq.	210	277	182	237	201	1107
recognition	Row%	18.96	25.02	16.47	21.43	18.12	100.00
	Col%	50.75	58.11	56.56	57.90	40.06	52.14
iter into civil	Freq.	40	36	36	48	104	263
unions	Row%	15.04	13.50	13.77	18.14	39.54	100.00
	Col%	9.57	7.45	11.24	11.65	20.78	12.39
gally marry	Freq.	164	164	104	125	196	753
	Row%	21.81	21.79	13.78	16.57	26.04	100.00
	Col%	39.68	34.43	32.19	30.45	39.16	35.46
)TAL	Freq.	414	476	322	410	500	2122
	Row%	19.49	22.45	15.18	19.30	23.58	100.00
	Col%	100.00	100.00	100.00	100.00	100.00	100.00

ote: Income: (8 d.f.) 71.1677 (P = 0.0000). Split sample item in which one-half of respondents were asked this
iestion. Question wording: "What is your view about same-sex couples? Should they be permitted to legally
arry, enter into civil union, or receive no legal recognition?"

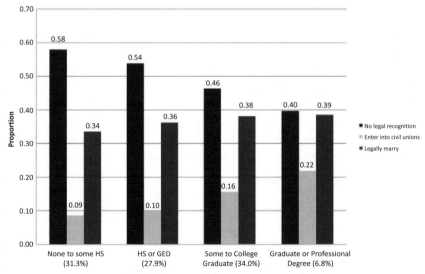

Figure 12.10. Support for Same-Sex Marriage, by Education
Question wording: "What is your view about same-sex couples? Should they be
permitted to legally marry, enter into civil union, or receive no legal recognition?"

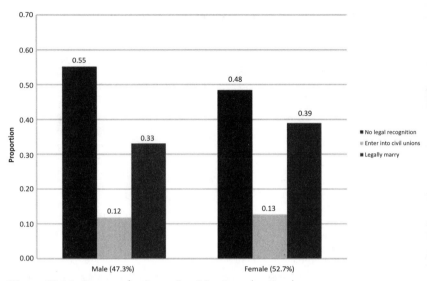

Figure 12.11. Support for Same-Sex Marriage, by Gender
Question wording: "What is your view about same-sex couples? Should they be permitted to legally marry, enter into civil union, or receive no legal recognition?"

Their differences from men range from 5 to 7 percentage points on these two outcomes, as shown in Figure 12.11. Among national origin groups, Mexicans and especially Puerto Ricans stand out, with both groups holding significantly more moderate distributions of opinion than Cubans; Dominicans; and other Central Americans, particularly Salvadorans; these interesting data are found in Table 12.26. We do not have a good systematic explanation of these differences, apart from the relatively greater familiarity of Puerto Ricans with other aspects and subgroups of American culture, and of course this explanation does not help us understand Mexican moderation or, for that matter, Salvadoran extreme opposition.

In the end, although the issue has not yet served to drive Latinos from their primarily Democratic identity, the belief that their views lean conservative on this social issue is not misguided.

Support for Legalized Abortion

Abortion is a salient issue for most Americans, and Latinos are no different in this regard (Bolks et al. 2000). Opinion is, as in other groups, divided. We find that support for some form of legal abortion increases

Table 12.26. *Support for Same-Sex Marriage, by National Origin*
Category: Political Views, Specific Issue Views

Response		Cuba	Dominican Republic	El Salvador	Mexico	Puerto Rico	Other Central America	Other South America	Other	Missing	Total
No legal recognition	Freq.	61	53	77	884	104	54	60	15	19	1326
	Row%	4.60	3.98	5.79	66.67	7.85	4.04	4.49	1.14	1.45	100.00
	Col%	55.48	55.22	75.75	50.51	46.40	57.78	43.20	57.40	61.26	51.60
Enter into civil unions	Freq.	21	9	3	197	33	10	32	4	5	315
	Row%	6.75	2.97	1.09	62.60	10.40	3.02	10.10	1.40	1.68	100.00
	Col%	19.32	9.77	3.38	11.25	14.58	10.25	23.05	16.74	16.90	12.24
Legally marry	Freq.	28	33	21	669	88	30	47	7	7	929
	Row%	2.98	3.60	2.28	72.05	9.42	3.19	5.01	0.73	0.74	100.00
	Col%	25.20	35.01	20.87	38.24	39.02	31.97	33.75	25.86	21.84	36.15
TOTAL	Freq.	110	96	101	1750	224	93	138	26	31	2569
	Row%	4.28	3.72	3.94	68.12	8.73	3.61	5.36	1.02	1.22	100.00
	Col%	100.00	100.00	100.00	100.00	100.00	100.00	100.00	100.00	100.00	100.00

Note: National origin: (16 d.f.) 61.6905 (P = 0.0005). Split sample item in which one-half of respondents were asked this question. Question wording: "What is your view about same-sex couples? Should they be permitted to legally marry, enter into civil union, or receive no legal recognition?"

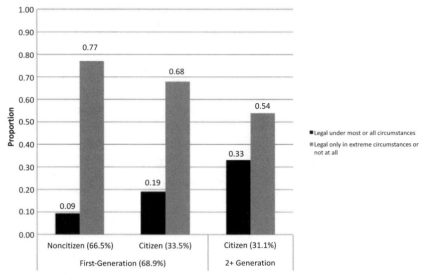

Figure 12.12. Support for Legalized Abortion, by Generation and Citizenship
Question wording: "Generally speaking, do you think abortion should be legal in all circumstances; legal in most circumstances; legal only when necessary to save the life of the woman or in cases of rape or incest; illegal in all circumstances; or are you unsure?"

across citizenship and generational status, but there are strong pro-life currents among all cohorts. Among first-generation noncitizens, for example, 53 percent of respondents would make abortion illegal except to save the mother's life or in cases of rape or incest, whereas an additional 23 percent would make abortion illegal in all circumstances.

Figures 12.13 and 12.14 indicate that income and education are positively associated with fewer restrictions on access to abortion. The majority of respondents do support some form of legal abortion, with limits. Note, however, that the two categories that could broadly be understood as consistent with abortion rights attract only about 18 percent of those with higher incomes and higher education. There is a hint of a gender effect in the direction observed among other groups, with women more supportive of access to abortion, but the differences are extremely modest, as reported in Figure 12.15.

We find mixed support for abortion rights across national origin groups. The majority of respondents support some legal restrictions on access to abortion, with the exception of Puerto Ricans (Figure 12.12).

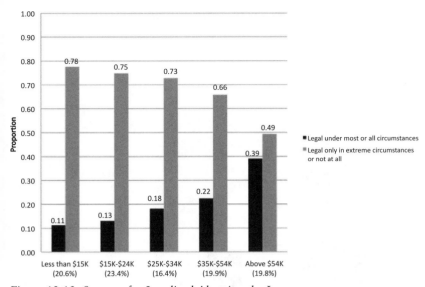

Figure 12.13. Support for Legalized Abortion, by Income

Question wording: "Generally speaking, do you think abortion should be legal in all circumstances; legal in most circumstances; legal only when necessary to save the life of the woman or in cases of rape or incest; illegal in all circumstances; or are you unsure?"

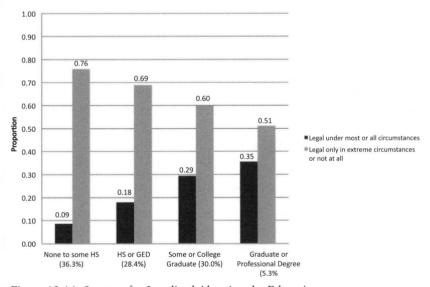

Figure 12.14. Support for Legalized Abortion, by Education

Question wording: "Generally speaking, do you think abortion should be legal in all circumstances; legal in most circumstances; legal only when necessary to save the life of the woman or in cases of rape or incest; illegal in all circumstances; or are you unsure?"

381

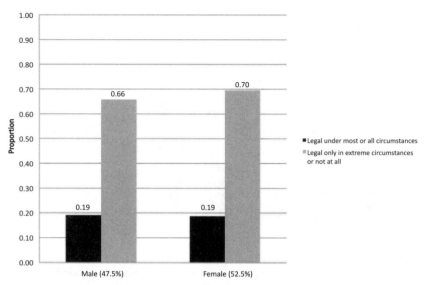

Figure 12.15. Support for Legalized Abortion, by Gender
Question wording: "Generally speaking, do you think abortion should be legal in all circumstances; legal in most circumstances; legal only when necessary to save the life of the woman or in cases of rape or incest; illegal in all circumstances; or are you unsure?"

For example, in Table 12.27 we see that about 56 percent of Cubans take one of the two middle positions – that is, support legal abortion only when necessary to save the life of the mother or in cases of rape or incest, or that abortion should be legal "in most circumstances." Only 13 percent of Cubans support legal abortion in all circumstances, whereas 12 percent feel that abortion should be entirely illegal.

Conclusion

It would be an oversimplification to declare that U.S. Latinos are liberals without offering some nuance or contextualization. Nevertheless, the results in our examination of disparate issues – a government-provided social safety net, Latino-specific issues such as immigration, and an exploration of the divisive social issues increasingly central to U.S. partisan identification – show strong evidence of Latino consensus on many issues. That consensus is, more often than not, left of the center of the political divide.

Category: Political Views, Specific Issue Views

Response		Cuba	Dominican Republic	El Salvador	Mexico	Puerto Rico	Other Central America	Other South America	Other	Missing	Total
Unsure	Freq.	32	14	33	420	34	18	17	5	5	578
	Row%	5.48	2.40	5.67	72.66	5.94	3.05	2.99	0.86	0.95	100.00
	Col%	18.46	9.15	17.62	13.73	10.77	11.47	8.58	13.12	10.19	13.34
Illegal in all circumstances	Freq.	21	27	53	597	62	31	38	8	7	845
	Row%	2.58	3.22	6.28	70.65	7.36	3.72	4.44	0.94	0.81	100.00
	Col%	12.72	17.97	28.55	19.53	19.53	20.50	18.64	20.88	12.61	19.51
Legal only when necessary to save the life of the mother or in cases of rape or incest	Freq.	76	81	77	1516	124	76	105	14	22	2090
	Row%	3.64	3.86	3.71	72.52	5.92	3.64	5.00	0.65	1.06	100.00
	Col%	44.34	53.31	41.66	49.58	38.89	49.61	51.92	35.60	41.13	48.26
Legal in most circumstances	Freq.	20	21	14	207	29	16	19	4	13	344
	Row%	5.81	6.20	4.14	60.28	8.40	4.63	5.45	1.24	3.85	100.00
	Col%	11.64	14.09	7.66	6.78	9.08	10.39	9.32	11.21	24.44	7.94
Legal in all circumstances	Freq.	22	8	8	318	69	12	23	7	6	475
	Row%	4.64	1.75	1.77	66.92	14.57	2.60	4.89	1.54	1.33	100.00
	Col%	12.83	5.48	4.51	10.39	21.73	8.04	11.54	19.20	11.63	10.96
TOTAL	Freq.	172	151	186	3058	318	153	201	38	54	4332
	Row%	3.96	3.50	4.29	70.59	7.35	3.54	4.65	0.88	1.25	100.00
	Col%	100.00	100.00	100.00	100.00	100.00	100.00	100.00	100.00	100.00	100.00

Note: National origin: (32 d.f.) 126.2320 (P = 0.0000). Split sample item in which one-half of respondents were asked this question. Question wording: "Generally speaking, do you think abortion should be legal in all circumstances; legal in most circumstances; legal only when necessary to save the life of the woman or in cases of rape or incest; illegal in all circumstances; or are you unsure?"

383

On the social welfare and economic security questions, supermajorities of respondents, across generations, gender, national origin groups, and income and education categories support or strongly support the presence of a social safety net to secure the income and health of the society. On questions related to immigration – an issue deeply rooted in the Latino experience – there is widespread support for immigrant legalization (though usually through a gradual, earned process), strong beliefs that immigrants strengthen America, and widespread opposition to punitive policies like the denial of in-state tuition to undocumented graduates hoping to attend college. Certainly, there is occasional variation in these views, and Cubans are often distinct from other groups, but it would be fair to characterize policy views as consensual rather than widely dispersed.

Social issues, consistent with earlier work, remain the exception to this left-of-center consensus. Support for same-sex marriage hovers around 36 percent, and opposition to abortion (apart from medically necessary abortion) remains strong. That said, our data also suggest that Latinos rate neither of these issues as particularly important.

As the political parties engage the rapidly expanding Latino electorate, the relative salience of the issues and the substantial consensus on ethnic-specific issues and the social welfare dimension would appear to be a substantial obstacle to GOP growth.

Bibliography

Bolks, Sean M., Diana Evans, J. L Polinard, and Robert D. Wrinkle. 2000. "Core Beliefs and Abortion Attitudes: A Look at Latinos." *Social Science Quarterly* 81(1): 253–60.

Branton, Regina. 2007. "Latino Attitudes toward Various Areas of Public Policy: The Importance of Acculturation." *Political Research Quarterly* 60(2): 293–303.

DeNavas-Walt, Carmen, Bernadette D. Proctor, and Jessica C. Smith. 2009. *Income, Poverty and Health Insurance Coverage in the United States: 2008.* Washington DC: Bureau of the Census. Current Population Report P60-236(RV). http://www.census.gov/prod/2009pubs/p60-236.pdf.

Lopez, Linda, and Adrian D. Pantoja. 2004. "Beyond Black and White: General Support for Race-Conscious Policies among African Americans, Latinos, Asian Americans and Whites." *Political Research Quarterly* 57(4): 633–42.

Nicholson, Stephen P., and Gary M. Segura. 2005. "Agenda Change and the Politics of Latino Partisan Identification." In *Diversity in Democracy: Minority Representation in the United States*, ed. Gary M. Segura and Shaun Bowler, 72–101. Charlottesville: University of Virginia Press.

Segura, Gary M., and Jessica A. Aylward. 2010. "Gender Attitudes, Race Differences and Gay Rights: Rethinking the Race, Religion and Demography Model of Attitudes toward Homosexuals." Paper presented at the annual meeting of the Midwest Political Science Association, Chicago, April 22–25.

Welch, Susan, and Lee Sigelman. 1993. "The Politics of Hispanic Americans: Insights from National Surveys, 1980–1988." *Social Science Quarterly* 74(1): 76–84.

13

Hope and Reality in Latino Educational Attainment

Latinos have long identified the education of their children as one of the most important policy challenges confronting their communities. Improving the educational attainment of Mexican Americans and Mexican immigrants was a primary goal of the League of United Latin American Citizens when it was established in 1929. This organization argued that communities needed to value formal education as a necessary resource to limit discrimination and promote their civil rights (Marquez 1993). Latino leaders and organizations were at the forefront of challenging the de jure segregation of Mexican and Mexican American children in California and Texas in the 1930s and 1940s that led to the dismantling of so-called Mexican schools in much of the southwestern United States (San Miguel 1987). More recently, Latinos challenged the de facto segregation of their children in the Southwest by filing lawsuits such as *Cisneros v. Corpus Christi Independent School District* (1970) and *Keyes v. School District No. 1, Denver, Colorado* (1973). The federal court decisions that followed determined that Mexican American and Mexican schoolchildren had histories of enrollment segregation that contributed to limited educational opportunities and low educational attainment more similar to the experiences of African Americans than to those of Caucasians.

It should not be surprising, therefore, that education ranks highly in recent polls that ask Latinos to list the policy issues of greatest concern to their communities. A survey conducted in 2004 found that when Latino respondents were asked, "What do you think is the most important issue to you and your family today – education, jobs and the economy, health care, terrorism, or immigration?" approximately 26 percent listed education as the most important issue. It was listed second only to jobs and the economy (Bendixen and Associates 2004). Also in 2004, a Pew His-panic Center survey of Latino registered voters education was listed by 54 percent of respondents as the issue that was most likely to determine whom they would support for president. Results from our 2006 Latino National Survey (LNS) reveal that when respondents were asked, "What is the most important problem facing the Latino community today?" edu-cation ranked third at 9 percent, behind immigration at 30 percent and unemployment and jobs at 12 percent.

Decades of research have consistently shown that, despite the efforts of Latinos to secure better educational opportunities and the high value they place on education as a policy priority, the actual experiences of a sub-stantial segment of Latino students in American schools remain tragically subpar. High school completion rates for Latino students are recently estimated at only 52 percent at best, measured through cohort analy-sis following students from the ninth through twelfth grade (Greene and Winters 2006). Their rates of racial and ethnic enrollment segregation are the highest in the country. The National Center for Educational Statis-tics (NCES) reports that in 2006–2007, 57 percent of all Latino students enrolled in public schools attended schools where 75 percent of students were Latino, African American, Asian/Pacific Islander, and American Indian and/or Alaska Native (Planty et al. 2009). The comparable per-centage who attended such schools for African Americans was 52 percent; for Asian/Pacific Islanders, 33 percent; and for American Indians and/or Alaska Natives, 29 percent. By contrast, the percentage of Caucasians who attended such schools was only 3 percent (Planty et al. 2009). These high levels of school segregation are often concentrated in high-poverty areas, where 75 percent of the student body is eligible for free or reduced lunch. Again, Latinos have the highest percentage of students who attend such schools: 35 percent of all Latinos students, as compared to 33 per-cent of African Americans, 25 percent of American Indians and/or Alaska Natives, 13 percent of Asian/Pacific Islanders, and only 4 percent of Cau-casians (Planty et al. 2009). With this in mind, it is not surprising that scholars continue to report that Latinos have among the lowest levels of educational attainment of any major segment of the U.S. population (Gándara and Contreras 2009). The most recent NCES reports show sub-stantial gaps between Latinos and all other racial-ethnic groups in both high school completion and college graduation (Planty et al. 2009).

This disjunction between the importance Latino communities place on education and their continued low educational attainment becomes even more significant when one considers that Latino students are the largest

388 *Latinos in the New Millennium*

Table 13.1. *Public or Private School, by Generation and Citizenship*
Category: Individual/Household Characteristics, Education

Response		First Generation			2+ Generation	
		Noncitizen	Citizen	Total	Citizen	Total
Public	Freq.	996	499	1495	516	2011
	Row%	66.62	33.38	74.34	25.66	100.C
	Col%	98.22	92.92	96.39	91.01	94.9
Private	Freq.	18	38	56	51	107
	Row%	32.14	67.86	52.34	47.66	100.C
	Col%	1.78	7.08	3.61	8.99	5.C
TOTAL	Freq.	1014	537	1551	567	2118
	Row%	65.38	34.62	73.23	26.77	100.C
	Col%	100.00	100.00	100.00	100.00	100.C

Note: First/2+ generation: (7 d.f.) 148.880 (P = 0.000). Citizen/noncitizen (first generation only) (7 d.f.) 65.570 (P = 0.000). Island-born Puerto Ricans are coded as first generation. Questio wording: "Is this child enrolled in public or private school?"

nonwhite racial-ethnic segment of all students attending public schools in the country. The NCES reports that in 2007 Latinos accounted for 21 percent of all students enrolled in public schools. This is a substantial increase from 11 percent in 1987 and 6 percent in 1972. In 2007, African Americans accounted for 15 percent of all students; Asians, for 4.1 percent; Pacific Islanders, for 0.3 percent; American Indians and/or Alaska Natives, for 0.8 percent; and students of more than one race, for 2.6 percent (Planty et al. 2009). Caucasians today account for 56 percent of all students enrolled in public schools, down from an estimated 78 percent in 1972 (Planty et al. 2009).

In this chapter we focus on three specific aspects of Latino families' experiences with schools: parent aspirations and expectations of their children's performance in schools, parent engagement with and participation in schools, and parent assessment of school quality. Questions were asked only of parents who currently had a child enrolled in school. Interestingly, 95 percent of all respondents indicated that their child attended public schools. As indicated in Table 13.1, although a slightly greater percentage of respondents who were first generation, 96 percent, reported that their children attended public schools, the percentage of second generation and beyond respondents who also indicated that their children attended public schools was again high, at 91 percent. Few Latino children attend private schools.

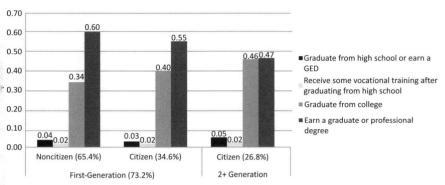

Figure 13.1. Aspiration for Children, by Generation and Citizenship. *Note:* Island-born Puerto Ricans are coded as first generation.
Question wording: "How far would you like to see this child go in school?"

Parent Aspirations and Expectations

The data in Figure 13.1 reveal that Latino parents have very high aspirations for how their children will do in school. Surprisingly, this is the case regardless of generation. Most respondents aspire to have their child either graduate from college or receive a graduate or advanced professional degree. Among first-generation respondents, just less than 95 percent of all respondents aspire for their children to graduate from college or receive an advanced degree; 92 percent of second generation and beyond respondents have the same aspirations. Only a very small minority of parents would like to see their children stop going to school once they graduate from high school, earn a GED, or receive some postsecondary vocational training after high school. Among the first generation, approximately 36 percent would like their child to graduate from college, whereas about 45 percent of the second generation and beyond aspire to this goal. Interestingly, the largest percentage of respondents who hope their child will receive a graduate or advanced professional degree are members of the first generation, at 59 percent. By comparison, only 46 percent of the second generation and beyond aspire to have their child receive an advanced degree.

Aspirations vary somewhat by level of parent education. Although the vast majority of parents, regardless of their educational attainment, would like their children to either graduate from college or attain an advanced degree, respondents with the highest education levels are most likely to find it desirable that their children earn a graduate or advanced degree, as indicated in Table 13.2. Seventy-seven percent of parents who

Latinos in the New Millennium

Table 13.2. *Aspiration for Children by Education*
Category: Individual/Household Characteristics, Demographics

Response		No High School	High School Graduate	College Graduate	Total
Graduate from high	Freq.	50	2	1	53
school or earn a GED	Row%	93.66	4.05	2.30	100.0
	Col%	6.28	0.53	1.07	4.0
Some vocational	Freq.	22	5	1	28
education after	Row%	79.20	17.74	3.06	100.0
graduating from	Col%	2.80	1.23	0.75	2.1
high school					
Graduate from college	Freq.	285	182	24	491
	Row%	58.08	37.07	4.85	100.0
	Col%	36.10	45.26	20.92	37.6
Graduate or professional	Freq.	432	213	88	733
degree	Row%	59.00	29.02	11.98	100.0
	Col%	54.81	52.97	77.26	56.1
TOTAL	Freq.	789	402	114	1305
	Row%	60.49	30.79	8.71	100.0
	Col%	100.00	100.00	100.00	100.0

Note: Gender: one way/chi-square (3 d.f.) 14.55 (P = 0.000). Question wording: "How far would you like to see this child go in school?"

were college graduates had such expectations, compared with 53 percent of those who were high school graduates and 55 percent of those who did not graduate from high school. Just less than half of those parents who were high school graduates, 45 percent, aspired for their children to graduate from college, compared with 36 percent of those who did not graduate from high school.

The data in Figure 13.2 reveal that Latino parents not only have very high aspirations for their children but also have very high expectations of them. We asked the question, "How far do you think your child will actually go in school?" This question was designed to temper the hopes that parents have of their children with the parents' past experiences and knowledge of the challenges that their children face in public education. However, much as it was with high aspirations, the vast majority of respondents also expect that their child will either graduate from college or earn an advanced degree. Slightly more than 82 percent of all Latinos expect their children to receive a university education or advanced degree.

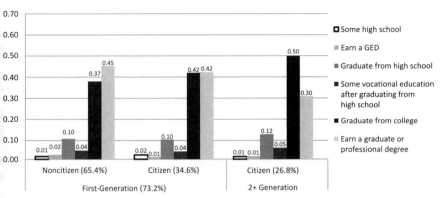

Figure 13.2. Expectation for How Far Child Will Go in School, by Generation and Citizenship. *Notes*: Island-born Puerto Ricans are coded as first generation. **Question wording**: "How far do you think your child will actually go in school?"

This applies equally to first-generation parents, where 83 percent have these expectations of their children, and to the 80 percent of second generation and beyond parents, who expressed a similar expectation.

There is variation in these expectations for parents who have different levels of formal education. Table 13.3 reveals that 96 percent of Latino parents who are college graduates also expect their children to either graduate from college or earn an advanced degree. These expectations are lower for those who graduated from high school, at 89 percent, and for those who do not have a high school diploma, at 76 percent. What is most significant, however, is the overwhelming majority of parents, regardless of education, who have very high expectations as to how far their children will advance in formal education. Only a very small minority of Latino parents expect that their children will only graduate from high school or receive vocational or job training after receiving their high school degree.

Parent Participation in Schools

We also asked a series of questions regarding parents' participation in their child's school. Although there is some variation by generation, gender, and education, the clear pattern is that Latino parents report very high participation in their children's schools across generations and genders.

Table 13.3. *Expectation for Children by Education*
Category: Individual/Household Characteristics, Demographics

Response		No High School	High School Graduate	College Graduate	Tota
Some high school	Freq.	15	0	1	16
	Row%	96.83	0.00	3.17	100.0
	Col%	1.96	0.00	0.45	1.2
Earn a GED	Freq.	20	2	0	22
	Row%	90.66	9.34	0.00	100.0
	Col%	2.53	0.51	0.00	1.6
Graduate high school	Freq.	112	22	2	136
	Row%	82.46	16.07	1.48	100.0
	Col%	14.18	5.43	1.76	10.4
Vocational or job training	Freq.	41	22	2	65
after graduating high	Row%	62.75	34.09	3.16	100.0
school	Col%	5.19	5.54	1.82	4.9
Graduate from college	Freq.	284	221	36	541
	Row%	52.52	40.81	6.67	100.0
	Col%	35.99	54.94	31.72	41.4
Graduate or professional	Freq.	317	135	73	525
degree	Row%	60.38	25.71	13.92	100.0
	Col%	40.14	33.58	64.26	40.2
TOTAL	Freq.	789	402	114	1305
	Row%	60.49	30.79	8.71	100.0
	Col%	100.00	100.00	100.00	100.0

Note: Gender: one way/chi-square (5 d.f.) 15.77 (P = 0.000). Question wording: "How far do y‹ think your child will actually go in school?"

As indicated in Table 13.4, there is virtually no difference by generation in the extent to which Latino parents have met with their child's teacher. Overall, 90 percent of all respondents indicate that they have met with their child's teacher. This includes 89 percent of first-generation parents and 92 percent of second generation and beyond parents. Table 13.5 does reveal that Latina women report meeting with child's teacher, at 93 percent, more often than Latino men, at 86 percent. However, this difference is overshadowed by the overwhelming majority of both Latinas and Latinos who report having had such contact.

Level of parents' formal education does reveal some differences, as demonstrated in Table 13.6. However, these differences – where 94 percent of parents who graduated from college, 91 percent of those

Table 13.4. *Meeting with Child's Teacher, by Generation and Citizenship*
Category: Community, Community Schools

		First Generation			2+ Generation	
esponse		Noncitizen	Citizen	Total	Citizen	Total
es	Freq.	898	489	1387	522	1909
	Row%	64.74	35.26	72.66	27.34	100.00
	Col%	88.56	91.06	89.43	92.06	90.13
o	Freq.	115	48	163	43	206
	Row%	70.55	29.45	79.13	20.87	100.00
	Col%	11.34	8.94	10.51	7.58	9.73
on't know	Freq.	0	0	0	2	2
	Row%			0.00	100.00	100.00
	Col%	0.00	0.00	0.00	0.35	0.09
efused	Freq.	1	0	1	0	1
	Row%	100.00	0.00	100.00	0.00	100.00
	Col%	0.10	0.00	0.06	0.00	0.05
)TAL	Freq.	1014	537	1551	567	2118
	Row%	65.38	34.62	73.23	26.77	100.00
	Col%	100.00	100.00	100.00	100.00	100.00

ote: First/2+ generation: (3 d.f.) 1.300 (P = 0.274). Citizen/noncitizen (first generation only): d.f.) 0.100 (P = 0.962). Island-born Puerto Ricans are coded as first generation. Question ording: "Here is a list of things that some parents have done and others have not regarding their ildren's school. Which of these things have you done? Met with my child's teacher."

Table 13.5. *Meeting with Child's Teacher, by Gender*
Category: Individual/Household Characteristics, Demographics

Response		Male	Female	Total
Yes	Freq.	706	1203	1909
	Row%	36.98	63.02	100.00
	Col%	85.84	93.13	90.30
No	Freq.	116	89	205
	Row%	56.78	43.22	100.00
	Col%	14.16	6.87	9.70
TOTAL	Freq.	822	1292	2114
	Row%	38.90	61.10	100.00
	Col%	100.00	100.00	100.00

Note: Gender: one way/chi-square (1 d.f.) 40.6412 (P = 0.000). Question wording: "Here is a list of things that some parents have done and others have not regarding their children's school. Have you met with your child's teacher?"

Table 13.6. *Meeting with Child's Teacher, by Education*
Category: Individual/Household Characteristics, Demographics

Response		No High School	High school Graduate	College Graduate	Total
Yes	Freq.	689	364	107	1160
	Row%	59.37	31.40	9.22	100.00
	Col%	87.37	90.79	94.26	88.96
No	Freq.	100	37	7	144
	Row%	69.59	25.85	4.56	100.0
	Col%	12.63	9.21	5.74	11.04
TOTAL	Freq.	789	401	114	1304
	Row%	60.49	30.79	8.71	100.00
	Col%	100.00	100.00	100.00	100.00

Note: Gender: one way/chi-square (2 d.f.) 8.7998 (P = 0.057). Question wording: "Here is a list of things that some parents have done and others have not regarding their children's school. Have you met with your child's teacher?"

who graduated from high school, and 87 percent of those with no high school education – are more reflective of a pattern in which high rates of meetings with teachers occur regardless of parents' educational background.

In reporting whether they had attended a parent-teacher association (PTA) meeting at their children's school, respondents demonstrated greater differences by generation. Table 13.7 reveals that 77 percent of Latino parents in the first-generation indicate that they have attended a PTA meeting, whereas only 64 percent of second generation and beyond parents report having done so. These percentages are noticeably less than the overwhelming majority who report meeting with a teacher, and it is surprising that the second generation and beyond report a significantly lower rate of PTA participation than the first generation. Nonetheless, a substantial majority in both generations report attending such meetings.

These differences, however, are much less significant when one looks at PTA participation rates by parents' educational background. Table 13.8 reveals that 76 percent of parents with no high school education report attending a PTA meeting, almost equal to the 77 percent of parents who are college graduates. The percentage reporting such participation is slightly lower for those parents with a high school education, at 70 percent.

It is in the area of school volunteering where parents, regardless of generation or education, report the lowest levels of participation in their

Table 13.7. *PTA Meeting Attendance, by Generation and Citizenship*
Category: Community, Community Schools

		First Generation			2+ Generation	
Response		Noncitizen	Citizen	Total	Citizen	Total
Yes	Freq.	784	419	1203	364	1567
	Row%	65.17	34.83	76.77	23.23	100.00
	Col%	77.32	78.17	77.61	64.08	73.98
No	Freq.	224	115	339	203	542
	Row%	66.08	33.92	62.55	37.45	100.00
	Col%	22.09	21.46	21.87	35.74	25.59
Don't know	Freq.	5	1	6	1	7
	Row%	83.33	16.67	85.71	14.29	100.00
	Col%	0.49	0.19	0.39	0.18	0.33
Refused	Freq.	1	1	2	0	2
	Row%	50.00	50.00	100.00	0.00	100.00
	Col%	0.10	0.19	0.13	0.00	0.09
TOTAL	Freq.	1014	536	1550	568	2118
	Row%	65.42	34.58	73.18	26.82	100.00
	Col%	100.00	100.00	100.00	100.00	100.00

Note: First/2+ generation: (3 d.f.) 110.364 (P = 0.000). Citizen/noncitizen (first generation only): (3 d.f.) 26.954 (P = 0.006). Island-born Puerto Ricans are coded as first generation. Question wording: "Attend a PTA meeting."

Table 13.8. *Attend PTA Meeting, by Education*
Category: Individual/Household Characteristics, Demographics

		No High School	High School Graduate	College Graduate	Total
Response					
Yes	Freq.	595	279	88	962
	Row%	61.87	29.01	9.12	100.00
	Col%	75.90	69.51	77.25	74.06
No	Freq.	189	122	26	337
	Row%	56.04	36.30	7.66	100.00
	Col%	24.10	30.49	22.75	25.94
TOTAL	Freq.	784	401	114	1299
	Row%	60.35	30.90	8.74	100.00
	Col%	100.00	100.00	100.00	100.00

Note: Gender: one way/chi-square (2 d.f.) 8.3398 (P = 0.045). Question wording: "Here is a list of things that some parents have done and others have not regarding their children's school. Have you attended a PTA meeting?"

Table 13.9. *School Volunteer, by Generation and Citizenship*
Category: Community, Community Schools

		First Generation			2+ Generation	
Response		Noncitizen	Citizen	Total	Citizen	Total
Yes	Freq.	437	304	741	378	1119
	Row%	58.97	41.03	66.22	33.78	100.0
	Col%	43.14	56.72	47.84	66.67	52.8
No	Freq.	575	231	806	187	993
	Row%	71.34	28.66	81.17	18.83	100.0
	Col%	56.76	43.10	52.03	32.98	46.9
Don't know	Freq.	0	0	0	2	2
	Row%			0.00	100.00	100.0
	Col%	0.00	0.00	0.00	0.35	0.0
Refused	Freq.	1	1	2	0	2
	Row%	50.00	50.00	100.00	0.00	100.0
	Col%	0.10	0.19	0.13	0.00	0.0
TOTAL	Freq.	1013	536	1549	567	2116
	Row%	65.40	34.60	73.20	26.80	100.0
	Col%	100.00	100.00	100.00	100.00	100.0

Note: First/2+ generation: (1 d.f.) 60.653 (P = 0.000). Citizen/noncitizen (first generation only): (
d.f.) 0.725 (P = 0.555). Island-born Puerto Ricans are coded as first generation. Question wording
"Acted as a school volunteer for your child's school."

children's schools. Only 48 percent of first-generation parents report volunteering, whereas 67 percent of second generation and beyond parents report doing so, as indicated in Table 13.9. The data in Table 13.10 indicate that more Latina women report volunteering, 56 percent, as compared to Latino men, of whom only 47 percent report doing so. The largest differences appear, however, in Table 13.11, which displays reported rates of school volunteering by parents' education. Parents who did not graduate from high school report the lowest rates of volunteering, at 42 percent. Parents who did graduate from high school report volunteering at a rate of 60 percent. It is parents who are college graduates who report the highest rates of volunteering in their child's school, at 69 percent.

Assessing School Quality

Obviously, the key question with regard to understanding how respondents themselves perceive the educational institutions that are available

Table 13.10. *Volunteer at School, by Gender*
Category: Individual/Household Characteristics, Demographics

Response		Male	Female	Total
Yes	Freq.	388	730	1118
	Row%	34.72	65.28	100.00
	Col%	47.39	56.49	52.96
No	Freq.	431	562	993
	Row%	43.39	56.61	100.00
	Col%	52.61	43.51	47.04
TOTAL	Freq.	819	1292	2111
	Row%	38.80	61.20	100.00
	Col%	100.00	100.00	100.00

Note: Gender: one way/chi-square (1 d.f.) 22.1518 (P = 0.000). Question wording: "Here is a list of things that some parents have done and others have not regarding their children's school. Have you acted as a school volunteer for your child's school?"

to them is their assessment of the opportunities available, and their experiences with, the schools their children attend. A first measure is the availability of English-as-a-second-language (ESL) programs. Table 13.12 displays responses to whether the school offered a specialized program for teaching English to predominantly Spanish-speaking children. Seventy-nine percent of first-generation respondents indicated that such a program

Table 13.11. *Volunteer at School, by Education*
Category: Individual/Household Characteristics, Demographics

Response		No High School	High School Graduate	College Graduate	Total
Yes	Freq.	331	239	79	649
	Row%	51.00	36.86	12.13	100.00
	Col%	42.05	59.93	69.35	49.92
No	Freq.	456	160	35	651
	Row%	70.08	24.58	5.35	100.00
	Col%	57.95	40.07	30.65	50.08
TOTAL	Freq.	787	399	114	1300
	Row%	60.55	30.71	8.74	100.00
	Col%	100.00	100.00	100.00	100.00

Note: Education: one way/chi-square (2 d.f.) 69.5707 (P = 0.000). Question wording: "Here is a list of things that some parents have done and others have not regarding their children's school. Have you acted as a volunteer for your child's school?"

Table 13.12. *Specialized Language Program in School, by Generation and Citizenship*

Category: Community, Community Schools

Response		First Generation			2+ Generation	
		Noncitizen	Citizen	Total	Citizen	Total
Yes	Freq.	728	260	988	58	1046
	Row%	73.68	26.32	94.46	5.54	100.0
	Col%	79.30	78.55	79.10	72.50	78.7
No	Freq.	190	71	261	22	283
	Row%	72.80	27.20	92.23	7.77	100.0
	Col%	20.70	21.45	20.90	27.50	21.2
TOTAL	Freq.	918	331	1249	80	1329
	Row%	73.50	26.50	93.98	6.02	100.0
	Col%	100.00	100.00	100.00	100.00	100.0

Note: First/2+ generation: (1 d.f.) 27.566 (P = 0.000). Citizen/noncitizen (first generation only): (d.f.) 3.873 (P = 0.164). Island-born Puerto Ricans are coded as first generation. Question wording "Was there a specialized program for teaching English to Spanish-speaking children in your child school?"

existed at their child's school. The responses of parents in the second generation and beyond were only slightly lower, at 73 percent.

We also asked parents if their child was ever in such a program. Not surprisingly, a clear majority, 63 percent, of first-generation respondents indicated that their children had been in such a program. As also indicated in Figure 13.3, the percentage for second generation and beyond parents was noticeably lower, at 37 percent. It is important to note, however,

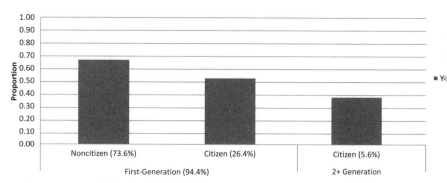

Figure 13.3. Child in Specialized Program, by Generation and Citizenship. *Notes:* Island-born Puerto Ricans are coded as first generation.
Question wording: "Was your child ever in such a program?"

Table 13.13. *Quality of Contact with School Officials, by Generation and Citizenship*

Category: Community, Community Schools

Response		First Generation			2+ Generation	
		Noncitizen	Citizen	Total	Citizen	Total
ery good	Freq.	565	299	864	293	1157
	Row%	65.39	34.61	74.68	25.32	100.00
	Col%	55.83	55.68	55.78	51.68	54.68
ᴐmewhat good	Freq.	318	178	496	215	711
	Row%	64.11	35.89	69.76	30.24	100.00
	Col%	31.42	33.15	32.02	37.92	33.60
ᴵot too good	Freq.	32	26	58	37	95
	Row%	55.17	44.83	61.05	38.95	100.00
	Col%	3.16	4.84	3.74	6.53	4.49
ᴵot good at all	Freq.	14	6	20	15	35
	Row%	70.00	30.00	57.14	42.86	100.00
	Col%	1.38	1.12	1.29	2.65	1.65
ᴵave had no	Freq.	83	28	111	7	118
contact with	Row%	74.77	25.23	94.07	5.93	100.00
school officials	Col%	8.20	5.21	7.17	1.23	5.58
ᴏTAL	Freq.	1012	537	1549	567	2116
	Row%	65.33	34.67	73.20	26.80	100.00
	Col%	100.00	100.00	100.00	100.00	100.00

ᴵote: First/2+ generation: (1 d.f.) 273.467 (P = 0.000). Citizen/noncitizen (first generation only): (1 d.f.) 15.604 (P = 0.008). Island-born Puerto Ricans are coded as first generation. Question ᴡording: "When you have had contact with school officials, would you say your experience has ᴇen very good, somewhat good, not too good, or not good at all?"

that just more than one-third of second generation and beyond parents is a substantial percentage. Because the parents are second generation and beyond, one might expect few of their children to have need for such a program. Our data indicate that many of their children still participated in this type of specialized instruction.

We were also curious about parents' assessments of the quality of their "contact" with school officials, shown in Table 13.13. A majority of first-generation parents, 56 percent, report that their contact was very good. A similar percentage of second generation and beyond parents, 52 percent, indicated that their interaction was also very good. When one combines the percentage of those parents who indicate that the quality of contact was somewhat good with those who indicate that it was

Table 13.14. *Contact with School Officials, by Gender*
Category: Individual/Household Characteristics, Demographics

Response		Male	Female	Total
Have had no contact	Freq.	54	64	118
	Row%	45.99	54.01	100.00
	Col%	6.62	4.94	5.57
Not good contact	Freq.	13	22	35
	Row%	37.36	62.64	100.00
	Col%	1.57	1.68	1.65
Not too good	Freq.	42	54	96
	Row%	43.48	56.52	100.00
	Col%	5.05	4.17	4.53
Somewhat good	Freq.	277	434	711
	Row%	39.02	60.98	100.00
	Col%	33.75	33.50	33.59
Very good	Freq.	436	721	1157
	Row%	37.68	62.32	100.00
	Col%	53.01	55.71	54.65
TOTAL	Freq.	822	1295	2117
	Row%	38.85	61.15	100.00
	Col%	100.00	100.00	100.00

Note: Gender: one way/chi-square (4 d.f.) 5.4732 (P = 0.466). Question wording: "When you have had contact with school officials, would you say your experience has been very good, somewhat good, not too good, or not good at all?"

very good, an overwhelming majority of both generations, 88 percent of the first-generation and 90 percent of the second generation and beyond, indicate that their interaction was favorable. Only very small percentages of parents indicate that their contact was either not too good or not good at all. There were not meaningful differences in the assessments of interaction between Latino men and Latina women, as indicated in Table 13.14 – 87 percent of Latinas report their contact as either somewhat good or very good, and 89 percent of Latino men report their contact as either somewhat good or very good – or by parents' level of formal education, as Table 13.15 shows. Eighty-six percent of parents who did not graduate from high school report that their contact was somewhat good or very good. The percentage for parents who are high school graduates was 90 percent, and 85 percent for parents who were college graduates.

Table 13.15. *Contact with School Officials, by Education*
Category: Individual/Household Characteristics, Demographics

esponse		No High School	High school Graduate	College Graduate	Total
ave had no contact	Freq.	66	9	6	81
	Row%	82.04	10.89	7.07	100.00
	Col%	8.33	2.17	4.99	6.21
ot good	Freq.	17	9	1	27
	Row%	61.51	35.01	3.48	100.00
	Col%	2.10	2.35	0.83	2.07
ot too good	Freq.	29	23	10	62
	Row%	46.87	36.46	16.67	100.00
	Col%	3.70	5.65	9.13	4.75
omewhat good	Freq.	254	146	31	431
	Row%	58.99	33.83	7.18	100.00
	Col%	32.25	36.34	27.24	33.03
ery good	Freq.	423	215	66	704
	Row%	60.13	30.53	9.34	100.00
	Col%	53.62	53.49	57.81	53.95
OTAL	Freq.	789	402	114	1305
	Row%	60.49	30.79	8.71	100.00
	Col%	100.00	100.00	100.00	100.00

ote: Education: one way/chi-square (8 d.f.) 36.6573 (P = 0.000). Question wording: "When ou have had contact with school officials, would you say your experience has been very good, omewhat good, not too good, or not good at all?"

Finally, we asked our respondents to give a grade of A, B, C, D, or fail to their "community's public schools." As indicated in Table 13.16, just more than one-third of first-generation respondents, 34 percent, gave their schools a grade of A. The percentage of A grades among second generation respondents was noticeably lower, at 20 percent. However, the percentage of first-generation and second generation and beyond parents who gave schools a grade of B was almost identical. Forty percent of first-generation respondents gave them this grade, as did 39 percent of second generation and beyond respondents. A higher percentage of second generation and beyond respondents gave schools a grade of C, at 28 percent, whereas only 16 percent of first-generation parents did so. Relatively few respondents, regardless of generation, gave their community public schools a grade of D or fail.

Table 13.16. *Grade for Community Schools, by Generation and Citizenship*
Category: Community, Community Schools

Response		First Generation			2+ Generation	
		Noncitizen	Citizen	Total	Citizen	Total
A	Freq.	1426	585	2011	544	2555
	Row%	70.91	29.09	78.71	21.29	100.0
	Col%	36.38	29.32	34.00	20.02	29.6
B	Freq.	1565	780	2345	1069	3414
	Row%	66.74	33.26	68.69	31.31	100.0
	Col%	39.92	39.10	39.64	39.34	39.5
C	Freq.	545	413	958	765	1723
	Row%	56.89	43.11	55.60	44.40	100.0
	Col%	13.90	20.70	16.20	28.16	19.9
D	Freq.	172	99	271	204	475
	Row%	63.47	36.53	57.05	42.95	100.0
	Col%	4.39	4.96	4.58	7.51	5.5
Failed	Freq.	212	118	330	135	465
	Row%	64.24	35.76	70.97	29.03	100.0
	Col%	5.41	5.91	5.58	4.97	5.3
TOTAL	Freq.	3920	1995	5915	2717	8632
	Row%	66.27	33.73	68.52	31.48	100.0
	Col%	100.00	100.00	100.00	100.00	100.0

Note: First/2+ generation: (1 d.f.) 38.014 (P = 0.000). Citizen/noncitizen (first generation only): (
d.f.) 6.500 (P = 0.078). Island-born Puerto Ricans are coded as first generation. Question wordin
"What grade would you give your community's public schools – A, B, C, D, or fail?"

There were, as Table 13.17 reveals, differences in the grade given to public schools according to parents' educational background. The largest percentage of parents who gave schools the grade of A, 38 percent, were those with no high school education. The percentage among those parents who were high school graduates was 19 percent, and 24 percent among those who were college graduates. The grade of B was given to schools by roughly the same percentage of parents, 36-42 percent, regardless of their level of educational attainment. It was parents who had graduated from high school and those with college degrees where a larger percentage, 27 percent and 26 percent, respectively, gave schools a grade of C. Among parents with less than a high school education, only 14 percent gave their schools a grade of C. Again, relatively small percentages of parents, regardless of education, gave schools a grade of D or fail.

Table 13.17. *Grade for Public Schools, by Education*
Category: Individual/Household Characteristics, Demographics

Response		No High School	High School Graduate	College Graduate	Total
A	Freq.	1136	339	102	1577
	Row%	72.03	21.47	6.49	100.00
	Col%	38.43	18.61	23.88	30.29
B	Freq.	1112	761	156	2029
	Row%	54.81	37.50	7.69	100.00
	Col%	37.62	41.80	36.39	38.97
C	Freq.	418	494	111	1023
	Row%	40.90	48.29	10.81	100.00
	Col%	14.15	27.13	25.78	19.65
D	Freq.	134	113	31	278
	Row%	48.24	40.77	10.99	100.00
	Col%	4.53	6.22	7.12	5.34
F	Freq.	156	114	29	299
	Row%	52.16	38.02	9.82	100.00
	Col%	5.27	6.24	6.83	5.74
TOTAL	Freq.	2956	1821	429	5206
	Row%	56.79	34.97	8.24	100.00
	Col%	100.00	100.00	100.00	100.00

Note: Gender: one way/chi-square (4 d.f.) 20.9525 (P = 0.011). Question wording: "What grade would you give your community's public schools – A, B, C, D, or fail?"

Latinos and American Public Schools

We are able to reach three general conclusions from Latino parents' responses to their and their children's interactions with public schools in the United States. First, Latino parents have both high aspirations and high expectations of how well their children will do in public schools. The percentages with aspirations and expectations for their children to graduate from college or earn an advanced degree are overwhelming. Importantly, this is the case regardless of generation. These data bring new insights into the old argument that many Latino parents, especially those from other countries and those with lesser formal education, do not value education and do not have high aspirations and expectations for their children's performance in school. There is some variation by parent educational background, but even so, high aspirations and expectations are the common pattern for the vast majority of Latino parents.

Second, our data reveal that Latino parents report that they participate in their child's school at very high levels, regardless of generation.
Extremely high percentages report meeting with their child's teacher and
attending PTA meetings. Again, there is some variation by parents' educational background, but the overall pattern is of very high participation.
There is less participation by parents as volunteers in schools, with variation by gender and by educational background, however; even the lowest
participation rates in volunteering, 48 percent of the first generation, is
slightly less than half of all Latino parents. Again, contrary to popular
belief about the disengagement of Latino parents with their children's
school (for a critique of the disengagement thesis, see, e.g., Quiocho and
Daoud 2006), our data reveal that many, and often most, Latino parents
do engage with their child's school.

Third, overall, Latino parents have favorable assessments of the public
schools in their communities. Overwhelming majorities of Latino parents
report that their contact with school officials was somewhat good or
very good, across generations, genders, and levels of education. Clear
majorities of Latino parents also give their public schools a grade of A
or B, although the percentage who do this among the first generation
and those with less formal education is higher than among the second
generation and beyond and those with more formal education.

On the whole, these data suggest that much greater thought and analysis must be devoted to further informing the apparent conundrum of high
aspirations, high expectations, high levels of school engagement, and
favorable school ratings with the reality that Latino students have low
high school completion, college attendance, and particularly low college
graduation rates. It would be unfortunate for many Latino families if the
explanation is that Latino parents are simply willing to accept the fates
that their children experience in schools. It would be equally unfortunate
for Latino families if educators were simply willing to accept that, despite
high parent aspirations and expectations, the continued low achievement
of Latino students is acceptable to teachers, educational administrators,
and policy makers at all levels of government. These data certainly suggest that the vast majority of Latino parents have values and attitudes
toward American public schools that educational reformers would consider resources. As we have argued elsewhere, how Latino parents view
educational opportunities; what they want for their children; and, to a
substantial degree, how they are willing to engage with their children's
schools, align fully with much of the emphasis of current education reform
efforts (Fraga et al. 2010). Perhaps what our data suggest most clearly is

that the major challenge to Latino students and parents, teachers, administrators, school board members, and other policy makers is to develop programs and policies that build on this alignment of values, aspirations, and expectations. The greater success of Latino students in our school systems will very much depend on the effectiveness of such alignment efforts.

Bibliography

Bendixen and Associates. 2004. "First National Poll of Latino Reaction to Bush Immigration Proposal: A Public Opinion Survey." New America Media. http://news.newamericamedia.org/news/view_article.html?article_id+f9e0a30c 7b390794b6469f6e10fcdldb.

Cisneros v. Corpus Christi Independent School District. 1970. 324 F. Supp. 599 (S.D. Tex.).

Fraga, Luis R., John A. Garcia, Rodney E. Hero, Michael Jones-Correa, Valerie Martinez-Ebers, and Gary M. Segura. 2010. *Latino Lives in America: Making It Home*. Philadelphia: Temple University Press.

Gándara, Patricia, and Frances Contreras. 2009. *The Latino Education Crisis: The Consequences of Failed Social Policies*. Cambridge, MA: Harvard University Press.

Greene, Jay P., and Marcus A. Winters. 2006. "Leaving Boys Behind: Public High School Graduation Rates." Education Working Paper Archive, University of Arkansas. http://www.uark.edu/ua/der/EWPA/approved/Leaving.

Keyes v. School District No. 1, Denver, Colo. 1973. 413 U.S. 189.

Marquez, Benjamin. 1993. *LULAC: The Evolution of a Mexican American Political Organization*. Austin: University of Texas Press.

Planty, M., W. Hussar, T. Snyder, G. Kena, A. Kewal Ramani, J. Kemp, K. Bianco, and R. Dinkes. 2009. "The Condition of Education 2009." NCES Working Paper 2009-081. Institute of Education Sciences, National Center for Education Statistics, U.S. Department of Education, Washington, D.C.

Quiocho, Alice M. L., and Annette M. Daoud. 2006. "Dispelling Myths about Latino Parent Participation in Schools." *Educational Forum* 70(Spring): 255–67.

San Miguel, Guadalupe. 1987. *Let Them All Take Heed: Mexican Americans and the Campaign for Educational Equality in Texas, 1910–1981*. Austin: University of Texas Press.

14

Latinos and the Future of American Politics

What might this all mean in the coming years? What will Latinos' attitudes and public opinion look or sound like after the second decade of the twenty-first century? Which factors will influence those views? The preceding chapters have drawn on the 2006 Latino National Survey and have considered an array of evidence on a wide range of substantive questions regarding Latinos' perspectives about issues central to their place in the American political and social structure. Along with learning much about what Latinos think regarding those issues, we have explored why that is, which variables and attributes may be related to and thus help explain their outlooks. In conclusion, we extend the assessment of those explanatory factors and consider their implications for Latinos in the (near) future of American society and politics, providing a discussion looking forward and extrapolating from the body of evidence presented in our analyses. In short, we offer some informed suppositions on what the future may hold.

To a considerable degree, what emerges from the chapters in this volume points to a modified assimilation story. However, the breadth and richness of our evidence has also allowed us to uncover nuance and variation in Latinos' views on an array of issues, which suggests a different, more complex outlook – one that might be characterized as neoassimilation – with Latinos both adapting to the larger society and the larger society changing in response, and with assimilation not precluding the retention of distinctive cultural ties. This conclusion highlights some of our most notable findings.

A central point is that we find on virtually every issue examined that citizens' views were different than those of noncitizens and that later generations differed from the first generation. Although such differences are broadly consistent with classic or standard assimilation claims, these patterns were not always simple or in the direction that would be predicted by such claims. Though consistently important, generation and/or time in the United States does not always lead to the same kinds of attitudes; in some instances, views become more positive about life in the United States and in others less so. For example, foreign-born Hispanics residing in the United States have significantly more positive views about government responsiveness than later generations, who are considerably more cynical. Furthermore, other variations appear in the data – in terms of socioeconomic status, national origin, and (occasionally) gender – that are not necessarily anticipated by assimilation arguments. Higher socioeconomic status is, for instance, associated with stronger reservations about inequality in life chances, which assimilation arguments would not predict as a matter of course or on which its predictions are not clear. Of the socioeconomic factors, income and education usually though not always have similar effects on the intensity of attitudes and opinions. Regarding national origin, we certainly see, for example, cases of Cuban exceptionalism in response to numerous questions but not others. In general, then, the convergent and simultaneously divergent evidence suggests an upward but hardly uncomplicated (linear) trajectory for Latinos' incorporation into American society, which is more or less manifest in the topics considered in previous chapters. In what follows, we expand on these themes, paralleling the topics of our previous chapters.

Public perception of Latinos stems in part from the rapid growth and geographic dispersion of this segment of the population, but it also is greatly influenced by widespread popular misperceptions, chief among them that Latino growth is driven primarily by immigration and that most immigration is unauthorized and illegal. A corollary is that Latinos are failing to assimilate into mainstream society. Recent data from the U.S. Census Bureau and the Department of Homeland Security Office of Immigration Statistics (2009) clearly refute the first and second popular beliefs, and our analysis of the demographic data in the Latino National Survey (see Chapter 2) equally disproves the premise of nonassimilation.

Chapter 2 presents data indicating that Latinos are indeed integrating into the mainstream – through English acquisition, out-group marriage, religious affiliation (e.g., increasing numbers of Protestants), and military service. They appear to be steadily advancing economically as citizens, and later generations are increasingly more likely than noncitizens to be college educated and homeowners with higher incomes – although there is some debate about whether these trends persist into the third and successive generations (Telles and Ortiz 2008; Kasinitz et al. 2010). With many Hispanic immigrants arriving to the United States with a lower educational base, even with substantial gains among their children, educational attainment continues to be a significant problem for a large segment of the Latino immigrant population. In general, there seems to be a slower rate of achieving socioeconomic parity with the mainstream than is the case with social and cultural assimilation.

Another demographic development with likely implications for how Latinos situate themselves and are seen by others in the evolving racial-ethnic order is their increased tendency to indicate "some other race" and to select "more than one race" in the LNS and in other surveys. Increasing numbers of Latinos indicate that they feel Latinos as a group are a race – perhaps reflecting the persistent racialization of identities that continues to characterize U.S. society, even as Latinos also seem to fit uncomfortably within the traditional racial hierarchy in the United States. A final demographic note is the continued overall youthfulness, as well as the greater proportion of younger Latinos that are native born. Hence, we see ongoing relative youthfulness and a larger American-born, and hence citizen, population is emerging.

Becoming part of a society involves various social, economic, and cultural dimensions, but Chapter 3 deals with another key aspect of incorporation: holding certain political values and beliefs. A neoassimilationist orientation seems evident in Latinos' attitudes concerning such core values as individual responsibility, a belief that hard work can lead to success, the importance of equality of opportunity, and support for political rights (e.g., freedom of speech). The powerful strand of individualism and work ethic are consistent with presumed American values, elements of the American Creed, and may also reflect an immigrant ethos. Given the large immigrant segment within the Latino population, this proclivity should continue to be prominent into the future as well, although it would be expected to evolve with time and experience in the United States (particularly so among immigrants compared to the native born).

At the same time, there is some drop-off by generation from extraordinarily high levels regarding self-blame (if there is lack of success) as well as belief that the poor can get ahead with hard work, which suggests that although a majority of respondents continue to exhibit a strong belief in individualism and the work ethic, there is also increasing skepticism, with 20 percent dissenting from those attitudes. Thus, the clear embrace of these values will likely continue, but their intensity may dampen over time and with increased socioeconomic status. Alternatively, it may be that later generations of Latinos are more cognizant of American ideals and juxtapose those to their own experiences in the United States. However, there appears to be a move from substantial to lesser acceptance of inequality of opportunity by generation (and, we would speculate, over time). Support for civil liberties is solid among the first generation and is even higher among the second generation and beyond, which may be attributable to the frame of reference: immigrants may be comparing their current situation with those left behind in their country of origin, whereas later generations are comparing themselves with others in the United States. In short, the strong sense of individualism and work ethic, which is especially present in the first generation and among the less well off (in terms of income and education), is likely to wane over time in the United States. The modest insistence on equality (of opportunity, or tolerance of unequal chances) becomes more pronounced in the second generation and among citizens; support for free speech is solid among the first generation and is higher among later generations.

As Latinos become more integrated into American society, then, their basic orientations will probably regress to the mean, becoming more like the "average" American, though arriving there from different directions. Again, the trend will likely be some kind of convergence and assimilation story, but with variation among or within Latinos, and with differences remaining between Latinos and the rest of society, with possible cleavages being race, phenotype, language, and class. Convergence to the mean will probably increase as a larger proportion of Latinos are native born, although these native-born residents may in some ways be less idealistic and/or accepting of certain social realities.

The findings in Chapter 4 suggest that the adoption of group identities can shape political participation, thus facilitating mobilization and participation as a group or, in their absence, leaving individuals to make their way in political life on their own. Much evidence indicates that Latino group identity may diminish over time. The data presented in Chapter 4 suggests, for example, that overwhelming majorities of Hispanics support learning English, and there is a strong shift, within the first generation and across subsequent generations, toward English as Hispanics' primary language. In addition, majorities support blending in to U.S. society, and this manifests through relatively high rates of intermarriage with non-Latinos. Over time and across generations, social ties with work and friends diversify, and increasing percentages of Latinos report "American" as their primary identity.

However, these indicators of social integration across generations are countered by data that show, for instance, that Latinos' attachment to their identities as members of an ethnic group – to being Hispanic or Latino – does not diminish significantly over time or across generations and that large majorities of Hispanics favor retaining proficiency in Spanish and a distinct Latino culture. The percentage of those who say Latinos should blend in to American society actually falls over time. Furthermore, the percentage of respondents who indicated that Latinos were a distinct racial group increases substantially across generations. These data seem contradictory, but in fact they indicate a process of social integration as Latino immigrants adopt a language, build friendships and choose marriage partners, consolidate a new ethnic identity constructed in the United States, and help redefine what it means to be American.

Seen in this way, the desire to maintain culture and language (often not carried out in practice, as Latinos adopt English as their primary language), and perceptions of Hispanic or Latino as a distinct racial group are reflections of a distinctly American process of ethnic construction. "Latino" as an ethnic identity, and particularly as a racial identity, occurs and makes sense only in an American context. This context is one in which all Americans define themselves and one another racially. It is also a context in which a substantial percentage of Latinos perceive discrimination, and one response to this perception of being singled out because of their accent, skin color, immigrant origin, or ethnic background is a strengthening of ethnic attachment and a sense that Latinos are a distinct racial group. Thus, the paradox is that even as Latinos Americanize, they may increasingly see themselves as part of a distinct ethnic or racial group.

How group identity among Latinos plays out will depend in large part on how the larger American society perceives them. Anti-immigrant sentiment, which has been particularly directed at immigrants from Mexico, has been a steady drumbeat accompanying American politics since the 1980s. There were particularly loud outbursts in California in the 1990s (exemplified by Proposition 187, which would have cut off state-level aid for all undocumented residents in the state, including for education, health, and welfare). This attempt to cut back support for immigrants swept across a much wider swath of states after the failure of comprehensive immigration reform at the national level in 2006. Arizona's Senate Bill 1070 – which instructed law enforcement officers to stop individuals they had good reason to suspect might be undocumented, ask for proof of residence, and arrest them if they had no satisfactory identification – is a prime example. Anti-immigrant sentiment is often perceived by Latinos in the United States as anti-Latino sentiment, and the perception of being singled out as a group certainly reinforces feelings of group identification and solidarity (Dawson 1994). What is most likely is that the sense of Latinos as a distinctive cultural group – with a distinctive culture or language – may be blurred over time, but the racialization of Latinos may be reinforced.

If anti-immigrant sentiment fades away with the passage of immigration reform, the tapering off of immigration to the United States, or a greater degree of integration of immigrants into American society, then ethnic boundaries between Hispanics and others may gradually diminish, as evidenced by the already significant out-marriage rates of Latinos in the United States. It may be that ethnic background may also become a more symbolic notion (Jones-Correa and Leal 1998). But if Latinos continue to experience negative stereotyping and racialization as a group, which seems more likely, then they in turn will increasingly perceive themselves in racial terms – something our data show is already the case for a majority of Latinos. This racialized group identity will be detached from an immigrant identity – again, something the data already suggest – as Hispanic residents experience more negative residential, educational, and occupational outcomes.

Immigrants to the United States arrive retaining ties to families, towns, and countries that persist for some time but that gradually, for the most part, fade away over time in the United States and across generations. As the evidence in Chapter 5 indicates, the decline in transnational ties is reflected by a downturn in the frequency of immigrants' contacts with friends and family over time in the United States; in the frequency of their monetary remittances to friends and family in their country of origin; in their support of children living in the country of origin; in their ownership of homes, land, or businesses in their country of origin; and in their plans to return to their country of origin. Within a few years of arriving to live in the United States, Latino immigrants overwhelmingly indicate that their plans are to remain in this country. Latino out-marriage to Hispanics from other national origin groups as well as to non-Latinos increases with time in the United States and across generations. These trends all point to a process of immigrant settlement and social integration in the United States.

The decline of such ties is uneven, though, across national origin groups and across forms of transnational behavior. Cuban Americans, for example, are at one end of the spectrum. Arriving in the United States as political refugees, they are much less likely to send remittances, travel, or plan to return to their country of origin than other Latin American immigrants, although this may be affected by public policy restricting the frequency and amounts of money that can be sent, as well as other activities. Dominicans are at the other end of the spectrum, showing greater persistence in their ties to their country of origin than other immigrants. Interestingly, our findings indicate that Puerto Ricans born on the island of Puerto Rico act transnationally in various respects (e.g., travel, remittances), as immigrants do, although they are formally U.S. citizens.

Although most transnational behaviors decline across time, not all do; for those that do, the percentage saying they engage in them never quite decline to zero, even across generations. In every generation there is a small percentage who indicate that they continue to keep up transnational ties. So although plans to return, remittances, and contact all decline, sometimes very quickly, with time in the United States, other behaviors – notably political contact and participation, which have low percentages of immigrants engaged in them to begin with – continue on, albeit at very low percentages. The story of transnationalism is that it declines over time and across generations, but it also persists among a small number across time and generations as well.

So, do small percentages matter? Given the large population of Latinos in the United States, it is possible that small percentages can translate into fairly large numbers: for instance, if 5 percent of Hispanics born in the United States say they still engage in the politics of their parents' or grandparents' country of origin, this could mean that several hundred thousand people participate in this way. The cumulative impact of this participation might not be insignificant. However, there are still many open questions. It might be that people's responses to the survey questions disguise differences across time or generation. It could also be the case, for instance, that those first-generation immigrants who participate in their country of origin's politics do it consistently, whereas later generations engage sporadically. In Chapter 5 we noted the possibility that, when later generations say they are active in hometown associations and other similar organizations, those associations have shifted their focus to the United States or keep a country-of-origin focus but are also attentive to U.S. domestic civic and political issues. There is a considerable body of research (Garcia 2011; Jones-Correa 2007; Segura 2007) that points to the complementary nature of transnational and U.S.-focused civic and political engagement. The behavior and participation rates of the first and following generations may look the same on the face of it but actually be quite different. So are survey questions being interpreted in the same way by respondents across generations, and do the answers they give describe the same thing?

If there is a pool of Latinos who express even intermittent engagement with their country of origin, this implies that there is a reserve of individuals who could be engaged transnationally under the right circumstances. If there were a natural disaster, a coup d'état, or a war, any of these could mobilize coethnics in the United States, in a manner similar, perhaps, to the way that Irish Americans were engaged in the struggles of the Irish in Ulster or that many Jewish Americans have ties to Israel. We do not know, however, when or how exactly Latino transnational ties might be triggered. In general, we need to know more about who participates transnationally in the longer term, when transnationalism might be mobilized more broadly, and what the consequences of these transnational ties might be.

Our examination of Latinos' experiences living in the United States ranged from assessing the opportunity structures available to them to assessing how they are treated. Although objective measures on the socioeconomic status of many Latinos indicate they are falling short of realizing their aspirations, there is at the same time a consistent belief that opportunities are open to those who apply themselves (see Chapter 3). So strong supportive attitudes of the American ethos seem to be less influenced by the reality of Latinos' day-to-day lives; this seemingly ironic combination warrants more attention in future analyses.

Our findings also showed that intra- and intergroup relations have been and will likely continue to be important aspects of Latino political development. There is, for example, clear evidence that across generational status Latinos perceive some degree of discrimination in public accommodations and the workplace. At the same time, there is a growing body of literature that corroborates a difference between actual experience with discrimination and perceptions of discrimination. The latter has been found to affect participatory orientations and behaviors. (Although we did not have direct questions or evidence to draw from in the LNS, future analyses might well examine variation of discriminatory experiences and perceptions among Latino subgroups as a factor affecting the strength of pan-ethnic identification.) Another of our findings was that another, or "fellow," Latino was the second most frequently identified perpetrator of discriminatory acts.

With regard to intergroup relations, our research shows a notable extent of linked fate with African Americans. Although there is some variation by generational status, our measures of linked fate – "how much does things going well with me (or my national origin group) depend on other Latinos (or African Americans) doing well" – indicate a sense of commonality in socioeconomic and education arenas, although it is less so regarding the (explicitly) political arena. In comparing the potential for coalition with other groups, specifically, African Americans and whites, both groups seem to be possible partners, but the data suggest a slightly greater affinity for the African American community. The growing body of research literature on collective group efforts needs to take better account of each group's resources, agenda priorities, and situational conditions to more fully determine the likelihood of cooperative endeavors.

Belonging to and immersion in social and civic organizations is generally thought to be of value in itself and to have additional benefits in fostering political participation. The low levels of civic engagement or group activity (discussed in Chapter 7) will probably give way to gradually increasing involvement with time and formal inclusion (especially regarding attainment of citizenship), but it may continue to be somewhat low, partly attributable to how recently citizenship was attained as well as to socioeconomic factors. Yet because Latinos' socioeconomic status will presumably continue to increase, more engagement would likewise be expected to occur, as research indicates is the case for the general population. In addition, these influences could also facilitate an increased tendency to address problems through organizations (rather than doing nothing or working informally), which would make Latinos' civic approaches more like (presumed) mainstream practices.

The composition of Latinos' social and cultural networks will become more mixed and will include more non-Latinos, projecting from what we currently find regarding generation, citizenship, and higher socioeconomic status (which will presumably increase somewhat over time), thus suggesting increasing sociocultural integration. Increasing contact of officials resulting from changed socioeconomic circumstances and with time, and contacting non-Latino officials, is also likely to grow.

The level of interest in politics, shown to be modest, is somewhat higher in later than earlier generations. Also, strikingly high levels of political alienation (for lack of a better word) were revealed; for example, respondents strongly believe that government serves mostly big interests; there is low trust that government will do the right thing very often; survey respondents believe they have very little influence or say in what government does; and they indicate that government is often difficult to understand. These attitudes do not necessarily improve or increase over time, by socioeconomic status or other factors, and would thus seem unlikely to foster political participation in the future. Going forward, it seems that Latinos' levels of political engagement will be affected by various internal and external influences and, importantly, the interaction of those influences. Among those influences is Latinos' attention and exposure to sources of social and political information, including electronic media.

The variations among Latino in terms of media use are, like numerous other dimensions we've addressed, affected by nativity and generational status. In addition, there are real differences between daily newspaper readers and television-news watchers regarding their levels of political knowledge, voting, and interest; exposure to news media sources, especially regular newspaper reading, does affect levels of civic and political engagement. These variations by nativity and generation raise questions for the future, such as how the content of materials found in newspapers versus television news compare; the relative accessibility of these sources is also something to consider.

Given the evidence of movement from the use of Spanish to more English across generations, how are bilinguals similar to or different, if at all, from monolingual Latinos (English or Spanish)? There has been a trend in Spanish-language media to engage in more public service and news coverage of American politics, as well as greater attention by the Democratic and Republican parties to Spanish language media. What implications will this have for reaching various segments of the Latino community, and does exposure facilitate greater political incorporation and awareness? Besides the news information gleaned from these media sources, what is the portrayal or representation of Latinos, and does this affect their attachment to and engagement in social and political processes in the United States? Finally, the digital divide still exists between Latinos and other Americans, even though there are internal differences (e.g., younger Latinos are greater users than older Latinos). Nevertheless, a slow closing of this gap will occur; hence, Latinos' use of the Internet (perhaps for political and social content) will be important for understanding if and how political outreach, which relies on social networks and Internet connections, engages Latinos. As more targeted mobilization efforts are directed at Latinos in general or at specific segments thereof, assessment of the impact of newer technologies on Latino political and civic engagement should follow.

Political participation remains a central challenge for Latinos. The story presented in our data suggests that some – though not all – of the resource difficulties will diminish over time. Intergenerational socioeconomic mobility improves registration and turnout, and the significant age disadvantage will eventually become a resource.

Data from the 2000 census revealed that 87 percent of Latinos younger than eighteen are U.S. citizens and will enter the citizen-eligible population (and potential electorate) merely with the passage of time. In the interim, those young Latinos who are eligible but – like other young people – do not vote, will mature, often into participating members of the electorate.

Some of those challenges, however, are beyond the reach of Latinos themselves. Contact by parties and candidates are underwhelming, which suggests both that there is work to do with getting parties to mobilize Latinos and that the upward potential for growth in the electorate is quite sizable.

Once in the voting booth, however, the two-party preferences of Latinos are remarkably consistent across almost every cohort and subgroup, with one major exception – Cuban Americans. (However, even among Cuban Americans party orientations may be shifting somewhat, becoming less heavily Republican among the later versus the earlier generations.) Perhaps most important, nonvoters have preferences that look very similar to those of voters. Significant growth in the Latino electorate is very unlikely to produce meaningful partisan shift, as those not voting look a great deal like those who do with respect to their candidate of choice. Over the coming several decades, voter education, registration, and mobilization remain the principal obstacles and opportunities for Latino advocates and policy demands.

If Latinos maintain the patterns of partisan identification indicated in the LNS data, their growth in the electorate will benefit the Democratic Party more than the Republican Party. Although the magnitude of this Democratic advantage varies among national origin groups and across states, the trend of a Democratic advantage appears in all groups and in all states. It is less the case in Florida, where the Republican Party has consistently had an advantage among Cuban American voters; however, even there Democratic gains are beginning to appear, as later generations are less tied to the Republican Party. Cuban Americans are a minority of the Latino population in Florida, yet the overall proportion of Latinos (more than 20 percent), the state's size, and its competitiveness in presidential elections will make these matters of significant for some time to come.

It is also apparent that Latinos generally have strong preferences for coethnic Latino candidates and for candidates who speak Spanish. These preferences decline across generations and with increasing income and education; however, they remain substantial across all generations. These patterns of preferences suggest that the political party that nominates the greatest number of Latino candidates and candidates who speak Spanish may have a strong advantage with segments of the growing Latino electorate. (However, some developments of the 2010 elections, such as the election of several additional Republicans to the U.S. House of Representatives, suggest the difficulty of predicting what the future holds.) The trends should also be considered, however, in light of our findings that levels of political knowledge are low, especially for noncitizens, but they are also low for foreign-born citizens and those in the second, third, and fourth generations. Whether levels of knowledge increase or remain stable will affect, and be affected by, various aspects of Latino social and political incorporation.

Other indicators of acculturation into American society are Latino attitudes regarding the appropriate roles of men and women in society – what they are and/or should be. Stereotypical characterizations of Latino culture portray Latino families as traditional and patriarchal in their gender relationships. Latino men are commonly described as macho, and Latinas are frequently viewed as submissive and as young mothers with babies in their arms. Contrary to these popular characterizations, respondents in the LNS displayed fairly egalitarian gender-role views. For every gender-role question asked on the survey – including support for equal pay, access to birth control, preference for male leadership, and child-caring responsibility – the majority of the respondents supported an egalitarian position. In general, we would anticipate that if this pattern increases, the stereotypes and actual intragroup gender relations will be altered, such that they are more consistent with the norms ostensibly prescribed in American society.

Our findings with respect to public policy were consistent with the literature and, more importantly, with the partisan predispositions of most Latino voters. Although it is not surprising that Latinos are left of Anglos on Latino-specific issues such as immigration, we also find that Latinos are, by and large, liberals on most policy issues. Notable examples include that Latinos favor active government in the areas of health care and income support for raising the standard of living. This finding is consistent with research on African Americans (Kinder and Winter 2001) and the more exhaustive examination of this question among Latinos by Bowler and Segura (2011).

The long-standing exception to these patterns is social or moral issues, where Latinos remain somewhat conservative on gay rights and very conservative on abortion. Here, however, we noted two important caveats. First, these issues never rank among the most important for

Latino voters when asked, and second, the trends of change across cohorts – comparing foreign born to U.S. born – and over time are likely to erode this exceptionalism. As Latinos assimilate into the U.S. cultural milieu, they become somewhat more accepting of the pro-choice argument and significantly more supportive of same-sex marriage.

Looking toward the future, what might we expect with respect to changes in policy preferences over time? Although there are modest trends away from some of the liberal social welfare policy positions across cohorts, there is little evidence of significant movement. Even among the highest income group, more than three-fourths of respondents supported or strongly supported government policies of income support, and 83 percent did the same for government intervention into health care. In terms of education, the numbers are even greater; the highest education group supports or strongly supports income assistance, at 86 percent, and supports health-care intervention, at almost 85 percent. In short, there is no evidence of meaningful erosion in policy liberalism as a function of socioeconomic mobility. If this policy liberalism remains resistant to change even as the group experiences socioeconomic diversification, it seems unlikely that conservative candidates and the Republican Party will have much success swinging a larger portion of the group into its electoral column.

One implication of the growth of the Latino population is that Latino students are increasing as a percentage of students enrolled in schools in all regions of the country, and no other racial-ethnic group is increasing at a faster rate. Nonetheless, Latinos have among the lowest school completion rates of any group in the country. Our data reveal that this is inconsistent with the overwhelmingly high aspirations and expectations that Latino parents have of how their children will do in school, and this is so regardless of generation. It is also the case that Latino parents report participating in their child's school at very high levels, again regardless of generation. Moreover, Latinos consistently give their children's schools favorable ratings.

There is an apparent – yet difficult to explain – disjunction. On the one hand, there are high aspirations, high expectations, high levels of school engagement, and favorable ratings of schools; on the other hand, there is the reality that Latino students have low rates of high school completion, college attendance, and especially graduation from college. If education is indeed the linchpin of American equality of opportunity it is commonly perceived to be, better understanding of the causes of the disjunction and explaining its consequences would seem essential for a variety of empirical theoretical and normative reasons. The LNS evidence indicates a possible opportunity for Latino parents and students to work collaboratively with education officials to develop programs and policies that build on a clear alignment of values, aspirations, and expectations among all of these educational stakeholders. The future educational attainment of Latinos and the socioeconomic and political well-being of Latinos will depend on building on this alignment in ever more innovative and creative ways. Although the evidence on Latinos we have provided in our study is both deep and wide and has informed our speculation about the future, the future itself is, of course, not preordained.

A common thread throughout our analysis has been some noticeable differentiation based on Latinos' generational status in the United States. A host of attitudes, behaviors, policy preferences, and other issues was examined, and immigrant status often revealed some results that differ from those for the native born. At times, immigrants are more positive and the second generation and beyond more negative, such as about whether one can or should blame oneself or the "system" regarding success in life. Examining when congruence and differences occur becomes a way to understand the development of Latino orientations toward American society, including the coexistence of national origin and pan-ethnic identity as related to American identity.

On the whole, our analyses present evidence of an assimilation story or immigrant-group model as well as a (related) socioeconomic-status model regarding various topics and dimensions. Changes occur from and/or by generation and with the attainment of citizenship in ways we might expect. Yet the socioeconomic status of Latinos is skewed toward the low side; thus, changes may seem slow and/or segmented. In addition, some notable qualifications or exceptions to overall patterns are apparent (e.g., national origin, especially Cuban, differences). Latinos' perceptions of the possibilities of upward socioeconomic mobility are overall quite positive, but their views of their ability to shape the governmental in the decision-making arena are quite different, where they indicate considerable reservations.

The good news for American society is that Latinos are becoming more like the general population, and thus embody the ostensibly common and presumably normatively preferred (standard) assimilation pattern. Yet the bad news is also that Latinos are becoming more like the general population in several respects. As Latinos have become and are increasingly integrated socially, they seem more skeptical politically. Embodying this irony of acculturation and assimilation, Latinos' attitudes and opinions are both stronger in some respects and weaker in other ways than are general patterns. However, in light of Latinos' unique conditions – regarding citizenship, generation, socioeconomic status, and national origin diversity, among other things – the full visibility and impact of all this may become apparent gradually, though steadily, thus barring some significant changes in immigration, birth rates, and other social and political factors. Yet the overall or aggregate volume of change in the society will be considerable because of the population's dramatic growth.

That growth, as conditioned by Latinos' demographic attributes; values, beliefs, and principles; sense of identity and commonality; civic and political involvement; policy preferences; and associated factors – in themselves and relative to their counterparts in the rest of the society – is fundamental. But as fundamental as it is, these are not the only critical elements for understanding Latinos in the United States in the new millennium. The reactions and responses of the political and social system (e.g., the orientations of political parties, the extent of acceptance of or discrimination toward Latinos, the implications of American governmental institutions and social structures) will affect the rate as well as the direction and forms of change. In short, it is a two-way street, with numerous intersections, stops and gos, and a host of regulations and restrictions. We have sought to acknowledge and engage many of those, although surely we have not been able to engage all of them.

Our analysis has addressed and examined both sides of the street and a number of the intersections and other dimensions thereof, thus detailing a massive array of contemporary evidence. In this final chapter, we have considered the implications for the future of Latinos in American politics and, to a considerable degree, the future of American politics. At minimum, we trust that the descriptions and analysis we have presented inform and stimulate readers as they ponder important issues and broader implications of the materials we have provided.

Bibliography

Bowler, Shaun and Gary M. Segura. 2011. *The Future is Ours: Minority Politics, Political Behavior, and the Multiracial Era in American Politics*. Washington, D.C.: Congressional Quarterly Press.

Dawson, Michael 1994. *Behind the Mule: Race, Class and African American Politics*. Princeton: Princeton University Press.

Garcia, John A. 2011. "Latino Immigrants: Transnationalism and Patterns of Multiple Citizenship," in David Leal, ed. *Latinos, Transnationalism and Immigration*. Notre Dame, IN: University of Notre Dame Press.

Jones-Correa, Michael. 2007. "Fuzzy Distinctions and Blurred Boundaries: Transnational, Immigrant and Ethnic Politics," in Rodolfo Espino, David Leal and Kenneth Meier, eds. *Latino Politics: Identity, Mobilization and Representation.* Charlottesville: University of Virginia Press, pp. 44–60.

Jones-Correa, Michael, and David Leal. 1996. "Becoming Hispanic: Secondary Pan-ethnic Identity among Latin American Origin Population in the U.S." *Hispanic Journal of Behavioral Sciences* 18, no. 2 (May): 214–54.

Kinder, Donald R. and Nicholas Winter. 2001. "Exploring the Racial Divide." *American Journal of Political Science* 45:439–56.

Krasinitz, Philip, John H. Mollenkopf, Mary Waters, and Jennifer Holdaway. 2009. *Inheriting the City: The Children of Immigrants Come of Age.* New York: Russell Sage Foundation.

Telles, Edward E. and Vilma Ortiz. 2008. "Mexican Americans and Education," Latino Policy & Issues Brief. Los Angeles: UCLA Chicano Studies Research Center.

U.S. Census Bureau and the Department of Homeland Security Office of Immigration Statistics (2009).

Index

collective discrimination as foundation
for, 148
common status goals within, 148–50
formation of, factors against, 149
ideological foundations for, 150
political, 149
purpose and function of, 147
socialization experiences as influence on,
148
collective action, for racial identity, 76–78
expressive benefits of, 77
free rider issues in, 76–77
from group mobilization, 77–78
incentives for, 76
in politics, 76–77
psychological benefits of, 77
as rational, 76–77
Colombia, Latinos from
by generation, 33
transnationalism for, 102
U.S. population demographics, 30
community schools, 402
competition, between Latinos, perceptions
of, 97–98
Congress, U.S., political knowledge of,
308, 309
contraception. *See* birth control, attitudes
toward
core values
in American creed, 56
democracy as, 56
equality as, 56
equality of opportunity as, 56
freedom as, 56
individualism as, 56–57
liberal tradition as, 56–57
liberty as, 56
self-reliance as, 56
crime, Latinos and
race of perpetrator, 159–60
as victim, 159
Cuba, Latinos from
contact frequency between, in nation of
origin, 106, 126
contact of government officials by, 202
contact with election candidates, 261,
262
discrimination against, perceptions of,
145
electoral participation, in nation of
origin, 121

equal rights support by, 71
equality of opportunity, perceptions of,
68
exceptionalism for, 407
extended visits by, to nation of origin,
111
in Florida, population demographics for,
11
by generation, 33
on government efficacy, 213
immigration law for, 354–55
interest in public affairs and, 209
naturalization of, 32
political contributions by, in nation of
origin, 122
political transnationalism for, 118
property ownership by, in region of
origin, 112
remittance practices for, 106
repatriation to nation of origin for,
108–109
Republican Party support by, 279
self-reliance as value for, 59
short-term travel by, to nation of origin,
115, 129
social group participation by, 191
success from hard work for poor,
perceptions of, 64
support for Bush by, 271
trust in government by, 217
U.S. population demographics, 5, 30
voter registration by, 251–53, 254
voter turnout for, 255
cultural discrimination. *See* discrimination
cultural isolation, as stereotype, 12–13
cultural stereotypes. *See* stereotypes, of
Latino community

democracy, as value, 56
social capital and, 188–89
voting and, 248
Democratic Party. *See also* partisanship,
political, for Latinos
educational level and, registration for,
288
generational support for, 283–85
income level and, registration for, 287
Latino support of, 20–21, 312–15
partisanship support of, 278–79
registration for, by nation of origin,
283–85, 286